DAILY LIFE IN

RENAISSANCE ITALY

Recent Titles in
The Greenwood Press Daily Life Through History Series

Behind the Iron Curtain
Jim Willis

Trade: Buying and Selling in World History
James M. Anderson

The Colonial South
John Schlotterbeck

A Medieval Monastery
Sherri Olson

Arthurian Britain
Deborah J. Shepherd

Victorian Women
Lydia Murdoch

The California Gold Rush
Thomas Maxwell-Long

18th-Century England, Second Edition
Kirstin Olsen

Colonial New England, Second Edition
Claudia Durst Johnson

Life in 1950s America
Nancy Hendricks

Jazz Age America
Steven L. Piott

Women in the Progressive Era
Kirstin Olsen

The Industrial United States, 1870–1900, Second Edition
Julie Husband and Jim O'Loughlin

The 1960s Counterculture
Jim Willis

DAILY LIFE IN

RENAISSANCE ITALY

Second Edition

ELIZABETH S. COHEN
AND THOMAS V. COHEN

The Greenwood Press Daily Life Through History Series

 GREENWOOD

An Imprint of ABC-CLIO, LLC

Santa Barbara, California • Denver, Colorado

Library of Congress Cataloging-in-Publication Data

Names: Cohen, Elizabeth Storr, 1946– author. | Cohen, Thomas V. (Thomas Vance), 1942– author.
Title: Daily life in Renaissance Italy / Elizabeth S. Cohen and Thomas V. Cohen.
Description: Second edition. | Santa Barbara, California : ABC-CLIO, LLC, [2019] | Series: Greenwood Press daily life through history series, ISSN 1080-4749 | Includes bibliographical references and index.
Identifiers: LCCN 2019020666 (print) | LCCN 2019020745 (ebook) | ISBN 9781440856938 (ebook) | ISBN 9781440856921 (print : alk. paper)
Subjects: LCSH: Italy—Social life and customs—To 1500. | Renaissance—Italy.
Classification: LCC DG445 (ebook) | LCC DG445 .C48 2019 (print) | DDC 945/.05—dc23
LC record available at https://lccn.loc.gov/2019020666

ISBN: 978-1-4408-5692-1 (print)
       978-1-4408-5693-8 (ebook)

23 22 21 20 19   1 2 3 4 5

This book is also available as an eBook.

Greenwood
An Imprint of ABC-CLIO, LLC

ABC-CLIO, LLC
147 Castilian Drive
Santa Barbara, California 93117
www.abc-clio.com

This book is printed on acid-free paper ∞

Manufactured in the United States of America

CONTENTS

PREFACE TO THE SECOND EDITION

We thank the editors at ABC-CLIO for the opportunity to revise a book that is almost twenty years old. The actual Renaissance, now long gone, has not changed a whit, but recent research has evolved and deepened so that we see that past differently. In the domain of daily life, social history has been partly subsumed, partly set aside by cultural studies in many forms. Renaissance scholarship has advanced far in studying topics that in 2001 were just opening up: spaces, urban forms, the environment, time, material culture, memory, oralities, slavery, human bodies, health, food, and sex. Bigger than all of these, the global perspective and an at least piecemeal recognition of the great diversity of human histories have reshaped the vision of, among others, those who study old Europe.

As the field of Renaissance studies elaborates, it is impossible to cover everything. In preparing a second edition, we have aimed to absorb some of the new scholarship and bibliography. Most novelly, we have added a new chapter on Italy and the world beyond its borders, on the varied people who came and went. We have also sought to rebalance our discussion on some classic topics such as religion and art-making and to better integrate material on women and gender.

As authors here, we are grateful to countless scholars, including many lively members of a new generation, who, witting or not, have informed and guided us. We are indebted, also, to the direction of the Archivio di Stato di Roma for help during the decades of archival work that enrich this book in many ways. Meanwhile, all errors and imprudent formulations are our own.

As authors we have heeded not only the many scholars who have influenced this book, but also the flow of history itself. The first edition came out just before the shock of 9/11. Since then, for urgent reasons, scholars and the general public have turned to the complex matter of Europe's long, rich exchange with the Islamic world. Italy in the Renaissance figures now as more thoroughly enmeshed in cultural, economic, political, and environmental connections with other places around the Mediterranean Sea and beyond. The first edition emerged at the new millennium, a moment much sunnier than today, when it seemed to us authors and to most readers that, unlike Italians of the Renaissance, we moderns could trust that our world was reasonably safe and, thanks to our competent sciences, generally in good hands and under control. The past two decades have taught us all instead to worry deeply. We are far less sure we have either our planet or our governance under hand; our anxieties push us closer in some ways to the mind-set of Renaissance persons, whose risky world often kept them on edge.

We conclude nevertheless in tempered hope for the future. The Nonni dedicate this edition to Axel and Shoshanna, and their new, bright, many-colored generation.

NOTE ON CHAPTER NOTES

Chapter notes have two principal functions. First, they identify the sources of quotations and of references to archival materials. Second, for those who wish to probe more deeply, the notes name some works of more recent scholarship in English related to the specific theme. The Resources and Bibliography section lists additional books and digital resources.

For sources cited several times, we have used short forms in the chapter notes. The full citations for those materials are here.

Archival Materials in Rome:

BAV: Biblioteca Apostolica Vaticana
ASR, GTC: Archivio di Stato di Roma, Governatore, Tribunale Criminale

Published Primary Sources:

Leon Battista Alberti, *The Family in Renaissance Florence,* trans. R. Watkins (Columbia: University of South Carolina Press, 1969).
Thomas Coryate, *Coryat's Crudities: hastily gobled up in five moneths travells in France, Savoy, Italy. . .,* vol. 1 (Glasgow: James MacLehose and Sons, 1905).
Giovanni della Casa, *Galateo,* trans. K. Eisenbichler and K. Bartlett (Toronto: Centre for Reformation and Renaissance Studies, 1986).

Fynes Moryson, *Shakespeare's Europe: A Survey of the Condition of Europe at the End of the 16th Century, Being Unpublished Chapters of Fynes Moryson's Itinerary (1617)*. Second edition (New York: Benjamin Blom, 1903; reprint 1967).

Secondary Works:

Rudolf Bell, *How to Do It: Guides to Good Living for Renaissance Italians* (Chicago: University of Chicago Press, 1999).

Thomas V. Cohen and Elizabeth S. Cohen, *Words and Deeds in Renaissance Italy: Trials Before the Papal Magistrates* (Toronto: University of Toronto Press, 1993).

Thomas V. Cohen, *Love and Death in Renaissance Italy* (Chicago: University of Chicago Press, 2004).

Edward Muir, *Ritual in Early Modern Europe* (Cambridge: Cambridge University Press, 1997).

TIMELINE OF EVENTS

1347–48	Black Death sweeps across Italy
1378–1417	Great western schism in the papacy leads to two, and then three popes
1402	Filippo Maria Visconti starts forty-five-year rule in Milan
1405	Venice expands onto the mainland, taking Padua and Verona
1417	After the Council of Constance ends schism, rebuilding of the papal state begins very slowly
1420	Construction begins on Brunelleschi's dome for the cathedral of Florence
1423	Vittorino da Feltre establishes humanist school at court of Mantua
1425–30	Venice continues to war with Ottomans over control of eastern Mediterranean commerce
1427	Masaccio's *Trinity* first uses linear perspective in a painting
1433	Aragonese Alfonso I, the Magnanimous, becomes king of Naples
1434	Cosimo de' Medici assumes leadership in Florence
1447–55	Papacy of Nicholas V, founder of the Vatican library
1450	Sforza family takes over rule in Milan
1453	Fall of Constantinople to the Ottomans

1465	First Italian printing press at Subiaco
1474	Mantegna completes *Camera degli Sposi* at Mantua
	Federico de Montefeltro, now formally titled Duke of Urbino, continues embellishing his palace
1478	Pazzi conspiracy in Florence; Lorenzo de' Medici, the Magnificent, assumes power alone
1480	Gentile Bellini paints Sultan Mehmed II in Constantinople
1482	Botticelli paints *Primavera*
1490	Aldo Manuzio founds his humanist press at Venice
1492	Isabella d'Este joins her husband's court at Mantua and begins a long career as patron of art and culture
	Christopher Columbus makes his first voyage to the Caribbean
1494	Charles IX of France invades, opening the Italian Wars
1497	John Cabot "discovers" the coast of Labrador
1498	Girolamo Savonarola is burned at the stake
1499–1502	Cesare Borgia, son of Pope Alexander, campaigns in Romagna and the Marches
1503–13	Papacy of Julius II, warrior and art patron
1504	Spanish viceroy is established in Naples
1506	Leonardo da Vinci finishes *Mona Lisa*
1507	Foundations are laid for the new Saint Peter's Church
1508–20	Raphael paints at the Vatican
1509	Venetians, routed at the Battle of Agnadello, barely conserve their state
1513	Machiavelli writes *The Prince*
	Michelangelo finishes frescoes in the Sistine Chapel ceiling
1513–21	Papacy of Leo X, patron of culture and target of Martin Luther
1516	Jews are readmitted to Venice, and ghetto is established
1525	Imperial coalition defeats French at Battle of Pavia
1527	Sack of Rome by imperial troops
1528	Castiglione publishes *The Courtier*
1530	Charles V is crowned Holy Roman emperor in Bologna
	Last Florentine republic falls; the Medici are installed as hereditary rulers

1532	Ariosto publishes his epic, *Orlando Furioso*
1535	Spanish governor rules in Milan
1540	Bull of Foundation of the Jesuits
	Death of Saint Angela Merici, founder of teaching congregation at Brescia
1541	Michelangelo completes *Last Judgment*
1542	Roman Inquisition is established
1545	Council of Trent opens
1551	Palestrina enters long career as papal composer
1555–59	Papacy of Paul IV, ferocious religious reformer
1555	Roman Jews are enclosed in a ghetto; fifty-five Jewish apostates from Christianity are burned at Ancona
	Florence conquers Siena
1556	Saint Philip Neri initiates Oratory of Divine Love
1559	Peace of Cateau-Cambresis ends the Italian Wars and seals
	Spanish primacy in the peninsula
	Roman Index of Prohibited Books is published
	Sofonisba Anguissola, portraitist from Cremona, goes to serve at the royal court of Spain
1563	Council of Trent closes
1571	Much-feared Ottoman fleet is defeated near Lepanto (modern Nafpaktos)
1576	Saint Carlo Borromeo, reforming archbishop of Milan, succors plague victims
1580	Court at Ferrara is adorned with a novel "concerto" of women singers
1582	Gregory XIII reforms the calendar
1585–90	Papacy of Sixtus V, energetic religious reformer and urban renewer
1586–96	Hunger crises and associated waves of brigandage
1590	Dome is closed on unfinished Saint Peter's basilica
1600	Giordano Bruno, philosopher, is executed for heresy
	Posthumous publication of Moderata Fonte's *The Worth of Women*

Italy in the Renaissance.

1

ITALY IN THE RENAISSANCE

The daily life of any place and time is a fascinating subject, and all the more so when the setting is so rich, varied, rambunctious, and inventive as Italy in the Renaissance. So central is Renaissance Italy to Western history, and so momentous are its achievements for the rest of the globe, that hundreds of scholars have studied its history. Much of this research bears, directly or at short remove, on the daily life of Italians in that important time. We two historians who wrote this book thus belong to a long, lively tradition of inquiry and debate. Like any view, ours is partial, conditioned by our own long research in archival papers concerning both Rome and its hinterland, by our finite readings in an inexhaustible literature on other parts of Italy, and by the habits and interests of our scholarly world. Like any history, this is a work of interpretation.

Let us begin by defining the terrain of investigation—its subject matter, time, and place. What does the title mean? "Daily life" itself is a more complex subject than first meets the eye. The term covers, of course, the simple facts of existence: what people wore and ate; how they worked, played, rested, took sick and recovered; and how they prayed, mourned, loved, and celebrated. Accordingly, a history of daily life might catalog the things and activities in a given time and place. In this book, we push further, to lay out the larger structures of social life and the cultural logic that made sense of them. How did Italians of the Renaissance experience, appraise, remember, and describe both their surroundings and one another? How did they communicate and deal with one another? And how, to their eyes, did they themselves act on their social and material environment?

DAILY LIFE

Renaissance Italians shaped their daily lives. *Agency*, a term from the social sciences, offers a useful model for understanding any society, for it lays out persons' powers to make things happen. Agency is not untrammeled freedom to do exactly what one wants. No one, in any social or natural world—not even the antisocial hermit in his hut—lives free of constraints. Agency is the capacity to make a difference under the conditions that hem one in. Italian men and women in the Renaissance lived with restrictions, both internal and external, both human and natural, very different from those that hedge us moderns. There are few better ways to see how they were both like us and very different from us than to study their lives with an eye to their ploys and stratagems to make headway in their world. The topic is harder than the history of material culture, for we must explore senses, feelings, and minds now five centuries gone.

Historians can never resurrect the dead; the deeds and consciousness of past people are out of reach. Nevertheless, scholars can reconstruct a likeness, and Renaissance Italians left rich sources for research. On paper they expressed themselves profusely, in letters, petitions, diaries, memoirs, commentaries, poems, ambassadorial reports, trial depositions, legal and commercial documents, and deathbed testaments. They also produced a rich imaginative literature—short stories, plays, epics, songs—full of details true to life. Alongside such literature, describing what one did, Italians also wrote a mass of normative prose, saying what one ought to do: statutes, decrees, sermons, and instructions. These prescriptions also offer abundant clues, since laws and rules barred activities people really did. These various papers survive in millions. Despite Italy's eventful history, its archives, with a few tragic exceptions, have been spared the many catastrophes wrought by war and revolution. They remain immensely rich and far from fully explored. Renaissance Italians left superb materials for a detailed and colorful portrait.

Two kinds of sources offer especially precious access to the lives of Renaissance Italians. First are accounts by outsiders, for, since the early Middle Ages, Italy has been a favored destination. Men and women came to view the holy places and the awesome ruins of ancient Rome, to petition the papal court on legal matters, or to seek the pontiff's blessing for their souls or their political ambitions. Artists and scholars crossed the Alps to admire, study, and imitate. Kings and armies came, bent on conquest. All this traffic left a rich literature on Italy by foreigners, useful to us precisely because they came from elsewhere. Travelers often note what locals take for granted. The best observers, like the French philosopher Montaigne, left incomparable records of the little things—the taste of wine and food in the inns, the courtesies, songs, dances, games, and festivals that gave daily life its savor, sound, movement, and color. The second treasure of information lies in the visual arts, especially painting and book illustration. Renaissance Italians, pioneers of naturalism, skilled at depicting their surroundings, left abundant images of their countryside, streets, houses, furniture, implements, and clothing and of their labors, wars, and celebrations. Foreign artists, among them Germans, Flemings, and Frenchmen, left pictures too.

No such records of the Renaissance, be they words on parchment and paper or images of wood, metal, stone, pottery, and canvas, for all their clarity, eloquence, and immediacy, tell a transparent tale. Like any sources for the past, they demand cautious, thoughtful interpretation. Doing history always involves decoding, detective work, and seasoned intuition.

RENAISSANCE

Renaissance, a famous term—not of its own time but of later date—evokes for us the dawn of modernity. It was coined in the nineteenth century by French literary historians to label a renascence, a re-birth, a stylistic revival whereby fourteenth- and fifteenth-century writings recaptured the polish of ancient Roman prose and poetry. As time went on, scholars generalized the word, applying it to all of Western Europe's high culture as the Middle Ages ended. We thus now speak of Renaissance painting, sculpture, architecture, and decorative arts, where first Italians and then other Europeans adopted, adapted, and transformed the themes and motifs of ancient Greece and Rome. Literatures in the vernacular—in Italian, French, Spanish, Dutch, English, Polish, and other languages—are also said to have had their renaissances, marked by the influence of classical models. The term stretches, for similar reasons, to cover the time's philosophy, theology, political theory, and natural sciences. Scholars have also stretched the term into zones where it loses much of its initial, classicizing sense, as in coining "Renaissance monarchy," to label a more competent, more ambitious state neither reborn nor especially Roman. In this latter sense, *Renaissance* comes merely to designate a period in history. So "Renaissance" society denotes social relations characteristic of the era of cultural rebirth. But most Italians of the time—shepherds, soldiers, wet nurses, washerwomen, weavers, merchants, notaries, and many others—spent little time creating or observing Renaissance high art and literature, a refined product made for and often by elites. Common folk did see, hear, touch, wear, consume, and inhabit Renaissance artifacts, but their everyday activities and social relations followed patterns having almost nothing to do with the rebirth of antiquity.

Thus, when it comes to daily life, *Renaissance,* a temporal tag, is not very informative. Nevertheless, scholarly and popular consensus has made the label stick. Historians of material and social life may also write "early modern" (c. 1400–1800), a useful term with longer stretch but we stick here with the label so tightly bound to Italy's image and fame.

Like most historical periods, the Renaissance had fuzzy boundaries. It began sometime toward the middle of the 1300s and ended in the later 1500s, when the Catholic Reformation censored cultural life. The Italians started the process; for some scholars, their Renaissance ended somewhat earlier than elsewhere. This book, a social and material history, explores the two flourishing centuries between 1400 and 1600, before the slow economic and political decline that long diminished Italy's place in West European civilization.

ITALY

Geography

"Italy," like "Renaissance," is largely a modern term, for the present Italian state is only a mid-nineteenth-century creation. Renaissance Italians inhabited a political hodgepodge united by historical memory, geography, general shared culture, and a language-family, but not by government. Whatever common traits they possessed coexisted with great diversity. *Italia,* in ancient times, had first meant a zone of allied peoples gradually co-opted by expansionist Rome; later it labeled a province of the empire of the Caesars.

In the central Middle Ages (781–1014), the name had attached to a segment of Charlemagne's empire, and then to a kingdom of his successors. For four hundred years, there had been no autonomous political entity called Italy. Nevertheless, Italians in 1400, when they spoke of Italy and Italian things, knew what they meant.

Geographically, Italy was edged by clear boundaries. Visitors had no doubts they had arrived. Those who came by sea stepped gratefully onto the solid land of the peninsula or the islands; the quay, or shore, marked distinctly where Italy began. The many others—French, Germans, Netherlanders, Englishmen, and Central Europeans—who descended on the peninsula by land had to cross the formidable barrier of the Alps. Once they came, visitors who traversed the length of the peninsula encountered an astonishing variety of terrain. Travelers trooping down the mountain passes would meet a linguistic frontier. The valleys widened; the climate softened; and the unfamiliar Mediterranean trees, fruits, and flowers first appeared on the terraced lower slopes. Passing the great subalpine lakes, they would emerge onto the fertile plains of Lombardy, thickly settled and strewn with cities and big towns. Then as now, the change—in climate, terrain, architecture, economy, speech, and culture—was dramatic. Early modern Europeans detested mountains. Gratefully, they left the Alps at their back and reveled in the lush flatlands that spread below. The memoirist Thomas Coryate, back in England in 1611 after his Italian travels, remembered:

> Surely such is the fertility of this country, that I think no Region or Province under the Sun may compare with it. For it is passing plentifully furnished with all things, tending both to pleasure and profit, being the very Paradise, and Canaan of Christendom. For, as Italy is the garden of the world, so is Lombardy the garden of Italy, and Venice the garden of Lombardy. It is wholly plain, and beautified with such abundance of goodly rivers, pleasant meadows, fruitful vineyards, fat pastures, delectable gardens, orchards, woods, and what not, that the first view thereof did even refocillate [revive] my spirits, and tickle my senses with inward joy.[1]

The well-watered, intensely cultivated valley of the Po River with its many snow-fed tributaries was not the only landscape that awaited those voyagers who pushed farther south. Italy is long, more than 750 miles of mainland, with Sicily below, half-closing the narrow stretch of Mediterranean that separates Europe from North Africa. By European standards, 750 miles is a long way. By crow flight, Milan, just below the Alps, is far closer to Paris, Prague, and Berlin than it is to Palermo, the capital of Sicily. From Venice, it is as far to Rome as to Vienna. In the Renaissance, when roads were often bad, and dangers, by land and sea, were many, those distances counted far more than they do today.

Italy was more than one long peninsula. There were three huge islands: Sicily to the south, and off the west coast, Sardinia and Corsica, which was not yet French. They, and, in a sense, the bordering seas, the Tyrrhenian to the west, the Ionian at the instep of the boot, and the Adriatic to the east, all arms of the Mediterranean, were parts of a larger Italian whole. Italians used these waters to fish, travel, trade, and wage war. Italian control was always partial; it was challenged at times by Ottoman fleets, North African slave raiders and Dalmatian pirates, and more peaceably by the merchant ships of other maritime nations. Still, all these familiar waters belonged to the Italian sphere.

Voyaging south, a traveler would meet sharp changes in landscape. The Lombard plains below the Alps are an exception; little else is flat. Down the center of the peninsula runs a range of mountains, the Apennines, lower and drier than the Alps but cool and wet enough to offer edible chestnuts, wood, charcoal, and summer pasture and rough enough to furnish little other wealth. They were ideal bandit and smuggler terrain. Flanking this range are zones of hills and valleys, in the Marches, Tuscany and Umbria, with tree-studded plots suitable for grain, vines, and olives. Ranging along the west coast, from Siena southward, is a series of volcanoes, all dead until one reaches rumbling Vesuvius near Naples, and many of them now filled with placid crater lakes. Below Vesuvius, the volcanic chain heads out to sea, reappearing at Stromboli, an island off Sicily, and at towering Etna, smoky and sulfurous on the east Sicilian coast. Much of the southeast of the peninsula, Apulia, is a plain, far drier than Lombardy, and much used in the Renaissance for winter pasture for vast flocks of sheep that summered in the Apennines. The whole peninsula is too narrow and too dry in summer to support readily navigable rivers, except those fed by the meltwaters of the Alps; elsewhere they carried at most small craft and rafts of timber. Many small streams are mere seasonal torrents, shrinking in summer to great gray streaks of dry boulders. At the same time, in premodern times many low-lying areas were swamp and marshland, precious to migrant waterfowl, but also hospitable to the mosquitoes that often carried the malaria endemic in the Renaissance. The low-lying Maremma (the name means "swamp") of the Tuscan coast and the rolling Roman Campagna were particularly plagued and fairly empty of people. Economic geographers argue that, for all this environmental variety, Italy has three basic landscapes: plain (and valley bottom), hill, and mountain. Each had its products and its needs; the complementarity of these zones and their nearness to one another encouraged interzonal trade and economic interdependence.

To the eyes of Renaissance travelers, Italy was densely settled. Yet its population, though always high by European standards, fluctuated in the course of the Renaissance. The first great wave of bubonic plague, the famous Black Death of 1347, was for Italy, as for the rest of Europe, catastrophic. Commentators who liken slow, insidious AIDS to that swift epidemic draw a false parallel. Plague more resembled Ebola, fast and terrifying. It killed within a week. It raged through cities, killing a third or a half of the populace, or even more, in a month or two. Further bouts of plague undermined recovery. By 1400, Italy was down to eight million, having lost three million in a century. For the next fifty years, numbers did not recover much; the Italy of the great Florentine Renaissance remained depopulated. Then, after 1450, although plague remained a danger, the population started to climb again. Throughout the sixteenth century, it rose steadily, reaching perhaps 13.5 million by 1600. Greater numbers did not always bring prosperity; on the contrary, in a world where most fertile land was already under tillage and technology moved slowly, rising population meant falling yields for land and labor and declining living standards. In the last two decades of the sixteenth century, Italy suffered severe food shortages and increasing poverty and vagabondage. By 1600, with a population only one-fourth today's, Italy was for its time overly full; the next century would see economic decline, lower living standards, de-urbanization, two massive epidemics, and a sustained fall in numbers. That sad story, however, lies outside our scope. Our Italy of the Renaissance remained prosperous; its manufactures were among the best in Europe, its merchants and artists highly skilled. Travelers saw not dearth but abundance and wrote admiringly of the luxuries they encountered.

The Italian Renaissance landscape had characteristic settlement patterns. With the exception of the coastal Netherlands, nowhere else in Europe was so urban. Many Italians were city dwellers, and many others inhabited large commercial or administrative towns. This was particularly true of the North and Center, where cities in the Middle Ages had often won political independence and come to control the surrounding countryside. By modern standards, cities' size was modest. Naples, at 200,000 or more, was well the biggest, followed by Venice, at 120,000. Florence in the time of the Medici had only 60,000 inhabitants. Many other urban centers were about half that size. South of Rome, despite the bulky regional capitals, Naples and Palermo, urbanization was weaker, as were commerce and artisanal production. These two southern cities were big, but they had few towns for company. This contrast between the South and the rest of Italy ran deep and involved more than the size and number of cities. In many ways, it continues even today to mark the politics, economy, and culture of the peninsula. The North was then, and remains now, richer and better linked to the rest of Europe than the South and the three great islands of Sicily, Sardinia, and Corsica.

Although Italy was unusually urban for its time, some 75 percent of its people were rural. Of these country dwellers, relatively few lived on isolated family farms of the sort familiar to North Americans (such outposts had, however, colonized parts of Tuscany and Lombardy); instead, most were villagers. Their villages were often big, sometimes almost agro-towns. Many perched on hilltops or mountainsides, often several miles from their fields. Peasants therefore often had to commute to work, on foot or donkey back. These tight, fortified villages to the casual eye look almost eternal; villages in fact were a product of the Middle Ages, as inhabitants abandoned the scattered villas of imperial Rome. Some gathered on higher ground for safety, at the cost of long trudges down and up to farm. A slow process, village fortification (*incastellamento*) began around 1000. The traveler, casting his eye over the hills, might see many villages at once, with their encircling walls and bell towers.

The Italian landscape, more than any other in Europe except perhaps the Dutch, showed the mark of human hands, for it had a very long history of dense settlement and intense cultivation and other use. Everywhere, the natural world bore the traces of intervention, much of it harmful. Although the fall of Rome had brought reforestation, the population growth of the central Middle Ages had reversed that process, so that by 1400,[2] much of the original or recovered forest had been degraded. Forests were a cherished resource, often protected by law and custom, but what woodland survived suffered pressure from woodcutters, herds, and tillers. In some zones, the stable Mediterranean *macchia*, a succession plant community of tough herbs and woody bushes, had replaced the original trees. For reasons of climate, economics, and institutions, the farther south one went, the more fragile the cover of the slopes became. The fatal sequence of cutting, followed by downhill plowing and overgrazing by sheep and goats, often produced catastrophic erosion. Today much of the mountain country of the South and Center is almost totally denuded of soil, a stark zone of deep environmental degradation. This process, well under way in the Middle Ages, accelerated in the Renaissance, thanks to the massive flocks of sheep that spent their summers in the high country of the South and Center. Deforestation and erosion had many consequences; springs dried up, summer rains faltered, and runoff sped up, altering the flow and ecology of rivers, leaving them murky and more often slack or dry in summer. It also encouraged the floods that inundated riverside cities like Florence and Rome. The down-washed soil often found its way to the coast, silting the lagoon of Venice, spurring the state to defensive engineering, or extending the deltas of the Tiber and the Arno. By altering drainage, the eroded soil may also have fostered the spread of coastal marshes. Most Italian states legislated to shield their rivers, to keep them potable and rich in fish.

Other human interventions, somewhat less deleterious, aimed to expand cultivable land. Terracing made hillsides more fruitful. Generation after generation, patient, vigilant labor kept in place the dry-stone walls that held soil to the slopes. Montaigne, traveling in the valley of Spoleto in 1581, marveled to see mountains terraced to their very summits, gray-green with olive trees. Another form of land engineering important in the Renaissance was the systematic draining of swamps, often under princely auspices, to grow food and drive off malaria. Other projects included the irrigation of the fields near the river Po, and the construction of aristocratic gardens and hunting parks.

Culture

The Italians had a shared culture that, despite regional diversities, created a sense of affinity. Thus, despite scattered non-Italian tongues—pockets of Albanian, Greek, French, Spanish, Croatian, and Yiddish for instance—almost everyone also knew and spoke versions of a common language descended from the Latin of the ancient Romans. In the Renaissance they seldom called this tongue "Italian," but rather Venetian, Milanese, Tuscan, Roman, Neapolitan, and so on. Their dialects were many and often mutually unintelligible. Nevertheless, with a little effort, most people could make themselves understood in a common speech, a peninsular amalgam that over the centuries, due to the cultural influence of Florence, took on Tuscan coloration. This approximately national speech, with its local variations, had no home territory or place-based name.

Renaissance Italians also shared religious and moral systems. Aside from the Jews, and a few others, almost all were believing Catholics. The great majority practiced a religion that offered a comprehensive vision of society, history, nature, and the universe, as well as a code of moral conduct, and a rich, complex set of rites and institutions that touched almost every aspect of daily life. At the same time, Italians, like many other Mediterranean peoples, ascribed to notions of honor. Honor provided its own ethics and a view of social and familial life sometimes sharply at odds with Christianity. Together, honor and religion combined to heighten Italians' senses of theater and ceremony. Furthermore, honor spurred a guarded, often anxious habit of rivalry. Competition at times set individual or groups at odds, but as often it mobilized the many solidarities to which people attached themselves, for cities, families, neighborhoods, guilds or corporate bodies, and bands of friends had their collective honor. Since men and women belonged to many groups at once, social life often required a delicate sense of balance as one juggled competing claims for support and loyalty. Renaissance values made for a sometimes-violent, often edgy, and almost always intensely competitive social life. Religion and lay ethics, both so important to the nature of everyday life, will appear often here, in Chapter 6 and elsewhere.

Politics

Politics did not unite Renaissance Italians at all, for there was no central authority. Their political map was so complex that, especially in the North, a traveler met borders everywhere. The many states varied in size and in form of government. They ranged from sprawling kingdom across a variety of rural and urban lordships to republics. Regimes had countless roads to power, from inheritance to election to assassination and stealthy coup d'etat. Some states were fairly big, and others were mere sovereign fingernails of territory. The smallest were autonomous feudal lordships, nominally parts of the Holy Roman Empire. That body, despite its name, was an elective monarchy of the Germans that still asserted residual claims to northern Italy. Though legally subordinate to the emperor, these functionally independent lords might rule a clutch of villages, presiding over their own tribunals and collecting fines and taxes. Somewhat larger were the self-governing cities, some, like Lucca, with modest territories a few dozen miles across, and others, like Florence, Ferrara, and Venice, capitals of fair-sized states with their own subject towns and cities. Some of these city-states were democratic, though suffrage was limited to elites, while others had fallen under the power of *signori*, lords who ruled in an autocratic spirit. Astride the peninsula was a principality like none other, the State of the Church. Centered on Rome, it ruled a great slice of the peninsula's waist. The pope was therefore not only the head of Latin Christendom but also an elected temporal monarch, with his army and navy, foreign policies and diplomats, local governors, judges, jails, and tax men. The mainland's southern third, down to its heel and toe, and Sicily, belonged to Italy's only kingdom, Naples.

Between 1400 and 1600, Italy's political fortunes changed radically. At the start, transalpine powers were weak. In France, war with England absorbed the monarchy. The German emperors, enfeebled, could not meddle, as traditionally, in peninsular affairs. Moreover, the papacy, divided by schism, was torn between Rome and Avignon. In the resultant power vacuum, the middling states of Italy made shifting coalitions free of external interference. After 1443, with the pope finally in command at Rome, a fairly stable system of five major states—Naples, the Papal State, Florence, Venice, and Milan—came to dominate political affairs. Since any three defenders could check two aggressors, no player could overwhelm the others. Italy knew, if not peace, at least a certain predictability. The end of the 1400s destroyed this stability as large, international powers—a revived France, a newly united Spain, and ambitious German emperors—made Italy their chosen battleground and goal of conquest. For sixty-five years after 1494, France and Spain, whose Hapsburg king from 1519 also ruled the German Empire, fought "the Italian Wars" up and down the peninsula. The Italian states strove to play the two combatants off but were too weak to determine the outcome. In the end, after 1560, the French, falling into four decades of civil war, gave up their Italian ambitions, leaving Sicily, Naples, and Milan in Spanish hands until the early eighteenth century. The entire peninsula heeded Spanish hegemony; not even the papacy escaped it.

The political institutions of a scene so mixed do not summarize easily. Some typical features stand out. First comes sophistication. Renaissance Italy pioneered in statecraft. The origins of modern diplomacy, and espionage, seldom far apart, owe much to Italian ingenuity. The medieval visiting emissary gradually evolved into the resident ambassador, with his chancery and his diplomatic immunities. The brilliant dispatches of the ambassadors of Milan, Florence, Mantua, Ferrara, and Venice, and of the papal nuncios, with their eye for local detail, were precious data-sources for the regimes that employed them, as they are for modern historians. Italian regimes were precociously literate and, by continental standards, complex and ambitious. States and cities devised various clever ways of financing their military, judicial, and administrative operations. They legislated with an eye to regulating the economy, the environment, urban spaces, public health, and private morality. On the other hand, do not overestimate their modernity, for many states' ambitions outran their powers of coercion. Early modern statecraft was a dialogue between an ambitious center and a recalcitrant periphery. Remote districts, subject territories, and privileged urban institutions and persons all strove to balk the will of governments. Weak regimes often compromised, granting and selling so many exemptions from the rules that it sometimes seemed that they governed as much by wrangling and exceptions as by decrees and laws.

Participation in power varied greatly. Some regimes were tightly held, others fairly open. In general, in states, towns, and villages, both elites and those of middling station desired public higher offices. Some positions came by appointment, others by ballot. Wherever elected councils sat, there were complex routines of nomination, election, and choice by lottery for offices of strikingly short duration—three months, six months, a year, seldom longer. The rapid circulation of council members served to spread the fruits of power and block anyone from becoming overly mighty; the subtle electoral machinery, with its lotteries and electors of electors, was designed to forestall alliances, connivance, influence peddling, and party faction. Alongside local councils, there were independent judges, almost always from elsewhere—for locals were thought to play favorites—and a corps of secretaries, notaries, and other lettered functionaries, plus a corps of lessor servitors. In all regimes, from autocratic to democratic, power was unevenly distributed. Women, the young, the poor, and even the less wealthy working classes had no formal role, but an informal politics of parish, guild, workplace, confraternity, neighborhood, and piazza animated almost everyone, whatever the age, class, or sex. In the ruling institutions, even in democratic regimes, the rich amassed the lion's share of seats, thanks either to the rules, often made by them, or to their influence. As the Renaissance went on, in many places, the base of power narrowed, in an aristocratization of elites.

Princely regimes gave rise to courts. A court was a social world gathered around a ruler, where his friends and friends of friends battened off his wealth and power. There the ruler exchanged patronage for the submission, loyalty, and services of his more privileged subjects. The richer the state, the more lucrative, though dangerous, courtly life could be. Courtiers, brokers of news and influence, traded in secrets, gifts, commissions, appointments, introductions, invitations, privileges, and other perquisites of power to build their own careers and to advance their kinsmen and friends. The court favored those who possessed tact, subtlety, and an exquisite sense of timing. It was a competitive, sometimes cutthroat place where the mastery of appearances, self-control, and smooth social graces were prize assets. There was little in common between the blunt public discussions of a republic's elected council and the veiled innuendo of much courtly talk.

Economy

With the usual regional variants, a lively economy sustained the states of Italy and fed, clothed, equipped, furnished, and housed their people. A great zone of production, involving both the peasantry and many specialized trades, provided food and drink. Italy also produced abundant goods for home consumption and export. The most important industrial activity was the manufacture of cloth—wool, silk, cotton, linen—both plain and very fancy, for much of the nation's wealth was worn on its backs. Also important were the building trades and the production of glass, leather, and metal goods, including weapons. A distinctive part of Italy's Renaissance economy was cultural: books, prints, art-works, antiques for the domestic and foreign markets. A large service sector, both sacred and secular, occupied and fed many. Providers of services included, beside male and female clergy, diverse lay workers such as lawyers, bankers, notaries, tavernkeepers, wet nurses, porters, and prostitutes. Italy, long commercially more advanced than most of Europe, had more sophisticated mercantile practices and banking methods. A diaspora of men and talents had scattered merchants, bankers, artisans, and artists across Europe and into the Middle East and beyond. Even after Italy lost its monopoly on the Asia trade, it remained important in East–West commerce into the seventeenth century.

Venice, as portrayed in a German world chronicle of 1493, shows off its distinctive island setting, its commerce, and its landmark buildings. The cityscape, an image of a town imagined from above, was a popular form for Renaissance print makers and armchair travelers. (Library of Congress)

Experience of Life

How did it feel to live as a Renaissance Italian in such a landscape, culture, political order, and economy? Much depended on who and where one was. Unlike modern North Americans and Europeans, Renaissance Italians did not think of themselves as citizens of a large country, members of a national group. Rather, their loyalties were intensely local, pinned to family, neighborhood, guild, town, and region. Men and women took much of their identity and sense of self from these alliances and these places.

The Renaissance self was thus a product of both individual impetus and group affiliations. A famous cliché posits that the Italian Renaissance saw the birth of individualism—meaning that in the arts and politics men (and a few women) began to act on their own, untrammeled by custom and social ties, and to cultivate their singular genius. This idea is an overstatement. Such an autonomous mind-set and sense of self did not fit the psychology of everyday Renaissance life. Rather, most people were so enmeshed in complex social relations that defined their values and their natures that they spent little time and energy on self-analysis or self-description. At the same time, in an intensely sociable world that had no word for privacy, they were often assertive, canny, and articulate in both self-presentation and the depiction of those around them. Their social life required intense bargaining. Commerce, politics, courtship, play, and sociability all demanded acute negotiating skills. Accordingly, self-mastery, the control of appearances, self-declaration, and the decoding of the theatrics of others were precious abilities. All the alliances and solidarities, with other men and women and with the saints, Mary, and Jesus, served as bulwarks against the dangers and insecurities that stalked the world. For many Italians, no one, not even a saint, was altogether reliable. It paid to be wary.

How did Italians shape their personal goals in a society so defined and circumscribed by hierarchy and by tight social relations? They lacked the optimistic modern notion of getting ahead, for much of status was inherited. Nevertheless, with luck and pluck, one could better one's position. Still, in a volatile economy that grew slowly, if at all, descent was as likely as ascent. Beset by a realistic sense of scarcity and risk and unable to fall back on a reliable state or strong institutions of social welfare, Italians spent a lot of energy securing and defending themselves. They worked hard to find protectors, both human and divine. Because much of security came from allies, they strove to advance and to protect not only themselves but also their associates, especially their families. They aimed at survival and safety, as well as pleasure and prosperity in this world, and at salvation in the next.

One aspect of self-experience was sensation. Here, premodern Italian life was different from our own. Consider sight. We moderns almost never see deep darkness, for our electricity has diluted night. Aside from a few flickering torches on palaces or from the flambeaux and lanterns some walkers carried, Italian towns were dark once the sun went down. Yet in good weather, stars were bright, and several days a month the light of the full moon helped peasants, soldiers, and bandits to move around at night. In the daytime, colors were sometimes brighter and sharper than they are today under Italy's often polluted skies. Sound too was different, for there was no roar and rumble of internal combustion to drown out the human voices, the sharp cry of summer swallows, the hypnotic, rasping click of the Mediterranean cicada, the shrill chatter of the millions of winter starlings, the sounds of livestock, and the pervasive clangor of church and civic bells that marked the divisions of the day. In the absence of raucous machines, Italians filled their streets and piazzas with social talk. They called and chided children, greeted friends, and hurled comments, insults, and challenges. From inside the house, the ears could monitor the social world of the street; noise of a fight would bring neighbors to the windows. Political life had its shouts of celebration, affirmation, anger, dismay, and supplication. There was also much music; peasants sang while working in the fields, friends played lutes and guitars on a summer evening, ambassadors arrived to the thump of drums and the blare of trumpets, holy processions sang hymns. The Renaissance nose, too, had its sharp experiences. The world was full of smells we moderns have banished. Seldom-washed human bodies carried acrid sweat and the gentler scent of hair, unmasked by deodorants and shampoo, though the affluent might wear scented oils or perfumes. The warm odors of baking bread and cooking often filled the air, competing with the pungent reek of stale blood at the butcher's shop, of garbage, and of animal and human excrement. The skin's sense of touch had to suffer the itch of fleas, lice, and bedbugs. It put up with cold, without benefit of central heating, and with stifling summer heat, unrelieved by air-conditioning. And few good medicines could begin to dull the body's frequent fevers, chills, or pain.

CONCLUSION

Daily life in Renaissance Italy thus had its geographic, political, and cultural setting. The actions of ordinary men, women, and young people played out against the handsome backdrop of a lovely countryside that, despite frenzied overbuilding, remains still visible today. The towns and villages, too, set a dramatic stage for work, play, and social life. The many institutions they housed, large and small, jostled for authority; Italians were adroit at using them and playing them off one another for leverage and protection. Society as a whole was very "face-to-face," to use a sociological term; transactions felt personal, and emotions went into play. Life was often neither comfortable nor easy, but even where tense or painful, it was seldom lonely. Existence, as a consequence, was at once very sociable and often intensely political. We will return to all these themes as we survey the many facets of the everyday life of Renaissance Italians.

NOTES

1. Coryate, *Coryat's Crudities*, 238. (Spelling modernized.)
2. On managing forests, Karl Appuhn, *A Forest of the Sea: Environmental Expertise in Renaissance Venice* (Baltimore, 2009).

2

SOCIETY: WHO WAS WHO

In Renaissance Italy, as in other premodern European societies, people's experience of daily life varied according to rank above all, and to age, gender, and, especially for women, marital status. Thus, to be a child, adult, or old person affected what one must, could, could not, should not, or need never do. For women, the status of wife was in ways the most constrained stage of life; widowhood offered more independence, though also greater vulnerability. Differences also followed from how and where people made their livings. When Italians met—to talk, do business, play, fight, pray—all these social traits, readily visible in body, bearing, speech, and clothing, governed expectations and options. Access to resources—not only material and economic goods like food or tools, but also good connections or legal privileges—shaped daily life. What one had to work with depended on one's birth family, for property and status passed mostly along lines of kinship. Nevertheless, inherited assets did not wholly set a person's place. Chance attributes, including health, looks, talents, and plain luck—what Renaissance Italians called "Fortune"—also determined where in society a person fit.

To visualize a cast of characters for our panorama of daily life, it helps to catalog the wide array of social roles or niches in which Renaissance Italians might improvise moves to play out their lives.

It lets us slot into a workable model of a social structure Italy's wel-ter of men and women, rich and poor, literate and illiterate, domi-nant and subordinate, urban and rural, worldly and otherworldly. Nevertheless, too neat a scheme risks distorting actual Renaissance experience. Therefore, we offer some historical examples to show how quirkily people might fit the types.

In a hierarchical society, social roles, one understood, stood higher or lower on a pyramid of prestige. Our portrait will begin at the top and work down. Note, however, that the most power-ful, while highly visible, were also few. Their daily lives differed greatly from those of the much more populous lower classes. Fur-thermore, many traits made up a person's place in society, and the hierarchies were many. We need to imagine Italy's social structure not as a simple ladder but as a multidimensional complex.

In this chapter we begin with the clergy, a social order with its own divisions and hierarchy. Next, we turn to the countryside, where the vast majority dwelled. In rural areas lived a spectrum of social types, from privileged landowners through hard-working peasants to landless shepherds and bandits. Then we turn to urban society. Cities, the site of prosperous commerce, artisanal produc-tion, and princely courts, supported a wide range of activities and ways of life. The chapter ends with a quick look at the least fortu-nate who made do with little.

CLERGY

The Christian clergy evolved through the Middle Ages into a separate order of society, committed to God's services. Its special, sacred task was to help all Christians conform their lives to divine will, so as to attain salvation after death, and, in their earthly lives, to win providence's favors. The clergy constituted a separate juris-diction. Mostly, its members answered to church authorities, not to local rulers. Furthermore, becoming a cleric represented, in theory, a break with family and with other ties to worldly status. By the Renaissance, the Roman Catholic clergy, both male and female, took vows of celibacy. To serve God and minister to all Christians alike, clerics were to be free of human ties to spouses and children (in fact, the wider family still made claims). Besides the spiritual rewards of renouncing fleshly appetites, there was an obligation of selfless service. This universal and godly mission not only set clergy apart but also earned them a conceptual primacy in the social order.

Within this churchly order, however, were many sorts of clerics with different powers, obligations, and lifestyles. By the Renaissance most though not all male clergy were ordained as priests. The largest cohort, the secular clergy, together shouldered the care of souls, an awesome burden that entailed many tasks. These men provided sacraments and other rituals, taught doctrine, offered moral counsel, supported charitable works and social services, and judged infractions of church law. They also administered the economic assets and physical plant that sustained all those activities. The secular clergy carried out this massive task through an elaborate institutional hierarchy descending from the pope, through the cardinals, archbishops, and bishops, and down to local parish priests. At the bottom were students who took the minor holy orders; they could later renounce these and often did so. Clerical status in the meantime entitled them to church benefices and, for certain crimes, spared them from answering to secular courts. The layers of the church varied greatly in power and affluence. Thanks to centuries of pious donations to support God's works and save donors' souls, the church owned great wealth. The prelates at the top, chief administrators of this great patrimony, disposed of vast resources. During the Renaissance, some were known for lavish living. The clergy's lower ranks, meanwhile, generally lived modestly, though few faced the hardships that racked their parishioners.

Besides these pastoral clerics, the church relied on clergy of another sort, who lived in obedience to an order's rules. Some among these "regular" clergy, the monks and nuns, usually dwelled in communities walled away from the world's distractions and devoted themselves to prayer, study, and good works. Others, especially friars like the Franciscans and Dominicans, carried their work to ordinary people and sought, through preaching and counseling, to bring Christ's aid to the poor, wayward, and desperate. So popular did the friars become with their novel Christian social work that the church soon put them to use in other ways. During the Renaissance, friars were everywhere, preaching moral reform, acting as confessors to both commoners and patricians, lecturing in universities, and even, with the Florentine Dominican Savonarola, directing an attempted revolution in city government. The friars' very ubiquity and prominence made them the butt of more and less good-humored anticlerical criticism, as in the stories of Boccaccio's *Decameron*. In the sixteenth century, some of the new Catholic Reformation orders, the Jesuits especially, joined the friars in apostolic work.

While abbesses led convents, women clergy could not administer sacraments or readily imitate the lifestyle of the friars, whose work moved them about the world. Although houses of female Franciscans and Dominicans did exist, like the older orders of nuns, they practiced cloister. Yet many spiritually zealous women wished to serve God and his poor directly. Some found an outlet for their holy ambitions as tertiaries, layfolk who took vows to live piously in the world, where they might serve the sick, prisoners, and other sufferers. Tertiaries had formal ties with the friars, but they had imitators who preferred autonomy. People on the church's borderland, uncloistered semi-nuns, home-made mystics, and hermit prophets, had a mixed reputation, mingling admiration with suspicion. Devout women who chose independence, in particular, invited gossip, occasionally with good cause; courts occasionally did try alleged prostitutes who, said the neighbors, made house calls dressed in holy robes.[1]

Profile: Angela Merici, Founder of a Religious Congregation

Saint Angela Merici (1474–1540), a mystic, founded the Ursulines, the first religious order devoted to educating poor girls. Born of modest parents in a small town on the shores of Lake Garda in Lombardy, she became an orphan at age ten; her older sister died three years later, suddenly and without last rites. According to Angela's hagiography, the first of her many visions occurred then; it reassured her anxiety over her sibling's salvation. Gratefully, she dedicated herself yet more fully to God, practiced great austerity, and lived a virgin in the habit of a Franciscan tertiary. Leading a cluster of like-minded young women, she began work with the local needy, a novel form of charitable service impossible for traditionally cloistered nuns. Her special project was to bring religious education to the neglected daughters of the poor. In Brescia, Merici oversaw the growth of a new kind of institution for religious women, dedicated to teaching, under the patronage of Saint Ursula. Its members worshipped and worked together but did not take vows or live communally. Merici and her institute attracted support from powerful and devout admirers. The company received formal papal approval four years after her death.

Before the Reformation, Italian clergy had much in common with those in all Western Europe. Nevertheless, Italy was distinct, in part because Rome was Catholicism's historic center. In the early fourteenth century the papacy moved to Avignon in southern France, but in 1378 popes returned to Rome. Despite four succeeding decades of schism, when two rival popes sparred across the Alps, Italy reclaimed a focus, still contested, of church politics. With the division resolved in 1417, the reunited papacy gradually made Rome once again a magnet for all those who sought spiritual uplift at its holy sites or had business with the central church. In addition, as landlord over vast properties, especially in Italy's Center and South, the church played a major role in temporal affairs. Therefore, although a small fraction of the population, the clergy were very prominent in Italian life. Powerful churchmen—bishops, cardinals, heads of religious orders, and their agents—were numerous and influential.

Profile: Cardinal Francesco Gonzaga

Cardinal Francesco Gonzaga (1444–1483), son of the ruler of Mantua, was one of the worldly prelates who served the pre-Reformation papacy. He received a cardinal's red hat at the precocious age of seventeen while a student at the university at Pavia. According to many art historians, the Gonzaga family celebrated this great coup by having their court artist, Andrea Mantegna, fresco a collective portrait in the famous Camera degli Sposi, at the Ducal Palace. Though not a priest, Francesco acquired through his career a number of benefices whose income was necessary, though ultimately insufficient, to sustain the heavy expenses incumbent upon a cardinal. These included maintaining a large household (in the first year of his appointment, Francesco's already contained eighty-two persons and fifty-four animals) and providing fittingly honorable accommodations for them in Rome and elsewhere. Pope Pius II, who had raised Gonzaga to the cardinalate, pressured him also to build a palace in the new summer capital at the tiny papal hometown renamed Pienza. When made bishop in his native Mantua in 1466, the cardinal faced squarely the inherent tensions of his position; his family wanted him to reside in his see and attend to the family's local interests, while his superior, the pope, demanded his service in the larger church domain, as in his posting as legate to Bologna. Like some other prelates of his era, he forewent clerical celibacy. His illegitimate son, known later as the "Cardinalino," was raised comfortably in Mantua under the eye of Francesco's mother.

RURAL SOCIETY

Land was the rural economy's key resource. Many rural folk owned some, but, in much of the countryside, most land belonged to a few large landholders. Typically, rural society divided sharply into those few who owned the bulk of the land and other resources and the many who did the work.

Landlords and *Signori*

Big landowners took their profits in several ways. Much income came from money rents or a share of the crops. Many landowners also held the legal status of *signori* (lords), a feudal rank entitling them to profit from their privileged intervention in the lives of their dependent peasants. As *signori* they administered justice, owned village facilities and services, controlled hunting and fishing and other uses of their domains, and commandeered labor for carting, for local maintenance and construction, and for their own harvests. A *signore also* collected fees and fines from villagers who sued or were convicted by his courts. He (or she) rented out the monopolies on the mill, wine presses, bakery, inn, and store. When he preferred not to exploit his fields, meadows, woods, and streams himself, he sold licenses to others. Some lords also bought the option to collect state taxes. Lords might encroach on the rights and revenues of the local churches and lay confraternities. And they lent money and seed grain to needy tenants. Thus, lords relied for their well-being on wealth exacted from the less-advantaged rural majority. In theory, elite privileges entailed responsibility. Both Christian charity and honor's magnanimity urged benevolence toward dependents and the needy. Lords and tenants sometimes did look out for one another's welfare. Yet the financial chasm between landlords and peasants and their mutual struggle for a bigger share of the land's production provoked latent conflict. Nevertheless, Italy's peasants, unlike those of Germany, France, England, Sweden, Hungary, Russia, seldom rose in violent rebellion. The sanguinary Friuli Carnival uprising of 1511 is an exception.

Although many landlords owned properties of different sorts and sizes, big holdings were often exploited as estates, run from a central village. There the lord had a residence. In the hills and mountains, it was often an old castle, once built for defense against endemic medieval violence. A massy building, it not only housed the landlord, his family, retainers, officials, and guests, but it also stored cash, papers, equipment, grain, wine, oil, produce, animals, and the weapons to protect it all. Often there was a lockup. Gradually, during the fifteenth and sixteenth centuries, especially in calmer zones, these elite residences lost their military functions and came to offer greater comfort and pleasure, acquiring handsome big windows and columned loggias. In northern and central Italy, near cities, some landowners put up new country homes, or villas, pleasure domes whose main purpose was neither economic nor political, but aesthetic and even intellectual. In most places, however, the lord's house still served the old needs. Although violence declined during the Renaissance, in the rural Center and South and in frontier zones like Friuli, routine mayhem persisted. Local big men had to be tough to fend off incursions from aggressive neighbors, ambitious central governments, and restive dependents. For some *signori*, private raids and wars remained a pastime.

Landownership took many forms. Families held big estates, and so did secular and religious institutions. The interests of ecclesiastical estate holders did not always align with the moral imperatives of Christian benevolence. Some landowners enjoyed a noble's title and prestige, while others only "lived nobly," claiming respect through lifestyle alone. Still others were commoners whose simple means ruled out pretensions. Meanwhile, landowners, noble and commoner alike, did not always live in the country. Increasingly, rural properties belonged to town dwellers. Outside many cities were little vineyards, retreats for quiet life or social gatherings, where a hired hand saw to the gardening and split the harvest with the landlord. Grand suburban villas, often palatial, were bigger operations on a similar model. Owners with careers in city or court often shared the country environment of their tenants and dependents for only part of the year. They might leave the running of their rural properties to hired estate agents or rent out their lands for months or years to capitalist enterprises that tilled and grazed the estate.

Profile: Giuliano Cesarini, Baron

Giuliano Cesarini (d. 1567), a proud man with a hot temper, pursued the lordly ambitions embraced by his forebears, a rising clan of wealthy barons. Thanks to Cesarini cardinals and some strategic marriages, the family had assembled villages and estates in the coastal lowlands near Rome, in the nearby mountains, and, finally, on the Adriatic coast. The Cesarini also had a prestigious sinecure, the ceremonial post of Standard-bearer of the Roman People. Flaunting this title, Giuliano paraded at civic festivals in gorgeous costumes studded with precious gems. His two palaces in Rome featured gardens adorned with antique statuary collected by his cardinal predecessors. His stable was full of fine horses, and, delighting in the hunt, he kept many dogs. Giuliano ruled his lands in absentia. Harsh but inattentive, he knew few tenants by name and had little knowledge of their needs and histories. He squeezed them hard through paid agents, laying on new feudal obligations, and amassing peasant lands defaulted due to debts and fines. He was also an ambitious castle builder, using unpaid village labor. By these means he financed his comforts and public life, a series of governorships and high military commands in the Papal State. His tenants loathed him; several of his villages rebelled.[2]

Village Elites

Running estates and villages, especially where landlords were routinely absent, fell to a local elite who mediated between the peasants and the outside world. Owners' agents managed the land, oversaw work on the lord's own acreage, and collected rents and dues. These deputies juggled contradictory demands: to serve their employer's interests, make their own way, and live among the often-impoverished and resentful tenants. This village elite also included professionals, often from elsewhere or linked to external institutions. Among these, priests, though often sparely educated, were men of weight. A board of senior villagers, a small version of cities' communal councils, spoke for local government. But the central official, called *podestà* or *vicario*, was an outsider appointed by the feudal lord or the rulers of the state. Commonly, assisting these administrators were resident or passing country notaries, who wrote and kept legal documents. Their outside origin, professional ties, and official power distanced officials from the rest of the rural community. They could command and punish in the name of external authority. At the same time, they mediated conflicts between the village and the larger world and between contentious locals.

Peasants

Peasants were Italy's largest social group. At home or migrant, they occupied, worked, and used the land. Some peasants owned land, but much terrain belonged to landlords or, in rougher country, was commons. For access to land, peasants normally paid money rent or delivered a share of their yield. They might also contract to secure livestock, tools, and gear to work their holdings. Many of them owed seigniorial dues in money, kind, or labor. They paid tithes to the church and, sometimes, taxes to the state. And, when times were hard, they often shouldered debt to cover obligations. Feudal and economic dependency restricted peasants' options. Commonly, they pieced together a livelihood from a mix of rural activities, in the home village or elsewhere, aiming to amass the assets to marry off their daughters and set up their sons. Women were crucial to this household economy. The peasant world was not closed; economic necessity spurred much migration in search of income. Peasants consumed part of what they grew, but, for most, some produce, directly or via the landlord, made its way to market.

The organization of agriculture differed by locale, with varied patterns of family and residence. Peasant livelihood derived largely from family labor, supplemented where useful by hired workers. In any region, the most productive size and form of the residential group depended on the crops, land-holdings, and tenure customs. Thus, smaller nuclear families suited the labor-light pastoralism of mountain regions, or specialized farming with very seasonal need for workers. Larger, more extended family groups—three generations or allied adult siblings—fitted well the sharecropped, mid-sized farms of the North and Center, units that required a substantial labor supply through much of the year. The lands a peasant household worked, especially in zones of mixed farming, were seldom contiguous and compact. Rather, the family might cultivate flax in one place, grain, fruit, and vines together in another, and olives yet somewhere else.

Besides relying for aid on family, peasants turned to peers. Villagers cooperated in collective work like ditching, threshing, gleaning, or washing clothes, and in local government, collective lawsuits or petitions, and festivals. This collaboration, not always harmonious, enhanced their capacity to cope. Even in dispersed settlements, mutual aid, probably scantier than in villages, was still crucial.

Peasants' prosperity was unpredictable. Many conditions shaped their fortunes: the fertility of the land, and shifts in the weather, the harvest, and market prices. In bad years debt piled up. Banditry and warfare could wreak havoc. As the population rose, scarce lands to work and many mouths to feed pressed on the entire peasantry. Yet some families fared better than others, whether through richer holdings, harder work, less greedy landlords, fortunate timing of births and deaths, or sheer luck. Some peasants lived well, expanded their resources, and hired hands to boost their yield. Many others scraped by, improvising to hold off creditors and keep their lands and goods.

Profile: Giacobo Caponero, Rich Peasant

At sixty-two, Giacobo di Giuliano, alias Caponero (Black Head), of Rocca Sinibalda had in 1556 probably gone gray or bald, but the old nickname stuck. He and Tomassa, his wife, had just married off a son. A rich peasant, literate and precise with numbers, he was of the village elite. He was a very active *massaro*, one of four aldermen who directed local government, and he had served as one of the *santesi*, officers who raised and oversaw parish and confraternity funds. Caponero's economic enterprises were diverse. He owned a hemp plot, a rig for trapping birds, woods, meadows, and vineyards, cattle, and the mule and donkey, which, as a feudal service, carried bricks for the castle his lord was building. In addition, he had leased from his lord rights to run the village mill. He lost badly on the contract and sold some lands to pay back his debts. He had also held the monopoly on the local sale of cheeses and other foodstuffs, and sometimes wholesaled salted pork and pigeons preserved in oil. He remembered hard times: the famine two decades back when his mother brought bread and acorns to starving prisoners in the castle; the war and sack, when armies had cut his vines and driven off his cattle. Yet he had recovered some if his prosperity.[3]

Landless Workers

Some peasants controlled no land; they were among the poorest. But the landless—and surplus members of landed families—could still earn a living. In some regions—the grain lands of the Southeast and Sicily—rather than rent parcels to families, landowners paid laborers to work their large estates. Elsewhere, harvesting and other seasonal field tasks offered temporary employment. And many areas needed herding, woodcutting, and carting. Such activities often required workers to leave their villages. In some places, rural industry offered opportunities. Making bricks was country work. At a few sites, workers extracted minerals: marble at the Carrara quarries; iron in parts of Lombardy; and, from the 1460s, alum, for fixing dyes in textiles, at the pope's mines at Tolfa. Elsewhere, the urban textile industries in wool, linen, and silk gave homework—spinning, weaving, fulling—to rural women and men. Often only part-time, such work seldom provided a regular living. Especially in hard times, another option was emigration, to seek work as a servant in the city, a soldier, or a brigand in the hills. The sharp insecurities of the landless often made their families fragment.

URBAN SOCIETY

City life differed sharply from country life in scale and tempo. Density did not make the difference, for many villages were, like cities, closely packed. Rather, cities were big, teeming, and diverse in ways of life. Many of them survived from antiquity thanks to a cathedral or seat of lay power, but they owed their eventual medieval revival to commerce. As they prospered, political, administrative, and cultural activities grew up around their markets and workshops. Urban society reflected these varied functions. Occupations and professions, wealth, legal status, and education combined to generate and define an urban social hierarchy. The elite included a politically active aristocracy and a stratum of affluent citizens, many of them large-scale merchants and entrepreneurs, plus a cohort of lettered professionals and bureaucrats. In the social middle was a mix of skilled artisans. Further down the scale came the semiskilled and unskilled, including male and female servants. At the bottom struggled the deeply impoverished, disproportionately female, as women earned less income. Many of the destitute were sick or disabled, and reduced to begging. They survived at charity's will or whim.

Patricians and Nobles

Urban aristocracies varied in origins and evolution. This class might include urban-dwelling members of the rural, feudal elite.

Urban families had merged with them to create an upper class called "magnates." In the Middle Ages, some cities, Florence and others, greatly fearing their power, had excluded magnates from political office; elsewhere, they were part of the governing class. Even where these nobles held some power, they had to share it with new, prominent rich families emerging from international commerce, banking, and manufacturing. A new urban upper class that we call patricians emerged from the coalescence of these two groups: noble and mercantile. During the Renaissance, these patricians consolidated their position, curbing political competition from other groups and hindering social ascent into their caste. This group rewrote municipal statutes and constitutions to define their privileges and monopolize major public offices. In those cities where the bar to mobility was stringent, patrician privilege might acquire hereditary legal status that withstood financial shocks. To reinforce their distinctness, privileged families also sought marriages within their group. Nevertheless, within patriciates not all was peaceful. Rival insiders—individuals, families, or factions—jostled energetically, using political manipulation, judicial repression, and not a little violence.

Many of Renaissance Italy's greatest cultural achievements involved these patriciates, as producers and as patrons. Especially in the North, this social group committed itself early to the new educational and intellectual program of humanism, based in renewed use of the ancient Roman and Greek heritage. These men saw the classical heritage as enriching and validating civic political culture. This elite also supported the efforts of visual artists, whose work wedded models from the classical past to new techniques of building, painting, sculpture, and crafting domestic goods. All this high culture enhanced and legitimated patrician superiority. In the sixteenth century, many patricians waxed aristocratic in tastes and values; more and more of their culture took on a courtly cast.

Profile: Alessandra Macinghi negli Strozzi, Patrician Wife

Alessandra Macinghi (c. 1408–71), the daughter of Florentine patricians, at age fourteen married twenty-five-year-old Matteo Strozzi, of a large, prestigious lineage. Over ten years she bore eight children. Political struggles between urban factions banned from Florence her husband and other Strozzi males.

Alessandra joined her husband in exile until his death, about a year later; around the same time, three of their children died of plague. She then returned to Florence, where she lived her remaining forty-five years as a widow. Alessandra dedicated her life to protecting and advancing her children and their patrimony, playing attentively her local contacts and Strozzi family networks. While her exiled sons pursued business, for years she penned them extensive letters full of worries, counsel, and practical information.

Merchants and Businessmen

Merchants and entrepreneurs spanned a wide range of stations in life. In Renaissance Italy, fortunes were volatile. One could get rich quickly; one could fall fast. At the group's top were very rich men who had everything in common with the patricians except their wealth's timing. Theirs was new money. Its sources were no different. Yet the tightened rules for entry into the governing class often kept newcomers from political roles commensurate with their economic clout. They did enjoy legal rights as citizens and sometimes had access to less prominent offices. And they lived well, gaining and spending with some of the best. Of course, not all merchants became or remained so affluent. While the wealth and skills of Italian businessmen made them visible throughout Europe, not all could aspire to international markets. Among those who bought and sold there were quite modest dealers in local trade and even itinerant peddlers. The dealer in recycled clothing was a more frequent, if less imposing, figure than a banker of Medici stature. In lifestyle, such small-scale entrepreneurs resembled their economic peers among the artisans. Prosperous merchants' wives do not appear to have engaged directly in the family business. Some widows, though, controlling family assets, invested in their own or others' ventures. And, in modest concerns, women at times worked on their own as retailers.

Those who lived from commerce and business had their own lively culture. They admired curiosity, ambition, prudence, and an eye for calculated risk, all traits that served them well in their work. They also valued education, though of a practical sort. They supplemented their ability to keep records, reckon accounts, and appraise both goods and men with knowledge of applied

A fresco from ca. 1500 at the Castle of Issogne (Val d'Aosta) suggests how food shopping brought men and women of diverse social and economic statuses face to face. (PHAS/Universal Images Group via Getty Images)

geometry, geography, current affairs, foreign tastes and customs, prices, currencies and exchange rates, and commercial law.

Profile: Gregorio Dati, Wealthy Merchant

Gregorio Dati (1362–1435) was a successful Florentine merchant, with many profitable partnerships dealing in wool, silk, and other merchandise. His career, however, especially early on, knew the vicissitudes characteristic of Renaissance business. For example, while he sailed to Spain as his enterprise's traveling partner, a role typical for young men, pirates stole all his goods, including a consignment of pearls, and his own clothes. He recovered from such losses, thanks in part to infusions of capital from dowries from four successive marriages. Later in life, he was honored to serve several posts in city government; his election to the prestigious office of Standard-Bearer of Justice marked his career peak. Over the years he wrote a "diary," actually an occasional record in which he kept accounts of his commercial and family life. Men of his kind pioneered this form of writing about the public and private self (Chapter 11).

Lettered Professionals and Bureaucrats

In medieval and Renaissance Italy, the demand for literate public servants promoted a new elite group living off the fruits of education. Their work demanded facility in reading and writing classical Latin, skills more accessible to those with family means to afford the schooling. Yet here was one avenue by which skilled modest men could rise.

Lettered professionals worked in several venues. Health care, with its university-trained physicians, and its craftsman surgeons and apothecaries, was one literate zone. Another domain employed the teachers and private tutors. With the elaboration of government and associated public institutions, demand for literate employees grew. More and more, records needed keeping, negotiations needed their paper trail, speeches and letters of praise and persuasion needed penning. Sensitive dispatches required encoding and decoding. The appetite for lawyers, magistrates, administrators, secretaries, copyists, and notaries was sharp. And then, the flood of paper needed archivists to file and find it. The new printing needed teams of workers who could read. Artillery called forth engineers, surveyors, cartographers, and military architects. Earlier, in the Middle Ages, literate work had clung to the church. Many Renaissance men who pursued careers in the expanding bureaucracies still followed ecclesiastical careers, as celibate clerics. It became more common, however, for men to combine literate work with marriage and family. In some cities, by the sixteenth century, the reproductive success of the lettered class contributed to its transformation into a closed, hereditary caste; only members' sons could apply to join.

Courtiers

In the course of the Renaissance, princes ruled more and more Italian states. Many traced their power to military prowess and coer-
cive takeover. Once in place, they tried to consolidate their authority
and establish dynasties where rule would pass within the family.
One strategy was to establish a court. Its site was normally a city,
albeit sometimes a small one such as Urbino. The function of a medieval court had been to guard the ruler and his government and to
secure advice from powerful dependents, whom he bound to his
person with hospitality and largesse. While the Renaissance Italian
court retained these military and political functions, its social and
cultural role blossomed. It became a lively center of social and artistic display and entertainment. Dispensing patronage and fostering
art and festivities to bolster their legitimacy, princes and their families attracted a prestigious entourage that mixed the well-born, the
well-connected, the beautiful, and the talented. Castiglione's famous
book *The Courtier* set the model: a gentleman accomplished in military skills, graceful in body, elegant in dress and manners, sage and
tactful in word and conduct, knowledgeable in letters, and appre-
ciative of the arts. He was to serve the prince as a soldier, adviser,
and diplomat. This male paragon had his counterpart in a lady also
beautiful in both body and soul, pleasing in bearing and conversation, clever, discreet, and wise. Besides those nobly born, courts
welcomed men and women of unusual artistic and intellectual gifts:
musicians, singers, dancers, poets, architects, painters, philosophers
and fine cooks, plus dwarfs, buffoons, and keepers of the horses,
hounds, and the exotic beasts. Their achievements and company
gave pleasure to the prince and his guests and allure to his regime.

Artisans

The productive core of urban society were artisans and their
families, who made and sold goods for both local consumption and
external markets. Typically, artisans worked with considerable independence, acquiring raw materials, working them, and then selling
directly to consumers. They produced some routine goods for general sale but often made more specialized products on commission,
to a buyer's specifications. Artisans filled the whole spectrum of daily
needs. Masons and carpenters designed and built. Many artisans,
including bakers, cooks, and brewers, processed food. Others made
hides into leather and leather into shoes, pouches, wall coverings,

book-bindings, saddles, and harnesses. Woodworkers made barrels, implements, and furniture. Soap, candles, paper, baskets, bird cages, musical instruments, ceramic and metal containers, weapons, jewelry, playing cards, books, and countless other objects all emerged from artisan workshops. The manufacture of textiles occupied many workers, especially in a city like Florence, which specialized in high-end merchandise for international trade. Textile production coordinated the efforts of carders, spinners, weavers, dyers, and fullers. The tight vertical integration of this major industry gave workers less autonomy than that of many other artisans. The cutting and sewing of clothing and the confection of special decorations like gold thread and lace occupied numbers of hands. In some cities, artisans produced luxury goods for markets throughout Europe, as did the glass-workers of the Venetian lagoon and the armorers of Milan and Brescia. Much of the art that makes Renaissance Italy famous—made by jewelers, metalsmiths, majolica makers, furniture makers, and printers as well as painters and sculptors—was produced by men working as artisans. (See Benvenuto Cellini in Chapter 6.) Like other groups, artisans varied in prestige and wealth. Workers in precious metals had more prestige than butchers and tanners, who handled carcasses and blood. The executioner was among the lowest. Also, within any craft, some men, more talented, ambitious, connected, or industrious, outdid their fellows.

The basic unit of artisan production was the household. Residence and workplace often occupied the same or adjacent premises. The master craftsman typically led the work of family members, assistants, and apprentices learning the trade. His wife frequently was active in the business; more rarely, she had a trade of her own, typically spinning, embroidery, or weaving. Many cities had corporations, or craft guilds, of artisans. These bodies oversaw the work, regulating quality and work conditions and supervising entry into the occupation. Often, they, or allied confraternities, also provided welfare services for members and their families. While some guilds claimed political representation, artisans were increasingly excluded from participation in government (Chapter 15).

Profile: Ginevra Rossi, Wife and Candy Maker

Ginevra (d. 1608), wife of Guglielmo Rossi, learned candy making from her husband. Together they developed a prosperous Roman business and also produced five children. So successful

were they that, said Guglielmo, they attracted the envy of
local competitors, who instigated an inspection by guild officials. During the Christmas rush, the consuls barged into the
shop and obliged Ginevra, then six months' pregnant, to hurry
about, hauling out boxes and climbing up and down stairs, to
show their goods. Several days later, the woman miscarried
and shortly after died. Her husband, blaming the stress the
inspectors caused, took them to court. He itemized his injuries,
including the loss of the child and of Christmas business and
the dishonor to his good name. The largest claims he made were
for the loss of his wife's work caring for the children and overseeing the shop (500 scudi), of her expertise as a candy maker
(2,000 scudi), and for her beloved companionship (4,000 scudi).
The huge sum, 6,500 scudi, could easily marry off 25 women of
her class; he was only posturing. But Ginevra's centrality to this
artisan family's livelihood was clear.[4]

Servants, Semi- and Unskilled Workers

Renaissance cities depended on the efforts of workers who had
brawn, grit, and patience but only mediocre skills. To migrants from
the countryside, such was the most accessible employment. Probably the most common form was domestic service. Where workplace and home merged, servants might participate in the economic
activities of their masters as well as keep their houses. Even very
rich families seldom had more than one or two servants, although
in the sixteenth century the numbers rose; the more aristocratic lifestyles of the later Renaissance called for more domestic support.
Servants typically worked on written or spoken contract, receiving
board, shelter, sometimes clothing, and either a salary, or a lump
sum at the end. Sometimes, loyal servants, through long service,
earned their master's lasting affection and protection, receiving
gifts in cash and kind in wills, and sometimes even burial in the
family's preferred church. Nevertheless, rapid turnover was normal. Accordingly, in the literature of the time, faithful old family
retainers appear less often than do deceitful servants who exploit
their intimate knowledge of the household to please a grateful master or embarrass a resented one. Both males and females worked
as domestic servants, with women increasingly outnumbering men
later in the Renaissance. For both sexes, service was often work for

the young—sometimes children from age seven, but mostly those in their teens and early twenties. Girl servants hoped to lay up pay toward a dowry. Many quit domestic work upon marriage, but some remained or returned. Married female servants had more status and security. Resident wet nurses could become very close with the employer's family. Some servants were elderly; employers occasionally described keeping an aged servant as a work of charity.

Profile: Camilla of Parma, Domestic Servant

By 1559 Camilla of Parma had served in the house of Roman notary Girolamo and his young wife, Giulia, for more than a year. Probably middle aged, Camilla had to support herself; any husband she once had was no longer part of her life. Her daughter lived in a local monastery, where Camilla sent her gifts of food scrounged from Giulia. While the servant had a room upstairs that was locked with a key, she passed much of her day in the company of her mistress. They shared work, such as organizing linens and clothing and sending old items out to be sold by Jewish secondhand dealers. Camilla also ran errands and carried messages, for Girolamo did not allow Giulia onto the streets and even locked her in the house. The servant's activities served recreation as well as work. Camilla encouraged and probably even initiated an amorous intrigue between her mistress and a gentleman neighbor, who came calling secretly through a hole in the upstairs ceiling. The servant also showed Giulia how to do bean magic to secure her lover's devotion and keep her husband under her control. The spell failed, however. Girolamo soon caught on, and Camilla ended up arrested.[5]

At the low end of urban society was a motley contingent of people without special skills and resilient social ties. This stratum included migrants and foreigners but also locals just doing their best. Many lived from semiskilled and unskilled work, usually at day or piece rates. For example, porters and drivers handled loads of goods entering and leaving the city, and, in bigger cities, to deliver drinking water. Other carriers removed garbage and sewage from the streets and latrines. Strong arms and shoulders shifted earth and stone at building sites. Women also worked in this scorned and poorly paid sector. Laundry, at public tubs and riverbanks, was a hard and lowly task. And almost any female could nurse the sick, although particular experience or gifts might single some out. Younger women might sell companionship and sexual services (Chapters 15 and 16). At the very bottom of urban society were those with little purchase or none at all: very casual laborers, beggars, and thieves. The city also had outsiders, including soldiers, scattered household slaves, and Italy's long-established, ever-marginal Jews, who were hard to place (Chapter 17).

CONCLUSION

The people who inhabited the Italian peninsula and islands during the Renaissance fell into many social types. The world was deeply hierarchical. Its classifications—patrician, courtier, artisan, servant, peasant, soldier, and so on—spoke to differences in the prestige, power, wealth, and life patterns. Nevertheless, Italians of whatever status never lived with their own kind alone. They needed allies on all levels for political, material, moral, and emotional support. So Renaissance Italy was at once sharply divided and socially promiscuous; across social boundary lines, there were frequent, routine exchanges and complex human relationships.

NOTES

1. ASR, GTC, Processi, 16th c., busta 8, case 4.

2. ASR, GTC, Processi, 16th c., busta 25; busta 34; busta 35; also, Sforza/Cesarini, busta 89, doc.12.

3. ASR, GTC, Processi, 16th c., busta 25; busta 34; busta 35.

4. ASR, GTC, Processi, 1600–1619, busta 74, ff. 138–79.

5. Cohen and Cohen, *Words and Deeds*, 159–87. On servants, Dennis Romano, *Housecraft and Statecraft: Domestic Service in Renaissance Venice, 1400–1600* (Baltimore, 1996).

3

DANGERS

Renaissance Italy was stalked by dangers, both individual and collective. Illness, disability, isolation and early death, financial ruin, fires, wars, plagues, famines, storms, floods, and earthquakes threatened well-being and haunted the imagination. Now no society knows boundless security. Our own twenty-first-century world lives with the memory of disastrous global wars and the unsettling facts of nuclear weapons and environmental degradation, both local and planetary. Our febrile media inform us daily of tidal waves, frightful new diseases, the collapse of states, acts of terror, and misery of refugees. And, for thrills, we flock to films about asteroids of doom and other celestial threats. Nevertheless, despite real and imaginary alarms, many of us today enjoy, in our daily lives (despite the planet's worrisome longer run), unprecedented physical security. We do have our anxieties, griefs, and tragedies. But they do not hit or haunt us as did the dangers faced by the men, women, and young folk of premodern Europe. Thus, to penetrate the minds and experiences of Renaissance Italians, we should scan the structural and cultural differences that made their world so much less safe than ours.

Renaissance people confronted many dangers. Some, to premodern eyes, had supernatural origins. Others stemmed from a natural world not easily controlled. Some perils had a double source, at once natural and supernatural, for God, and at times the devil, had a pre-sumptive hand in catastrophe. A third set were human—the result of the political and social organization of the Renaissance world. To Renaissance folk, however, supernatural, natural, and human dangers often ran together. As people sought to navigate the shoals of earthly life, nature's signs could be divine messages that stimu-lated wary speculation. As omens, catastrophic earthquakes and floods announced God's displeasure with men's impiety. Signs, too, were the natural realm's gentler surprises, many of them from the sky—unusual rainbows, strange clouds, shooting stars and the occasional fallen meteorite, and even the odd swarm of red but-terflies. The birth of what the age called "monsters," deformed ani-mals and humans—a four-legged chicken, a two-headed child, for instance—could stir both excited commentary and anxious symbol-reading. In the face of perceived threats and real calamities small and great, men and women contrived to secure themselves.

THE SUPERNATURAL

From late antiquity and the Middle Ages, Christianity had inher-ited a strand of bleak pessimism about this world. Woven across this theme was a slighter thread praising God's creation and preaching the terrestrial benefits of righteous human works. (Religion runs throughout this book; here we stress its cosmic vision.) God, for all his benevolence toward humankind, could also deal out harm. He and his saints, but also the arch-enemy, the devil, and his min-ions could be unpredictable and dangerous. In its anxiety in the face of God, premodern Christianity stood apart from most mod-ern versions of the faith. To Renaissance Catholic eyes, the earth, although of God's making, was no securely happy place. Rather, the true domain of peace, order, and good government lay outside this temporal world, in the eternity of heaven. But, as preachers and moralists were quick to remind their flocks, many dangers to body and soul stalked the world. Fear the vanities of earthly hope, they warned, and stake all on the afterlife! Meanwhile, lesser spir-its haunted the worldly landscape. Gentler ones like wayward ghosts might be good for divination. Demons, on the other hand, as tempters and mischief-makers, could wreak much harm; worst of all they could possess a person entirely and patient exorcism sometimes failed to expel them. One message of the world's dan-gers was "aspire to heaven," a safer realm above. Spliced to it was a second admonition: "flee sin to ward off disaster here on earth!"

This double reading of terrestrial life reflected the Christian's two main goals: other-worldly salvation and this-worldly providence.

Salvation was the sin-bound soul's eventual redemption. Thanks to earthly traps, not everyone won this heavenly prize. For those who lost it, there was hell, which the Renaissance took dead seriously. Hell was no mere metaphor, but an agonizing reality of flames, molten metal, sucking toads, and biting snakes. People saw lively images of its gaping jaws and gleeful, eager devils in countless mosaics, frescoes, altar-pieces, and sculptures. Purgatory, too, was a real, but extraterrestrial place, a cleansing painful suburb of the true inferno and the temporary abode of all but the purest souls. Salvation therefore was serious work, an individual and collective endeavor that absorbed great energies. The clergy prayed, preached, and delivered sacraments. The laity meanwhile worshipped, did penances, fasts, and charitable works, and invested heavily in masses for themselves, their kinfolk, and other allies. Premodern religion was bleaker than now about a soul's chances. Preachers, confessors, and devout books urged a life of anxious, vigilant self-control, to master sin. Hope there was, but tempered with a darker vision of the moral cosmos.

The second goal of Christian life, providence, much concerns us here, for, as a conception of the world's working, it heightened the pervasive premodern sense of insecurity. A notion far more central to earlier Christian thought than now, providence is God's justice wrought on earth. With an eye to fairness and to instruction, he, the Virgin, and the saints keep a firm hand on the terrestrial tiller, afflicting and rewarding. Why did it hail on our crops? It must be our sins! And why did the fleet go down? We blasphemed! And why do our affairs prosper? Virtue rewarded! This notion of divine providence shaped worship and colored the worldview. There was a double message: first, that catastrophes are a divine chastisement, ordained and just, so we, all sinners, must expect them; second and less bleak, that all our scourges are neither meaningless nor entirely beyond human control. Plagues and earthquakes, locusts, and wars invited moral actions—rectitude, charity, chastity, and devotions such as fasting, prayer, a solemn procession; virtuous and pious action might buy or beg them off. Sometimes, providence even rewarded the hapless or undeserving with miraculous rescues or signs of favor. Not only individuals and families but also states, towns, and villages therefore at times of crisis looked to providence—to God, Mary, and the saints. People turned to specialist saints, like Saint Rocco, good against plague, or Saint Nicholas, for safety on the seas. Whole communities sought help at local cult sites, praying, for instance, to the ancient black Madonnas deemed especially powerful and holy. Collective vows, pilgrimages, and processions with wonder-working images and potent relics aimed to stave off disaster.

Such were the long-standing supernatural dimensions of risk. The great majority of Italians kept faith with this traditional, medieval cosmology through the Renaissance. Nevertheless, especially during the religious turbulence of the sixteenth century, several currents jostled these familiar truths and stirred anxious, new uncertainties. Challenges to the universal magisterium of the Roman church came not only from outside Italy but also from local spiritual reformers and intellectual mavericks, from high philosophers to everyday folk like the miller, Menocchio. A broader cultural disorientation that also touched some of the most militant Catholics followed from Europe's explosive earthly venture into "new" worlds. To many this moment bore the signs of approaching apocalypse.

NATURE'S DANGERS

Nature, God's good creation, was often perilously out of hand. Not that it was more potent than today; rather, people in the past faced the world with technologies far feebler than our own. True, the Renaissance helped bring on modern science; there was lively experimentation and avid investigation of the natural world. Nevertheless, in practical matters, progress was slow. Italians of the fifteenth and sixteenth centuries had nothing like our present upper hand, mostly, over matter and energy, over the landscape, and over pain and sickness. Moreover, natural science was still a dispersed activity and not yet a pervasive culture, set of institutions, and enlightened public policy. In the popular imagination, science had no name, concept, or robust identity to assuage anxiety. One could not think, as we sometimes do, "Surely science will find a way." If wounded nature does overwhelm our best technologies, the old pessimism may reawaken. To earlier Italian eyes, it was not human sway and masterful response, but natural power, unpredictable and dangerous, that caught the fancy and stirred the feelings. Italy, for all that it seemed to travelers' eyes a balmy garden, like any Mediterranean terrain was often a dangerous land. The sharp swings of climate could work havoc, as could a restless tectonic underground. As always, when nature stirred, human environmental tampering shaped the suffering.

Italy suffered from heavy weather. Environmental historians' "Little Ice Age," lasting some five centuries but coldest from 1580 to 1620, hit hard.[1] Italy always knew fearsome storms: hail ruined grain, lightning might kill a watchman on a castle tower, and, in the mountains, heavy snow could block the passes. Even summer seas could be churned by sudden blasts of down-rushing Alpine air, furious cold-front winds called *tramontana* on the west coast and *bora on* the east. Wrecks took their toll in mariners' lives and goods, off Italy's coasts and farther away. Another feared natural force was flooding. The heavy rains of fall and spring often pushed rivers over their banks, and heavy deforestation made matters worse. A famous passage in Machiavelli's *Prince* likens "Fortune," as he calls the force of chance in human affairs, to a river: "I compare Fortune to one of those violent rivers which, when they are enraged, flood the plains, tear down trees and buildings, wash soil from one place to deposit it in another. Everyone flees before them, everybody yields to their impetus, there is no possibility of resistance."[2] The power of raging waters caught the Italian imagination. Leonardo da Vinci, as artist and engineer, was entranced by the swirling power of rushing waters. The same was true of less educated folk; Romans often pegged memories to the city's floods: "That was when the river grew."[3]

A believer offered an ex-voto to hang in a church to thank the Virgin Mary or a saint for special rescue or protection. This early modern example from near Naples shows gratitude for surviving a fearful storm at sea. (De Agostini Picture Library/Getty Images)

These floods were full of lessons, moral and practical. Their biblical echoes stirred anxieties. In Italian, as preachers and ballad singers remarked, little distinguished an ordinary flood (*alluvione*) from Noah's deluge (*diluvio*). Raging waters therefore often seemed a sign, for they expressed aptly God's wrath against sin. Prayer and contrition might help keep back the waters. However, Machiavelli went on, in his same text, "Yet such is [the rivers'] nature, it does not follow that when they are flowing quietly one cannot take precautions, constructing dikes and embankments so that when the river is in flood it runs into a canal or else its impetus is less wild and dangerous." As a Florentine official who had helped lead a failing campaign to divert the river Arno, in hopes of retaking rebellious Pisa, Machiavelli remembered here his frustrated hydraulic engineering. Especially in the North, by long tradition, Italians built and repaired dams, dikes, and sluices to control raging waters. As with Machiavelli's "Fortune," foresight sometimes helped, but floods remained a problem.

Italy's geology is never quiet. Although the great volcanoes, dire Vesuvius that buried Pompeii and Sicily's smoky Etna were docile in the Renaissance, both reawakened soon after. Earthquakes, seldom still, are harder than flooding to anticipate or limit. Almost the whole of Italy, from the Alps to Sicily, is seismically active, with many zones prone to catastrophic quakes. One in1456 shook all of southern Italy. In 1570 half of Ferrara crumbled. Around Naples in 1626 tens of thousands died. Scholars have tallied more than four hundred reported earthquakes for the seventeenth century, only twenty-eight of them so grave as to leave an echo in the age's incipient journalism. Like floods, earthquakes could be read as portents of God's semi-inscrutable will. The Venetian diarist Marin Sanudo drew surprising comfort from the accidents of a disastrous quake that in 1511 rattled Venice:

> First there fell four marble kings that before had stood over the facade of the church of St. Mark. . . . There fell a woman in marble who represented Prudence, even though she was standing among other virtues. . . . The upper portion of the decorations over the great balcony of the Great Hall of the Major Council, which was high, fell, [along] with a Justice that was there, but a marble St. Mark [the patron saint of Venice] held firm and did not fall. . . . A marble merlon [a piece of a parapet] decorated with a plaster seal bearing a lily blossom fell, and many held this to be a good sign, because the lily, which is the crest

of France, will fall and come to ruin, which is what God wants for the good of Italy, sorely tried by barbarians.... And I saw the holy Mark, who remained intact on top of a palace.... Thus this city will be the savior of Italy and of the faith of Christ by chasing the barbarians [i.e., the foreigners] from Italy.[4]

Venice was struggling to recover from a stinging military defeat that had nearly annihilated its mainland domain. Sanudo linked the details of his city's damage to the day's tumultuous politics.

BETWEEN THE NATURAL AND THE HUMAN

Another scourge, hunger, haunted Italy, as it did the rest of Europe. Unlike floods or earthquakes, a famine was not a simple "act of God." Rather, famine arose from a complex ecology, an interaction between humans and their surroundings. By delivering too much water, or too little, or excessive heat, or unseasonable frost, nature damaged the sowing or the harvest, so that a district could not feed itself. Nevertheless, often there was more to it. In the short term, war could disrupt production, driving off the peasants or hindering the flow of supplies. A siege could starve a city, and international politics could block shipments.[5] Across Europe, hunger also rose and fell with demographic changes. Greater population pressure added environmental stress; peasants crowded the terrain, dividing their lands among their heirs, so, over generations, families had ever less to till. Meanwhile, since agricultural techniques improved at a slow amble, land-hunger fostered more precarious forms of cultivation. Peasants cleared marginal tracts unsuitable for sustained agriculture. In a hungry search for plow-land for grain, they colonized steeper slopes and marshy plains, destroying forests and driving out wildlife. They also encroached on pastureland, for, when food was scarce, animals and meat were luxuries. Thus, denizens of a crowded landscape were far more vulnerable to vagaries of climate. In the emptier Italy of the fifteenth century, meat was agreeably abundant, grain cheap, and famine rare. Italy usually fed itself by regional shipments, with Sicily a great granary. As the population rose through the sixteenth century, resource pressure impoverished many peasants. Low yield-ratios of grain to seed and inefficient transport made things worse. The 1590s saw widespread famines, often due to rain that rotted crops; in response, cities and their merchants mustered massive, costly shipments of Polish wheat.

Italian governments worked hard to manage these scarcities of food, especially bread. The wealthy, aware of the risks, sometimes stockpiled in their houses grain enough to last months, even hoarding the precious seeds in chests in bedrooms. Meanwhile, cities, and villages too, had public grain hoards and systems of emergency relief. Urban authorities closely regulated bread's price, weight, and quality, both to secure the welfare and survival of the poorer classes and to discourage riots. To supply the city's bakers, the Roman grain office, an organ of papal administration, sold importation rights to political favorites. This cozy system, sometimes tinged with graft, could bring merchants handsome profits, at the expense of the hungry populace. To the annoyance of rural landlords and peasants, a producer was supposed to sell to the capital's agents, even if he could make better profit shipping his grain elsewhere to a hungrier market. Often, as with such rules, growers retaliated by smuggling. In general, the cities, politically stronger, espoused grain policies that fed their inhabitants at the countryside's expense.

HUMAN THREATS

In many forms of both private and public violence, human beings posed dangers to one another. Damage both to bodies and to goods was a constant risk in a weakly disciplined society. At the same time, states and governments, seeking steadily to monopolize violence for themselves, acquired means to awe or ravage their own populaces and those of other rulers.

Personal Violence and Crime

Although bloodshed varied with the territory and the time, personal violence was by modern standards common. Some city-states were fairly well policed, but, in most of Italy, everyday life was often combative. Family, goods, and honor were chronically at risk. (On honor, see Chapter 6.) People had to mind their words, gestures, and dealings lest they provoke a fight. Simmering vendettas and sudden brawls, often over trifles, flared with little warning to take their toll in life and limb. The need for self-defense nurtured a culture of male violence. On the alert against attack by enemies or hired thugs, men were quick to draw the knives they always carried, or their swords where those were allowed, and to grab clubs, torches, pikes, scythes, or firearms. Though their weapons were more often words or broomsticks, lower-class women might also fight. Surveying the record books of the barber surgeons, required by law to report all wounds they treated, a historian has calculated that sixteenth-century Rome was far more dangerous than the cities of the United States today. Rome had ten serious woundings a day and about thirty-five homicides a year. Had it Rome's per-capita rate, modern New York would see daily a thousand woundings and ten murders.

Another mode of private mayhem was robbery, banditry and piracy. Englishmen in Venice reported on bravoes who attacked strollers in the depth of night, nabbing their valuables and rolling any corpses into the nearest canal. In the countryside, banditry was a menace. As courts often exiled malefactors, homeless men without income would flock together, to rob or kidnap travelers or raid settlements. The practice flourished in the worse-governed states, in rough terrain, and near frontiers. In the sixteenth century, Tuscany, for instance, was reputed safe, while the mountainous country behind Genoa and much of the Papal State, especially the Adriatic coast and the mountainous and wooded Neapolitan frontier, were notorious, as, in Italy's deep South, was Calabria. To avoid the bandits' depredations, travelers often went in large armed groups. Another recourse was to disguise one's wealth, dressing shabbily and hiding one's gems and coins, preferably gold because it is more compact than silver. One sewed the valuables in unlikely secret places—inside shoe's soles or a jacket's lining—or stowed them deep in baggage. These stratagems did not always work; highwaymen were hard to fool. But a Polish gentleman in 1595 had a lucky scrape. He was walking, he reported, when:

> after the sun had sunk into the bushes before Spaccafurno . . . some robbers emerged. After scuffling with me and finding nothing, they went off into the forest, one of them giving me two *testoni*—just over twenty *grosz*—as a sign of their supposedly great mercy (for I had indeed pleaded with them) and to make up for the disrespect they had shown me in their hope of finding spoils. They shook me all over, including my bundle and jerkin, so violently that I was lucky to get away alive; but God's grace was my guardian, because I had eighty Hungarian gold coins sown into the soles of the linen socks I was wearing, and on top of these I had my worn-out shoes and linen stockings, where it was hard to imagine they'd look, both because of my bad shoes and because of my ease in walking.[6]

One recourse, in empty country, was to hire a carrier (*vetturino*), who arranged pack animals, wagons, and inns. In some zones, these ancestral travel agents and guides were widely believed to be in cahoots with the bandits; one paid them well for safety's sake. Even honest *vetturini* thus profited from their fellows' ill repute. In the sixteenth century, piracy grew more dangerous, partly due to Dalmatian freebooters but mainly because of North African ships that, in the Sultan's name, scoured the seas and coasts for loot and captives. Inhabitants decamped inland, leaving whole districts thinly peopled. The corsairs ransomed some prisoners on the spot and took thousands more away to enslave them on land or in the galleys, to keep or sell back later. Christian fleets—Malta's Knights of Saint John and Tuscany's Order of Santo Stefano—plied in reverse the same cruel and cynical trade.

The Intrusive State

Another source of insecurity, alongside the private depredations of enemies and criminals, was the heavy hand of the state: its wars, its regulations, and its sporadic judicial force. Warfare was not too burdensome in the fifteenth century, when small armies battled for limited objectives. The sixty-five years between the French invasion of 1494 and the French-Spanish treaty of 1559, however, made the peninsula the theater of operations for dynastic struggles that convulsed much of Western Europe. The forces were now larger, the battles bloodier, and civilian damage far greater. In 1512, the Spanish army slaughtered thousands in the streets of Prato. In 1527, mutinous troops starved for unpaid wages sacked Rome hideously for weeks. The city's physical fabric, population, and artistic culture took decades to recover. Soldiers were usually mercenaries, often backcountry types from other parts of Italy, or Switzerland, Germany, and the Balkans. Outsiders unchained by local ties, these armies harmed not only by killing, maiming, or sacking foe. They also looted, raped, and bullied supposed allies and neutrals unluckily in harm's way. With their primitive systems of supply, premodern armies tended to live off the land. Soldiers were dangerous even when demobilized; veterans, especially when, as often, barely paid, easily stooped to theft and highway robbery. Crowded and unsanitary, armies also often left in their wake a widening trail of disease. In the last forty years of the sixteenth century, on the other hand, Italy, though bedeviled by banditry, saw little warfare.

A second state intrusion, aiming to keep peace and order, used rules, police, and courts. Owing to its organizational weakness and to the erratic actions of the privileged, Renaissance government itself often provoked anxiety. We today have become accustomed to the protection of a large, efficient, generally even-handed state, restrained by its own laws. Despite the inefficiencies, blunders, and inequities of which they are capable, modern governments guarantee reasonable stability and well-being. In contrast, Renaissance regimes, not altogether masters of their territories, could prove for their citizens far less comfortable. In some ways, Italian city-states and principalities anticipated modern aspirations, for they were zealous legislators of public and private behavior. Nevertheless, one should not read their laws and rules as banishing from civic life either disorder or privilege. Governments often seemed disconcertingly arbitrary. Justice could deal harshly with the unlucky few whom it caught to cow the many who escaped. Public authority tended to protect the elites, though sometimes one at the expense of another, and its decrees and punishments often served less as controls than as inducements to buy exemptions. The ideal of consistent treatment for all was tempered by the habit of exceptions, to the point that Italy was a quilt of special arrangements and privileges sold, granted, or appropriated. Inhabitants less powerful or privileged could not easily parry the state's penal and administrative intrusions into their lives. In the face of overweening power, one played one's well-placed connections and addressed petitions as best one could. Thus, government itself became a source of danger to pocket and to person.

One uneasy place where a person often confronted intrusive administration was in crossing the many frontiers. There, against smuggling, banditry, unwanted migrants, and epidemics, regimes stationed gates and guards. In northern Italy, where states were many, borders were ubiquitous. Long-distance merchants and other travelers therefore had to navigate customs offices, again and again. Since cities and states made ready money by taxing the goods that passed, the guards wanted to find what wayfarers preferred to hide. The English traveler Fynes Moryson reported his dilemma: if you showed your valuables, the guards taxed you; if you hid them and they ransacked your baggage, they confiscated what they found and you had to bribe it back. The regulations themselves produced not clarity and certainty, but occasions for bargaining, with unpredictable results. Here, as often, public authority was a mixed blessing, at once protective and a little dangerous.

Renaissance states by their nature used judicial process as a chief tool of administration. Their tribunals engaged with business of every sort. In criminal matters especially, their proceedings could menace. The law, with its imposing majesty, and its arcane codes, books, and formulae, upheld an ideal of impartial justice, but its apparatus might feel intimidating and highhanded. Every procedure and legal paper had its fee that fed the system and regime. Criminal courts tilted steeply against the accused. The police, a novel device for civic safety, were little better than the thieves they chased and were themselves a frequent threat. Procedures were opaque and sometimes cruel, and defense was arduous. Punishments targeted goods and bodies; criminal courts fined, confiscated, banished, whipped, branded, and hanged. To a degree, such official violence and bureaucratic rapine did counter widespread disorder and help calm civic life. The courts also gave Italians a potent means to keep battling private enemies. All in all, for many, especially for ordinary people, the judicial system, with its political vagaries and penal ferocity, did both good and harm. (See Chapter 7).

CONCLUSION

For Renaissance Italians in their daily lives, far more than now, many forces inflicted harm and fostered anxiety. The causes were economic, political, social, and natural, with the supernatural also active. This situation hardly reduced Renaissance men and women to quivering jelly. It did, however, alert them to take what steps they could to protect themselves from risks. In their own lives and in their relations with their fellow humans and with the saints, the Madonna, and God himself, they strove to secure themselves against a sea of troubles. How they did this is the subject of later chapters.

NOTES

1. On climate, Geoffrey Parker, *Global Crisis: War, Climate Change and Catastrophe in the Seventeenth Century* (New Haven, CT, 2014).

2. Niccolò Machiavelli, *The Prince* (Harmondsworth, 1961), 130.

3. ASR, GTC, Processi, 16th c., busta 48, case 13, f. 19v.

4. Quoted in Ottavia Niccoli, *Prophecy and People in Renaissance Italy* (Princeton, 1990), 31.

5. For war's dire impact, see Lauro Martines, *Furies: War in Europe, 1450–1700* (New York, 2013).

6. Antoni Maczak, *Travel in Early Modern Europe* (Cambridge, 1995), 161–62.

4

FAMILY AND OTHER SOLIDARITIES

Renaissance people faced lives full of risk. To get on as best they could, they relied on relations with other people—in particular, on ties to networks and groups. Of these bonds, the most important was family, but webs of patronage and friendship, brotherhoods, professional associations, and alliances based on neighborhood or shared origins also gave support. Men and women built their very social identities by cultivating such associations, so crucial when state institutions had barely begun to attain their modern competence and strength and when the stable assistance programs that many Europeans and some North Americans now rely on did not exist. The Renaissance state, though expanding its powers and concerns, could neither quell all violence nor stave off famine, plague, or other calamities (Chapter 3). Church-funded institutions provided some help, mostly in cities. Hospitals sheltered the indigent but had few beds and little capacity to treat most illnesses. Schools remained small and largely taught boys whose families could afford to pay. Charitable bodies helped some of the poor and disabled, but they did not reach everybody. No modern arrangements, public or private, such as health, unemployment, or life insurance, buffered the hard times that swept across Renaissance lives with frequency and vehemence. When, as often, people needed help, they fell back on their social solidarities.

The nature of these affiliations varied. Some associations were loose, others very formal. Some linked people as rough equals, while others reached up or down the social hierarchy. Sometimes, as with family, birth determined membership. In other settings, birth, and the social place that followed, might position a person handily to forge a link, but belonging still involved a choice. Other connections were purely voluntary. Frequently these associations bound one person to others, but institutions too could enter into bonds with individuals.

All solidarities, whatever their origin, required sacrificial gestures. To belong entailed exchanges, with benefits and obligations accruing to both parties. Both parties used the rhetoric of benevolence, gift, and service, and tended to deny their real self-interest. Nevertheless, payback would come, but, as gift theory suggests, it was seldom direct, precisely balanced, or the same in kind. Thus, a client might convey a rich present to his patron, who would respond with goodwill, and good words dropped in the ear of an ally who could offer the client's nephew a job. Nor was the exchange always prompt; an act or gesture now might well be repaid later. Renaissance Italians never knew when they would need a favor. They thus found it prudent to entangle themselves in a supple web of mutual obligations, cultivating connections and storing up claims against the next good chance or plight. Now and then, the law defined these affiliations and claims, but typically such exchanges lacked the precision and guarantees of formal contract. Indeed, one strength of this way of dealing was its flexibility. These precious solidarities were vulnerable. Therefore, one invested not only effort and material assets but also gestures and feelings. As people pursued practical ends, they also expressed their commitments, bolstered their claims, or veiled their self-interest in the language of strongly felt loyalty and love.

FAMILIES

Family was the primary solidarity. One was born into family; one could not choose to join or easily opt out. Family was a general institution, an organizing model or template hedged by laws, dogmas, and customs that set its profile and common features. It was also a constellation of living people, whose configurations and internal dealings varied hugely. In an environment where few could make their way from rags to riches on their own and public institutions offered little consistent support, people relied greatly on their families, so as to survive, inherit, get on in life, and defend themselves from physical, political, and moral assault. More than in our society, the Renaissance family served a wide gamut of human needs: material and economic, social and political, personal and emotional.

As the prime mediator between people and the larger world, the family both provided essential benefits and made heavy demands. On the one hand, family was the main conduit for many life-sustaining resources. It controlled the property that purchased shelter, food, and other necessities and funded economic activity. Since inheritance determined station in life, parents wielded power. Often, the family also taught economic skills. Social status, reputation, and connections all often passed through the family, as did political rights and alliances. Family found you work, and championed your connections. It laid money on your future, saved for dowries, paid for school, and purchased positions. On the other hand, family could not deliver these goods and services without compliance and support. Thus, people had to defer, cooperate, and obey, accepting responsibility for others, and often sacrificing their own appetites, inclinations, wealth, or safety. Family and its formal and informal leadership had regularly to deal with structural and personal tensions among members. Renaissance law and social practice did not recognize the individual rights that modern political thinking has entrenched, but there were ways of staking claims. Like its present counterpart, but with very different stakes and moves, the Renaissance family often required negotiations to adjust the needs of each member to the welfare and stability of the whole.

As family loomed larger than most other institutions, it mattered that bigger and more powerful families had greater assets. A family rich in resources—material, social, political, educational, and honorific—had more to give its members, who in turn had stronger motives to maintain ties. Such a family could make heavier demands, impose tauter discipline, and mobilize more effort to enhance the collective well-being. Thus, among the rich, nobles and patricians especially, one finds the great, many-branched families that so often figured in politics and culture. Such families had the cohesion to wage the factional struggles that racked many a Renaissance city.

Further down the scale of privilege and wealth, fewer assets meant more vulnerability and, typically, smaller and more fragmented families. Death often came sooner and more disruptively to families that were economically fragile. Death aside, too little land or food to provide for everyone more often broke up poor families, through migration and abandonment. Nevertheless, some poorer country families soldiered on without splitting. Larger peasant households held together because their abundant labor gave them access to land and income. Elsewhere, self-defense in feuds reinforced kin solidarity.

Family Identities

In Renaissance Italy, many families cultivated their collective, public face. They invested in marking themselves and in courting the respect of others. While the elite were especially energetic in this campaign and had more means, the less privileged also protected familial honor keenly. In public dealings, families identified themselves to the ear and the eye. Back then, not all families had a stable name, passed down the generations. Lineages of nobles and patricians proudly did call themselves by a collective name, often, though not always, ending in the "i" of the Italian plural: Grimaldi, Medici, Orsini, Contarini. But there were also the singular Sforza, Doria, Caracciolo. Many humbler Italians, however, continued to use either patronymics, or tags built on occupation or place of origin, or on nicknames. Thus, in daily life the many men called "Giovanni" were distinguished by phrases like "son of Bernardo" or "the tailor" or "Neapolitan" or "Lefty." Married women were generally known as the "wife of so-and-so" (Chapter 11). Although such non-lineage names ignored collective family identities, people knew where they and others belonged.

Families also marked their identities in public space. Family was closely linked to the properties it owned and occupied. In the city, the house, or *casa*, with its facade was a conspicuous site of family honor; the great would place their name or emblem. Wealthy families also reached into other spaces to claim recognition. Adorning a tomb or chapel was a favored investment. Such pious architecture, and endowments for public use, such as fountains, might bear a family name or shield. Those with truly aristocratic ambitions sometimes sent their liveried servants about town, trumpeting the family colors on their bodies.

Who Is Family?

Family was a term with many Renaissance meanings—some tight, others stretched across space and time—and the unit's composition varied with the sense in play. On the one hand, *family* denoted a group bound by chains of biological continuity, described meta-phorically as blood, or by marriage. These ties defined kin. On the other hand, *famiglia* in Renaissance Italian also designated a household or group that lived, and often worked, together. By this meaning, servants, dependent workers, or a powerful man's entou-rage, often not their master's kin, were also of the "family." Thus, in spatial terms, *family* might mean, quite narrowly, all those who shared a residence or, very broadly, it might signify those linked by kinship but housed in assorted places, or already in the grave. For many purposes, what most mattered for everyday life was the fam-ily that dwelled together. But from time to time, a ceremony, a trag-edy, a crisis, an ambition would call on the more scattered family.

The co-resident family could take several forms. Many people lived in a nuclear family, just a married couple and their children. As the life cycle and high mortality did their work, this simple basic unit fluctuated. A married couple lived alone before their children were born and after all left or died. Or one widowed parent carried on raising the offspring. Often servants, apprentices, and some-times an unattached relative or a boarder filled out a nuclear house-hold. There were also households structured on a more complex core. Three generations might live together, although the heavy death toll kept this brief and rare. In the city, for example, aging parents often lodged with an adult offspring. In the country, pat-terns of labor and tenure reinforced this practice. The benefits of consolidated agricultural labor fostered an extended household, where brothers co-resided, with their wives and children. Over time, demographic and economic circumstances could shift a fam-ily's composition between nuclear and extended forms.

Large and complex families were commonest among society's upper ranks. Patricians often created elaborate households stretch-ing vertically across generations and laterally among siblings, and even incorporating remoter kinsmen without homes of their own. In cities such as Genoa, Florence, and Naples, networks of such kin-linked households would occupy nearby buildings and dominate the neighborhood. Keeping these complicated families going cost money and effort, but the economic and political advantages paid off. Note, though, that these powerful families did not mirror the strategies of most other people.

Family also meant persons linked through time, to past and future. A family had its own life cycle; its living membership changed as the parental generation aged and died and as the chil-dren matured and produced their own offspring. As souls and

This composite, later sixteenth-century painting of an unidentified, North Italian family by Girolamo Forni includes figures added over stages, likely by other artists. As here, a family portrait might represent not a snapshot in real time, but an imagined gathering. (The Metropolitan Museum of Art)

memories, the dead remained part of the family, acknowledged in memorial rites to ease their afterlife, and invoked by the living as they plotted family strategies. Old names given to new babies linked the living to the dead. This sense of family underlay lineage, the institution that linked people, especially males, across generations. Thus, for Renaissance Italians, family name, property, and reputation passed from ancestors (even, not rarely, imaginary ones) to grandfather to father to son and on down. Men claimed the achievements of their ancestors to enhance their own honor and enjoined their descendants to remember, preserve, and live up to the family's tradition. So, too, disgrace marred not just an individual's reputation but that of his sons. The family memoirs, or *ricordanze*, written by Renaissance Florentines and others reflected the potent impulse to create such a sense of family history. So did the half-fantastical genealogies that claimed to trace a bloodline back to the Caesars or the Trojan War.[1] These attitudes flourished among the well-born, with most to crow about, but even ordinary Italian men knew they belonged to a line. Thus, some trailed a chain of patronymics three or four generations long. "I, Giorgio di Pietro di Antonio di Francesco," might begin a legal deposition.

Family Dynamics

Because it provided both essential resources and protection, the family housed many of life's key power relationships. Family operations bore on people and property, not only in the present, but also in past generations and into future ones. As with many Renaissance dynamics, both formal law and institutions, on the one hand, and the play of social customs and values, on the other, worked to shape family choices and strategies. Old Roman law with its deeply patriarchal habits set the overarching legal model and governed much of the transmission of land and goods. City statutes set local rules about inheritance rights and claims, legal capacity, age of majority, guardians' powers. emancipation, adoption, and other matters. Canon law bore especially on marriage, of which the consequences were not only sacred but also civil. These several layers of law gave rise to litigation in a panoply of tribunals. Renaissance law thus bequeaths to us today not only a corpus of detailed rules about family but also the records of myriad adjudications where clear legal doctrine confronted the murky complexities of real life.[2]

Law and custom, between them, shaped family strategies and tactics. The unquestioned authority of the male household head, supreme in principle, often prevailed in practice too. But knotty conflicts arose where the law ground slowly and solutions proved hard. What happened when the patriarch died, leaving no suitable male heir to step into his shoes? What if he were long absent, or rumored dead, but no one knew for sure when or where? What if he were sick, demented, or gravely delinquent? To whom then fell responsibility, and what credited his or her actions? Formal law was not the whole story. More fluid, less institutionally enforceable, but still influential in family fortunes were customary social roles and agreed-on obligations that also shaped the division of resources and the distribution of the burdens of care.

Each household had a head, usually the senior male, cast in the roles of husband, father, and master. When the male head died or left temporarily, women often stepped in. In big cities, women might head 20 percent of households, most of them small. The head enjoyed full authority over all the household's dependents: younger men, women, children, servants, and any others there. The law did place some curbs. If a man's wife failed in her duties or proper submission,

for example, he could beat her—but not too much. With this legitimate power came responsibility—the obligation to care for the economic and moral well-being of all family members. The head had to
administer property and other assets so that all got their present and
future due. Children were entitled not only to food and shelter but
also to training and a start in life. For city boys, that might mean an
apprenticeship, a role in the family business, or startup capital for
their own enterprise; in the country, land was key. For a girl, family
should muster a dowry so she could marry. Poorer parents sought
to place daughters in domestic service, to help earn marriage money.
Widowed wives were owed their dowries back, to pay their keep.
Decisions to attain these goals fell to the family head, who had to balance competing interests, as others lobbied for their concerns.

Central to family dynamics was property—its administration and
distribution. A family's material assets, fundamental to the well-
being of all, passed from generation to generation through legal
and customary arrangements. The bulk of property followed blood,
but some bequests heeded a testator's judgments and affections. By
Italian law, inheritance was partible—divided among all eligible
descendants, usually male—not concentrated in a single heir, a
practice in some other countries. This pattern recognized the claims
of all offspring but risked so fragmenting resources that nobody
got enough to live on. Families therefore contrived to balance two
imperatives: providing something for everyone and conserving a
patrimony that sustained position and honor. One solution was to
restrict the number of heirs. Another was to bind future generations by grave contract (*fidecommissio*) never to split a noble estate.

The focus of all these calculations was marriage. From the perspective of property and reputation, marriage of offspring had both
great benefits and substantial costs. Marriage served to secure wom-
en's honor and extended the family into the next generation. But successful reproduction multiplied claims on family resources. Second,
marriage created links with other families through which to consolidate assets, both property and social and political connections. But
such links went both ways, and families expected not only to receive
but also to pay out. To make a match, both families had to com-
mit material resources, to assure the new couple the means to support themselves and future children. With the dowry, however, the
bride's family outspent the groom's (Chapter 11). Daughters therefore were seen as a liability, since they carried off hefty assets that
benefitted another lineage. These asymmetrical marital exchanges
were also slow to balance out, as daughters married far younger

than did sons, who fetched in eventual dowries. Also, the parents' property devolved to girls at marriage, while a son inherited only at his father's death. Legal doctrine barred dowered women from further claims on the estate. A family with offspring of both genders saw flows both out and in; the net depended on gender balance and the size of settlements. Marrying off the daughters wove alliances and secured family honor, but at a price.

Elite families often turned to the church for other ways than marriage to provide for progeny. For girls this was often an economy as convents demanded smaller dowries than human bridegrooms. So many surplus daughters went to live as nuns that some communities became respectable repositories for unwed women, with little holy calling. Other girls, socialized from childhood in convents, chose the religious life willingly. A few even felt profound vocations. In saints' lives daughters sometimes fight for permission to take Christ as bridegroom. Elite sons could make useful and even brilliant careers as clerics; to become a prelate, or even a cardinal, however, usually required heavy financial and political investment.

Renaissance Italians' preoccupation with property in family relations seems foreign, indeed mercenary, to modern observers taught to exalt romance as the core of marriage and sentiment as the great domestic bond. Historians have much debated the quality of parental love (Chapter 11). As for matrimony, in courtship, with future prosperity and survival at stake, couples might put strategic and material needs first. Certainly, the psychological climate of Renaissance families differed from our own. Our present cultivation of marital affection is a luxury. Weaker control over life's conditions urged pragmatic matches. Nevertheless, rather than change the basic feelings, the divergence between Italians' sentimental expectations and ours probably just shifted emotion's needle. We too pick our spouses with an eye to social status and economic prospects, but seldom say so loudly. And, though affection's language seldom came first, Renaissance people clearly felt love and loyalty toward their families. And a host of other feelings—jealousy, gratitude, anger, delight, anxiety—also colored familial relations. In everyday Renaissance lives, emotions are hard to trace and gauge, but we should never underestimate them.

Family Relationships

The central family relationships—of husbands and wives, and of parents and children—were complex. Over wives, as over children and servants, husbands wielded undisputed authority. Commentaries on proper family life, by elite men, placed obedience and deft submission among a wife's prime virtues. The fifteenth-century Venetian patrician Francesco Barbaro, for example, wrote, in the humanist tradition, *On Wifely Duties*; admired perhaps more for style and classical examples than for its fleshless content, the treatise was widely read. For marital harmony, Barbaro propounded both a wife's obedience and her skill at emotional management:

> Cyrus, that great man and emperor, used to tell his troops that if the enemy advanced making a great noise, they should withstand the assault in silence, but if the enemy approached silently, then his men should go into battle with great noise and clamor. I would give the same advice to wives. If a husband, excited to anger, should scold you more than your ears are accustomed to hear, tolerate his wrath silently. But if he had been struck silent by a fit of depression, you should address him with sweet and suitable words, encourage, console, amuse, and humor him. Those who work with elephants do not wear white clothes, and those who work with wild bulls are right not to wear red; for those beasts are made ever more ferocious by those colors. . . . Wives ought to observe the same thing; if, indeed, a particular dress is offensive to a husband, then we advise them not to wear it, so that they do not give affront to their husbands, with whom they ought to live peacefully and pleasantly. I think that ear guards . . . are far more necessary for wives than for wrestlers, for the ears of the latter are subject only to blows, but indeed the former are subject to bills of repudiation accompanied by deep humiliation.[3]

This prescriptive literature on marriage urged the well-born husband to teach his new wife how to manage the household and to please him. In the Florentine Leon Battista Alberti's famous dialogue *On the Family*, one fictional character gave this account of his experience:

> After my wife had been settled in my house for a few days, and after her first pangs of longing for her mother and family began to fade, I took her by the hand and showed her around the whole house. I explained that the loft was the place for grain and that the stores of wine and wood were kept in the cellar. I showed her where things needed for the table were kept, and so on through the whole house. . . . Then we returned to my room and, having locked the door, I showed her my treasures, silver, tapestry, garments, jewels, and where each thing had its place. . . . I wanted none of my precious things to be hidden from my wife. I opened to her all my household treasures,

unfolded them, and showed them to her. Only my books and records [documents] and those of my ancestors did I determine to keep well sealed both then and thereafter. These my wife not only could not read, she could not even lay hands on them. . . . I made it a rule never to speak with her of anything but household matters or questions of conduct, or of the children. Of these matters I spoke a good deal to her. From what I said, and by answering me and discussing with me, she learned the principles she required and how to apply them.[4]

Alberti never married. These colorful descriptions portray some men's self-comforting ideals, not the loose ends of untidy reality. Nevertheless, in the elite readers' families, husbands and wives evidently lived separate lives. This image of molding one's bride as fresh clay must have most made sense when, as among the Florentine patricians, older men wed quite young women. The age gap reinforced marital hierarchy.

A wife's experience was complicated. On the one hand, a patrician wife's place was insecure for, as the daughter of another lineage, in her husband's home she was ever an outsider. Doubts about where, in the crunch, her loyalties lay could haunt a marriage. On the other hand, especially as a marriage matured, wives often became central to family affairs. A matron who carried out her housewifely duties, bore children, lived honorably and discreetly, and tended her husband's family's interests deserved her spouse's ear. Husbands sometimes appointed wives to execute their wills and oversee the children and the inheritance. Even during the husband's lifetime, when he was ill, absent, or delinquent in his duties, a wife might take responsibility. Furthermore, her dowry and her ties to her natal family, where both were weighty, raised her credibility. The marital ideal did not extoll cozy companionship; still, mutual responsibility and common concern softened the inequality. Further down the social scale, it is harder to see clearly how spouses dealt with one another, but precepts could not translate neatly into the shifting demands of everyday life. A smaller marital age gap may have fostered relationships both less distant and more symmetrical. Among the working classes, the husband and wife certainly shared the work that kept the family fed and might underpin prosperity.

Relations between parents and children were also strongly hierarchical. Sons and daughters owed deference even as adults. Fathers enforced their authority through their hand on the property, open or niggardly, on which offspring depended for their futures. When distributing property, through wills or sooner, women did the same, although they might be more generous to dependents disadvantaged by patrilineal claims. Poor parents with little to bequeath had less control; their children often ventured into the world to fend for themselves. This maneuvering around money and goods did not preclude deep sentimental ties. To the Renaissance mind, the fear and obedience progeny owed their parents did not inhibit filial love. And fathers and mothers reciprocated. Their emotions often became most visible in expressions of grief over the death of a beloved child. Parents did not, however, share the modern obligation to love their children equally. Favoritism was for them indeed a mark of authentic feelings.

Although elite families shed excess daughters into nunneries, this was not abandonment. As with marriage, here too a daughter's persistent sense of lineage loyalty was often strong. Her interest was reciprocated; although a nun remained enclosed for life, her kin could visit, passing news and gifts of food and clothing through the cloister parlor's grill. Wealthy families patronized favorite houses, depositing their women there as nuns or pensioners, befriending other sisters, leaving legacies, storing valuables, and hoping for an abbess in the family. The nuns themselves remembered their own ties and often followed keenly affairs of kin. Meanwhile, the nunnery took on traits of a surrogate family, the abbess serving as a "mother (superior)" for her "daughters," the house's "sisters." While male monasteries less often served as depositories for surplus sons, they used the same familial vocabulary and ideology.

Family relationships were thus tenacious. So central was family to society's structure that Italians usually remembered and respected its claims no matter where their lives took them. Nevertheless, they balanced obligations to kin with those to other groups.

PATRONS AND CLIENTS

Another useful solidarity, lesser than family, was the patron–client bond. In the face of pervasive scarcity, patrons offered protection, information, and assistance, in return for clients' services and loyalty. Like family, this alliance was built on both hierarchy and reciprocity of obligations. Unlike family, it was voluntary. While long habits, even decades-long and crossing generations, sometimes linked patrons and clients, to make and keep the tie took choice. Although some shared project might call forth legal papers, the association itself was not contractual. Typically, it was couched in protestations of mutual love, loyalty, and concern.

Patron–client ties were conveniently flexible. The two parties expected eventual but imprecise mutual benefit. A connection might vary in intensity as needs came and went. Both sides would gain, but reciprocation might come later, and in different form. Nor were alliances exclusive. A patron might have many clients, and a client several patrons. Informal networks could arise, where one person's client was another's patron, or co-clients made common cause. But such alliances were fluid and liable to internal rivalry and rupture. Thus, one nurtured the bonds one cherished; they were never to take for granted.

The core nexus was an exchange between a well-perched patron and a lower client. Hierarchical position was relative. The privileged could be clients of their own superiors, and modest folk might patronize those beneath them. For the client, the advantages were obvious; vertical ties offered preferment and work, help, protection, and privileged news. Patrons would stake their reputations to vouch for clients, a precious service in an opaque world where most social memory was oral and elusive. Less evident to modern eyes than to patrons then were the gifts, skills, labor, solicitude, admiration, information, and support a client offered. Some clients offered a reservoir of political or military force that a patron could rally. Others supplied useful gifts or money for spendthrift patrons strapped for cash. Still others did dark deeds or had connections in dim corners that elite persons could or should not know. Clients also fed a patrons' prestige. Those who earned honor by their own gifts and achievements flattered a patron's vanity. Likewise, being seen to nurture worthy dependents reflected well on the provider. Thus, for both parties, these vertical ties bolstered reputations and enlarged resources.

Up and down the social scale, patron–client relationships had many goals. One was to promote business arrangements inside ongoing patronage links. For example, patrons commissioned works from artists and architects. There might be a detailed contract spelling out what the creator would make, with what materials, how soon, and for what pay. This agreement often signaled a broader alliance between the two in which the artist visited, advised, and flattered the patron, while the patron not only paid but also entertained, encouraged, chided, and defended his protégé. Many other relationships echoed this model. Thus, an army was a veritable patronage-pyramid, where men served loyally not the state, but their own leaders. Commanders advanced their favorite captains, who meanwhile courted their loyal officers with gifts and protection, feeding them well at table and, not rarely, conniving to defraud the state through pay to phantom infantry on their padded muster rolls. Patronage also surfaced in the realm of charity and worship. Godparents, fictive kin who sponsored newborns at baptism, could serve their social as well as spiritual needs in later life. Institutions serving the needy dealt with their charges—the sick, orphans, dowerless girls—as clients and expected reciprocation in prayers and gratitude. And, very commonly, people went as clients to propitiate and beg from patron saints, clients on high of God. Supplicants petitioned holy protectors, with whom they cultivated personal ties, for help in exchange for gifts, prayers, and thanks.

OTHER SOLIDARITIES

Alongside the hierarchical relationships of family and patronage, Renaissance people used a range of other, more egalitarian solidarities. Some of them were firm and durable, others more improvised or flimsy. While some alliances harmonized readily with family and state, others served to curb or counterbalance the chief social obligations. Even when people banded together for less weighty ends, their groups had their cohesive pull, an amalgam of shared feeling and mutual obligation.

Brotherhoods and Academies

Among the solidarities of peers available to Renaissance Italians, the most institutionalized were corporate brotherhoods. One sort, the guilds of merchants or artisans, such as silk dealers or shoemakers, typically had a formal structure, with foundation statute, by-laws, officers, and a governing board selected from the membership. To practice a guild trade in a town, one had to join. Entry depended on qualification and a vote. Within the bounds of the confraternity, brothers acted toward one another as if equals. The guilds promoted good business and the craft's repute; they fostered fair practices and good standards, defended against outside competition, assisted members and their families, and cultivated their patron saints.

Confraternities, similar in structure, highlighted religion. Gathering laity and clergy, many organizations were male, while some included women. A few, like Florentine boys' groups, assembled age-mates (Chapter 11). Confraternities had their officers and councils, and sometimes chapels or meeting halls. Membership was voluntary, but confraternities often mirrored other solidarities, such as guilds. Some drew their members from a trade; others assembled a parish or adherents to a shrine or a devotion. Confraternities sponsored regular gatherings for prayer and held occasional processions and special celebrations. They also often took up charity, ministering to needy members or outsiders: pilgrims; the sick; prisoners languishing in jail or facing execution.[5] Confraternities multiplied in cities, drawing broad support across the community. Among the most flamboyant were the hooded flagellants who on Good Friday and other holidays beat themselves bloody through the streets as penance on behalf of all sinners. Many confraternities expressed their religious fervor in less gory fashion, singing psalm cycles or staging devout plays.

Other assemblies gathered for a range of more secular pleasures. Learned men, philosophers, artists, and their noble patrons gathered in academies to debate ideas, read poetry, and share high culture. The more formal groups had their statutes, scheduled meetings, and officers, and became lasting institutions that cultivated new forms of knowledge. More lighthearted were festive groups who banded for pleasure and relaxation, to stage dances, jousts, plays, and sometimes mischief. For example, through the Compagnie della Calza, young Venetian nobles organized lively spectacles, including boat races and mock naval battles.

Friends and Enemies

Friendship was torn between an altruistic ideal and pragmatic interest. Humanist writing echoing the ancients could hail the friendship between adult men as the most reliable and candid precious bond. At the same time, calculated friendships often linked more and less powerful men, sometimes older with younger, to serve mutually beneficial social aims. So, a patrician Florentine, Giovanni Morelli, counseling his sons, advocated the careful cultivation of "friends" to ward off the hazards of public life. There, friendship looked much like an egalitarian parallel to clientage.

Intellectuals wrote of friendship as a highly philosophical or spiritual meeting of minds. For most ordinary people, however, friendship grew out of proximity and common experience. A friend was a companion you lived or worked beside, a person with whom you might share meals, wine, gossip, recreation, and even beds. Friendship was one of the looser peer alliances. In the mobile urban population, it could be improvised and flighty. Its

connections were often modest in their claims and benefits, but at
critical moments their support could be valuable. Friends might
stand you to food or drink, lend you cash, gear, or clothing, or
store goods; they might take you in if the police pursued you or
your husband threw you out. Before the law, they might bear witness to your contracts, stand surety for your obligations, or baldly
perjure themselves for you in court. In the street they might stand
up for you in a brawl or counter nasty gossip. They could also let
down their guard and spill their secrets, a sign of trust. Many were
the risks one took for others, Renaissance friendship's quintes-
sential gambit. Nevertheless, no clear code defined what services
friends should do. In the world where disorder was endemic, family fragile, and governance erratic, friends often were the people
who were there. You hoped that, when need arose, they would
come through.

Although friendship imposed no specific obligations, enmity, its
recognized opposite, had sharper boundaries and better-defined
rituals. It constituted a kind of antisolidarity. An enemy was an
oddly intimate foe, as obligated to hurt you as was your friend
to help, a person with whom you shared nothing, often not even
words. Not to be on speaking terms was one of antagonism's characteristic, more benign expressions. All the while enemies were not
speaking to you, their words did injury as they badmouthed you
to all and sundry and tattled to the authorities on your spied-out
lapses. At other times, enemies engaged in slanging matches, which
often sparked violence. Men lashed out with rocks, clubs, knives,
swords, and guns. Women scratched, pulled hair, and wielded
broomsticks. Sometimes such hostilities persisted for months or
years, as feuds. To have many enemies marked your social stature
and strength, honor's embattled signature; it thus mobilized your
friends. Still, enmity was a costly, ambiguous asset, and means of
resolution were available. With time, as courts became more accessible, a lawsuit was one recourse; in less institutionalized settings,
a negotiated private peace reconciled enemies. Sealed with a kiss,
and wine plus cake or a common meal and sometimes solemnly
notarized, and underwritten by courts with their threats of expensive legal forfeits, a peace ritually marked the end of an exchange
of injuries.

The same associative habits that sustained family, patronage,
friendship, and enmity also fostered militant networks we call factions. In some cities, such coalitions arose, to vie by fair means and
foul for dominance. At times, their conflicts could reduce a town

to endemic civil war or end in the exile of whole alliances. At other times, factions functioned more benignly as semi-legitimate political parties and benevolent associations.

Compatriots and Neighbors

The choice of friends often owed to happenstance, as accidents of life and work threw people together. Some alliances grew out of shared geography—common birthplace or residence—encouraging a loose, structurally egalitarian association useful for support. Informal ties to region, city, or neighborhood did not obligate compatriots to demanding mutual service. But these links might shape behavior. When away from home, people felt and used geographical bonds. Settled migrants would often form communities with their *paesani* (compatriots), and travelers, in a foreign town, would seek them out for lodgings, company, and help. Thus, in Italy or abroad, Genoese or Neapolitans would band together to live, socialize, do business, and defend themselves. In the goldsmith Benvenuto Cellini's experience, in Rome an attack on a Florentine rallied Florentine defenders. Boundaries between territories also invited dramatic enactments of local patriotism. Wars to expand borders were the most serious such expressions. These were mirrored in less harmful ritualized competitions such as the district-based horse races of the Palio in Siena or the massed battles between the youths of different neighborhoods in Venice, Pisa, and other towns.

Neighborhoods were alert self-protective units; artisans at their shop doors, women at the windows, eyes on the street, watched for intruders and trouble-makers. Neighbors gossiped so much that people often had a substantial local reputation. Often one heard in court "in all the neighborhood she (or he) is known as a person of good repute." Courts often tapped this local *fama* (reputation) to make a case. Thus tribunals and local solidarities collaborated, informally, as mutually supportive agents of social control.

Solidarities on the Social Margins

Society's margins offered few opportunities to join established solidarities. Strolling players, prostitutes, vagabonds, thieves, rural brigands, hit-men, beggars, and their like had meager social credit. With their families often fragmented or far away, such persons lacked the respectable trade, juridical rights, stable local ties, or money to join most formal organizations. Exposure to risk threw

them back on one another; common vulnerability urged cooperation. They relied on their own subcultures, convening over food,
wine, and dice to share jokes, lore, news, and support. Seldom
able to use the state with its courts and contracts, they improvised
bonds with solemn oaths of loyalty, gift giving, reciprocal debt, and
shared risks and secrets. These insubstantial devices were fallible;
betrayal was a constant danger.

CONCLUSION

Renaissance Italians had a range of solidarities on whom they
depended for the support that public institutions and private enterprise did not provide. Some, notably the all-important family, were
imposed, not chosen. As was the dependency of peasants under
oath to an hereditary lord. Most other alignments, whether hierarchical or egalitarian, being elective, required cultivation. Most
Italians belonged to several such groups, for diverse purposes.
Membership was far from random, for solidarities often lined up
and reinforced one another. Two kinsmen might well belong to the
same guild, confraternity, religious house, or outlaw band. Italians
often stood as godparents to their clients, neighbors, or other allies.
Thus, each solidarity easily intersected many others. To live was
to negotiate the convergent or competing claims of many solidarities. All transactions required nimble, conscious calculations about
the obligations, needs, and risks of family, patrons, friends, faction members, neighbors, ritual kin, and other associates. Renaissance individualism, such as it was, was trammeled in collective
obligations.

NOTES

1. For example, Cellini, *Autobiography* (Harmondsworth, 1998), 2–5.
2. On family and law, Thomas Kuehn, *Family and Gender in Renaissance Italy, 1300–1600* (New York, 2017).
3. Francesco Barbaro, *On Wifely Duties*, excerpted in *Civilization of the Italian Renaissance*, ed. K. Bartlett (Lexington, MA, 1992), 142.
4. Alberti, *The Family*, 208–9.
5. For example, Nicholas Terpstra, *Cultures of Charity: Women, Politics, and the Reform of Poor Relief in Renaissance Italy* (Cambridge, MA, 2013).

5

HIERARCHIES

A VISION OF THE WORLD

To make sense of their world and, as best they could, to keep it orderly and safe, Renaissance Italians liked to arrange it into hierarchies. Imbued with legitimacy, even sacrality, hierarchy offered an interpretive framework and a set of organizational structures. Under the supreme eye of God, Renaissance spiritual and intellectual life was deeply imbued hierarchical ideals. These arrangements carried moral values, ordered from top to bottom, from greatest to least. A stratified vision, in turn, pervaded Renaissance politics and social orders, both big and small. Hierarchies—real, imputed, or imagined—did not, however, fix every person or family into an immutable place. Rather, hierarchies were frameworks within which people moved, as they made their way, sometimes smoothly, and sometimes amid hard bargaining and sharp strife. This chapter scans the hierarchical ideals, processes, and structures by which Renaissance Italians worked to fend off all too threatening disorder.

Cultural Roots

The Renaissance Italians' fascination with vertical ordering marks their social and moral philosophy as unlike ours. They understood

the universe as designed by a just God with hierarchy as its fundamental structure. Twenty-first-century science, on the other hand,
sees the earthly world as the product not of divine purpose, but
of complex, interactive, and unfinished processes. Transposed into
social organization, our ideas differ as well. We too applaud those
who come first, usually crowned in specific domains: in sport,
who won the champion's title? in music, whose song sold best? In
school, who was the top of the class? We attend little, however, to
who was second, third, and fourth. Renaissance thinking instead
aimed to fit everyone into an imagined procession of precedence.
Also, like the Renaissance, we live with social inequalities. But our
social and political principles are democratic; they insist on a fundamental, if fictitious, equality of persons. These ideals are a modern
luxury, owing much to our relative civic security. Although real life
enacts these aspirations very imperfectly for some, the conceptual
commitment to equality differentiates twenty-first-century democracies from early modern Europe. Inherited rank and unearned
prerogatives were then far less often questioned than are today's
inequities. While the Renaissance principle of hierarchy justified a
very uneven distribution of powers and privileges, it also doled out
responsibility. Those higher up had some charge for the security of
those below. For Renaissance Italians, hierarchy was a good and
necessary ideal, a divinely ordained foundation for human well-
being in the natural realm, in the cosmos, and in the world to come.
    The Renaissance's hierarchic vision had long intellectual roots in
ancient Greek philosophy, especially Plato and his many followers.
In Christianized form, this heritage pervaded most medieval and
Renaissance thought. Natural philosophy and religion agreed that
God had built a hierarchically ordered world. The cosmos, composed of four elements, ascended from base, heavy earth through
ever nobler spheres of water and air, to the exalted realm of fire,
dwelling place of stars. In parallel, the metals ascended from base
lead to noble gold. Animals climbed in vertical order from worms
and slugs to lions and eagles. Among body fluids, hot blood lorded
it over chilly phlegm and the two biles, yellow and black (Chapter 14). Among beings, humans hovered midway between the
beasts and the angels, who lodged under God.
    Across medieval Europe, this hierarchic vision shaped models
for political and social order and justified the forms of many major
institutions that the Renaissance inherited. Kingship, lordship,
family, and the Latin church all stressed authority and subordination. In the communal centuries, Italian city governments built as

well on elected councils and corporate bodies. Yet, as warring factions and class quarrels raged, many cities slipped under the hierarchic rule of princes and tyrants. Even where democratic practices and principles survived, regimes championed subordination as a bulwark against subversion and party strife. From the fourteenth century, by different paths, the political classes narrowed. Renaissance aristocratization sharpened social distinctions, amplifying their expression and hampering access to the top. In parallel, the Catholic Church reacted to disruptive Reformation challenges. Protestants translated Bible and liturgy from Latin into common speech, demoted clergy by denying their sacramental powers, and raised up instead the congregation of all the faithful. In response, at the Council of Trent (1545–63), the church reaffirmed its holy magisterium, Latin as religion's language, and the adamantly hierarchical structures that made salvation possible.

Precedence

On a more local scale, one common way to show hierarchy was precedence, a horizontal enactment of vertical schemes. Wherever two or more people came together, their relative status likely came into play. Who sat or stood where and who walked first mattered hugely. The seating at a banquet or a meeting diagramed prestige and power. Great processions, as at the summer feast of Corpus Christi, put a city's clergy and male elites on show. All the worthies, in their robes of office, paraded with hymns, crosses, banners, and gorgeous monstrances for the holy wafer. Their wives and daughters watched from windows and doorways, while the lower orders thronged the streets to see the passing show. Men marched in groups according to their rank, clergy first and then secular officials—the bishop, the friars, the lay confraternities, the magistrates, the guilds. Within each contingent, the best went first. Thus, the whole parade was an ambulatory image of the local hierarchy. The order of festive march was no joking matter. A newsletter of 1555 reported a typical moment of social agonism, at a great procession of the *Possesso*, the installation of a new pope as bishop of Rome:

> Last Monday the pope went to San Giovanni Laterano accompanied
> by all the court, and the soldiers, and the Roman people in arms, to
> take possession of his bishopric according to the ancient ceremonies.
> A minor brawl broke out between Papirio Capizucchi, who was in
> command of a unit of soldiers, and [men of the] districts of Ponte and

Trastevere, about precedence. Things got really rough, and Papirio was wounded with a pike wound in one thigh, and about 15 or 20 others on one and the other side were hurt, and there would have been a blood-letting if the cavalry had not gotten in between them, and Cardinal Carafa came running at the uproar, dressed in crimson, with his cardinal's hat in his hand, and he got in between them and, with his authority and bearing, he made everything settle down.[1]

This story illustrates that precedence mattered not only for leaders. And often it was not clear who should come before whom, or on what basis to create the right order? Renaissance Italians in fact would never all fit into a single line of prestige, good for all times and places. In everyday life, social place had too many components, and myriad circumstances changed the calculus. How did a middle-aged lawyer with a doctorate address the teenaged son of a minor baron? How did the trusted nurse of a patrician family treat the peasant who brought chickens to the kitchen?

Power, Prestige, Wealth

For gauging status, classical sociology offers a handy formula with three ladders—power, prestige, and wealth. On the ground, the interactions among these factors were complicated. In Renaissance Italy, power came from inherited rank and high office, but also rested on skilled deployment of fear and force, as famously rendered in Machiavelli's *Prince*. Prestige, often conceived as honor, accrued to power, to position, to living and consuming nobly, and to a careful defense of status. Yet honor played not only at the top, but also, adapted in its particulars, way down the social scale and even among the disreputable. Much of this chapter describes the many ways to cultivate prestige, and we return to honor as a competitive moral system in Chapter 6.

Wealth, which is so central to modern assessments of status, had for several reasons less direct correspondence with social position during the Renaissance. Perhaps 10 percent of the people were what we might call well-to-do, their wealth mostly inherited, but sometimes achieved through business or professional work. The sizes of these fortunes, however, were hard to know. Much wealth was tied up in property and credit, and little cash circulated. Yet all was not stable. Across generations, landed patrimonies could fragment and dissipate. Commercial riches, especially, could be volatile. Consequently, even the rich seldom knew exactly how much they had, and did not want others to know in any case. Furthermore, among this moneyed 10 percent, many of the nobly born had relatively smaller means than successful members of the non-noble citizenry. In a classic marriage strategy, a cash-poor noble scion offered his prestigious rank to the richly dowered daughter of a rising mercantile clan. A family's assets relative to its peers also mattered among peasants and among middling folk, but there few substantial changes of position were in play. Although there were many ways to use money to improve a family's lot, it seldom of itself advanced its standing.

Although in the Renaissance birth and inheritance counted for much, and personal efforts availed far less than in our more mobile modern world, real-life hierarchies incorporated many ambiguities. These left plenty of room to maneuver, to jostle, to negotiate on behalf of self and family. Much energy went into fine adjustments of hierarchic relationships.

HIERARCHY AND INBORN IDENTITIES

Family

The paramount determinant of social rank was family. Especially for the upper classes, families owned property, managed wealth, waged politics, imposed collective discipline, and advanced their members' welfare. Together, they had reputations to proclaim, cultivate, and defend. Increasingly, social hierarchies consolidated. Everyone could name the best and the better families. In an increasingly princely society, the hierarchy of real power attached closely to birth. In families invested with hereditary rule of states, the patrimony normally went to the first-born surviving male, but if a father held several lordships, he might spread them among his sons. Lacking brothers, an heiress could wear her father's title and bequeath it to her descendants. In many cities, family membership also came to confer the right to election to high public office. Venice, for example, in 1315 restricted admission to its ruling councils to families later inscribed in a Golden Book. Such constraints spread widely in the fifteenth and sixteenth centuries. At the same time, elites turned inward for sociability, alliances, and marriages. A similar process of closure infected the professions in many cities. Thus, genealogy, not merit, governed entry into the ruling "colleges" of notaries, lawyers, or physicians. Even village elites often intermarried. The working classes and the poor, however, looked less to family background and more to individual traits and immediate opportunities.

Gender

Gender had, in theory, a simple binary hierarchy: male rightly dominated female. Real-life relations were less neat. Despite recognizing variant bodies such as hermaphrodites, early modern European culture expected everyone to live as either male or female. From a belief that man represented the human ideal and woman an inferior replica, there followed expectations about physical and intellectual abilities. This high culture view aligned with a widespread popular misogyny. These principles in turn justified differential access by gender to power and resources, especially as mediated through formal institutions. Catholicism, while acknowledging that all souls were alike before God, allowed only men to be priests and prelates, although women could become nuns and run convents. In formal institutions of the secular realm, including governments, armies, and universities, authority and power belonged, with few exceptions, to men. Nevertheless, in many settings the other hierarchies, notably that of social rank, disrupted the privileges of masculinity. Thus, most men did not, in fact, hold high position and were dominated by other men. Those same lesser men had also to defer on occasion to well-born women. There were also many kinds of informal power in which women participated. In the household, large or small, men were heads, but wives were important auxiliaries. Often, with no man to serve by reason of death, illness, travel, or ineptitude, women from duchesses to stocking-makers stepped up, and their families depended on their being able to do so. Women had restricted legal rights tied often to their status as wives or widows, but they could own property, participate in transacting business of various sorts, and testify in criminal court. So, in the hierarchical scheme of things, women came second, but that did not mean all were, by gender, powerless or enslaved.

Age

Although the counting of years was often approximate, greater age might mean more social weight. Unpredictable mortality led the age pyramid to taper sharply after people reached their forties, and the relatively few who reached sixty or seventy or more could claim a certain venerability. Premodern societies with weaker technologies for storing and distributing knowledge turned more readily to their elders as fonts of wisdom and oral lore. Inheritance customs also nudged younger generations to cooperate with their aging grandparents and parents before property passed down. Usually, however, a respect for age accrued mostly to those who had other claims to hierarchical prestige like wealth, accomplishment, or a big family. Poor, solitary old widows got little deference. An alternate view of the life cycle was a stairway that rose by steps from babyhood to mature adulthood and then started down again. Rather than corresponding to a specific age, maturity was marked by physical vigor, good judgment, authority, and for most men and women marriage (Chapter 12). This view rewarded age only to a point. On the down slope, popular custom sometimes mocked the geriatric decline of physical powers, looks, and acuity. For example, a favorite theme of stories and plays was the rich old widowers who, taking young brides as they often did, invited teasing and snide doubts as the new wives' contentment and fidelity.

OFFICES AND TITLES

Italy, from courts to towns to villages, was awash in officialdom, both professional and amateur. Shaped by institutional hierarchy, office-holding furnished not only pay and power but also pomp. Governmental or political offices were prominent, but guilds, professional colleges, confraternities, and learned academies also had leaders and functionaries, some elected, others appointed. In many cities, each high post had its magnificent robes in which to process on solemn occasions. Lesser officers like the town crier and the civic watchmen, the captain of the constabulary, trumpeters, and doorkeepers also bore their insignia and special clothing. Access to public offices, and their perks, often extended to a fairly large portion of male citizens. From among those who did qualify by family, gender, age, corporate affiliations, or other criteria, the next round of officers were chosen by nomination, lottery, or election. Since terms of office were often short, many had a chance to take their turn and share the glory. Eligibility often came in degrees as a man matured, and older men usually ran things. Membership in one elite body sometimes granted admission to the ballot in another. Thus, the pinnacles of leadership readily became an interlocking directorate of the privileged. Alongside the elected officers, there were the many professional officials, who held their posts by appointment, purchase, inheritance, and pull: magistrates, ambassadors, secretaries, treasurers—an officialdom, often trained in law, whose career paths let them climb in power, prestige, and salary, and in privileges, sometimes less than licit. They could rise locally, or zig-zag from town to town, aiming for top spots in important places. Unlike citizen officials, successful professionals served long, invest-ing in careers, hoping to rise steadily.

A separate, hierarchical pathway of office shaped the careers of the upper clergy. A classic pyramid of rank and authority reached down from the pope to cardinals, archbishops and bishops, the heads of religious orders, monsignors, and so on. Popes, rare celi-bate sovereigns, owed their office to the cardinals' vote in consis-tory. Most other ranks came by appointment and were attached to specific benefices that provided income to support the office's work. Preferments came more and less fat, and invited intricate politicking that often roped in the churchmen's secular kin. Church office, even without simony, was very much part of great families' maneuvering for ascent. Before Trent's reforms, a careerist aimed to snap up plural benefices by the handful. He would be addressed by his best title and esteemed for the whole collection.

Renaissance Italians used a finely tuned array of terms and titles to delineate social hierarchy. Noble titles attached to lordship and ancestry. Among them were king (*re*), duke (*duca*, in Venice *doge*), marquis (*marchese*), count (*conte*), and down to knight (*cavaliere*). These honorific labels passed between generations along with pat-rimony. Wives, too, as consorts, carried female analogues to their husband's titles and commensurate prestige. Some less exalted titles came with offices: *ambasciatore, segretario,* and the like for gov-ernment officials; *colonello* and *capitano* for commanders of troops; *monsignore* for high clergymen; *padre* or *don* for priests; *fra* for fri-ars; and *suora* for nuns. The holder of a university degree deserved *dottore*. Other words, *signore* and *signora,* for example, had a more fluid range of meanings. Although today *signore* just means "mis-ter," in the Renaissance this word of feudal origin meant "lord" and demanded serious deference. The term served both as a title, Signor Alfonso, and as a free-standing noun. Thus, villagers might call their masters *i signori*. Indeed, even God was called *il Signore,* as with our English "the Lord." On the other hand, in Rome, neighbors respect-fully named a prominent courtesan *Signora Settimia* or *la Signora*. In Venice, where noble titles were banned, one called patricians, but not others, *clarissimi* or *magnifici*. More generally, in terms that were not titles, a man of elite presence could be called a *gentilhuomo* and a woman a *gentildonna*. The title *messer* originally attached to lawyers and notaries but by 1500 extended to many prosperous urban men. A master artisan, however, went by *maestro*. In parallel, the term *Madonna*, for women, had a huge range that went from the mother of God to burghers' or tradesmen's wives. The poor lacked titles, but varied words for underlings served to describe and to address. Some, like *poveruomo* (poor-man), invoked pity and Christian charity, while others, like "Jewish dog" dripped ugly contempt.

As the Renaissance went on, this language got fancier. Even pronouns elaborated to show degrees of respect. Like some modern European languages, medieval Italian had two forms of "you" for individual persons: a singular *tu* reserved for intimates, children, and inferiors, and a respectful plural, *voi*. Aristocratization favored yet another version in the third-person pronoun, *lei*, that meant an even more deferential "you." In the same spirit came a swarm of circumlocutions. For example, "may I go now" might become "does his most illustrious lordship grant me license to depart?" Giovanni Della Casa in his book of manners, *Galateo*, grumbled in 1555 that stilted sycophancy was infecting speech. Nevertheless, he grudgingly counseled his readers to follow fashion, but moderately:

> Let us remember, therefore, that formalities—as I said at the beginning—are not necessary by nature. In fact, one could do without them as our nation did until not so very long ago. But someone else's ills have made us ill with this and many other infirmities. For this reason, once we have obeyed custom and used such permissible lies, anything more is superfluous; however, it is impermissible and forbidden to go further than custom allows, because formalities then become an unpleasant and boring thing for men of noble spirit who do not indulge in such games and pretenses.[2]

Della Casa lost his battle to keep courtesies plain; the new titles flourished and long endured.

CULTURAL PERFORMANCE

Place in the social hierarchy for a family or individual much depended on the circumstances into which they were born and the ranks, offices, and marriages that might follow. Competition was stiff, and for many families the battle was to hold position. Major ascent, if it happened at all, usually took more than a single lifetime. Nevertheless, there was room for maneuver and the possibility for the accomplished, the deft, and the lucky to shift and even rise a bit. Misfortune and miscalculation might end up in slippage downward.

To enact and, maybe, enhance their standing, Italians fashioned the best possible version of themselves. In this jostle for position, everything one did could be matter for appraisal and judgment. There were endless ways of fouling up. People garnered prestige, or owned their honor, by knowing what mattered and performing well in several different domains. Social, cultural, and intellectual capital all served in these negotiations. Players in a hierarchy needed to know people: their superiors and patrons; their clients and dependents; their peers. It served to know these people's connections and networks, their personal quirks, their pleasures, and their enmities. Success also turned on learning and displaying, with finesse, those admirable traits of character, appearance, and self-expression that suited one's own place. It was necessary to fit in, but also to stand out. Besides the presentation of self, it was useful to know, select, consume, and display prestigious things. The models for all of this came from princely courts.

A Renaissance novelty was the how-to book not for princes or rulers, but for courtiers. The most famous and subtlest of these, by Baldassare Castiglione, became an instant and enduring classic. Although addressed to society's highest men and women, among whom competition for position was both intense and refined, the treatise's lessons resonated well outside the court. The book, framed as a discussion among the members of the court at Urbino, described *virtù*, the mannerly and moral conduct that ideal men and women should display. Social and cultural capital was not inborn but learned. Its deployment followed from a person's knowledge of not only what to do and how to please, but also when and where to act and how to fit his conduct to his company. A known coward, liar, cheat, or drunkard lost standing in the eyes of all, while a person of firm probity and moral or physical courage gained. *Virtù* would not, however, dislodge persons from their social place; a virtuous commoner owed an immoral nobleman gestures of respect. However much the commoner might feel morally superior, the rules forbade his acting so. The immunities of the powerful might rankle and stir up fruitless literary debate by learned underlings about right precedence: nobility of soul or nobility of title. Soul, of course, would win the bookish argument to no practical effect whatever.

The Renaissance word *virtù* also meant skills and lives on in both the English and Italian in term *virtuoso*, still applied to artists and other adroit performers. Yet, rather than flamboyant showing off, however, the mark of the truly superior was restraint.

Castiglione distilled the polished courtier's essential trait as *sprezzatura*, strictly "putting a low price to it," but usually translated as "nonchalance." It meant making the hard look easy, making an intricately artful performance look natural. *Sprezzatura* was, in a sense, ancestral "cool."

Virtù of the Body

Renaissance Italians used a codified body language to enact place in the social hierarchy. Over and over in daily life, people performed deferential gestures of respect: raising the hat, bowing, kissing hands, lowering the gaze, and stepping back. To express radical inequality, inferiors knelt. Supplicants, imploring grace and mercy, fell on their knees or faces, clasping the powerful by the knees or ankles. This desperate gesture of subordination recognized a superior's political and social status, and often his or her moral authority. Superiors, meanwhile, used eyes, stance, and movements to assert pride and station. All such moves had their modulations of duration and intensity. An inferior, for instance, encountering a man of higher rank, should doff the hat first. If his better too removed his hat, the inferior should wait until his better replaced it before donning his. In Venice, where by civic constitution all patrician men were theoretical equals, etiquette was tricky. Moryson remarked that two gentlemen meeting in the street would raise their hats and hold them high, passing one another with caps aloft and taking care not to look back, so that neither could say the other had been the first to cease paying his respects.[3] Sometimes, however, the expression of priority was inescapable. Since only one man at a time could pass through a narrow doorway, portals provoked elaborate protestations, as courtesy demanded each to offer the other first place. Similarly, in narrow Venetian pathways, the superior walked next to the wall, while in broad streets, when three walked abreast, the middle had precedence, followed by the right, and then the left.[4]

More generally, bodily decorum marked the elite: graceful posture, quiet gestures, a measured gait. Courtesy manuals inveighed against the florid body language so useful to an oral culture—that use of head, hands, elbows, indeed the whole torso as an eloquent supplement to speech. To this day, less bourgeois Italians have a rich gestural repertoire; paintings, stories, and trial testimony prove the same was true five hundred years ago. We moderns are heirs to this Renaissance campaign to civilize and veil the flesh. It is the

The often-painted biblical scene where the returning Prodigal Son begs paternal forgiveness offers many enactments of hierarchy: by age and social rank, and by roles in family and service. This early sixteenth-century version is attributed to Palma Vecchio. (DEA/G. DAGLI ORTI/ Getty Images)

Italian fork that chased our fingers from the stew. By our standards, premodern Italy was neither squeamish nor inhibited. Against this backdrop, courtly manners taught that many acts that call attention to the body and its functions should be banished from sight and mind. Today's readers of Della Casa's *Galateo* find many of its earnest strictures hilariously absurd, for nobody would do such disgusting things. For example, Della Casa wrote, "It is not proper for a well-mannered gentleman to prepare to relieve his physical needs in the presence of others." Further, he inveighed against sneezing in people's faces and admonished servants not to handle their private parts while waiting on the dinner table. The Renaissance saw a gradual spread of fastidious distaste for bodily functions that began at the top and, after 1600, gradually infiltrated downward.

The body itself was an instrument for expressing social hierarchy. Although age and disease hit the well-born, a beautiful and healthy body could signal high status. Hard work, exposure to weather, injuries, and bad diet were the lot of the poor. Signs of menial labor, such as callused hands and feet, singled a body out as lower class. Noblemen cultivated physical strength and agility in fencing, horsemanship, and hunting, and trained for their traditional profession as soldiers. So, elite men could sport a sun-tanned skin, but for their women, pallor was desired and lent prestige. The fifteenth-century writer Agnolo Firenzuola reflected on female beauty: "The cheeks must be fair *[candido]*. Fair is a color that, besides being white, also has a certain luster, as ivory does while white is that which does not glow, such as snow. If the cheeks, then, in order to be called beautiful, need to be fair, and the bosom needs only to be white"[5] (Chapter 13). Renaissance elites, men and women alike, were also schooled in physical inhibition that contrasted sharply with the exuberant physicality of the less privileged majority. Although Castiglione cautioned against women's riding and handling weapons, some noble ladies, notably Isabella d'Este, risked their complexions on the hunt. More suitable activity for gentlewomen was elegantly restrained dancing.

Virtù of Mind and Tongue

Intelligence and intellectual mastery of valued topics and activities served in wrestling for prestige and influence at all social levels. Renaissance Italians prized cleverness of many sorts—witticisms, good stories, wily schemes, and practical jokes. They also admired pragmatic know-how, agile handling of human relations, and many sorts of special knowledge that pertained to particular social niches. In courtly culture, one had to know much and to offer it publicly with apt ease. Shared cultural capital brought together noble amateurs with others we might think of as professional virtuosi—intellectuals, artists, musicians, astrologers. Princely patronage raised the position of the specialists but did not make them aristocrats.

Speaking well was one important domain of prowess. The great cities and courts set local ideals, but all scorned village patois. Castiglione's *Courtier* recounts a virtuoso prank in which a nobleman convinces several court ladies that a well-dressed peasant who speaks in an almost impenetrable and to their ears execrable dialect from the countryside near Bergamo is in fact a noble so clever that he can ape rustic speech. The gullible ladies, completely fooled, extol the peasant's genius for speaking the only way he can. The story illustrates perfectly *sprezzatura*—strenuous effort (here only an illusion) on the part of the elite to appear altogether natural. It also points out linguistic snobbery. There was more to elite speech than an urban dialect. Precise enunciation, pleasing rhythm, the right words, and literary allusions all gave prestige. With the aristocratization of the later Renaissance, language became even more a salient device for marking hierarchy and setting barriers to social ascent. One mark of status was the mastery of *cortesia*, the words and gestures of good manners. As preached by Castiglione and Della Casa, courtesy was a modulation of responses, calibrated to give not offense but pleasure. Well-chosen words and actions masked true feelings where necessary, smoothing social relations in the competitive world of princely courts. With time, the courtly model of polite restraint spread across the elites and seeped into the middle classes.

Written language and intellectual dexterity also counted. Latin erudition earned respect, especially humanism's literary cult of ancient authors. A polished style and adroit quotations from the classics glorified both the writer or orator and his audience. The visual arts, with their rich, clever allusions to ancient models and stories, likewise strove for prestige through learning. Not universities, but rather courts and a swarm of new academics—clubs of cultured men who discussed literature, philosophy, statecraft, or natural science—were the sites for display of this fashionable scholarship. Not all intellectual life looked backward to the classics. Italians also cultivated skills of contemporary observation, especially in unfamiliar geographical or scientific terrains. Ambassadors, for instance, aspired to advance their careers by vivid reports on their travels. Heads of household, especially Florentines, wrote down maxims and comments on the world, to pass on to their descendants as domestic intellectual capital crucial to the lineage's success. Although women of the upper classes took no part in public competition for intellectual reputation, a good head and a ready tongue, if not too biting, did their standing good. A handful of middling rank women and an occasional "honest" courtesan reaped male admiration and some recognition for their exceptional literary skills in Latin and Italian.

In addition, a courtly aspirant cultivated connoisseurship, the mastery of esoteric knowledge of horses, dogs, weapons, gems, painting, furniture, tableware, cookery, and myriad other beautiful things valued by elite society. All the arts, including dance and music, invited refined appreciation and sometimes performance.

Collecting the rare and the curious became a serious intellectual pastime. One might amass antique statues, coins, or cameos; it paid to know one's Mars from Hercules. A man chose carefully when to show his treasures, to whom, with what ceremonies of revelation, knowing well that, as he displayed his belongings, he staked his social self. While courting admiration, one ran the risk of indifference or scorn. Successfully deployed, informed, tasteful display bolstered social standing, but its impact was never closely measurable.

Prestigious Consumption

As today, elite groups competed through conspicuous consumption. The display of wealth contributed, but even more important was the exercise of good taste and connoisseurship—the prestigious knowledge of pleasing or exotic or venerable things. Our cultural snobberies thus have a venerable history. Although there were medieval precedents in the court fashion and the cult of chivalry, the Renaissance saw a flowering of forms of knowledge and taste that, by defining elite groups and making entry harder, served as instruments of hierarchic competition. The very Renaissance itself, a glorious bloom in so many arts, was itself a spectacular investment, individual and collective, in cultural capital. Competition for standing, though not its only source, was crucial to its verve.

Social competition spurred conspicuous extravagance. There was no top to more. Clothing, especially for great, festive occasions such as weddings, was a favored site for expenditure and self-declaration. Consequently, many city governments passed "sumptuary" laws to curtail lavish outlays. Detailed strictures regulated the use of fur trim, cloth of gold, expensive dyes, jewelry, fancy buttons, wide sleeves, slashings, and assorted other costly fashions.[6] At some moments, these apparently leveling strictures also had an anti-aristocratic slant. More commonly, however, the protocols respected and reinforced hierarchy by calibrating permitted ostentation to rank. And the less lofty could often buy a license to break the rules. Another frequent argument in all-male city councils was that extravagance was the fault of wives, who drove their husbands to ruin by trying to keep up with the neighbors. Could not such money be better spent on the defense of the republic or the advancement of trade? And, churchmen added, reprovingly, women's fancy dress and low-cut bodices fostered vanity and lust. Practice, however, discounted these misogynistic arguments. Although women sometimes had a say in choosing their wardrobes, it was men who held the purse strings and indeed wanted to show off the family's taste on their womenfolk and not less on themselves. Despite the laws, both sexes seldom hesitated to embellish themselves as best they could. In contrast, the dull, rough homespun and patched garments of the poor marked their low status.

Elite houses, or, better, palaces asserted high status and often marked a neighborhood's identity. The architecture itself—a rusticated facade, a balconied window on the Grand Canal, classical cornices, and pediments—announced the family's pretensions. In the fifteenth century, great families sometimes held their banquets in their street-side porticos, so the whole town could gawk and marvel. The same sumptuary laws that sought to regulate clothing aimed also to cap the size and cost of wedding parties and funerals. These elaborate familial rites of passage called for public events that proclaimed status and cultivated alliances with pomp, hospitality, and largesse. Private transportation such as fine horses, sedan chairs, and gondolas also made their claims. Closed coaches were the prestigious novelty of the later sixteenth century. It helped, too, to have servants, sometimes in livery, running at one's stirrups or before the carriage to hustle pedestrians out of the way. Inside, although by our upholstered habits furniture was often sparse, tapestries, gilded leather wall hangings, a carved wood ceiling, or a credenza stocked with silver and glass spoke of taste as well as wealth. Collections of antiquities, marble busts, finicky metal ornaments, and paintings of many sorts displayed their owners' expertise.

Let us imagine a gentleman's afternoon call at a Renaissance Roman palace. When you ride through the elegant doorway into the arcaded courtyard, servants help you to the ground. With bows and lowered voices, they ask your name and go off to announce your arrival. Your host, as a mark of high respect, comes to greet you at the head of the wide stairway that leads to the *piano nobile*, the lofty second floor. He salutes you with courteous words, embraces you (if you are male), and then, acknowledging your substantial standing, leads you through a chain of ever more private rooms into the intimacy of his study. There in a space more private than his bedroom, he may show you his treasures. At the end of your visit, he escorts you back to the spot at which he first had greeted you. For a lesser personage, he would have come less far out and perhaps talked with you only in that room. Had you been his better, he would have met and saluted you at the foot of the stairs, or even at the portal, or better yet, have escorted you from and to your lodgings.[7] Yours is a simple visit, not a meal, where the business of who sits where and who eats first would have brought yet further mannered niceties. All this seems fussy and uneasily subservient now, but to a sixteenth-century Italian it was second nature, and indeed necessary to get on in the world.

CONCLUSION

Hierarchy was a fundamental and righteous principle of Renaissance cosmology, theology, and social organization. In an uncertain world the ideal of careful calibration of persons and things offered security. The notion that every person had a place translated into the interactions of daily life in countless strategies, ceremonies, and forms of speech. At the same time, whatever precedence imagined, there were many ladders for measuring standing, with no consistent correspondence among them. Therefore, the fine gradations and abundant codes did not lock Italians in. Rather, while acknowledging the hierarchical order, men and women, individually and in groups, jockeyed energetically for position.

NOTES

1. BAV, Urb. Lat. 1038, f. 98r.
2. Della Casa, *Galateo*, 28–29.
3. Moryson, *Shakespeare's Europe*, 417.
4. Coryate, *Coryat's Crudities*, 462.
5. Agnolo Firenzuola, *On the Beauty of Women* (Philadelphia, 1992), 15.
6. On sumptuary law, Catherine Killerby, *Sumptuary Law in Italy, 1200–1500* (London, 2002).
7. On palace courtesies, Patricia Waddy, *Seventeenth-Century Roman Palaces: Use and Art of the Plan* (Cambridge, MA, 1990), 3–13.

6

MORALITIES: RELIGION AND HONOR

The solidarities and hierarchies of Italian society lived in complex symbiosis with its moral values. There, as in any place and time, institutions fostered values that in their turn propped up institutions, in intricate feedback loops. To study moralities, we need to distinguish ideals, customs, and the pell-mell untidiness of everyday life. At face value, moral precepts, typically legitimized by divine will or other weighty power, laid out what a good person should and should not do. Authorities urged compliance with instruction, counseling, inspiration, and threats. There might be formal enforcement as well, although we easily overestimate the disciplinary force of early modern governance. But in real life, people dealt routinely with oughts that, by choice or necessity, they could not fulfill. Local communities were a more useful monitor than officialdom of a less idealized range of morally acceptable behavior.

Two elaborate moral systems, Christian virtue and a code of honor, shaped the lives of Renaissance Italians. So contrary do these two seem at first glance that one might expect people to have spent their days baffled and torn. Honor urged vengeance, pride, display, and partisan loyalties, all deplored by religion. Religion, meanwhile, preached peace and mercy, humility and a universalizing social ethic at odds with honor's deep particularism. Of the two competing codes, the Christian ethic had the far sharper, more coherent formulation, and perhaps a prior claim to attention and adherence, backed as it was by the potent institutions of the church, a rich tradition of theological explication, and God himself, who held eternal souls hostage to enforce good behavior on earth. Meanwhile, honor shaped much everyday interaction. Not formally encoded nor written down, and open to wiry adaptation from case to case, honor was learned, practiced, and enforced in the endless exchanges, routine and extraordinary, of daily life. It had stylized written models, in, for instance, chivalric literature, but its foundation rested on a broad oral culture. Alongside these first two ethics were other, less sweeping, but still potent moral codes, anchored in the law and in the customs of family and of group solidarity. These complicated the picture yet further.

As we survey this conundrum of Renaissance ethics, a caution is in order. Moderns looking at the past sometimes mistake moral rules for inviolable commands. They are puzzled to see people flout the very ethical principles they propound. They query, for instance, the sensuality of some Renaissance popes or Christian cruelty to those outside the faith. "How could they do such a thing? It was against their values!" Furthermore, moderns sometimes imagine, ahistorically, that premodern institutions can effectively enforce their will and punish those who deviate. Such readers therefore expect past peoples to be far more consistent in precepts and conduct than we ever are. Medieval and early modern Italians held deeply the values that guided their choices. Yet their behavior corresponded to these rules in as mixed and nuanced a way as does our own conduct when it heeds our own contradictory moral strictures.

In fact, discordant moral codes are common, now and then. Indeed, they are useful, for, amid the complexities of all human social life, they give elbow room to individual action. Agency is the capacity to choose, even when constrained. It thrives on contradictions. Moral values help designate the possible choices. They set a price and a benefit to every option, making some courses cheap, others costly, even prohibitive. But they often do not dictate the decision. Often one must choose between two goods, or two evils. This fact, though it burdens the choosing, gives us humans a leeway. Moral dissonance sparks discussion and eases bargaining, two activities central to Renaissance Italian life.

RELIGION AS A MORAL CODE

Morality by Institution

Behind Catholic morality stood a vast, sophisticated, immensely wealthy institution of great prestige. The church not only embodied a morality but also propagated and enforced it in pulpit, confessional, school, and tribunal. Nevertheless, the Renaissance church, for all that it had a central government in Rome, a chain of command, and, for the times, efficient lines of communication, was very far from the monolithic, proto-totalitarian regime that moderns sometimes project back onto it. It remained polycentric with ample room for local initiative. Leaders—among them bishops, friars, scholars, and zealous lay men and women—all pursued a righteous Christian polity, but they sometimes walked different paths, worked at cross-purposes, or quarreled. Only in the mid-sixteenth century, with the Council of Trent, did the Rome-centered church begin to tighten its hold on the whole, but without simple unanimity or clarity.

The church taught Christian values by many routes. Clergy, themselves often poorly educated, were in short supply, especially in country parishes. Priests there provided occasional sacraments and oversaw rites of passage, but did not preach. They shared the rural lives of their flocks, and, as counselors and peacemakers, brokered social and political relationships. The cities were better served. Urban clergy did confess their flocks, but most parishioners went only rarely. It was a reform when Trent insisted on communion, preceded by confession, at least once a year at Easter. Preaching, however, was very influential. The specialists for reaching the large populace were the friars. Franciscans and Dominicans, above all, from the thirteenth century on toured Italy's cities and towns, teaching basic doctrine, devotional practice, and moral living. In an age where information was scarce, the friars combined the roles of entertainers, broadcasters, inspirers, prophets, scolds, and social facilitators. A truly charismatic preacher, like Bernardino of Siena or Girolamo Savonarola, was a political force to reckon with. Such men could evangelize a city, bringing about, for a while, dramatic changes in public and private behavior.[1] Moral teaching also employed other media. Didactic Christian art ornamented houses, street-corner shrines, and countless churches and chapels. Recognizing saints, who posed with their standard emblems, and picking out gospel stories about Jesus and Mary, Italians recalled familiar lessons. The church also relied increasingly on print and literacy to spread its word.

To separate the sacred from the profane, though central to the Christian vision and its moral aspirations, was impossible. Catholicism was itself of two minds about the virtues of being apart from the world or in it. The monastic impulse had always hankered after withdrawal and seclusion. An otherworldly environment favored the spiritual achievements of God's athletes, monks and nuns. Although their ascetic, often-cloistered rule of life was not intended for most people, they modeled prayerfulness and charitable care to travelers, pilgrims, and the sick and poor. On the other hand, "church," in its original Greek (*ekklesia*), meant "gathering" and hence community, not of clergy alone but of all the faithful. This church could not stand outside society, which constituted it. Except for the Jews, all Italians thought of themselves as Christian; indeed, as a noun *cristiano* was a word for a person. ("Lutheran" [*luterano*], on the other hand, meant a Protestant, an alien.) While the clergy were legally a separate order with great power, the laity, especially some members of its elites, had ample initiative in some religious activities such as overseeing parish property, organizing pilgrimages, leading confraternities, and promoting reforms. Furthermore, the church's broad responsibilities for spiritual and social leadership, for education and welfare, depended on the management of its huge economic resources and, so, embroiled its institutions in practical affairs. And, entangled in the world as they politicked for good appointments, Renaissance prelates, to the annoyance of church reformers, were notoriously quick to remember their alliances with families and friends.

The Spirit of Christian Morality

Although theologians laid out morality as a skein of interlocking rules, when Italians invoked or followed Christian values, they often heeded as much a rhetoric and mood as specific strictures on conduct. For them, to be Christian was to imitate the life of Jesus, or, like a musical string, to resonate in sympathy with his example. He, as God in human form, had suffered at the hands of other men, had forgiven them, and, by his sacrifice, had given all humankind a chance of salvation. To be Christian therefore entailed renunciation, pain, charity, and mercy. The premodern Jesus had also a sterner streak, less often emphasized in modern Christianity, as the formidable judge at the end of time. Human imitators of Christ were always flawed, for, unlike him, men and women were fallen creatures full of sin and subject to divine wrath. The threat of hell, demons, and damnation warned Italians to be as virtuous as possible. Nevertheless, for their inescapable weakness, Catholicism offered sinners understanding and support. Unlike her awe-inspiring son, Christ's mother, Mary was a softer being, who knew suffering and endurance, and practiced mercy. Many stories told of her forgiveness and aid to the hapless and unworthy. Saints, male and female, provided inspiring models for virtue. Martyrs suffered grisly deaths—by the toothed wheel, grill, sword, thicket of arrows, or pot of oil, but in altarpieces they never flinched or raged, but rather bore calm witness to steadfast faith. Other saints showed the way with acts of profound charity, extraordinary service to the church, or mystical union with God. Saints in their turn offered not only universal paragons but also help to particular protégés: Saint Ivo championed lawyers, Saint Luke painters, and Saint Nicholas sailors and dowerless girls; Saint Margaret protected childbirth, Saint Lucy eyes, Saint Christopher travelers, Saint Sebastian and Saint Roch plague victims, and so on.[2]

In a well-known composition, the members of the Holy Family appear to be flanked by the donors, a well-dressed man and his wife on their knees. This painting by Dosso Dossi from around 1514, probably commissioned for a chapel, celebrates the values of both family and piety. (John G. Johnson Collection, 1917. Philadelphia Museum of Art)

Itself a richly complex assemblage, Christian morality had a subversive streak that often undercut both lay values and habits, and also many of the institutions that governed Italian life. This ancient tension between sacred ethics and everyday life marked the faith profoundly. In Italy, where religion encountered life's needs and pleasures, struggle often ensued. The church extolled: against warfare and civil strife—peace; against worldly ambition— heavenly salvation. Against the patrimonial strategies of lineage, religion preached fat bequests to churches, clerical celibacy, respect for monastic vocations, and not divorcing a barren wife. Against indulging sexual desire, piety urged continence; against feasting— periodic fasts; against Sundays spent carousing—sober church attendance. Christianity could also offer utopian moments of with-drawal or social transformation. At gatherings of their penitential confraternities, Italians could shelter from the tensions of civic life. Or, when a preacher galvanized their town, they could turn against much that honor prized, making private peace, forgiving enemies, stoking bonfires of "vanities"—playing cards, dice, fine clothes, amorous paintings of Mars and Venus—and purging the city of all the usual vices. Such reforms never lasted, but they had a cathartic effect that helped balance the demands and impulses of discordant codes of action. Nevertheless, Christianity's subversion was only partial, for it relied on and sanctified the very institutions—family, state, and church—that it also hedged and chided.

Everyday Religious Practice

For church authorities, a moral life included proper religious observance. Some people, mostly in cities, attended church for spe-cial festivals and, less commonly, daily Mass. In sixteenth-century Roman courts, women more often than men spoke of doing these public duties. Taking communion, on the other hand, was seldom frequent, and many couples lived together without church wed-dings. The Christian calendar also set out special times for prayer and penance, including fasting or meat-free diets, and abstinence from sex and worldly recreations. Although it is tricky to general-ize, piecemeal evidence suggests that many Italians observed these obligations, More than once, in Rome, a prostitute reported eating fish with her client on a fast day. The taverns that supplied take-out meals served fish on these days, presumably to many people. Were customers making a choice not to eat meat? We should not, in any case, presume the prostitute a hypocrite, for her trade did not render her an irreligious person. More generally, a residual respect for sacred persons, places, objects, images, and words was widely shared.[3] Those who profaned them felt pressure not only from the law but also from their peers.

The religion that infiltrated the everyday life of layfolk was less ceremony than informal praxis. Christianity suffused the language of prayers and blessings for moments of stress and rites of life passage. It surfaced whenever people evoked charity or extolled compassion. Landscape and city streets abounded in local shrines and images, over gates, on corners, by doors, as did rooms in homes.[4] Feeling their protection, people gave thanks as they passed, or sought out these holy figures at times of need. Special seasons, too, had their popular ceremonies, pilgrimages, and festivals that mingled piety with a hope for worldly well-being. Amulets worn around the neck or on the wrist had a holy tinge. Indeed, much magic and divination worked on religion's fuzzy boundary, incorporating saint's names and prayers, and looking to the arcane power of supernatural, sacred figures.

Some Italians from time to time not only neglected their Christian commitments but also spoke or acted in ways deemed explicitly offensive to religion. For example, the clergy, and perhaps most abundantly the friars who worked among the laity, were the butt of many jokes and stories. Although unwelcome to church authorities, such anti-clerical opinion did not necessarily signal a rejection of religion. Indeed, such lay complaints figured prominently in the reform movements that in the early sixteenth century sought to purify Christianity and its practice. Also, very common, though less earnest, were blasphemy and godless recreations such as gambling. Oaths could be colorful: "by the breasts of the Virgin!" But, as with us, routine and automatic profanity, though offensive, did not signify revulsion toward Christianity. Especially as Catholic reform gained momentum, ecclesiastical discipline worked to repress such low-grade ungodliness, but the high stakes attached to heresy were another story entirely.

HONOR AS A MORAL CODE

There was more to Renaissance Italian ethics than Christian precept and sensibility. Religion's enterprise had, in honor, a less formal complement and serious rival. Honor's force was this-worldly and deeply social. Unlike Christianity, it had neither institutional structure nor economic assets. Rather than a formal code of behavior, honor was a set of practices and a fluid calculus of human worth. Renaissance Italian habits had much in common with a larger cultural complex much discussed by anthropologists of the Mediterranean. This package of ideas and practices, in fact, comes in varied flavors and also shows up elsewhere in Renaissance Europe. Still, the notion helps to grasp an elusive but central structure of premodern Italian mentality. The ethic's main traits were prickly male pride, energetic payback for harm and help alike, firm bonds to family and allies, a sharp distinction between males and females, and a fierce joint custody for one's own women's chastity. At its core, honor was a social quality, the distillation of reputation.

External to the self, honor lodged in the judgments of the perduring circle of family and friends who monitored your doings, as well as in the thoughts of casual onlookers. While praise left its glow, sharp was the sting of shame, what Italians called *vergogna*. Honor's social utility was tied to its odd vulnerability. It did have some resilience, as a good name was an inexhaustible social asset; one cashed it in repeatedly without its losing any worth. Nevertheless, honor was also a liability, for it was easily harmed at the hands of others. This notorious fragility of honor engendered thin-skinned prickliness, boastful swagger, and tussle for position. Easily damaged, honor functioned as collateral, readily pawned among peers. Renaissance Italy, where government was often flimsy, needed noninstitutional ways of enforcing agreements and verifying claims. Honor, as liability, made one reliable. One pledged it: "Upon my honor, I will do it!" "Upon my honor, I speak the truth!" So honor readily stood hostage.

Honor, which pervaded the whole social order, was alert to hierarchy. Standing set social regard, and, by delineating peer groups, lodged honor's contests within narrow bounds. Underlings, even peasants, thieves, and prostitutes, possessed a strong sense of it, but only among their equals. In their struggles for face and standing, they could not aspire to filch honor from their social betters. Nor could their superiors gain by taking honor from them. Rather, contests for honor engaged near-equals. A gentleman could shrug off an inferior's insult; indeed, to take it to heart was to stoop and risk derision. Or he could avenge the offense by some scornful act that inflicted pain and shame without engaging his own honor. Certainly, to challenge an underling would have looked bizarre. Honor came into agonistic play among peers, be they lords or stable hands, where real adjustments to prestige could happen.

Thus, as a social practice, honor both expressed and supported Renaissance hierarchy; it was a conservative ethic.

Honor reinforced solidarities, for its combative ethos welded men and women to their groups and assigned them collective responsibilities. Both honor and its obverse, shame, were as if contagious. One caught them from the company one kept. Families above all, but also cities, trades, professions, neighborhoods, patrons with clientele had a notional shared honor that they imparted to their members. There was group dishonor in yielding place, especially if pressed. Many tumultuous and even bloody conflicts of daily life stemmed from struggles not over tangibles but over reputation. Within families, sustaining honor designated different duties to males and females. Nevertheless, as with most moral codes, custom and practice called for behavior that was more nuanced than theory prescribed. Furthermore, although we associate the discourses of honor most closely with the noble ranks, versions of this ethic can be heard in Renaissance Italy up and down the social scale, from prelates to thieves, and among women as well as men.

Honor inhered in persons as both a moral potential and a social record. Everyone was watching what a person did. So potent was the bearing of witness that others' judgment must have often seemed to constitute one's very self. Honor thereby acquired an inward aspect, as knowing that you had so acted that others plainly approved underlay your self-esteem. The ethic inspired proud display, manly swagger, and much legal and political jostling over where one sat at table or stood in a line of march. To merit the claim, "He is a man of honor," several traits weighed. Honor accrued not only to power and wealth but also, crucially, to virtue. Paramount was fidelity to word. A person of honor told the truth and kept all promises, no matter the risk or cost. In all life truth-telling was a luxury, indulged only by those who could afford it. A weakling would twist the truth. Thus, honesty signaled prosperity and strength. A second potentially expensive virtue was generosity. This took two forms: largesse and magnanimity. Largesse was open-handedness: one gave gifts and offered food and hospitality. Magnanimity was greatness of soul: one forgave enemies and forbore, without vexation, others' faults. The last virtue was courage, which put life and well-being at risk. All these costly, strenuous virtues, fundamentally male, descended from the ethics of the medieval warrior. Women too might derive honor from such behavior, yet the essence of female honor lay elsewhere.

Female Honor

In the schema of Mediterranean honor, women's virtue resided primarily in her chastity and fecundity, both valued highly among family assets. The task of male kin—fathers, husbands, sometimes brothers—was to prevent sexual approaches to their women and to be seen to be keeping them out of harm's way. Edgy vigilance was necessary, for women's gender, the notion went, made them weak and fickle, and so vulnerable to seduction as well as force. A man whose woman suffered, willingly or not, public compromise reaped deep shame. By the code, the only recourse was violent revenge, against the lover, but also, sometimes, against the daughter or wife as well. To avoid this fate, the woman's job was to collaborate by cloaking her sexuality in thick veils of self-restraint. Honorable women sought to escape the disapproval of others by diligent modesty. In contrast to the corrosive shame of *vergogna*, this voluntary, preemptive, good shame, called *pudore* (modesty), called for downcast eyes, a bridled tongue, quiet bearing, and, at moments of notice, a virtuous blush.

Wifely adultery deeply offended family honor, but probably the more common threat was the defloration and, worse, pregnancy of nubile girls. Girding the women on whom rested family's reputation was easier for the high born and wealthy, who could afford to chaperone them closely or shut them in a cloister. Among ordinary people, the material realities of life—the need to work, jumbled domestic spaces, an unpoliced outdoors—put young women at risk. In Matteo Bandello's novella about Giulia of Gazuolo, a would-be lover of higher rank stalks and eventually rapes a poor man's daughter in the fields where she works alone. Giulia afterward dresses in clean clothes and drowns herself in the river to cleanse her family's honor. The storyteller marvels at the high-minded conduct of a lowly woman who sharply shames her betters. In real life, however, despite its harsh ethical precepts, honor involved endless social negotiation. For example, everyday culture offered some remedies for the problem of a daughter no longer virgin. A father need not languish in lifelong infamy, nor need the daughter's sexual misuse doom her to prostitution and social exclusion. One course was to marry the couple promptly, although, unsurprisingly, seducers often could not or would not oblige. With a dowry, perhaps somewhat larger than customary, there could be a marriage to some other willing male. The culpable man, pressed informally in the neighborhood or by a judicial proceeding, might cough up some money. In some cities, a young woman might mend her honor in a monastic asylum for errant women, before a charitably arranged marriage or placement in domestic service. Either destination respectably absolved her father of his responsibility and placed the girl under suitable discipline.

The iconic tale that follows is true, but all the more startling because it was not very common. In the eyes of honor, its logic is crystalline. The better recompense for a visibly wrecked reputation was cash for a dowry. Barring that, this father felt compelled to take his due in lovers' blood.

An Honor Killing in the Family

Here is a piteous story from 1555, from the Sabine mountains east of Rome, told by Nuntio of Rocca Sinibalda to the pope's magistrate. One day, he informs the magistrate, he was working in the fields when his brother arrived with an urgent summons to Uncle Barnabeo's, in a nearby town. Why? asked Nuntio; the brother would not say. Arriving at his uncle's house, Nuntio found all his kin there, crying. What is wrong? It is your cousin, Bernardina. She is pregnant, and she was a virgin! Nuntio too burst into tears. Who did it? The village judge! But don't worry; we have his house surrounded, and the priest is negotiating to secure a dowry. All afternoon and evening they parleyed, but to no avail. The next morning, the feckless judge chose to make a run for it, jumping out his window and down the town walls. Dashing for freedom across the terraced gardens, he failed to reckon on Barnabeo's lurking kinsmen. They cut him down. At once, word came to the father: the judge is dead! Aware that with the seducer had died the promise of a dowry and of familial honor redeemed, the father took his daughter by the elbow and, under the eyes of the whole village, led her across the field to her lover's corpse. There, as all watched, he slit her throat.[5]

While the cultural logic of honor made agency male and restraint and subjection female, in daily life women, notably those far down the social scale, took active part in the ethic's play. In their neighborhoods women collaborated with their menfolk in aggressive protection of their family and its local reputation. The language of honor and especially its inverse, vituperation, clothed the dynamics of much street sociability. Women's slanging matches began with words but sometimes migrated to battering with wooden slippers and hair-pulling. Women's initiative sometimes prodded male family members into action. Other times, men and women worked for peacemaking, which also rested on honor-laced rituals for much of its force.

Shamelessness

The antithesis of honor, *vergogna* (shame), had a triple sense—at once a state of mind, a painful social purgatory, or for some a trait of character. The first was anguished embarrassment, the second passing or permanent disgrace. As to the third, in Italian eyes, people "without shame" (*senza vergogna*) discounted public scorn; they were too base or foreign to observe honor's rules. Shamelessness was in some an involuntary flaw of status or identity, in others a wittingly chosen occasional or habitual role. Among those deemed categorically shameless by respectable people were executioners, jesters, dwarfs, prostitutes, and Gypsies (Roma). A more individual shamelessness attached to a persona that, for example, inverted gender norms, such as a passive male sodomite or a woman who was forward, loud, or violent. Shamelessness, though costly in some terms, could also offer advantages. Those with little reputation to lose grasped transgressive liberties to serve, for tips and favors, more confined insiders. Thus, a shameless go-between reaped benefit from a freedom of movement denied to her lady.

Related, but less deeply rooted in personal character, was the concept of *sfacciatezza*. The term literally meant "lacking face." Since the head and especially the face was the body's chief seat of honor, a person metaphorically without a face was unreadable and dubious. More broadly, *sfacciatezza* suggested nerve or impudence, the refusal to restrain oneself within the canons of good shame and proper conduct. With its love of wit, play, and tricksters, the Renaissance was fascinated by *sfacciatezza* and made place for it across its secular culture. In Carnival many people donned masks to toy with impertinence, social inversion, and sexual license. *Sfacciatezza* was the stock in trade of actors, and comedy regularly featured subterfuge and guile, often practiced by servants and underlings at the expense of their more honorable employers. In Pietro Aretino's *Dialogues*, prostitutes voiced the author's sharp critique of patronage, clerical and lay. Criminal trials show *sfacciatezza* put to work in real life, too.

Agonism and Honor

The agonism so typical of Renaissance social life provoked many contests for honor. Often squabbles with roots in other domains, such as material goods or emotions, were converted for resolution into battles over honor. The social and psychological dynamics of protecting, acquiring, defending, challenging, and losing honor were complicated. From one perspective, as in an economy of limited good where land and wealth were finite, honor was precious and there was never enough to go around. To retain its value, people could not hoard honor but had to keep their assets in play and thus at risk. A contest might then take the form of theft, of piling up your own honor by taking someone else's. On the other hand, in practice the supply of honor was not fixed or measurable. Nearly everyone claimed to have honor, or public repute, that could be mobilized or eroded in the restless shifting of Renaissance daily life. The quota of honor staked in a given confrontation depended on the particular contestants, their skills, resources, connections, and hopes.

A classic honor contest had a loose choreography of challenge and response. From myriad possible sources, at some moment friction between two men of roughly equal standing began to coalesce into confrontation. The setting was likely public, with a chorus of associates or perhaps only idle bystanders who could attest to the propriety of the moves. One party, feeling his social integrity at risk, would issue a challenge in honor's terms. Since honor and truth-telling vouched for one another, the most direct way to defy a man was to call him a liar. For example, a first man affronted another with the insult "Cheating coward!", to which the challenger retorted, "You are lying through your throat!" For the first speaker, to refuse a legitimate contest was shameful; he lost at once. But to respond was to stake not only reputation but also body or other assets. So, at that, out came the daggers. There ensued clash, decision, picking up the wounded, and commentary from *publica vox et fama* (gossip and reputation). Some affronts were almost codified, as when two antagonists undertook to settle a quarrel by duel. The sixteenth century elaborated a complex etiquette that occupied many printed treatises: an initial insult; the reply ("You lie"); the arrangement of time, place, and seconds; the choice of weapons. Dueling was almost as rule-bound as chess, and no less open to improvisation in the fight itself, and to punctilious debate about what moves were proper.

To enhance one's honor by challenging another's, there were several terrains of encounter. First was the corporeal person. The head and face were the noblest parts of the body, along with the hands and chest. The belly was a transition zone, while the private parts, by their very nature, both embodied and engendered shame. The head was a favorite target for attack. One might throw an enemy's hat to the ground or pull his beard, or drag a rival by the hair. The assailants might also bare their victims' nether regions or spank them. Far graver was an injury to the flesh, especially if it left an enduring mark. A permanent scar on the face, a *sfregio*, was a terrible blow. A lopped-off ear or nose brought shame, whether lost in a private contest or as a public punishment. Such damage appeared far too often in the court records to be mere brawling accidents. Similarly, since a man's honor was tightly bound to autonomy, any act that trammeled his body could be taken as an affront. To deny a man access or to challenge his progress in the street invited a fight. To bind a man prisoner was an affront so vile that it polluted not only the captive but also his captors. The police were especially scorned because their profession made them tie men up (Chapter 7).

By extension of the body, honor also attached to a man's house or other spaces under his control. To invade a man's dwelling or lands gave affront, as did theft or injury to his goods and livestock. Not only his family and womenfolk should be safe within the house but also his guests. As the symbolic face of the household, the dwelling's facade attracted the shaming attentions of enemies. Often a response to aggrieved honor, the practice of "house-scorning" had a rich repertoire of moves that caught the eyes and ears of neighbors. In Rome, under the cover of darkness, assailants attacked their victim's walls, doors, and windows, defiling surfaces with vials of ink or papers smeared with excrement, breaking window coverings and unhinging shutters with hurled stones, kicking or torching doors. The scorners also sang bawdy songs, made rude noises, and sometimes scrawled derogatory symbols such as the cuckold's horns. In the morning, those assaulted, sometimes with neighbors' help, worked quickly to erase the shaming marks and sometimes initiated criminal charges. Notably, many prosecutions involved the houses of prostitutes, assailed by rejected would-be clients. Here we see the complexity of honor culture in practice, as the city courts allowed women in a shameless profession to proceed against men who had offended their honor.

A Workplace Contest for Honor

The boastful autobiography of the goldsmith Cellini includes this lively yarn of a workplace competition between himself, an employee, and the shopmaster, the silversmith Lucagnolo. Following the typical rhythm of a contest for honor, the story begins with a duel of mutual boasts. Lucagnolo then sets the formal challenge: to make the more intricate and precious work in metal. He also lays out the game's terms, that both will finish their work at the same time and then compare how much the buyers will pay. Workmen and neighbors would act as both witnesses and jury.

> While I was working on this project, that skilled fellow, Lucagnolo . . . took it badly, saying again and again that I would have much more profit, and more honor if I worked on big silver vases, as I had started out to do. I answered that I could make big silver vases any time I wanted to, but that the things I was doing now didn't turn up every day, and that in what I was doing now there was no less honor than in big silver vases, but a lot more profit. Agnolo scoffed at me, saying, "You'll see, Benvenuto, because, while you finish working on your job, I will hurry to be done with this vase, which I started when you began with the jewel, hoping that it will be clear how much profit I get from my vase, and what you get for your jewel." I answered him that I was glad to have a match with a man as able as he, for in the end of the work we would see which one of us was deluding himself. So both of us, with a slightly scornful smile, bent our heads proudly, eager to finish the job. So that, at the end of ten days, both of us had finished his piece very cleanly and cleverly.[6]

As Cellini's tale goes on, when he delivers his jewel to the beautiful Roman lady, who has commissioned it, she challenges him to name his price. He replies with a strategic counterchallenge to her generosity by protesting that her satisfaction is pay enough. Cellini, if we can believe him, returns empty handed to the shop, to find Lucagnolo clutching his payment. Invited to finish the contest, Cellini begs off until the following day. In the morning, a messenger brings him a not-unexpected packet of coins from the lady, whose honor lies in recognizing her artist's great talent and rewarding him with largesse.

To Lucagnolo, it seemed a thousand years till he could match his packet with mine. As soon as we were in the shop, in the presence of twelve workmen and other neighbors who came crowding in to see the end of the contest, Lucagnolo took his packet and, laughing scornfully and crying out three or four times, "Ooh, Ooh!" he noisily poured his coins out on the counter. There were twenty-five scudi worth, in [silver] *giulio* coins. He thought I had four or five scudi in cash. Suffocated by his racket, and by the stares and laughter of the people standing around, I peeked in my packet and, seeing that it was all gold, I cast down my eyes and, from one side of the counter, in total silence with two hands raised my packet up way up high, and poured the money out as if from a mill hopper. My money was half again as much as his, so that all the eyes that had been fixed scornfully on me suddenly switched to him. They said, "Lucagnolo, this money of Benvenuto, because it is gold, and because it is half again as much, makes a much prettier show than yours." I was sure that, for envy and for the affront he suffered, Lucagnolo would surely have died on the spot.[7]

Cellini, in his telling, is deft and graceful, as nonchalant as one of Castiglione's imagined courtiers. Without the judgment of witnesses, however, all would have been in vain. Applause was only half the watchers' job; they also must show their scorn. Their eyes were avid to see not only triumph but also humiliation for, far more than we, Renaissance Italians enjoyed derision. In honor contests, onlookers sometimes did judge both sides winners, but often, as here, a clear victor walked off with reputation's prize.

A Violent Family Fight

In another story, retold in a trial of 1557, an honor-driven fight rends a professional family and its house. The tangled back-story features a festering quarrel over both money and precedence inside the family. The contenders, Roman gentlemen, are brothers. Ascanio, the oldest, is the black sheep: a notorious cheat at cards and dice, with a shocking courtesan wife and a reputation for shamelessness. A teenaged sister died during the afternoon, and Ascanio, for his vices, has been left out of her will. Standing in the courtyard, he pleads in vain with his younger brothers for a share of the substantial money. Second by age and the leader of the respectable brothers, Pompeo, dressed for dinner, without even a dagger, descends the stairs into a confrontation with the elder. The move from words and gestures insulting honor to swordplay follows a familiar social script. Later, the brawl spills from the family courtyard into the street. In a common second phase of honor contests, bystanders, including soldiers, then work to break up the fight.

Pompeo: "Ascanio, what is this? What is this you are saying? What is all this shouting about? Your sister's will was well made. There's no need to get you dragged into this! You know that already."

Ascanio: "What do you think I am?"

Pompeo: "You know well enough what I think of you. You mean nothing to me. Go on, get a move on! Get out of here! You have no business being here. I think you are . . . I think you are a mortal enemy!"

Ascanio: "There are other things than this that I should spend my time on with you!"

He then bites his finger at Pompeo, who at once spins around, thrusts his bottom at his brother, and roars:

"Ascanio, I want you to stick all the nose you've got up my ass!"

Ascanio, reaching for the dagger at his right hip and lunging toward Pompeo, shouts: "You have assassinated me!"

A dinner guest leaps at Ascanio, clasping him to prevent an attack on Pompeo. Pompeo rushes at Giuliano, Ascanio's servant, who is standing by the courtyard wellhead, grabs the youngster's sword, draws it, and dashes toward Ascanio. Several bystanders converge to seize Pompeo. In their hands, he trips and falls; Giuliano's sword goes flying. At once, one of the servants picks it up and hustles it out of range. The air rings with profanities. Pompeo recovers his balance, breaks away, scampers up the steps into the garden, and returns brandishing his own sword. Soon the household servants rush in with battle-axes. There ensues a melee that, miraculously, produces only a small cut to Pompeo's thumb before soldiers in the street first join in to defend the underdog and then calm the brawl.[8]

NAVIGATING BETWEEN RELIGION AND HONOR

Between Christian ethics and honor, as codes of conduct, rhetorics, and habitual practices, tensions abounded.[9] In its moral

teachings, Christianity was universalistic. It posited the brotherhood of all believers and urged equal love for all. Honor, meanwhile, was in principles and actions always sharply particularistic;
it lauded whatever favored kin, allies, and dependents. Honor fostered pride and its display. A person of prowess, talents, and skills
was to show such assets off, albeit without silversmith Lucagnolo's
braggadocio. Christianity instead, with an eye to Jesus, extolled
humility. Honor encouraged the display of wealth. But Jesus, the
moralist would recall, had loved the poor; poverty was a Christian ideal, propagated by monks, and later by friars. In practice,
of course, many Christians, including the church itself, relished
riches, but the principles of charity urged sharing with God's ever
present poor and needy. Honor, in parallel, praised generosity,
especially largesse to allies and clients and splendid hospitality that
vouched for the giver's greatness. Furthermore, the tussle for honor
bred wrath and retribution: "If you shove me, I shove you back,
and harder. Seduce my daughter and I slit your throat!" To the
Christian moralist, the life and words of Jesus argued instead for
meekness, mercy, and peace. With magnanimity, honor sometimes
forgave, but only if mildness betokened strength, not cowardice.

The two ethics both valued chastity, but with different concerns.
Here, again, religion was universalistic; all wrong sex was wrong,
while honor, as usual, took note of who was who. Christianity had
long distrusted sex. Not especially biblical, this unease had tangled
roots in the philosophy, ascetic movements, and monastic practices
of late antiquity. Sexual pleasure came to epitomize vanity, the
emptiness of the worldly things that obstruct the path to heaven.
Sex also showed how the imperfect body mired the perfectible soul
in earthly things. Yet the Christian message was mixed. To marry
was the lesser path but still holy, and marital sex was not only tolerated but, if chastely done, even good, for procreation. Adultery,
however, violated matrimony's sacred bonds, and unmarried cou-
pling was also a sin. On chastity, honor, with an eye not to God
but to lineage and social standing, was more tolerant for men, but
very hard on women. Hence, a wife's adultery or the seduction of
a daughter or sister cried out for vengeance and might, as we have
seen, bring death for the woman, too. But free men, married or
single, who trafficked with slaves, servants, prostitutes, and with
other women of low status risked no moral jeopardy. A man of
rank could seduce or violate the women of his inferiors without
much fear of the sluggish law or her low-ranking male protectors.[10]

In the transactions of everyday life, honor's imperatives were often harsh and quick. Christian ideals of peace and mercy, evoked in religious rhetoric, sometimes sought to stay the violence and to break long chains of killings. Here is a report from 1549 from a Jesuit missionary in the mountains north of Florence, a zone where long vendettas still roiled the countryside.

> In the end, when [the Jesuit] saw that he had humbled those hearts which a little earlier had been like those of lions, he called to the pulpit the head of one of the warring parties, whose name was Giovanni Corso. He said, "Father, what do you want me to do?" "That you forgive all your enemies and that you ask pardon of all those whom you have offended in any way," said the Father preacher, "and that for God's love and mine you make peace with all." At once, the fellow threw his weapons on the ground, and, prostrate on the earth, began to shout loudly "Peace! Peace!" And the opposing party did the same.[11]

Both Corso, the clan head, and the villagers of both factions, lived strung between two value systems. The Jesuit, writing to headquarters in Rome, depicted this moment as a successful, definitive conversion: farewell honor, welcome Christian love. He may be right; another, less partisan reading would see Corso and his fellow mountaineers as juggling two value systems as they manage their many conflicts. The Christian language of love and peace could help negotiate a truce, but need not end the war.

The ideals and rhetorics of both honor and Christianity also played out among the perils of the criminal court. Facing judicial torture, social and moral position shaped people's moves. Torture seldom befell the well-born or well-placed, because they were persons whose honor gave their word weight. Rather, the magistrates singled out for pain those poor, weak, and ill-famed "vile persons" who, in the larger frame of things, lacked honor. Humble folk, the court believed, lacked a social motive to speak the truth, because their reputation so low that lying would not hurt it. Lacking the stake of honor, the judge believed, they needed a second jeopardy: to pain of limb. Prisoners, hoping to parry the magistrates' urge to string them up, paraded a third jeopardy that they insisted kept them honest. Their souls, they protested, were in hock with God. "Your lordship, if I do not speak the truth, may God never let me into Heaven!" If such rhetoric failed and a person was put to torture, they invariably called on Jesus or Mary for mercy. In bargaining, before torturers and other overweening tormentors, Christianity was the usual refuge of the weak.

As always, to live moralities every day, practice was less clear than principles. Nevertheless, wide gaps of style separated the path of Christianity from that of honor. Divergent codes sometimes created stress, other times opportunity. For example, following a challenge, "Why did you not strike the rascal dead?" "Am I not a Christian!" Depending on the play of circumstances, one could summon up either religion or honor to explain one's action or inaction. Still, the coexistence was uneasy, and Italians had to step adroitly to straddle both.

OTHER MORAL CODES

Although much of Renaissance Italian life can be read as a restless dialogue between two ill-matched moralities, other ethical rhetorics complicated the scene as well. One of the most pervasive and influential was the law. Renaissance Italy had a rich legal tradition, with intellectual roots in ancient Roman codes, church canons, old Germanic legislation, and feudal practices. In towns and country alike, Italians were accustomed to dealing with the courts and to running to notaries, scribes, secretaries, chancellors, and other officials. All such men heeded legal language and ideas. The law offered notions of legitimate authority, equity, impartiality, due recompense, respect for form, proper consent and consultation, verification, fair arbitration, and conditional and unconditional assent or agreement. Its terminology infiltrated the speech of every social class. In general, like religion, the law bolstered the notion of a public interest. In this idea, it countered honor's moral particularism, advancing the principle of a more abstract, impartial fairness, guaranteed by due process. Besides the law, there were other rhetorics, closely tied to family, professions, and other solidarities and to neighborhood. These discourses had much to do with roles: the love of parents, the loving obedience of sons and daughters and the loyalty of servants, the solidarity of colleagues, and the mutual help and discretion of neighbors, who, despite their vigilant surveillance of good local order, should never stick their noses in other people's business. This last double injunction was flatly contradictory. It reminds us once more that no moral code, large or small, is ever internally consistent. Whatever unity any set of values possessed was thematic, more rhetoric than logic. A precious larger lesson for historians, often overlooked, is that, however much past values illuminate some bygone time, they never fully explain its actions.

NOTES

1. On sixteenth-century preaching, Emily Michelson, *The Pulpit and the Press in Reformation Italy* (Cambridge, MA, 2013).

2. On complexities of the sacred in southern Italy, David Gentilcore, *From Bishop to Witch: The System of the Sacred in Early Modern Terra d'Otranto* (Manchester, 1992).

3. On the material culture of piety, Maya Corry, Marco Faini, and Alessia Meneghin, eds., *Domestic Devotions in Early Modern Italy* (Leiden, 2019).

4. On healing images, Marco Faini, "Everyday Miracles and Supernatural Agency in Sixteenth-Century Italy. The Case of the Marche," in *Saints, Miracles and the Image: Healing Saints and Miraculous Images in the Renaissance*, S. Carderelli and L. Fenelli, eds. (Turnhout, 2017), 169–87.

5. ASR, GTC, Processi, 16th c., busta 34, f. 44r.

6. Benvenuto Cellini, *Vita*, ed. G. D. Bonino (Turin, 1982), 40 (our translation).

7. Ibid., 42 (our translation).

8. Cohen, *Love and Death*, 101.

9. On tensions between honor and religion, Ronald Weissman, *Ritual Brotherhood in Renaissance Florence* (New York, 1982), 43–105.

10. On the sexual double standard, Guido Ruggiero, *The Boundaries of Eros: Sex Crime and Sexuality in Renaissance Venice* (New York, 1985), 16–44.

11. From Ottavia Niccoli, *Perdonare: Idee, pratiche, rituali in Italia tra Cinque e Seicento* (Rome, 2007), 176 (our translation).

7

KEEPING ORDER

Renaissance Italians approached their problems of insecurity and disorder in varied ways. Their solidarities, hierarchies, and moralities of religion, honor, and law all helped ward off chaos. Now we turn to the mechanics of social discipline. Alongside institutions—the church, governments, courts, and the police—much enforcement fell to less formal groups and practices. To highlight their importance in a society whose state, though expanding rapidly, had yet to achieve full modern competence, we look first at these pervasive and fluid habits of persuasion and coercion and then turn to the formal bodies that wielded power.

SOCIAL CONTROL

Social control is the shaping of individual and collective behavior by promoting cooperation, rewarding or enforcing conformity, and squelching deeds deemed harmful. In Italy as elsewhere, some of this task fell to governing bodies—public institutions, and the courts and police of both state and church—and some was at the hands of informal groups, that is, of society itself. By setting models, praising, shaming, blaming, and dealing out rewards and punishments, Italian government and society shaped behavior. In this process, both official laws and social codes of conduct counted.

If statutes and moral rules were tyrants, social control would be a simple matter; set standards and people would just obey. But ethical codes have never ruled the world. Rather, simply by being there, they prove that people sometimes flouted them. The same holds true for laws; states seldom ban what subjects never do (no law bars parking elephants at school). Social control does use laws and morality, but the connections are always subtle and complex. Furthermore, Renaissance Italian social control differed from ours today. Governments weighed less than now; they were smaller, less funded and equipped, and far less organized or informed. Their paltry powers of coercion barely overawed private violence. Consequently, social control fell less than today to states, towns, and functionaries and more to society itself, which used "self-help" to police its members. Coined by social science, this term denotes the regulation, persuasion, and coercion by which informal bodies solve problems and maintain social discipline without calling in the state. While self-help routinely embraces peaceful coercion and surveillance, it often uses private violence to deter or punish offenses. This chapter surveys Italy's mechanisms, both informal and formal, for shaping behavior. We begin with social and economic processes and then pass to regimes: governments and the church.

The Political and the Social Intertwined

Our distinction between social and institutional processes is tricky, for the line between society and state blurs. Social groups always have their internal politics, and any polity inevitably is also social. True everywhere, this statement holds especially well for premodern Italy. There, wherever power lay, politics intruded, even in institutions so intimate as the family. Meanwhile, kinship, friendship, and clientage ran rife in every governing body. For instance, in Rome, the chief prosecutor received melons from his constable and gambled evenings with his own court's suspects; every polity had its social side.[1]

Unlike Renaissance Italy, modern democracies extol the impersonal polity. We think that our civil servants, when at work, should put their friends and rivals out of mind. We prefer our institutions, public and private, to treat people as equal, at least in chance to rise and in claims to consideration. Pay, promotion, tasks, and services should all be blind to who one is, to who one's kinfolk are, and to all gifts, favors, and quarrels. When organizations fall short of this ideal, we tar them with bias, favoritism, or corruption. The institutions of Renaissance Italy were very different. They were rife with social life; alliances were everywhere. The gravitational tug of kinship, friendship, and clientage often outpulled the common good. The state was a pig trough at which one fed, as was the church; the powerful therefore strove to lodge their favorites' hooves for cozy swilling. Public bodies were therefore full of friends and friends of friends, and shot through with social loyalties and conflicts. Italians did laud impartial government and professional conduct, but these ideals were locked in combat with the ingrained cronyism of life.

Several Italian routines aimed to drive social impulses out of political institutions. One was swift rotation of office. The longer a man stayed in place, the more he would be ensnared by affection, gratitude, and obligation, so high officers often had to move on within a year or two. A second measure was to employ outsiders as judges, as if in a kin-centered, friend-encumbered world only a stranger could do justice. A third was electoral lottery. The Venetians, in choosing their doge, raised this device to a high art: men selected by lot elected committees, which ran new lotteries for nominating committees, on and on, five cycles in all. Chance and remoteness of outcome hobbled backstage machination. Less elaborate systems often faltered; the influential Medici in fifteenth-century Florence saw to it that, despite lotteries, their friends and clients still packed the urban councils. In general, by the sixteenth century, small circles of elites often scratched one another's electoral backs. Yet another device for impartiality in offices was formal review of an official's conduct at his end of term. Scrutiny's risks were real: high officers were often prosecuted; many were punished and disgraced, though not a few bounced back. The charges were the usual ones: negligence, graft, cronyism, and ruthlessness. Furthermore, all governance was subject to legal standards; there was growing zeal for orderly records and reporting; paperwork exposed officialdom to judicial oversight. Nevertheless, the campaign to squeeze the social out of government never triumphed.

At the same time, things political also percolated through social life. Italy's solidarities were often semi-institutions. Factions, guilds, parishes, confraternities, and colleges of officials gathered not only for fellow feeling and mutual help, but also to do good works, to lobby, and to politic (Chapter 7). Many such bodies had their statutes, tribunals, rotating councils, and elections. Wherever there were committees, laws, and policies, the political intruded. But politics went further, penetrating non-statutory groups as well: clienteles, bands of cronies, neighborhoods, and, above all, the family, the central social institution, where stakes were often high. There, though prestige and the control of resources fortified the household head, all members, male and female, down even to the servants, who could have allies or know secrets, might make their influence felt (Chapter 4).

Political activity often worked as social control. Renaissance politics was non-economic exchange, a barter where material goods, services, power, prestige, position, information, and backing were all commodities. One might promise good for good: "Assign me the job, and I will slip you secrets." "Kill a man for me, and I will put you in the cavalry." But power could also harm. Consequently, one might extort: "Do it or I disinherit you!" Extortion could be veiled or silent; heirs, for instance, could bend on tacit knowledge that a legacy hinged on their compliance. No society lacks such politics. What distinguished Italy was lively agonism, precise calculations, and alertness to the stakes.

Bargaining Tactics

The politics of daily life involved much bargaining. Italians lived in a state of perpetual negotiation. Their bargains varied in rhetoric and form. A historian of Florence once posited two contrasting modes of dealing: "contract" and "sacrifice."[2] Deals of either sort could buttress social control. Contract was tit-for-tat agreement. It spelled out actions, and set their times and places. Sacrifice refused contract's sharp reciprocity: it took the generous pose: "I am yours!" "It is yours!" Honor and religion both exalted sacrifice and scorned the niggardly contractual commercial spirit. So, at first glance, sacrifice might seem bargaining's negation. With hand on heart or Bible, one affirmed one's gratitude, generosity, loyalty, and love. A second glance reveals that sacrifice, real and feigned, did not ban trading but, by veiling it, just extended it by other means. Sacrifice was slower and less precise in its claims than was contract. It was more often broad-band in its offerings and expectations, and open-ended: payback had no fixed date. But sacrifice did cash in. A vengeful lord reminded a servitor that he had always "eaten the bread of the house" before asking him to kill a man.[3] Sacrificial words and deeds were ploys that entangled other persons. True, some acts of kindness or mercy expected no reward, but the usual habit of dealing eyed an eventual gain.

Economic Exchanges

Social control also pervaded the economy. Commerce, in theory, is a nonsocial, nonpolitical exchanging of money, goods, and services. You want my chicken; I want your cash. Done! A simple sale, with narrow bandwidth and sharp closure; neither the personal nor the political enters. But Renaissance Italian commerce belied this picture; at the trade's end, one was seldom altogether "done." Rather, the commercial, the personal, and the political tangled. Closure came slowly, for transactions ramified. In a cash-short economy, one often paid in credits. Debt was ubiquitous. Rich and poor were enmeshed in webs of money and goods owed. Rather than put the cash on the barrelhead, many buyers proffered credits on third parties and promises of future payment. Buying and selling thus often created and adjusted myriad debts and obligations. Moreover, for big items like an estate, a house, or an expensive office, purchasers often tapped private mortgages, not banker's loans, and, for funds, tapped their social allies. Moreover, even modest purchases themselves, rather than simply exchanging money for finite goods, frequently stoked a continuing relationship between the buyer and the seller. Webs of economic alliance thus both hedged and fostered social or political action (Chapter 15).

Borrowing and Lending

Outside commerce too, borrowing and lending also cemented alliances and shaped behavior. Renaissance Italians exchanged clothing, furniture, food, houseware, tools, weapons, draft animals, services, and privileged information. They borrowed from equals and unequals. Friends and neighbors loaned gear or lodging, courtesans and their lovers borrowed one from the other, and needy peasants turned to their landlords for seed. Such borrowing was in part an economic activity, a response to scarcity, where allies helped tide one over. Indeed, willing lenders provided a communal safety net. But credit had a political aspect too. In an insecure world, coils of obligation engendered trust—edgy trust, as debtors might default. Many a quarrel arose over debts neglected or denied. Nevertheless, indebtedness bloomed; Italians embraced it to cement their social ties.[4]

Gifts and Social Control

Borrowing was not debt's only source. Any sacrificial act that awakened reciprocity created social debt. Here, it was not economic and legal obligation that staked a claim, but gratitude and propriety. Gift giving, as anthropologists note, creates bonds. Until the recipient responds, in measure if not in kind, a hovering sense of asymmetry binds the giver and the taker. Our own world's attitudes to wedding invitations, Christmas cards, and kind words on social media confirm this fact. Gift giving, a universal custom, varies much in scope and customs.

Renaissance Italians, stoking alliances, were avid givers. Rites of passage—marriages and births especially—called gifts forth, as did myriad social ties. Clients plied their lawyers with hams and wine; villagers feted magistrates come to hear their case; suitors showered girls with pears, slippers, necklaces, hairnets for their dress-up dolls, and even books. Humanists smothered well-lodged patrons with fulsome praise. Commoners cemented fellowship with jugs of wine or veal and pigeon at the osteria. Gentlemen, for friendship, sent presents. Montaigne in Italy received wine and precious early figs by the horse-load, marzipan, quince jam, lemons, and oranges. Princes regaled one another with trains of horses in cloth of gold and bejeweled tack, ancient art, fine armor, plus dwarfs, giraffes, or elephants at which their subjects gaped. Scholars exchanged rare manuscripts, and naturalists traded in cuttings or stuffed exotic beasts. In all exchanges, social control might enter.

Building Trust Through Pledges

Because institutions were often weak, and their enforcement of obligations faltered, trust was hard. Trust was both quality of person, called *fede*, good faith, and a transactional expectation, a confidence in the outcome. To bolster both, Renaissance Italians used various exchanges, both economic and social. To win trust, they often put themselves in hock. There were two standard moves: to surrender valuables, be they tangible or symbolic, as pledges, hostages to an obligation, or to bind oneself to abandon them if ever in default. In the first case, one became an actual creditor, in the latter, a potential debtor. State and society exploited both devices. For legal actions, one posted sureties; in society, one put one's name at risk. The two sides of social control, by state and community, neatly converged when friends promised big sums to assure a court a suspect would not flee before his trial had ended. From then on, to save their goods the friends would police good behavior. Putting goods at risk was very common. For instance, small loans often came from pawnshops. Chronically short of cash, Italians often pledged their goods.

Nobles pawned their tapestries and ancient statues. Townsmen deposited arms, clothing, jewels, and furnishings; peasants hocked their vineyards, woods, and pastures. In social exchanges, analogously, Italians made hostage their moral capital—their honor: one said, "By my faith, I speak the truth" (Chapter 6). Honor was not the only guarantee. Other ploys could cement the slippery loyalties of, for instance, a band of thieves. Malefactors spilled their secrets and, on a joint operation, incurred mutual guilt and risk; in both cases, they gave one another the gift of trust, for each could turn the others in: "I am in your hands, so you can rely on me." As for thieves, so for all; in social life, one fine route to trust, where trust was precarious, was a sense of your partner's vulnerability in your regard.

Social Discipline

In daily life, much social discipline is quieter than power politics, market transactions, and gift exchange. It is also far gentler than armed self-help. In any society, the company we keep molds our actions. Countless small things in others—a blush, smile, averted eye, tear, choking of the voice, a kind or harsh word—both attune our dress, posture, movement, or vocal timbre, and shape our speech and deeds. Usually we are barely conscious of this process, though embarrassment sometimes makes us blushingly too aware. In a face-to-face place like Italy, with its dense neighborhood and village life, such forces mattered hugely; still, historians seldom detect them, for, ephemeral and subtle, they left few material traces.

One powerful form of social control was gossip. The records of police courts overflowed with it. Renaissance cities were small and neighborhoods tight. Newcomers did not long stay strangers. Street and piazza were arenas for social interaction, while, at their balconies and windows, the women, especially, witnessed what went on below. They not only watched; they also commented to one another and to people in the street. Their remarks surface often in the records of the courts: "In the whole neighborhood he has a bad reputation." In general, the women were the more local voice and conscience; male gossip ranged wider.

Neighborhood was more than just an arena of gossip and social pressure. It also protected its denizens. Faces at the windows and doorways kept a watchful eye on playing children and passersby and a cautious lookout for fishy strangers and breakers of the peace. When a noisy fight broke out, residents came running to their doors and sills. They might later testify to court or neighbors as to fault and consequences. Witnessing was a potent social control. A person wronged in public could bellow, "Everybody bear witness to what just happened." The very presence of onlookers often checked violence. Neighbors might intervene to break up a fight. At a wounding or a fire, they came running to the rescue.

Sharper than gossip was ritual defamation. Italians often assaulted the good name of one another's houses. There was a familiar repertoire of familiar insults. The *mattinata* (morning song) was a caterwauling nocturnal serenade under a victim's windows, lampooning the virtue of folk inside. Enemies also attacked houses, throwing rocks, mud, ink, or excrement at walls and doors and windows. They also hung insulting pictures, sometimes embellished with demeaning doggerel, or draped the house with cuckolds' horns. If a feud was earnest, the enemy might use turpentine to kindle the front door. The assailant wanted everyone to see and smell the havoc; neighbors flocked and murmured, and sometimes stepped up to help the victim, who was scurrying to repair the insult to both house and local reputation.

The pervasive petty quarreling, though disorderly, itself served social control by policing behavior. People curbed themselves, sometimes, to dodge gossip, insults, or fights. In the country, hostilities often began with work long owed, boundaries moved, or one man's pigs in another's garden. In town, the first cause might be a straying pet, a children's spat, slops and garbage, or a disputed place to hang laundry. Very often, women carried out these low-grade hostilities. They used not just words, but fists and fingernails, clogs, and broomsticks. Their fights might draw in male servants and even senior men. These petty battles could escalate from shouted insults to blows and vandalism. Heavier enmity (*inimicitia*), usually male, was the inversion of friendship (*amicitia*). It was a familiar social condition, semi-codified, widely understood, swiftly labeled, and readily suspected whenever some affront or crime lacked a clear culprit: "which enemy might have done this?" Often, before hostilities went too far, neighbors or allies brokered a settlement. When local efforts faltered, the state might step in, on its own or summoned, to impose or guarantee a formal peace, under pain of fines. All this squabbling was the most vocal expression of the complex social pressures that shaped behavior.

Self-Help

Where government was weak, self-help flourished. Transgressions could provoke a violent response, but closure was untidy.

Strong bonds of personal solidarity could make for chains of reciprocal mayhem as kinsmen, friends, and clients, taking matters into their own hands, turned to weapons to avenge a recent injury. When the series of affronts ran long, one spoke of a *vendetta*, a feud. Some classes—nobles, soldiers, peasants—were more prone to feuding, as were remoter zones less controlled by urban governments. A serious feud could last for years or decades and draw in skeins of allies.

Vengeance and feud were less chaotic than they seem. Like the petty quarreling, feuding helped enforce order and social control.[5] The likelihood of feud inhibited; one hesitated to hurl insults, cheat, steal, ravage, wound, or rape, fearing incalculable repercussions for oneself and all one's allies. The specter of reprisal could urge peace feelers and deter retaliation. Renaissance Italy, like any feuding society, strove to contain violence, for feuds troubled communities. Italians therefore evolved rites of mediation and settlement. The passage from enmity to amity was ticklish; go-betweens stepped in when warring parties loathed talking eye to eye. Here, churchmen did good service. By their station, they were exempt from violent honor culture, and their values preached reconciliation. When at last enemies patched up their quarrel, they celebrated a formal ceremony, sharing wine and cake, embracing and kissing on the mouth, and often shedding cathartic tears. The state might stand as guarantor, demanding forfeit money in case of breach. Yet such pacifications might fail.

In Europe, self-help gradually yielded to public policing and justice. In parallel, health, education, and welfare all migrated from the private to the public sphere. Between 1400 and 1600, Italy evolved. States and cities extended their spheres of competence, and, in many zones, self-help did indeed recede, so that, if not by 1600, at least by 1700, life had grown less sanguinary. This evolution was both gradual and easily set back. For instance, in many zones, the end of the 1500s, a time of hunger, saw an epidemic of self-help—a wave of brigandage that challenged the rural authority of princes. The 1630 bubonic plague, ravaging Bologna, unleashed a local wave of grudge-based murders. Geography influenced self-help's rate of recession; some zones, such as Venice and much of Tuscany, were swifter to supplant it. In general, cities had solider government than the countryside; the remoter the district, the shorter the law's arm.

Governments did not simply squelch self-help; rather, the expansion of state power was subtler, and more collaborative. So do not

imagine two opposing spheres, one public, the other private, struggling to hog social control. Rather, everywhere there was fluid symbiosis. Although public authorities sometimes strove to quell social
violence, they also harnessed it to extend their reach. Bounties on
outlaws' heads are a case in point; if you lack police to catch or kill
a bandit, reward his fellow countrymen instead. Meanwhile, ordinary Italians appropriated courts and constables for their quarrels.
The neighbor's call to witness might do just this. Many a judicial
action masked someone's campaign for leverage or revenge.

INSTITUTIONS HELP KEEP ORDER

As, in the Renaissance, church and state extended their reach and
grew stronger and more competent, authorities strove to mold society. Keen to control behavior, they legislated, policed, and prosecuted. Success was mixed; often their ambitions outreached the
grasp and competence of their forces of coercion. Nevertheless,
governments and church institutions did make a difference, and,
with time, their impact grew.

Governance itself was complex. States came in many shapes and
sizes, and, despite their shared routines and legal culture, institutions varied. There was a baffling kaleidoscope of official bodies.
Jurisdictions overlapped, and offices, courts, and constabularies
vied for authority and precedence. To start with, major towns,
unless sovereign republics, had lords or governors. Almost always,
they also had local councils of leading citizens. Guilds of professionals, merchants, and artisans often wielded regulatory powers.
Furthermore, diverse officials for health, roads, markets, and the
grain trade deployed quasi-judicial powers. Bishops' courts judged
morality, marriage cases, and ecclesiastical rights. After the 1540s,
Inquisitions joined the bishops in policing matters touching faith.
All such bodies produced a welter of decrees, laws, and judgments
that bore on social control. Although villages were somewhat simpler places, there too the centers of control were many. There was
often a resident judge-administrator—either the feudal lord's or
the state's. State magistrates might come through on circuit or for
special cases, in the name of higher authority. Lords often stationed
an estate agent to squeeze their tenants and, in the fort, placed a
castellan with a small garrison. At the same time, like the towns,
villages often had their statutes and elected councils, with perhaps a secretary or chancellor with divided loyalties to community
and lord. The village priest was half insider, half servant of higher

authorities, often of both lord and bishop; he was not at all autonomous, and a council of villagers oversaw his church's physical fabric. Thus, nowhere in Italy was there a dearth of governance. What was often lacking, rather, was coherence and effectiveness.

In the face of such varied governance, politics suffused daily life. Political action took many forms, touching men, and women too, on almost every social level. The forms of action were many: with so much collegial governance in church and state, one discussed, voted, decided, and communicated official resolutions, in writing and out loud. And, atop that, one staged the ceremonies that gave legitimacy and heft to power. That was on the inside of institutions. On the outside, Italians talked, argued, lobbied and petitioned abundantly, litigated, protested raucously, and, in a pinch rebelled. And they also decamped; one political act, sometimes coerced, sometimes voluntary, was departure or formal exile. And, once outside the borders, one often conspired with allies still inside.

Laws

Italians had a welter of doctrine and legislation. There was no overarching code but rather a vast mass of *ius commune* based on ancient Roman compilations, learned medieval commentaries, and case law, to which one defaulted when other laws fell short. On top of this were local statutes. These rambling collections of semi-coherent legislation and occasional decrees set procedures of governance and established rules about many things, from inheritance rights to commerce, garbage, and stray beasts in street and garden. Statutes were conservative; they brimmed with archaic bans on things no longer done and rehashed ancient rules, for they evolved slowly. Meanwhile, governing bodies legislated fast, spewing out decrees on nocturnal lanterns, the width of sleeves, clothing marks for Jews and prostitutes, hue and cry, gambling, swearing, street litter, market stalls, and keeping holy days. Legislation waxed and waned with the ups and downs of regulatory zeal. New decrees were posted in "the usual places"—on the doors of major churches, by government buildings, in the marketplace, on the city gates—and read aloud by official criers on foot or horseback, often to the blare of trumpets. By the sixteenth century, they often appeared in print as broadsheets, under bold woodblock insignia of their official authors.

In this vast swarm of laws and rules, some thematic concerns stand out. One was health; decrees sought to free the town of garbage and dung, confine and cure the sick, and quarantine travelers

Feudal lords and city authorities employed heralds and messengers to circulate public and private communications. The display of insignia, such as this fifteenth-century badge of enamel on metal, identified official employers and legitimated the agent's passage. (The Metropolitan Museum of Art)

from suspect places. A second charge was the good order of public space: zoning issues like the lay of buildings and the freedom of the public way from private encroachment, and also the upkeep and operation of public facilities like walls and gates, markets, and fountains. A third issue was public safety. Legislation not only curbed violent acts and insulting gestures but also regulated weapons and strove to ban the occasions for fighting. Rules about circulation after dark aimed for calm, as did the campaign against gambling, a notorious spawner of brawls. A fourth concern was warding off offense to God. The masters of Venice, to fend off divine wrath, instituted a magistracy against blasphemy. Rules to foster respect for holy times and shield churches from ribaldry courted providence. Social regulation also policed beggars and the idle poor, who might be banished or, toward 1600, confined to a zone or a workhouse, for their own supposed benefit. Sexual conduct, too, attracted regulation. Although Italian cities seldom outlawed prostitutes, they hedged them; in Rome, by 1600, such women could neither wear the gentlewoman's veil, nor ride in coaches, nor eat in wine shops, nor entertain armed men at home. They were also banned from lodging on the better streets, unless they bought exemption. Homoerotic conduct sometimes fell under the jurisdiction of special morals courts, as did other breaches of the sexual rules.

Almost always, in Renaissance Italy, where there was a law, exceptions abounded. Many regulations aimed as much at raising money as at squelching behavior; again and again, the authorities sold exemptions. Thus, although massive, Italian legislation had uncertain reach, for wealth, power, and privilege knocked enforcement full of holes. Not all exceptions to the law were bought; police jurisdiction had territorial vacuums. Churches were sanctuaries; those who ran inside ducked arrest. Embassies, and their precincts too, had extraterritoriality. Police who made an arrest in their shadow risked indignant drubbing by the ambassador's servants. Nobles sheltered protégés in their palaces; not rarely, the authorities hesitated to take a magnate on. Many rural outlaws therefore huddled under the protection of the great.

Police and Courts

Central to governmental control of society were the courts. Tribunals came in many kinds; some were civil, others criminal, ecclesiastical, or administrative in scope; not rarely, one magistrate combined several functions. Courts had their judges, notaries, summoners, turnkeys, and executioners, and in their orbit hovered a swarm of prosecutors and advocates. In general, they were sticklers for procedure; they loved paper, keeping complicated records, often in Latin. To uneducated Italians, courts seemed imposing, with their obscure formulas in a learned tongue, their rituals, robes of office, harsh methods, and heavy punishments. Yet, far more than most of us today, Italians knew the insides of courtrooms from rich firsthand experience, for they often took part in proceedings, as parties to a civil suit, witnesses, technical experts, guarantors, suspects, or prisoners for unpaid debts. Their testimonies show that they usually understood the rules and rituals and knew how to use them to advantage.

Of all state organs, the criminal courts tried hardest to control society. There the rules tilted sharply against a suspect. Examined in a closed room, with neither friends, nor counsel, nor public observers, unsure as to the charges, accusers, and evidence, the accused was on edge. As there were no detectives, inquiry fell to prosecutors and judges, so a trial's first stage investigated, via interrogation, to build a dossier. The magistrates questioned cagily, first circling around the issue, probing for clues and inconsistencies, and only gradually tipping their hand as they closed in on the suspected crime. When stories clashed, at their discretion they called the other witness for face-to-face confrontation. By theories of proof, a conviction required strong evidence from at least two credible witnesses or confession. Sometimes, lacking good witnesses and hoping for that crucial confession, judges tortured. They usually targeted suspects of low estate. They also sometimes strung up witnesses and, to verify a charge, even tortured the crime's victim.

An extension of inquiry, torture had several common methods. Commonest was the rope; the court's men stripped suspects to the waist, tied their hands behind the back, put a rope to the wrists, and hoisted them. If they did not confess, they might give the cord a painful jerk, a *strappado*. Other devices in the repertoire varied in severity. At the mild end were sundry instruments to squeeze feet or fingers, sometimes applied to women. The direst were long sessions spent seated in painful postures, or fire to the feet, an ordeal so hideous some jurists condemned it. Whatever the torment, all the while the court notary wrote down each piteous moan and imprecation; on the ancient paper the old agony still shakes a modern reader. Do not confuse this investigative judicial torture with the cruel punishments after sentencing. The investigating magistrates were often harsh, but torture did follow rules. It should not maim. Suspects with broken or damaged limbs were not to be hoisted up, nor women menstruating or pregnant. Furthermore, if torture ran too long or came too often, the defense lawyer might plead abuse to invalidate the case. For the judges, torture was a means to an otherwise elusive end. Without it, a stubborn or wily criminal could stall forever. Even with it, the strong sometimes toughed it out and escaped condemnation. Understanding the risk that the innocent might confess falsely to flee pain, courts insisted that all who confessed under duress return the next day to ratify their words. Those who retracted usually faced another session on the rope; this ominous prospect, however, aroused little judicial skepticism about post-torture ratifications.

To enforce its will, government needed a constabulary. Larger cities had several competing troops, each under its captain. The countryside made do with small local detachments, plus city-based squadrons that sortied. Nowhere were the police reliable. Recruited from the poorest classes, they had no prestige, little discipline, and a healthy appetite for loot. People loathed them; *cop* and *cop's woman* were sharp insults. The police roughed up prisoners and grabbed their belongings. They bound their captives, an action seen as vile (Chapter 6). They readily broke into houses without a warrant, snooping for stolen goods or sexual misdemeanors. They bullied the weak but cowered before the strong. Paid for each successful arrest, they showed greedy zeal that blackened their repute.[6]

Allied to the cops were informers tarred as "spies"; the word was a common insult hurled any snoop. Authorities in bigger cities like Rome and Venice made energetic use of them, some on retainer, others cashing in diversely. In Rome in 1555, two shady Spaniards persuaded the chief constable to permit them an illegal gambling house at the Campo de' Fiori market in hopes, they said, of learning military secrets from Spanish soldiers. After a few months, the authorities concluded that the constable and his spies were merely raking in the take, arrested the police chief, and fired his agents.[7] Not all spies, real or bogus, were steady employees. Lacking detectives, authorities needed the informants. Very often, they promised snitches a cut of penalties. Here, the campaign for social control subverted trust and solidarity. Using similar devices against rural brigands, states dangled pardons in front of any bandit who ratted on his comrades.

Most malefactors escaped the hands of justice. Inefficient police and holes in jurisdiction lamed the courts. Moreover, territories were small and borders near. A miscreant's allies often warned of impending arrest. Suspects, wisely mistrustful of justice, fled *en masse*. Extradition seldom worked. Repeatedly courts tried *in absentia*, issuing dire sentences to be carried out if ever they caught the fugitive. In the meantime, they outlawed him and seized his goods. Then began the bargaining for a settlement, a "composition," that, for a price, allowed the malefactor back to his house and wealth. For the state, justice was so lucrative that the zeal for funds drove both punishment and forgiveness.

Executions and Other Punishments

If one had the bad luck to be caught, harsh treatment often loomed. Not only were courtroom rules stacked against a suspect, so too was sentencing. Condemnation was likely, and penalties were sometimes severe. Weak states with inefficient organs of repression used the few they caught to set a horrible example for the many who got away, for justice was meant to teach a lesson. Punishment therefore might employ public spectacle.[8] For lesser crimes, the state used public shame, putting malefactors in the stocks, often with a peal of bells and explanatory placards. Those who had spoken ill of state or church might find their tongues pierced or put in bridles. Other middling offenses earned a public whipping or *strappado* hoists on a high pole in the market or at the gate. For graver misdeeds, the authorities might mark a convict's body with a shameful stigma that testified to the law's power and grandeur; they cut off the nose or tongue, an ear, hand, or foot, or gouged out an eye or two.

An execution was a major drama for both state and church. It could draw a crowd. Then, several kinds of social control converged; many were the actors and the themes. The authorities demonstrated their implacable majesty to awe the people into compliance. Executions therefore had their vengeful solemnity. To inflict both pain and shame before their victim died, they might attack his body with knives or incandescent pincers. After death, to drive home the lesson, for major crimes they might quarter, otherwise dismember, or burn the corpse, and then expose it to the air, to crows, to the awed gaze of passers-by and the anguish of kinfolk who chafed for decent burial. The means of death itself varied with both crime and jurisdiction. It was nobler to be beheaded like the saints than hang like Judas. Swords and devices like stationary guillotines were normal. For commoners, hanging was the rule; gallows, empty or with crow-picked carcasses, were a familiar admonitory sight. There was special infamy in hanging upside down, as there was in burning, a fate reserved for heretics and desecrators, most of whom, kindly, one killed first. Assorted other methods, strangling, shooting, cudgeling, drowning, tossing from the battlements, were much rarer.

Meanwhile, alongside this grim, vindictive, rather Old Testament *mise en-scène*, executions had a second drama with Gospel coloration. Its themes were reconciliation, grace, and salvation. There were confraternities of lay "comforters," who visited the condemned on their last night to prepare their souls for death. This delicate task also fell to clergy. Despair was the great adversary. The helpers strove to convince the condemned that, if only he (rarely she) repented, the body's loss would buy the soul's redemption. Despite the famous proverb, a looming execution did not readily concentrate the mind. But unremitting prayer, night-long consoling talk, and the contemplation of holy images might keep mind and heart from straying. As the authorities carted their victim through the streets toward "the place of justice," visiting his sites of crime, the comforters marched below the cart in hooded penitential garb, while some aboard the wagon held painted tablets of holy scenes before his eyes. Image in hand, they even climbed the ladder to the noose. Onlookers joined this struggle for the criminal's soul, a high drama where their own prayers counted. They could kneel for his soul's sake, and, if he repented and begged his victim's kin for grace, they might cry tears of compassion and joy. A good death reenacted holy martyrdom, while the crowd's rapt call for blessings helped reconcile all parties, closing accounts, salving grudges. A defiant convict who struggled, cursed, or protested his unjust conviction clearly went straight to hell, another satisfying moral spectacle. Preachers might round off the event with a stirring sermon from the scaffold about sin, repentance, and redemption, or sure damnation, all just seen by all.

Such executions were special events, hardly daily. Courts far preferred cash to blood. Most convicted murderers suffered only confiscation and banishment. Many other crimes too were fined. Unlike us, Renaissance Italians eschewed long prison sentences, both expensive and unproductive. Jail served for holding debtors and persons awaiting trial, not for punishment. The naval galleys were far more useful; a few years spent rowing, chained to a bench, was a common penalty, often fatal. Italians of lower station often spent time in jail. A villager could molder for weeks in the castle tower while raising money to pay a fine; courts locked townsmen up as suspects or important witnesses. Until done testifying, one stayed in isolation. Jail cost money; inmates had to pay their keep, while the rich bought what comforts they could. The mighty, often imprisoned for reasons of state, might purchase good quarters while awaiting a happier turn of Fortune's wheel. Like all other cogs in the machinery of justice, jails were lubricated by lucre.

Banishment was common, cheap, and, given the many borders, easy. States shoved malefactors across frontiers and dispatched their bloody-handed nobles to Hungary to fight the Turks; villages just pushed men out of town. The exiled peasants often hovered just down the road or behind the woods, so that wives could scurry out with bread, cheese, and freshly mended shirts. But even this short-range banishment was disruptive; when a man could not work his lands, his family suffered. Without much income, the banished man (*bandito*) often fell back on banditry; our English word shows the old linkage between banishment and brigandage. Thus, as a device for social control, banishment often exacerbated things, putting rural lives and goods at risk.

Alongside severity, Italian authorities also practiced mercy, sometimes for a fee. To bestow grace combined honor's magnanimity with Christian mercy. It might also evince political acumen. Rulers read petitions in abundance: "five poor virgins still unmarried, and now to be without a father!" They pardoned. They invited back their exiles, restored estates, and commuted death sentences, in the nick of time or posthumously. Their God-like arbitrariness in dispensing grace increased their stature; like the Divinity, they garnered prayerful supplication and fervent gratitude. This mitigating clemency tangled further justice's snarled up skein. However dire the wages of crime, punishment remained capricious.

THE CHURCH AND SOCIAL CONTROL

Like the state, the church worked to control society. Down to the Council of Trent (1545–63), the campaign was polycentric and tentative; thereafter, it grew more coordinated and assertive. This great reforming Council exalted and energized bishops and called for a trained and disciplined parish clergy. Episcopal campaigns to impose Christian morals came to have real effect. A second movement, older than Trent but fostered by it, elevated new religious orders, the Jesuits and others, that practiced social activism, to transform lay conduct and belief. The Jesuits, for instance, ran internal missions in remote districts to instill orthodox beliefs and practices. They and others also ran schools where morality suffused the curriculum. While the Jesuits staffed bold elite colleges offering classics, the Scolopians opened modest schools to teach the poor to read. Counter-Reformation orders championed frequent confession, in lieu of the annual Easter habit; as the usage spread, parish priests gained moral influence and access to secrets.

Two other Catholic Reformation devices addressed social control. The Index of Prohibited Books (1555) worked less directly, as it oversaw reading and writing, not behavior. Nevertheless, the campaign for intellectual and moral propriety in print reshaped judgment and action. The Italian Inquisitions (1542) were a blunter instrument, a centrally directed set of tribunals to police right belief and action. Inquisitions have had a bad press, sometimes deservedly. At times they meted out drastic punishments for irregular ideas and, where converts relapsed to Judaism, they were often pitiless. The Italian Inquisitions, however, were milder than their Spanish counterpart. Most victims, if willing to recant, escaped with reprimands or light penalties, plus warnings to desist. Much Italian inquisitorial activity dealt not with cult and doctrine, but with morality, superstition, magic, and witchcraft. There, the tribunal, even by Italian standards, was careful and firm but fairly moderate. Therefore, unlike much of Europe, thanks to judicial care with evidence, Italy saw few long witch hunts.

CONCLUSION

At the close of the 1930s, Norbert Elias, a German Jewish sociologist, argued that European history has seen a continual "civilizing process," a victory of genteel self-restraint. Though grimly ill-suited to the dire year of its publication, his argument, debated and revised, has been hugely influential for the interpretation of European history. Elias saw the Renaissance and Catholic Reformation as great steps toward self-control. The boisterous violence of the Middle Ages subsided; brawling feuds shrank to polite duels with punctilious etiquette. Some dueling faded to snubs and pamphlet wars. Medieval hungry reaching and eager gulping gave way to table manners, and zestful gesticulation yielded to genteel poise. Bathroom matters and everything sexual went private. Shared beds, shared goblets, and shared food on a common plate all disappeared, forks triumphed over fingers, and lapdogs vanished from the tabletop. And, increasingly, restraint replaced expansiveness. There is much general truth here, especially for elites. Together, states and church did extend their controls, reshaping culture and taming society. Elias's transformation lives with us still.

NOTES

1. Cohen, *Love and Death*, 132–35.

2. On the notions of contract and sacrifice, Richard Trexler, *Public Life in Renaissance Florence* (New York, 1980).

3. Cohen and Cohen, *Words and Deeds*, 35; on the workings of the criminal court, 15–20.

4. On debt and its social dynamics, Daniel Lord Smail, *Legal Plunder: Households and Debt Collecting Collection in Late Medieval Europe* (Cambridge, MA, 2016).

5. On feuding, Edward Muir, *Mad Blood Stirring: Vendetta in Renaissance Italy* (Baltimore, 1998), 28–38.

6. Steven Hughes, "Fear and Loathing in Rome and Bologna: The Papal Police in Perspective," *Journal of Social History* 21 (1987), 97–116.

7. ASR, GTC, Processi, 16th c., busta 36, ff. 262r–65r.

8. On executions, Nicholas Terpstra, ed., *The Art of Executing Well: Rituals of Execution in Renaissance Italy* (Kirksville, MO, 2008).

8

COMMUNICATING: IMAGES AND WORDS

Everything a civilization does sends signals, whether intentional or inadvertent. Not only do images and words communicate, but so do physical structures and human bodies. Fortifications proclaim a regime's competence and might; private buildings signal wealth and power; clothing and body language broadcast gender, age, station, and ethnicity. Renaissance Italy was hypersensitive to the signs and symbols of prestige. Meanwhile, its visual arts, a rich medium, incorporated a new naturalism; its writing made deft use of the new print technology. So, there were new media, and new messages, touching religion, politics, education, and social relations. Although propelled by elite appetites, these innovations affected daily life for all. Our history traces authorities' communication, and its demotic reception. The masses had cultures of their own, largely oral and so elusive. Yet these distinct points of view are well worth the sleuthing.

Renaissance communication, for lack of motors and electricity, were on a human scale. Both transmission and reception of messages relied on human bodies and their senses, sometimes modestly amplified by bells, fires, banners, paper, and other devices. Theologians and philosophers scorned sensation for its mutable, fleshly uncertainties. Sensory knowledge, they held, was inferior to revelation and pure thought, channels held to be more spiritual, secure, and eternal. Nevertheless, daily life, even for the erudite, ran on communications more mundane and humanly embodied, especially in sight and hearing, plus sometimes touch. For us now, the smells, the tastes, and most sounds of Renaissance life have vanished, as indeed has much of what one saw or handled. The communications that we still do possess are largely matter for the eye: images, scripts, and objects of many sorts. All bore Renaissance messages that we now seek to decode in order to glimpse the elusive, larger picture.

THE ARTS IN RENAISSANCE LIFE

Artful expression embellished and energized Renaissance life. Some works in paper, wood, clay, and stone survive for us to admire. Embodied performances such as music, dance, public ceremony, and even theater are more elusive. Institutions and elites commissioned and funded the visual masterpieces that today mark the Renaissance, and lesser work too. These pieces speak mostly for their privileged patrons. Nevertheless, art, broadly understood, carried meanings across society; ordinary folk both perceived them and produced their own.

For Renaissance persons "art" did not mean what it now does for us. Even though our modern notion began with the Renaissance, the term's present meaning constricts our sense of the arts' past scope and value. In our world, Renaissance arts are cantoned in special venues—museums, concert halls, theaters—accessible by pricey tickets that fund the art's protection and display. In a museum, a work of art, however beautiful, is wildly out of place and time. It lacks the cultural and social meanings that gave it resonance. Often, too, what we see is only a part of a larger composition. Many an altarpiece or illuminated book has been dismembered, sold piecemeal for fatter profit. Even if still on view in a church, a painting, lit anachronistically bright by a coin dropped in the box, rarely conveys the liturgical and spiritual power its patrons sought. Modern curators also draw a misleading boundary between high art and lesser forms, discounting as merely "decorative" all the wall hangings, brocades, jewelry, tableware, musical instruments, carriages, horse gear, weapons, armor, and festive pomps that the Renaissance spent on lavishly.

Renaissance society did not isolate and subdivide its arts, their messages, and their consumers.[1] Contemplate those artistically complex ephemeral public spectacles that church and state staged in streets and *piazze*. Drawing on many arts, they enlivened the senses of high and lowly. Both religion and politics loved a parade. Dramatic processions marked major holy days like Good Friday and Corpus Christi. A victory, a political marriage, the installation of a prince or pope spawned gorgeous ephemera; public rituals raised pavilions, platforms, and triumphal arches of wood, plaster, and papier-mâché, draped with paintings and bedecked with statues. These temporary structures punctuated the march, inviting a pause to hear a speech or hymn, or to watch a winged youngster in angel dress descend by cable, warbling celestial greetings. The best painters, sculptors, architects, composers, and poets collaborated in these elaborate productions, of which we have tattered records, for the installations were made to be destroyed. Sometimes, to public glee, as a grand finale, fireworks packed inside blew them spectacularly to bits. The festive program had propaganda messages, either clear or recondite. Speeches, songs, and tableaux with statues and living performers—semi-clad or sumptuously garbed allegories of tranquility, harmony, industry, peace, the happy concord of the elements, and the submissive loyalty of conquered towns—regaled a visiting monarch or ducal bride. The populace too had roles: to marvel, to applaud, and on occasion to mock their betters. We know of these because print began to immortalize this pageantry, sometimes with elegantly illustrated books, but more often with humble pamphlets adorned at most with rough images.

Visual Arts

To depict the world, between 1400 and 1600, Italian visual art enhanced its communicative skill. Figurative arts acquired ever more refined powers of depiction. Greater naturalism applied close observation to the representation of people, nature, things, and, by extension, ideas. The new science of linear perspective and a growing mastery of light and shading gave images remarkable three-dimensionality. These technical advances enriched art's capacity to inform and enhanced its emotional force. Renaissance arts bore meaning in many ways: they described, evoked, symbolized, glorified, and just plain pleased the eye. Living surrounded by art, Renaissance people responded to its messages, sometimes in unintended ways.

A great motive for having and making art was holy devotion. Even modest households might own images of the Madonna or a saint. An ordinary woman's prayer book could have pictures besides the words. Although such everyday holy objects were everywhere, the great sacred art of the Renaissance most often graced churches, chapels, and monastic halls. There visitors and supplicants could view it, if dimly, by the glow of candles or the thin daylight filtering through high windows. Religious art was dense, with general messages of adoration, petition, and transcendence, plus targeted signs to particular groups or persons. An altarpiece told a complex story, linking the relics in the altar, the holy figures with their familiar tales and emblems, and the donors, often figured beside their patron saints, while their heraldic symbols bedecked the architecture. A rich family's chapel might be its lineage burial place, crammed with images—portrait busts or supine figures of the dead, fancy sarcophagi, and flattering Latin inscriptions with vital dates and boastful details of the defunct's career. The chapel glorified at once the family's saints and the patrons who, with art, paid them, and themselves, homage. Guilds and confraternities also decorated chapels to promote their corporate solidarity and piety. Churches were densely packed, inside and out, with symbolic messages, often readily legible even without words: who built, staffed, and patronized the church; who was buried there; what holy personages it worshiped; plus all cosmic truths evoked, biblical and contemporary events commemorated, and spiritual benefits conferred. Lively spectators, Italians both appreciated technique and felt religious meanings.

The Renaissance artistic revolutions reshaped secular works as well, with more naturalistic images, as of the human body, often unclothed. For many patrons, both lay and clerical, the boundary between worldly and spiritual art was not sharp. Although the Council of Trent set out to police the sacred's boundaries, allegories of power, justice, and virtue still aligned church and state. Like the churches, the edifices of government used art to proclaim authority. City walls and gates, portals to official buildings, town halls, and markets all sported emblems, legible and assertive. Palaces, outside and in, proclaimed the power and taste of families who built and occupied them. The wealthy acquired fine things to ornament their rooms and lives, and to impress the guests. Some amassed antiquities, with the missing bits often "repaired" for effect. Collectors also commissioned new works, on antique and other themes. With the growing elitism of Renaissance culture, some high-end art took on esoteric meanings for insiders' delectation; they could enjoy being in the know.

Art was also a commodity, and most artists, now long obscure, were general embellishers of objects and places. Although most of them were not celebrities, they honorably shared the prestige of skilled craftsmen like the jewelers, tailors, armorers, and confectioners who also devised fine things. Seldom an exercise in self-expression, art was mostly business. To make the Renaissance's art took the efforts not just of the outstanding masters but of many workers, more and less skillful, specialized, or well paid. Particulars varied with the medium, but the need to muster financing, materials, skilled labor, work space, and good design required teamwork. Everyday pieces, domestic Madonnas and saints, for instance, or the occasional portrait, by single hands or a small workshop, circulated through a growing art market. Meanwhile, the art that we now admire in museums and churches, the big projects that consumed months or years, began with a commission. The patron— a family, ruler, religious house, or corporate body—and the chief artist agreed on the size, materials, and price, but also on the style, theme, and details of the content. The artist then rendered a design and, as impresario and manager, divided the labor among members of his workshop or hired outsiders with special techniques. As the work developed, the artist oversaw and revised, often putting his own hand to central or demanding parts. Heroically, Michelangelo frescoed the whole Sistine ceiling, but he too had technical support. His helpers, often very practiced, erected the scaffold, mixed plaster and paints, applied coatings to the walls, and affixed the paper *cartone* outlines that showed the master where to apply his brush. Major paintings were often the work of many hands. Novices laid on general backdrops, while specialist helpers might do landscapes or decorative borders; the master did what counted most, the faces and fine drapery. When a work was finally finished, cost and payment remained, as in much Renaissance business, fraught. The expense of materials (gold leaf and ground lapis lazuli were costly; marble outpriced canvas or paint) and the fame and hand of the master helped set an anticipated price. The patron's eventual pleasure with the completed piece was less easily predicted. Sometimes, third-party appraisers were called in to name a just price. And, like other dealers in a cash-short, debt-ridden world, artists and customers often fell in arrears, with product or payment.

During the Renaissance, from several currents, emerged the idea of the artist's nobility. In the later sixteenth century, theorists opined that the finest art, distinguished by "design" and 'invention," required not just a good eye and manual finesse, but also high intellectual skills. Here, painting and sculpture took the lead; new academies advanced the intellectual life of the profession and of trainees. Courtly dexterity among his princely patrons was another artist's asset. Prestige, handsome gifts, and gentlemanly titles could come from service to a lofty family. A court artist, Giulio Romano at Mantua answered to his prince for all things of beauty, from the architecture and decor of palaces to jewelry and the serving dishes on a banquet's *credenza*. Others devised dance costumes or sugar sculptures for tables. Leonardo da Vinci, with his plans for fortresses, was not the only court artist to rig his state for war. Although the romantics' notion of the great artist as a genius displaying his temperamental, inner soul would have baffled Renaissance Italians, outstanding talent did earn celebrity. Some heroes of our idealized Renaissance, like Michelangelo and Raphael, were in their own time renowned. Others then admired have fallen into art historical shadows, including a few women.[2] The majority of artists could but aspire to high recognition and its perks.

SPOKEN LANGUAGE

More pervasive even than visual art was language, a medium that took distinctively Renaissance forms. What we know survives largely in many sorts of writing, At the time, however, most language was not written, but spoken. Since this great mass of oral utterances has evaporated, we labor to make sense of Renaissance language and culture by relying heavily only on written materials. Mesmerized by the wonderful survivals, we often forget that they were only part. About spoken words and the larger messages embodied in their delivery, we are left to infer from some sorts of written texts—sermons, plays, judicial transcripts—and from pictorial images of people orating or talking.

As in all Renaissance Europe, Italy's culture was predominantly oral. Although writing gained scope and weight, most messages still were spoken. Many people were, at best, partially literate, and even the best educated conducted much of life with tongue, not pen. There was a vibrant culture of speech, song, and gesture, and of memory, and mental navigation. As public life in courts and streets was highly theatrical, transactions had an artful streak. Talk's assorted gambits—inquiry, contest, insult, cajolery, exhortation, negotiation, agreement, and proclamation—structured economic transactions and the restless play of power. Many business deals were both arranged and sealed without writing. Memory, too, both personal and collective, lurked only in people's heads. Oral practices, however, helped families, institutions, and communities to curate their collective past. Legends, songs, rituals, and festivities, all preserved, and transformed, stories of past events. Such tales leaned on material things: treasured relics and decorated monuments helped anchor and stimulate narration. And, in the countryside, the names of fields, valleys, brooks, and springs spoke to villagers of their past. Moreover, prayers for one's own dead fostered community with those beyond the grave.

Oral culture is distinct. Its communications are ephemeral, kinetic, embodied, and interactive. For transmission, speakers and listeners must be in earshot. Furthermore, oral knowledge is plastic— conveyed one way, heard another, and processed and mobilized once more differently. Meanwhile, in a preindustrial landscape, largely rural, sound was calmer and more informative than today. In the open countryside, nonhuman sounds most often broke the quiet. In villages and in the city, where people lived close-packed on cramped streets, in buildings pierced by stairways and courtyards, and in rooms with jumbled activities and, often, flimsy walls, human voices carried well. Speech was therefore stronger, though it vied with other sounds: nature's water, wind, and thunder; animals and birds; and machinery—hammers, bells, wheels, rigging, guns, seldom loud devices. Addressing listeners, voice's range and expression varied—whispers, shouts, orations, songs—but word could never reach far, to attain an ear or expand the audience, without a relay. Thanks to intermediaries, spoken words strayed to casual or unintended hearers, sometimes to ill effect. Complex devices helped assure communication. Where not all words were true, how to trust a message? In a face-to-face world, orality looked to the messenger's looks, behavior, manifest state of mind, and reputation. It used not only hearing, but sight and touch and even other senses. Thus, orality's messages were broadband, reactive, and tied to speakers' moving, breathing bodies, and settings.

Linguistic pluralism complicated oral communication. Italian itself, especially when spoken, was not one language. Although Dante and Petrarch's Tuscan was gaining ground, most Italians spoke dialects not readily understood by outsiders. The dynastic ambitions of the French and, most successfully, the Spanish brought many speakers of those tongues into the mix. And there were pockets of minority languages: Greek and Albanian, for example, and occasionally German or Portuguese among Italy's Jews. Not only foreigners but also many locals, on the road or in cosmopolitan cities, navigated a hodgepodge Babel. For a lingua franca, educated Italians adapted the hybrid speech of princely courts, *cortegiano*, which in the sixteenth century assumed ever more Tuscan colorations. In some places this language trickled down into daily life. In Rome, for example, judicial scribes heard dialects from witnesses, but made largely *cortegiano* transcripts for legal use.

Authorities Communicate

To reach diverse audiences in a world only partly literate, authorities adopted a mix of aural and visual media. In parallel, church and state issued regulations, laws, news, and summonses to join rituals. To broadcast speeches and announcements, they often used the *ringhiera*, a high balcony on a town hall or palace. Criers moved around the city to proclaim public messages. Regimes also posted notices, and wall posters alerted travelers to bandits or plagues. The literate could read these out to those gathered around. Cannon fire and bells rung in distinct rhythms could call to arms or salute a princely birth or marriage. On their buildings, rulers might use heraldry to vaunt their strength or public art to insult their enemies. They had criminals or defeated foe painted upside down, hanging by the feet, or depicted their palaces of government, shamefully inverted.

Reviving the ancient Roman custom of monumental inscription, the mighty also carved stately words on public masonry. The Middle Ages had for its rare inscriptions used a barely legible, tight-packed gothic hand borrowed from the written page. The Renaissance returned to antiquity's ample capital letters, rotund and bold like our present upper case. Princes, prelates, and great families chiseled magniloquent self-congratulation over doorways, on window frames, on plinths and plaques. Generally, in Latin and aping the lettering on the ruins, they were meant to impress. Yet even men who commissioned these messages could sometimes barely read them. In 1556, a papal judge asked baron Giuliano Cesarini to explain an abstruse Latin motto over his town's gate where, likening his name punningly to Caesar's, he seemed to pose as greater than the pope. The baron, who did know Latin, retorted defensively, "I never heeded those words and don't know what they mean." The lines were, said he, just his learned secretary's concoction![3] (See Chapter 2.) Still, even literate Italians who lacked Latin could often pick out the name of the patron, whose heraldry often sat there too.

Preaching

Sermons were another authoritative meeting place between oral and written culture. Preaching took place in churches, but also often outdoors. To minimize distractions, men and women often occupied separate sections, as depicted in paintings where make-shift barriers partitioned the piazza. The great preachers were highly educated men, capable of long Latin disquisitions to learned gatherings. But, to reach the common folk, they spoke Italian. They did not read these sermons, which lasted hours, but composed them on the spot. The good preacher had a sense of path and des-tination, but, like a jazz musician, played off his own performance and his audience's response. He commanded a hoard of proverbs and lively stories, cribbed from anthologies and life. Though his central message had deep roots in written culture, his artistry was oral. Notetakers in the audience sometimes captured these perfor-mances, if incompletely, in writing. In an exceptional case, when a Florentine notary did record entire speeches of the charismatic Savonarola, "the very least word and act being inscribed exactly, without a single iota wanting," citizens called the feat "superhu-man" and a miracle.[4] More normal were abstracts, like good lecture notes, that caught some of the original's sense and feel. These then circulated the good word and its forceful delivery among the liter-ate, including other preachers.

Here is an excerpt from a lively sermon for the common peo-ple by Saint Bernardino of Siena (1380–1444), as recorded by a member of his audience:

A Sermon from Saint Bernardino of Siena

I once fell prey to the wish to live like an angel. Not like a man, I tell you. I got the notion to live on water, and on greens, and I got it into my head to go live in the woods. I began to say to myself, "What will you do in the woods? What will you eat?" And I answered, talking to myself just like that, "It'll be just fine. Doing it the way the Holy Fathers did. I will eat greens when I am hungry, and when I am thirsty, I'll drink water." And so that was my plan, to live on the model of God, and I planned to buy a Bible to read, and a pilgrim's vest to wear. I bought the Bible, and off I went to buy a chamois skin, to keep water from coming in the sides and getting the Bible wet. And, with my plan in mind, I went looking for a place to perch. . . . I began to gather me a salad of chicory and other wild greens. And I had neither bread, nor salt, nor oil. And I said, "Let's start, for this first time, to wash it and scrape it clean, and the next time we will scrape it without any other washing, and when we are more used to it, we will do it without cleaning it, and finally we will do it without even picking it." And, calling on the blessed name of Jesus, I started with a mouthful of chicory, and, sticking it in my mouth, began to chew it. Chew! Chew! It wouldn't go down. I couldn't swallow it at all; I said, "Enough of that! Let's start by drinking a spot of water." Heavens! The water didn't go down; the chicory was still in my mouth. In the end, I drank a lot of gulps of water with one mouthful of chicory and I couldn't get it down. . . . With one mouthful of chicory I washed away every temptation.[5]

Popular forms of oral culture also diverted, warned, and spread news, offering a different take on public affairs. Entertainers called *cantastorie* (story singers) or *cantimbanchi* (stage singers) made a living in the streets and piazze.[6] They performed old favorites, but their repertoire also included current events such as battles or murders. Sometimes, the singers sold pamphlets to carry their news further. Less commercial were the prophets of doom, who garnished their dire prognostications with notice of recent disasters or portents: odd rainbows, swarms of red butterflies, two-headed calves, and ghostly armies clashing in the sky.

WRITTEN LANGUAGE

During the Renaissance, writing spread. Authorities and common folk penned more contracts, sent more letters, filled more registers, and devised better systems for storing papers and finding them again. Although moveable type brought new cascades of words, it did not replace handwriting. A scribal culture of taking notes, making copies, and passing around manuscripts long survived print's advent. Skilled professionals—scribes, copyists, and notaries—worked on the boundary between the oral and the written. Where literacy was partial, communications often involved collaboration and compromise: professional letter writers for the illiterate; sample books to craft a fitting letter; notarial routines of reading legal papers back "in a loud and intelligible voice" to assure that unlettered parties grasped the terms. Few practiced silent reading; instead, the literate often read aloud, to themselves or to others less skilled. Meanwhile, listeners who could write might record things heard. Adaptively, many a message bounced back and forth between speech and ink.

Love intrigues from Roman trials, for example, illustrate the gendered complexities of an inconsistently literate culture. In one story, the illiterate wife of a prominent notary received letters from a neighbor proposing adultery. The gold coins folded inside made the amorous message plain, but, for the sweet words themselves, the woman had to enlist her sisters, nuns who could read.[7] Another trial record from 1602 included a bizarrely uneven missive from a teenaged scribe-in-training to his illiterate girlfriend next door. The boy's mother having discovered the sexual liaison (that the young people had consummated in the girl's basement during Carnival), she banned her son from the room where, like Pyramus with Thisbe, he had courted his beloved through a chink. Disconsolate, the young man penned a letter in fine school hand that began poetically, "Most worthy lady . . . heart of my life." His literary and emotional register then sinking, he griped about his interfering mother and at the bottom scrawled bawdy doggerel. He decorated the margin of the letter and the outside space for the address with sketches of organs, male and female, with the owners' names attached. The girl understood the art but could not read the words, so she took the letter for decoding to a nearby brass smith. To receive the whole, even if compromising, message, both women needed and sought out collaborators who bestrode the gap between written and oral cultures.[8]

A rural story shows how far written culture's zigzag paths could ramble. In 1574, peasants in the hilltop village of Aspra at a notary's instigation staged a raucous carnival play containing, among other blasphemies, a holy hermit who, frustrated in romance, hurled his rosary to the ground. Anonymous denunciations landed the amateur thespians in their bishop's court, where they recited their parts—the devil, the necromancer, the nymph-besotted hermit, the amorous shepherd, the wily servant. The illiterate actors had learned their lines by hearing them read from a published text. The slapstick script parodied a Renaissance high literary genre of classical pedigree, the pastorale. Aspra's real peasants acted out their own take on a written spoof on the Renaissance imitation of the imaginary literary peasants of ancient Athens, played out in front of real villagers, and local clergy and officials. Here, thanks to the printing press and a village notary, the Renaissance revival of ancient literary art, re-rusticated, found its way full circle, back to genuine countrymen.[9]

Professional Writing

Writing became an increasingly important part of different kinds of professional work. The written transmission over long distances of timely news helped shape not only commerce but also international politics. Closer to home, chanceries and bureaucracies grew, and paperwork, both its creation and its orderly storage, multiplied.

Renaissance Italians, owing much of their collective wealth to their prowess as traders, had since the Middle Ages trawled the world for news. Because international business relied on networks of far-flung partners and agents, successful merchants had to be masters of communications. All news from far away—of weather, crops, supplies, prices, currency fluctuations, pirates, bandits, and foreign rulers' whims—was germane to trade. Precious information traveled by private letters. Merchants kept careful copies of

From the *Nova Reperta*, a series of plates on new inventions, this image highlights printing. The engraving was made after a drawing of around 1590 by the Flemish artist known in Florence as Stradanus, who worked for the Medici. (The Metropolitan Museum of Art)

their correspondence and mustered all their accounts to keep intricate business in clear view. For secrecy, they often used codes that their agents carried with them. Mails, however, were slow and often erratic. From Italy, Spain was a month away, by sea, as were the Netherlands and England, via Alpine passes. The eastern Mediterranean took longer yet. Even though carried by galleys that did not depend on the wind, word took months to come back from Alexandria.

Renaissance rulers and councils of state, like merchants, sought a view of the world both panoramic and precise. Imitating trade, Italian states took to posting permanent ambassadors to princely courts. These diplomats, as required, sent back abundant letters abrim with information and astute political observations. These too, for safety's sake, used veiled language, code names, and numerical ciphers. Unofficial political inquiries engendered a parallel system of information gathering on retainer, a proto-journalism called *avvisi*. The writers, scrounging for rumors foreign and domestic, sent weekly compilations to the prince who paid their keep. These bulletins, barely secret, were copied and distributed widely.

Recordkeeping and formal documents, both governmental and personal, touched many everyday lives, even of those who could not read them. Italians, pioneer paper-pushers, were adroit makers, copiers, keepers, and occasional fakers, of state papers and legal records. Administrative bookkeeping, of mercantile origin, was rapidly adopted by public institutions. Churches kept note of tithes; the city grain office registered the bushels bought and sold, tribunals logged the fines and fees collected. Private landlords, too, expected their estate agents to track all income and outlays. To manage all the paper, Renaissance institutions elaborated archives, adding storage and devising systems to make retrieval easy.

At the center of the burgeoning business of legal paper were notaries, who served all across Renaissance Italian life, from major government bodies to private individuals. More than secretaries, less than lawyers, notaries drafted written documents according to legal forms and protocols, prepared final versions, and kept reference copies in registers. A will, marriage contract, bill of sale, inventory, lease, or peace-pact: each had its habitual order and standard phrases. Usually laid out in Latin and reinforced with precise dates and names of participants, the transaction's prose was lumbered with stock formulas and legalistic redundancies. At the bottom came the place and the names of witnesses, and often the notary's own elaborate sign.[10] Although agreements could have legal force without written documentation, Renaissance Italians kept notaries busy. Dozens of them worked in any big city, while others served towns and villages. Families, especially propertied ones, often patronized a favorite notary, who might also serve as family adviser, and they might store the key papers in a strongbox in the master's bedroom or study. Artisans used notaries, too, but less often, in part to spare fees. Modern scholars, including art and cultural historians, have learned much from painstaking study of these notarial records.

Printing

Printing brought a great change to communications. The technical novelty was movable, cast-metal type. This German invention of the 1440s swiftly spread to Italy, where the first press, in 1465 at the Subiaco monastery, soon had imitators. By 1500, Italy had far more printshops than Germany. As often, one new thing spawned many others. Handwritten books had been rare and expensive; princes and rich churches cherished prestigious tomes of calfskin parchment, decorated by skilled painters. Less elegant and costly were the practical volumes of the professions, works on medicine, law, or theology. Usually devoid of art and color, these books were dense blocks of text in angular gothic script, flanked by massed commentaries and serried notes, packed onto wide margins. Elegant presentation manuscripts gradually gave way to high-end, embellished hybrids, printed volumes where artists custom-painted coats of arms and ornaments in blank spaces left for decoration. Meanwhile, reference books not only fell in price; they also became standardized. Zeal to publish an authoritative edition stimulated humanist scholarship; men of learning at printing houses sifted conflicting manuscripts to recover the original ancient texts. There were positive feedback loops; better books produced cannier readers, who hungered after reliable volumes from printers, who, with more sales, hired more scholars. Thus, print stimulated both itself and a nascent transnational intellectual community, later called the "republic of letters."

Yoked to capitalism, print brought texts of various sizes and quality to an ever larger public. No sooner did commerce embrace the printed word than marketing set in: printers vied for customers, who benefited as competition improved the product. Good books, both old and new, were suddenly abundant. By the early 1500s, Italians could buy readily portable editions of the classics, published in Venice by Aldo Manuzio. Their clear Aldine typeface, named for its inventor, is with us still. Most modern print descends from it. On what scholars then believed to be an ancient Roman model, the Aldine letters were round, open, and serifed. The page, with its ample white space between words and lines, was easy on the eyes. Renaissance books usually sold as a stack of loose pages or quires. Binding depended on the purchaser's tastes and means.

Capitalist production both concentrated intellectual expertise and served the diffusion of ideas. For the information industry of the sixteenth century, Venice was Silicon Valley. The city's privileged position between Italy and Central Europe, its Eastern trade connections, and its polyglot population all fostered big publishers, printing serious tomes on religion, law, and medicine, for peninsular and international markets. The gathering of producers attracted expert workers and fostered a local culture where information mattered. Venice also became a center for nascent journalism. Alongside the fine humanist tomes, presses also churned out cheap editions, pamphlets and broadsheets, poorly printed, hastily edited, on flimsy paper, sometimes full of dubious information. This low-end product was more likely to enter daily lives down the social scale. Print robbed the written word of some of its aloof mystique.

Printed image-making also developed rapidly. With engraving, prints became high art. They often embellished books, as decorations or enhancements to the text. Although the great bulk were devotional, prints now lent themselves to scientific illustration, and to maps, and city views. A new visual geography appeared, thanks to atlases, costume books, and plates depicting beasts, plants, and artifacts from newfound distant places. Some prints were by artists of genius; many others, by lesser talents, helped propagate the fine designs they reproduced or imitated. Yet many images still lacked technical finesse. Plain line drawings drew readers' attention to things well known—costumes, games, tools, labors, portraits, events, places, and saints and holy tales, plus emblems and allegories in plenty. Printed images also enlivened the cheap publications that purveyed news of marvels: floods, monstrous births, and victories over the infidel.

As books multiplied, libraries grew. When, in 1450, Pope Nicholas V founded the Vatican Library, he owned only twelve hundred volumes, all handwritten. By 1600, Italy had libraries with many thousands, most of them printed. The early Renaissance library, like its medieval ancestors in universities and monasteries, usually displayed its precious volumes, prudently chained to the furniture. The reading room, in shape and feel, was much like the pillared monastic scriptorium, with books set out one by one on lecterns. By the end of the sixteenth century, as books multiplied, bookshelves appeared in libraries, often wonders of elegant carpentry so high that catwalks spanned the upper shelves. The soaring hall often took on palatial grandeur. Many of these beautiful Renaissance libraries are still in business. Some were open to the public; at the Angelica in Rome (1614), by statute, no one was barred. Today, ascending the marble stairs, one still encounters a neat plaque warning readers in Latin that anyone who stole or hurt a book would suffer the pope's thundering anathema. The admonition's language tells us that the library assumed high literacy even in vandals who abused its books.

Authorities Manage Print

Print created new opportunities for the rapid diffusion of new ideas and messages both approved and unsanctioned. Broadly, as the price of the written word tumbled, wider literacy threatened to undermine the power of educated elites who had hitherto hogged knowledge. While expanding literacy and access to schooling did allow some Italians to rise, the Renaissance saw no broad social democratization. Instead, the two centuries that ushered in print also brought the elites' growing closure and a sharper distinction between high culture and low. More acutely, the specter of Protestantism, with its vernacular Scriptures and its encouragement of the laity to read and discuss them, alarmed Italian authorities.

The Catholic Church acted on several planes to curb the risks of print's technological revolution. Aghast at the Protestants' doctrinal confusion that, in their eyes, menaced immortal souls, Catholic reformers resolved to squelch all translations of the Bible and to damp speculation and home-grown spirituality. All doctrinal writings, church legislation, and higher instruction would remain in Latin, a language accessible only to clergy, lawyers, physicians, and those rare others who could afford a long, arduous education. Furthermore, by Trent's decrees, to read sacred Scripture, even the educated needed a bishop's permission. For the literate laity, Catholic authorities did allow some devotional works in Italian. Encouraging memorization and sometimes illustrating doctrinal points with woodcuts, these usually taught catechism or promoted good conduct and piety. Some, intended for charity schools, featured lively vignettes of sins. The tone was moral and clear, not speculative, for the faithful needed faith, reverence, and virtue, not high theology.

The highly centralized church of the Catholic Reformation also strove to control what came out in print. All books both Latin and vernacular, and even handwritten news sheets, passed before censors. Learned officials reviewed texts, imposed revisions, and granted or stayed publication. Works printed earlier, or outside Italy, could end up expurgated or placed on the Index of Prohibited Books. Thus, the educated too came under intellectual tutelage, and those declared heretics were disciplined and even burned for their printed opinions. Protestants also banned books, but never so coherently. Meanwhile, the church also used print to advance the Catholic cause, publishing polemics and news of missionary exploits.

Yet, even in Rome, where the censorship was especially strict, surreptitious criticism of the church and state sometimes appeared on the pedestals of a few "talking statues." At night, polemicists crept up to these battered antique marbles to affix satirical remarks, often in pungent rhyming dialect. Romans copied these on the sly to pass around the town. The most famous statue, still impudent today, a stumpy relic fondly called "Pasquino," gave his name in several languages to "pasquinade," the anonymous topical satire.

LITERACY AND SCHOOLING

Literacy

With print, literacy came to matter more, and it spread, but slowly and unevenly. Our term in fact covered several distinct skills that people mastered in different measures. Reading itself divided between skills in Italian and in Latin. Writing overall was less widely known. Elementary reading and handwriting were often learned informally and at varied ages, but higher accomplishments usually required concerted study. Unlike quirky English, Italian is phonetically simple; with the alphabet and patience one could sound out simple vernacular prose. Some people learned to write wobbly sentences with an unsteady hand and a crude sense of where words stopped. The clear typography of print began to set a model even for the unschooled. Without formal training, however, polished penmanship and composition were largely out of reach. Measuring levels of basic literacy is difficult, but we get some sense of social distributions. Except for some clerics and estate officials, literacy remained rare in the countryside. Cities had much better rates. Many more men could read and sign their names than women. Thus, estimates from late sixteenth-century Venice suggest that one boy in three and one girl in eight spent some time at school. Many male artisans were semi-literate, and big merchants needed solid competency to succeed. Even for nobles and patricians, who did not have to write their own letters, high skills became increasingly valued. Even a clutch of exceptional women corresponded in humanist Latin.

Latin literacy remained the foundation of high learning. It formed the base of professional success for swelling cohorts of officials and bureaucrats. In the millennium since imperial Rome fell, the language had evolved to suit new uses. The Middle Ages bequeathed to the Renaissance a practical Latin, with rich, specialized vocabulary. This remained the language of many learned treatises on theology, law, medicine, and natural science. Churchmen, lawyers, notaries, and some administrators wrote this workaday Latin fluently, and often spoke it readily. Debaters at a university or advocates before a judge could wrangle in it. Meanwhile, the intellectual movement we call humanism rebelled against this workaday Latin to promote the refined language of the classics. This elevated Latin, sometimes an end in itself, embellished eloquent letters, poetry, histories, and philosophical dialogues. As elite men learned to write literary Latin at school, it acquired cachet and bespoke social finesse. A polished letter, witty epigram, or elegant oration both gratified recipients and advanced state and church careers. Yet few educated men could actually converse in this refined tongue. At some stricter boarding schools, however, pupils were supposed to speak it, and student spies ferreted out backsliders.

The Renaissance also saw the expansion of the use of written Italian. As none of the larger Italian states overawed the rest, politics did not impose a national language. Unlike Latin with its long-fixed grammar and spelling, the motley of regional vernaculars including Venetian, Lombard, Tuscan, and Neapolitan lacked standardization. Yet as serious literary texts in varied genres—lyrics, epics, plays, tales, dialogues, and conduct books—proliferated, models for good usage gelled. Print, assuring that many people read the same versions, much reinforced the process. Thanks to Dante, Petrarch, Boccaccio, and others, Renaissance Tuscan had an edge, but major authors assured a readership for some of its rivals: Castiglione in Lombard, Ruzzante in Venetian, Basile in Neapolitan, among others. Roman, however, scrambled by heavy immigration and the Sack, faded as a literary language.

Schooling

In modern times, education is often equated with formal schooling. But during the Renaissance only a small part of the learning that prepared young men and women for their adult roles took place in specialized institutions or came from professional teachers. Much training in the basic skills that sustained a livelihood or advanced a family's interests happened in a domestic household, which for many, among elites as well as working families, was the site of not only domesticity but also production and business. Concerning education, as well as elsewhere in Renaissance life, we need to set aside our anachronistic assumption of a clear separation between private and public domains. In the household, parents, masters and mistresses, or other adults modeled skills and behavior and corrected novices, girls and boys, as they progressed from simpler to more demanding tasks. This informal mode of instruction served, as well, to convey elements of basic literacy to many down the social scale.

Patricians and nobles sometimes hired private tutors to teach their sons, and occasionally daughters, in the household the specialized knowledge and accomplishments that set the elites apart. Such education at home could deliver high mastery, including of Latin. The few, but exceptional woman humanist writers owed their training to this domestic model, and often to the support of fathers or kinsmen.

Nevertheless, during the Renaissance, schools became increasingly important for literacy, book-learning, and some other skills. There were two educational streams matching Italy's two chief languages: vernacular and Latin. In neighborhoods, teachers received for pay small groups of pupils in their homes and taught them to read Italian and to memorize Latin. There was no curriculum; the students, mostly boys, attended when they could and progressed or not, at their own pace. Children started with hornbooks, wooden boards holding a single page, with a cross at the top and a model alphabet, in gothic or Renaissance script, to trace and copy. The name came from a sheet of translucent horn that protected the paper underneath. After letter Z, the page often laid out all the syllables that made up Italian words as well as, in Latin, the Lord's Prayer. Beginners then went on to a primer, a little book of twenty or so pages, with more Latin prayers to learn by heart and simple readings in Italian. In the sixteenth century, in the wake of Catholic reform, charitable Sunday schools taught catechism and doctrine in this way, alongside ABCs.[11]

Beyond these often hodgepodge elementary classes, some schools offered more systematic instruction to larger numbers of students. These taught more advanced vernacular reading and preparation to study Latin, and some trained future merchants and businessmen in a kind of practical mathematics called *abbacco*. This arithmetic for commerce, using real-life problems set in textbooks, dealt with weights and measures, currency exchange, interest on investments, estimating volumes, and gauging costs. Although Machiavelli, for one, studied at both Italian and Latin schools, the second, shaped by humanism, rose with the Renaissance aristocratization that drove a wedge between merchants and the governing classes.

Not just churchmen and intellectuals, but also rising numbers of secular professionals and bureaucrats needed good Latin. University studies in the liberal arts, theology, law, or medicine rested on it. Higher Latin schools, mostly taught by clerics, proliferated during the Renaissance to meet these demands. Early on, a teacher with several assistants might direct the education of several dozen students at a time. After 1550, the new religious orders like the Jesuits set up bigger schools more like the ones we know, where a student moved from grade to grade, each with a different instructor. The humanist curriculum cultivated not workaday medieval Latin but the eloquence of classical Rome. Pupils studied a few famous authors including Caesar, Ovid, and Virgil. Cicero, a master of rhetoric and author of many elegant letters, was especially useful as a model for the Latin correspondence that kept the wheels of Renaissance government turning. This instruction taught imitation, not originality or discovery; it cultivated able readers, good speakers, fluent writers who adapted tone to task at hand. Therefore, pupils filled their notebooks with model sentences from the accepted works, in hopes of imitation. Latin schooling also paraded Roman models of the moral public life. It taught no practical mathematics, just a smattering tied to ancient Greek philosophy.

MEMORY

All Renaissance media—script, image, speech, melody, pageantry, and even buildings and their material contents—served individual and collective memory. Religion, lords' desire for legitimacy, community spirit, family pride, and legal and commercial imperatives all looked to the past for validation and rhetoric. Interested parties turned to media in their campaigns to construct a useable past linked to present needs and ambitions for the future. History was curated memory.

The rise of public historical thinking stimulated private family records of several sorts. Tracking domestic events and personal doings, *ricordanze* (memory books) generally intended to lay down life lessons useful to their heirs. Some compilations, for example, Gregorio Dati's (see Chapter 11), smacked of the merchant's ledger: enter each wife and dowry and each child's birth; debit one by one the many deaths. Other men kept diaries, a finer scale account if not always day by day, in which they reported not personal thoughts, but rather public events like wars, factional strife, and natural calamities that might bear on business. Marcello Alberini, a Roman nobleman, linked the personal and the political. Writing just for family, he placed his own life, marked by the Sack of 1527, amid the struggle between his class and the papacy over who ruled Rome. Not all family history, however, picked up Alberini's sense of historical moment. Other sixteenth-century noble houses hired genealogists to trace their remotest ancestors; with luck, effort, and abundant self-delusion, one might thread back to a consul, emperor, or veteran of the Sack of Troy.

Meanwhile, far more than the Middle Ages, the Renaissance as a cultural enterprise invested in constructing public memory through writing history. Educated Italians began, self-consciously, to revive the high literary genre of history modeled in ancient Greece and Rome. They composed histories of their cities and even, boldly, of Italy itself. Some works aimed to retrieve the past to inform the present and others to record the present to instruct the future. Scholars also devised tools to describe and appraise the institutions, actions, and ideas of the ancient world. Such study fostered a sense of historical difference, of the deep pastness of the past, a notion now taken for granted, but alien to medieval thinking.

CONCLUSION

Like all people, Renaissance Italians sent, received, and transformed communications of many sorts. Yet the Renaissance added some distinctive features. The arts, and especially the visual arts, acquired brilliant new dimensions, as they informed and embellished public and private spaces used by the elites but also by ordinary people. Language—oral and written, Latin and vernacular—pervaded life in many rich forms. In an oral, only semi-literate world, speech and script interpenetrated in countless ways.

Italians used their visual, verbal, and material media to address God and each other, to pass judgments, to transmit practical information, to describe the world, to bond solidarities, to express and adjust hierarchy, to exercise social control, and to foster a sense of continuity with bygone days. The new technology of movable type promoted literacy and empowered readers. Print extended reach, enhanced precision and consistency, and thickened communication for the solitary reader in a private chamber, the studious community of intellectuals, and the foreign merchant long years and many miles from home.

NOTES

1. An overview, Evelyn Welch, *Art and Society in Italy, 1350–1500* (Oxford, 1997).

2. See essays by Sheila Barker, Sheila ffolliott, and Cecilia Gamberini, *Women Artists in Early Modern Italy: Careers, Fame, and Collectors*, ed. S. Barker (Turnhout, 2016).

3. ASR, GTC, Processi, 16th c., busta 29, case 7, f. 10r.

4. Luca Landucci, *A Florentine Diary from 1450 to 1516* (London, 1927), 130.

5. Quoted in Marco Masuelli, ed., *Letteratura religiosa e società del medioevo* (Turin, 1975) (our translation).

6. On street culture, Rosa Salzberg, *Ephemeral City: Cheap Print and Urban Culture in Renaissance Venice* (Manchester, 2014).

7. Cohen and Cohen, *Words and Deeds*, 159–87.

8. Elizabeth S. Cohen, "She Said, He Said: Situated Oralities in Judicial Records from Early Modern Rome," *Journal of Early Modern History* 16:4–5 (2012), 403–6, with illustration.

9. Cohen and Cohen, *Words and Deeds*, 234–77.

10. On notaries and their practice, Laurie Nussdorfer, *Brokers of Public Trust: Notaries in Early Modern Rome* (Baltimore, 2009).

11. On schools, Paul Grendler, *Schooling in Renaissance Italy: Literacy and Learning, 1300–1600* (Baltimore, 1989).

9

SPACES

Renaissance Italy had its distinctive spatial culture. The spaces it inherited or created, urban and rural, public and private, reflected modes of seeing, and shaped life. The Italian ambiance had a very distinctive look, unlike our own. Nevertheless, in some ways, the Renaissance is the intellectual progenitor of our own spatial sense, for thanks partly to its contributions to cartography and graphic arts we readily conceive of space abstractly and geometrically. For us, miles and kilometers are mathematical measures, laid across emptiness like giant rulers aligned with compass points. Our travels, by air or along smooth highways, eat up distance with monotonous regularity; we readily calculate arrival times from speed. Our maps are precisely scaled miniatures of real spaces, and our cities and farm plots, especially in lands Europeans once colonized, are often grids laid out by eighteenth- and nineteenth-century surveyors who cavalierly imposed abstract Cartesian geometry on what was, for them if not for the dispossessed indigenous peoples, blank terrain. The ruler-based map became the mother, not the child, of landscapes.

The Renaissance advanced our present geometric view of space. The painters' invention of linear perspective was a mathematical operation. Early practitioners often set the Madonna's throne on a tiled floor, the two-dimensional equivalent of a ruler receding correctly toward the vanishing point. The painters' device soon invaded both cartography and architecture. One of perspective's first theoreticians, Leon Battista Alberti, famous for his many talents—writer, mathematician, proto-scientist and architect—also pioneered the surveyor's science of angles and baselines for the exact mapping of cities. At first, little came of this innovation of the 1430s, but, seventy years later, Leonardo da Vinci, using a similar system, drafted an exact urban map for the ambitious military plans of Cesare Borgia, Pope Alexander's ruthless son. In the late sixteenth century, precise cartography of cities and the countryside developed swiftly, using both surveying and the methods of late medieval marine charts, based on compass bearings. At the same time, a passion for geometry swept architecture; the ubiquitous Alberti was an early pioneer. From the late fifteenth century, the delight in measurement and line inspired a new kind of urban planning that imposed abstract geometry, with its straight lines, precise angles, and clean circles, on actual buildings, streets, and squares.[1] At the end of the Renaissance, Galileo brought to both his physics and his astronomy a profoundly geometrical conception of body, space, and motion. It lives on still.

Meanwhile, a military invention, the siege cannon gave geometry another boost. By the middle of the fifteenth century, military engineers began to use the new surveyor's tools to site and sight their guns. Against this new threat, in the early sixteenth century, an Italian invention, the star-shaped fortress with its sloping bastion walls and geometric moats parried artillery's challenge. This military novelty soon swept both Europe and its expanding empires. The new fortifications were a geometer's delight; a tighter angle here, one wider there for better line of fire, a steeper wall to storm, a deeper ditch to cross might make the difference between victory and surrender.

Despite these technical innovations, everyday life usually gauged and experienced space in older ways. To most Italians, distance was exertion; our modern, everyday geometric vision befits a world where travel's frictions are far less than in Renaissance Italy. Back then, exertion measured distances. How far to the market? Two hundred steps! Two stone throws! A crossbow- or gun-shot!! The mile (*miglio*) was still, as in ancient Rome, as its name implies (*mille* means thousand) a notional thousand paces. Often Italians measured travel in hours and days rather than in abstract distances. Area, likewise, was often labor, or yield. Peasants sometimes measured their woods and vineyards in "labors" (*opere*) or their fields in "days of work" (*giornate*). Grain land might come in yields: "cups" or "bushels" (*rubbie*). A villager could say, oddly, that this bad year his ten "bushels" of land had yielded only eight bushels of grain. Acreage and yield could be loosely linked.

RURAL LANDSCAPES

Italy's varied landscape itself conditioned everyday spatial experience, on every scale.[2] Every natural setting combined with patterns of agriculture and local habits of building to set rural space's look and feel (Chapter 1). Suburban land, dense with high-walled gardens, was unlike the open plow land farther out from town. The wealthy, crowded North differed from the sparsely populated, often poorer South. Structures of land tenure also counted; solid sharecropper farms in the Center contrasted with great southern estates with huddled, shabby housing for their hired laborers. Everywhere, land type shaped human intervention: mountains, hill country, and plains always had very a different look.

The rugged mountain landscape was seldom out of sight. Italians used the mountains, taking wood and charcoal, and edible chestnuts from the woods, driving pigs for acorns, and herding goats and sheep to upland pasture. In the Renaissance, millions of sheep converged on the high Apennines in summer, wreaking ecodevastation, but earning rulers a good income from the transit rights they paid. A sixteenth-century traveler remarked that the many shepherds' tents and fires in the high Abruzzi looked at night like an invading army. The mountains were therefore laced with paths and trails. Renaissance Italians had none of our romantic love of mountainscape; they saw it as rough country, full of rough men and real dangers, but also useful.

On the other hand, Italians loved the hills. They preferred their nature softened by a human touch. The hill country near Venice, Padua, Florence, Siena, Rome, Naples, and Palermo was like a giant garden. Its settlements both fed and refreshed the city. Around each village extended a zone of walled, hedged, or ditched plots, given over to carefully planted rows of fruit trees strung with grapevines, and to olives, hemp, cane, melons, and garden vegetables. This garden zone was often full of farmsteads, with their many outbuildings and constructions: stables, granaries, hay sheds, tall dovecotes, threshing floors, cisterns, vats for grapes and olives, troughs for livestock. In hill country, beyond the gardens was an emptier outer zone of grain and then common pasture and woodland, where walls were fewer and property rights less absolute. In these hills, one saw a good deal of geometry—not the imperiously precise mathematics of the surveyor but the pragmatic, responsive geometry of agriculture. Where the hills were steep, walls and terraces of earth and stone balked erosion. To shore up fields on slopes, the Renaissance saw a spate of terrace building; the crazily perpendicular lemon groves of the Amalfi coast, for instance, often date from then. Terrace walls conformed to contour lines of hills, and fields and trees aligned themselves in orderly ways that pleased both painters and agronomists. The more suburban hills also delighted the wealthy, who, especially after 1500, built themselves commodious villas, refuges from politics and summer heat. There they installed ornamental gardens, geometrical feasts for all the senses. A statue glimpsed at the end of a tunnel of tall cypresses or well-trimmed live oak, a mock-grotto full of dripping mosses, or a hemicycle of antique sculpture and tinkling fountains might delight and impress a guest or lift the owner's weary spirits. By design, such gardens were complex spaces, full of modulation and contrast.[3]

The plains varied greatly in look and economic use. Lombardy, well-watered and full of wealthy cities that invested in the land, increasingly showed the hand of human intervention. Its excess water required careful ditching, with canals to carry runoff. These ran ruler straight, and the lines of mulberry trees or poplars, often strung with grapes, that lined their banks, laid out the precise geometry of the big fields. Well-watered meadows supported livestock good for meat and cheese. Other northern zones, off the beaten track, were however still swamp, heath, or woods. Another plain, the Terra di Lavoro behind Naples, was full of gardens to feed Italy's biggest city. In dry Apulia, Italy's flat Southeast, great estates grew wheat and fed sheep in winter; its towns were few and poor. The plains near Rome and stretching northward into coastal Tuscany were strangely empty. There, in the Renaissance, to escape abduction by corsairs, the populace fled inland, tillage declined, and sheep and goats took over. Depopulation permitted swamps that fostered malaria and drove off yet more occupants. Travelers to Rome often remarked on the desolation of the lonely landscape—green in spring and sprinkled with sheep, but yellow and deserted in malarial summer.

Whether mountain, hills, or plain, the Italian landscape was emptier of human habitation, wilder, and better wooded than today.

Modern Italy is 21 percent forest, much of it uphill; in 1500, woods covered some 50 percent of the peninsula, and they were then more varied, more robust, and far fuller of wildlife. In the sixteenth century, there still were bears in the Casentino valley near Florence, storks and beaver in the marshes near Ferrara, and, along the Tuscan coast, pelicans aplenty. In many zones, wolves abounded, and there was big game, enough to keep noble hunters happy. In 1515, on a single outing, Pope Leo X and his party bagged fifty deer and twenty boar right by Rome. Extensive forests in the Venetian Alps, Tuscany, and Calabria enjoyed protection by states keen to preserve them for beams for cathedrals, palaces, and ships' timbers, and for turpentine for naval caulking. But, in many zones, the sixteenth century's rising population, and lax administration encouraged the illegal clearances, overzealous cutting, and heavy foraging and grazing that eroded the forest. As deforestation and marsh drainage evicted wildlife, the hunt declined.

Settlement Patterns

Although some regions had their scattered farmsteads, much of the rural population dwelled in villages. While there was no single village architecture, there were patterns. Villages often were tightly packed, sometimes inside girdling walls with gates that shut at night. In the hills and mountains, they often perched for safety, high above armies and the worst mosquitoes. They might have a fort, or a palace for their lord's officials, or both, usually solid, plain structures, with here and there a heraldic emblem on the wall. Almost always there was a square, perhaps beside the church or the hall where the council sat. Village streets were almost always narrow, some no more than paths or stairs, one laden donkey wide. Arches and overhanging houses might make streets dark, and cool in summer. In the seventeenth century, when painters first depicted country life, they portrayed villages as ramshackle places, with humble trim, cracked plaster, missing bricks, abundant rubble, and broken gear, artistic convention perhaps, but probably often true.

In many parts, especially the South, outside villages there were few structures. Near town would be shacks in the vineyards of townsfolk, and imposing villas of the rich. Farther out, on roads and streams stood inns and mills. Other zones had isolated farmhouses; these were increasingly common in the North and Center, and present in Sardinia, eastern Sicily, and elsewhere. In Lombardy, solid, defensible buildings around courtyards housed several families, who worked a big estate. In the lowland outside Rome, big *casali* (farmsteads) sheltered estates' gear and administration, while the dozens of poor migrant laborers spent pasture season heaped in awful shacks. In the grain lands of Apulia and central Sicily, hired laborers left big villages of mean houses to work vast *latifondi* (estates), leaving wives behind to tend their modest garden plots. Some country buildings were not for agriculture; in coastal zones, isolated towers, *torri saraceni*, offered quick refuge should a Moorish ("Saracen") slaving raid storm through, and relayed smoke signals along the coast, warning of the enemy's approach.

Place Names

One very sharp difference between Italy and English-speaking New Worlds is the density of the names the landscape bore. Centuries of use draped over the ditches, springs, brooks, woods, shrines, lanes, paths, fields, and valleys a thick quilt of nomenclature. Some names commemorated persons or events; others signaled the land's use and features. The people of one central Italian mountain village worked Toadstool Plain, Field of Flowers, Long Clearing, the Cutting, Stick-Stockade, Little Tower, and Dark, Green, and Chain-Link Valleys, plus hills called Swamp, Ditch, and Pigeon. They also used Charcoal-Burner's Place, the Fig Tree, and the Little Live Oak, not to mention Little-Pole Chestnut, Rosettes, the Holy Image, Big Crow, Blind Ditch, Little-Market Bridge, and woods called Cat, Sun, Mountain, and Well, plus Long and Mountain Hill; they tapped springs named Marble, Swamp, and Cold. They had many other toponyms, some now obscure. Such local names bore associations outsiders would not know, anchoring village lore and collective memory of lands' improvement or damage, and of gifts, dowries, legacies, sales, confiscations, quarrels, crimes, fines and penalties, crops, bandit raids, floods, lightning strikes, and holy visions.[4]

URBAN SPACES

The Evolving Urban Fabric

As spaces, Renaissance cities still carried many marks of their medieval past. They still had sharp boundaries: high walls, with towers and imposing gateways with great doors that shut at night. They remained tightly packed behind defenses; land-hungry outlying monasteries and road-side inns did attract some settlement, but warfare made extramural sprawl imprudent. The older urban quarters were often a jumble of closely set buildings, some with jutting upper stories. Arching buttresses and elevated passageways vaulted the streets, blocking out the sky. Footing was cobblestones or mud. The streets, narrow and irregular, bent and twisted; a walker seldom saw far ahead. The older parts of Viterbo today still have this jumbled quality. Amalfi apart, Italian cities were less tangled than those of North Africa or the Middle East, but to outsiders their medieval back quarters were not swiftly legible. The major streets were easier to follow; linking gates and major squares, they cut through the mazes, roughly straight. Then the Renaissance, with its nascent passion for rational geometry, inspired a new urban planning. Regimes wanted a transparent city, its long vistas lined with elegant facades. Reason, not tradition or utility, would lay out the town. Geometry testified to princely power. Princes and popes waged campaigns to widen squares and cut broad thoroughfares through medieval tangles to impose clean grids on districts. One device was a focal monument set at the end of an urban vista; in Rome, famously, sixteenth-century popes re-erected old Egyptian obelisks, stone needles once shipped in as booty by the Caesars. The pontiff Christianized them a little, perching sacred emblems at the apex and, on the base, inscribing pious boasts. Major streets, arrow straight, converged on these monuments. This fashion for straight lines and long prospects would live on long, in Paris and Washington, with their convergent avenues, and in our grid cities.

The spatial features of Italian cities almost always owed much to the ancient world. Venice is the great exception, for only at the empire's turbulent fall did mainlanders take refuge on its islands. Otherwise, there is usually a pre-Roman or Roman core or, as in Naples, Siracusa and other southern places, an ancient Greek colony. The shrunken cities of the early Middle Ages cannibalized the ancient buildings for masonry and fancy marble, colonized and fortified them, or recycled them as churches. Often, later buildings perched on ancient foundations. Thus, thanks to cellars, in many cities the street pattern of the ancient Roman city still survives today. A satellite image, a good map, or the view from the cathedral roof will still show the characteristic tidy grid of square blocks, aligned neatly with the compass points. This is true of downtown Florence, and Piacenza, and Verona (where the river has nipped off two corners), and of many other places. Naples still has the un-Roman long parallel streets and oblong blocks of its Greek ancestor. In the late empire and the early Middle Ages, towns threw up a protective wall, a tight perimeter around the Roman core. After 1100, as they prospered and grew, they put up a second defensive ring and then, in the thirteenth or fourteenth century, to accommodate still more growth, built an ambitious third circuit. The geography of these outer zones lacked the Romans' prim geometry. The new walls captured radial roads heading from the original gates; these trade roads determined both the shape of neighborhoods, which had begun as extramural suburbs, and the location of the gates in each later perimeter. Sometimes the lesser streets and alleys of the expanding town had once been lanes between old fields. Many cities, anticipating yet more growth, had thrown out a wide circuit of fortifications not long before the Black Death of 1347, and then, hit by recurrent waves of pestilence, had shriveled. Even in the sixteenth century, many cities still had fields and gardens inside the fourteenth-century ring.

Many big cities had a citadel, a Renaissance fortification built for the age of cannons. Usually it housed the troops of a lord, foreign or domestic, who held the town, sometimes against its will. The term *cittadella* means "little city"—with reason, for this great fortress was often a world apart. Customarily, the citadel sat on the edge, an anchor to the circuit of walls. Girt with stronger defenses than the rest of town, it was a tougher nut to crack. On its townward side might lie a zone empty of houses, a free field of fire, so that, were the town to fall to an enemy or rise up against the regime, defenders could lay down a withering barrage.

Streets

Streets often had a very intimate feel. Even main ones were seldom wide. In the North, vaulted arcades often lined the sides, holding up the upper stories, protecting commerce and strollers from rain or sun, and, at night, sometimes hiding assailants behind the pillars. Fear of nocturnal ambush, hopes of easing traffic, and Renaissance tastes in palace architecture caused some regimes to knock these convenient shelters down, but in many towns they survive today. Streets were busy places, as full of social life and trade as they were of transport; commerce spilled into the roadway as merchants folded their shutters upward to make a sloping overhang against the sun and rain, and heaped their wares on jutting benches. In many cities, even palaces, their prestige untarnished by the commerce, housed ground-floor shops and sometimes rented merchants lodgings behind their shops or on a mezzanine upstairs.

Renaissance streets, despite concerted efforts to clean them, were also often messy. With their livestock, they smelled much like a village. Herds and flocks, mule trains, oxen pulling wagons, horses harnessed or saddled all dropped their droppings. Pigs rooted underfoot. Householders, against the rules, left slops and heaps of steaming stable sweepings. Markets spread rotting detritus. Smelly water sat in ditches. Where unpaved, roads alternated between mire and summer dust. Renaissance grandeur often rose amid squalor.

As Italians walked or rode through city streets, they felt the continual modulation of their space. There was visual and kinesthetic drama in the passage from tight to open, and then back to tight. Few sights are more splendid than a great square, when you debouche from a narrow, crowded alley. And it stirs the soul to enter a handsome courtyard or soaring church. Density, variety, and spatial complexity are enlivening; they keep the senses on their toes.

Other Structures

Renaissance towns had a lively skyline. Many still sported private towers, tall fingers of fortification common in medieval Italy. Noble families had built them for prestige and prowess in civil war, sometimes linking several with high galleries to fortify a whole city block. Striving to impose internal peace, urban regimes sometimes knocked towers to the ground or lopped them to a legislated height, but many of these austere, almost windowless pillars still vied with church belfries and the town hall tower. As the Renaissance progressed, ever more palaces sported peaceable rooftop pavilions called *belvederes* (the name means "good view"). There, the elite took the evening breeze and enjoyed the panorama. Meanwhile, although the great age of dome building would come after 1600, early cupolas already bellied upward among the prickly towers.

The urban fabric contained a great variety of structures. There were churches big and small, weighty seats of government, and arcaded market halls. In the fifteenth century, there appeared a new kind of house, so elegant and grand as to be called a palace.[5] In the rest of Europe, the medieval political elite, being rural, had invested little in urban real estate. In time, other countries would copy this imposing domestic structure, an Italian Renaissance innovation. The city's grander structures were very solid. Walls could be six feet thick or more, all stone. Lesser buildings were flimsy and often small; they are less likely to have survived. A substantial house or church, with its thick walls and few windows, resisted summer's heat; as now, Italians often passed from the dazzling midday sun to the dim cool of interiors. Winter, sadly, offered no corresponding indoor warmth.

The piazza was a crucial feature of urban life and layout. An invention of independent medieval cities, it served for civic and church ceremonies, commerce, games, and social conversation. The bustling urban piazza, enclosed, paved, and uncluttered by structures, became common in Europe (and rare in North

This busy sixteenth-century scene, evoking the Mercato Vecchio of Florence, represents a mixed crowd that includes dignitaries, soldiers, servants, market women, and children buying, selling, strolling, chatting, feasting, and ogling the spectacle of a sword dance. (De Agostini/ Getty Images)

America, where squares are mostly given over to greenery and lonesome statuary, if not to a noxious swirl of traffic). These Italian spaces varied in shape, size, and function. Cities often had three major ones—for the market, main church, and seat of government—each with its own functions. One square might do several jobs, and markets and sacred sites might multiply. There were also lesser local squares. In Venice, for instance, the *campo* (field) in the center of each of the many little islands remained open, functioning as the communal public space for neighbors who lived within their girdle of canals. Many other cities also had small squares, the focus of a quarter. One felt safer there, among one's own.

City Space Divided

Although Italians were fiercely loyal to their cities, they often felt just as devoted to neighborhood. Most cities had "quarters" or "sixths" or tracts by other names, often assigned to defend a segment of the city wall; these might also serve as electoral districts. These urban territories possessed their insignia, banners, patron saints, places of march in processions, and, often, their well-marked boundaries. Districts sometimes fielded teams in civic races and other games, or built floats for carnival festivities. Some cities, Pisa and Venice, for instance, divided in two, the halves of town waging great mock battles on bridges on the boundary line; the heady partisanship spilled over into endemic skirmishing and taunts (Chapter 16). Other divisions were less formal. In many cities, strong families colonized whole zones, buying and building houses and, in earlier centuries, towers along a street or around a square. Their dependents and allies crowded around them; often such elite families chose spouses and business partners from nearby streets. These local loyalties could ramify, to cover much of the city. In Rome, for instance, in the fifteenth century, the Orsini barons, papal partisans, and their allies dominated the approaches to the Tiber bridge to the Vatican, while some blocks to the east camped their ancient enemies, the imperialist Colonna and their clients. In the middle dwelled noble families who tried to steer a neutral course amid street warfare. When a city was full of violence, men watched their step when off their turf. One goal of pacification was to make the whole town safe for all.

Economic and social forces might shape a city's spaces. There were richer and poorer parts. In some cities, the elite built their houses close together, not rarely around the square of government. Poorer districts often lay along the walls, far from the seat of power. Nevertheless, there was less segregation by wealth than in modern cities; elite families' mutual suspicion kept them from withdrawing to a shared enclave, and the rented shops in their palaces, their clientele of underlings, and their many servants all assured social mixing. Economic segregation sometimes reflected trades; certain professions and crafts would settle all in one place. Several forces concentrated trades. It might be zoning regulations, as against smelly tanneries or butcher shops, and fiery glass-makers, or perhaps a local resource, such as plentiful water for dyers and millers, or ports and roads that drew taverns, cargo-handlers, and prostitutes. Or it might be convenient to have colleagues near at hand, as with bankers (Chapter 15). Another kind of segregation was ethnic or religious. A nationality might cluster around favorite wine shops or the church it sponsored. Jews, even before sixteenth-century legislation forced them into ghettos, usually lived together for safety and easy access to their synagogue.

All these divisions produced a complex local geography. Often the names of streets and squares reflected city life: families, trades, activities, or worship. As in the countryside, town nomenclature was dense with meaning. There were no street numbers and no useable street maps. People navigated in nonmetric ways. They described events as happening by a familiar palace, or at the crucifix near the bathhouse, or down by the elm at the blacksmith, and assumed that their hearer also knew well the texture and layout of the town.

Sacred Spaces

One other great division of the city involved the sacred. For Renaissance Catholicism, sacredness was never smoothly spread. Although God was in principle everywhere, special holiness adhered to sacred persons, times, words, gestures, and, what is germane here, to objects and places. Images of Jesus, the Madonna and the saints, relics (bones, hair, dried milk and blood, clothing, other storied materials), and the wafer of the consecrated host, concentrating God's grace and power, all demanded reverence and protection. Much such holiness inhered in the many parish and monastic churches and local chapels. A city had its patron saint, chief protector and focus of civic cult, resident in the cathedral.

Meanwhile, the Virgin, babe in lap, smiled down from many street corners or sat in roadside shrines, where citizens paid their respects with small gifts and burning candles. These Madonnas were legion; Venice had more than four hundred. They discouraged blasphemy, protected the poor, advanced peace, and warded off disease and danger. Around these icons, the faithful, to acknowledge miraculous help, nailed ex voto plaques recording the grace received. Whole cities put up monuments in thanksgiving for deliverance, especially from the plague. Thus, although a city's main sacred places and most powerful images lay in churches, under custody of clergy, a local sacrality scattered across the town, protecting the little spaces, and admonishing citizens to respect the holy and keep the peace.

GENDER AND SPACE

In the use of space, as in other domains, Mediterranean cultures distinguished male from female. If less sharply than among Muslims, with Christians or Jews gender did matter. Everywhere, domestic spaces were comfortable terrain for women, while more distant, less familial reaches—the fields, the main street, the square, and the inn—were male. Practice, however, varied markedly with social rank and livelihood. In Italy, in general, the higher the woman's status, the less freely she moved about, and, when she sallied forth, the more she turned to chaperones and vehicles. In paintings of great processions, resolutely male, the windows but not the streets were full of female faces. The threshold was a habitual domestic boundary, but the nearby neighborhood also belonged to women. In Venice, elite women might leave their house, but seldom the confines of their parishes. In Rome, ordinary women, sitting in their doorways to spin, watch children, and share news, together policed their local turf. At the same time, most working women, in both city and country, had regularly to venture beyond their doorsteps; they were too useful to coop up at home. The well and the collective wash tubs or river bank were places where the women gathered, and the market often had its female sellers. Female servants moved around town delivering messages and doing errands. In Rome, by law, women were not to go about at night unless accompanied by a male relative; yet the police reports prove that they sometimes did venture out alone.[6] Village women, too, roamed widely, picking fruits and olives, fetching water, and carrying washing.

HOUSES AND PALACES AS SPACES

Houses varied hugely in structure, shape, and size. Since every region had its own architecture, general remarks are hard. Some distinctions matter here: urban versus rural, rich versus poor, old versus new. Urban houses were often suited to trades, rural ones to farming. The former often had shops, workshops, storage rooms, and an open front for street-side commerce, while the latter often housed livestock and stored tools and supplies. In some zones, country houses were solid and spacious, in others often mean and squalid. In walled villages and cities, houses less often built safe-guards against attack than did isolated farmsteads. As for wealth, the houses of the very rich in the Renaissance were proper palaces, with a sumptuous architecture that made dramatic use of space to delight and to impress. Those of the well-to-do shared some of the same features, especially the desire for convenience and comfort. The urban poor, meanwhile, very often, dwelled in a room or two alongside other households, or shared a bed and room, in a build-ing neither grand nor solid nor agreeable. Older buildings in the Renaissance, and they were many, still had medieval lineaments: military trim, tight windows set at random, a jumble of parts. Newer ones took on the traits of a rapidly evolving architecture that prized classical motifs, grandeur, symmetry, light, air, and comfort.

Whether grand or humble, Renaissance buildings had some com-mon spatial traits. An important one was the courtyard. Almost all palaces had at least one great central space and often several minor ones. One came in through an imposing central door, passed down a vaulted corridor, and entered a shapely interior yard, paved, and lined on most sides by columns and porticoes. The palace court-yard was a ceremonial space, embellished with works of art and the emblems of the patrons. An imposing staircase led to galleries one flight up. Simpler houses had humbler central spaces. They were utilitarian expanses, convenient and fairly secure. There might be a well and doors to storerooms; tradesmen arrived with donkeys to unload gear. Children played there under watchful eyes, safe from street traffic, and men and women of the several households in the building could meet and gossip. A second common spatial configuration was the loggia, an arcaded porch or balcony. In the Mediterranean, a covered place to take the air while sheltered from sun or rain made excellent sense. The colonnaded walks around courtyards met this need, as did the covered roadside passages of many cities. Some loggias were on the public street; palaces offered them magnanimously to passers-by or used them to hold banquets under the envious public gaze. As the Renaissance progressed, this last custom receded; the move to privacy and class segregation encouraged indoor loggias, facing the back garden. More modest houses might also have such galleries. On an upstairs loggia, women might mind children, hang laundry, comb flax, spin, embroider, dry their hair and let the sunshine blond it, observe the men's activities, or flirt from a discreet distance.

Whether grand or modest, houses used the ground floor less for living than for work and storage. Often, to ward off trouble, downstairs windows had great iron grills. Above this utilitarian level, there might be a modest mezzanine that housed the proprietors of the shops below. Next higher, in a palace, came the *piano nobile*, the "noble floor." There, a wealthy resident received honored guests, entertained, and lived; on higher floors slept the household's lesser members. Simpler dwellings were no grander on one floor than another. Although palaces invented variants, all houses had two basic rooms: the *sala* and the *camera*. The *sala*, the bigger, accommodated the more public gatherings, while the *camera* almost always served for sleeping. Nevertheless, our customary division—public "living room" and private "bedroom"—does not fit the Renaissance, where the distinction was far less sharp. People sometimes slept in the *sala* and entertained guests and transacted business on or by the bed, often in the *camera*. The *sala* was the room most likely to have a fireplace. In simpler homes lacking a kitchen, people often cooked there (Chapter 13).

The urban palace made assertive use of space. On the outside, the palace was not only big but symmetrical, harmonious, and ornamented with motifs from ancient architecture. It put a bold face to the street; owners sometimes bought up nearby houses, knocking them down to make a square out front, the better to overawe the neighborhood. The truly powerful might even gut several blocks, to lay a perpendicular street that terminated impressively at their front door, making it the focal point of a linear perspective. Although the ideal palace had an internal symmetry that delighted architects, many real palaces were in fact an internal jumble behind a deceptively regular facade. And they might shelter more modest families and assorted trades. Palaces, and houses too, often grew haphazardly, swallowing older dwellings and reusing their spaces and bearing walls. As families grew, they annexed neighbors or built upward. And, when brothers split an inherited building, they might partition it. Because walls were thick and sturdy, a wealthy family's city house might rise five or six stories. The Davanzati house in Florence, a wonderfully preserved fourteenth-century complex from the pre-palace era, now a museum, grew so tall that the tight central courtyard, with its steep stairs and hanging runways, feels like an ample light well. The spatial impact is dramatic; from the bottom, the whole household seems to loom overhead, while a high perch feels like a domestic overlook. It is an architecture of almost cloistered intimacy. Renaissance cities had many such relics of medieval architecture, now mostly vanished.

The urban palace differentiated internal domestic space. It had more shadings than the modest house. On the inside, it interposed between the very public *sala* and the master's bedroom a suite of rooms: perhaps a *saletta* for more intimate meals, and an *anticamera* (antechamber). Behind the bedroom were spaces even more private, including, very often, a *studio* for books, important papers, and art treasures. There were no corridors; guests passed from room to room, penetrating the deeper into private space the more the host wished to pay them honor or take them into confidence. The whole series of the master's rooms came in the Renaissance to be called an *appartamento*. Normally the lord's wife had one too, similar in layout. These big buildings also featured many specialized rooms for household activities.

CONCLUSION

Renaissance Italians had spatial experiences of many kinds, most of them quite distinct from ours. Their landscapes, villages, towns, and houses had characteristic shapes. Their space was thick with messages about identity, memory, status, power, and security. Italian habits of perceiving, occupying, and using spaces, as their arts inform us, were part of their larger civilization and culture.

NOTES

1. On urbanism, see Nicholas Adams and Laurie Nussdorfer, "The Italian City, 1400–1600," in *The Renaissance from Brunelleschi to Michelangelo: The Representation of Architecture*, ed. H. A. Millon and V. Lampagnani (New York, 1994), 205–30.

2. On the rural landscape, Emilio Sereni, *History of the Italian Agricultural Landscape* (Princeton, NJ, 1997).

3. On villas, David R. Coffin, *The Villa in the Life of Renaissance Rome* (Princeton, NJ, 1979); Ovidio Guaita, *Italian Villas* (New York, 2003).

4. These names come from Rocca Sinibalda, near Rieti: ASR, GTC, Processi, 16th c., busta 25, busta 34, and busta 35.

5. On the design and use of palaces, Richard Goldthwaite, *The Building of Renaissance Florence: An Economic and Social History* (Baltimore, 1980).

6. Elizabeth Cohen, "To Pray, To Work, To Hear, To Speak: Women in Roman Streets, c. 1600," *Journal of Early Modern History* 12:3–4 (2008), 289–311.

10

TIME

Time, as a frame of understanding, is so embedded and implicit in a culture's consciousness that outsiders cannot easily grasp its shape and habits. Nevertheless, as a concept, perceptual habit, and frame for memory, time has its own a history. For us, time is universal, uniform, and impersonal. With watches and phones that display not just hours and minutes, but seconds and their fractions, plus dates, we now know at any waking moment exactly what time it is. Furthermore, we expect others to work with our same time, to arrive at appointments or to know exactly how late they are. We expect classes and flights still months off to start on their scheduled minute. Furthermore, we rely on this capacity to measure time precisely to run complex, global organizations, to sustain communication networks, and to pursue maximum efficiency with no time "wasted." Renaissance time was less abstract and consistent, less closely measured. Time-telling was more shaped by sequence and human activity, but it worked.

Renaissance Italians understood time in three interconnecting forms: natural, sacred, and administrative. Natural time was cyclic, sacred both cyclic and linear, and administrative largely linear. Nature's time derived from the movements of heavenly bodies. Solar time governed day and night, and also the year. Lunar time marked the months. The rotation of the seasons from spring around to winter looked to the cosmos and to the weather. As for sacred time, God lived in eternity but instituted on earth a temporal flow from the Creation to the Apocalypse, punctuated midway by Christ's incarnation. Christians meanwhile arranged their lives cyclically according to daily rhythms of prayers, annual rotations of religious holidays, and every twenty-five years a Roman jubilee. The state's version of time, though newer, was a growing force. With its abstract dates on documents, this system recorded history's linear progression. Experientially, people lived all three patterns, their time as twisted strand.

With early modern Europeans, we share a basic structure, tracing back to the ancient world, of the calendar and its temporal units—years, months, days, hours, and minutes.[1] In the Renaissance, precision about dates began to appear in, for example, chanceries' administrative paperwork. And better technology for measuring and announcing time gradually reached more ears and eyes. Yet most everyday time-telling relied instead on flexible reference points—dawn, dusk, church bells, the midday meal—and on a sense of sequence. So, even testifying formally in court, an Italian would say "I'd been with my friends at the inn, and then we went to my courtesan's house and waited at her door, and then she came home and we went up and heard a lute-player."[2] When people did speak of units of time, they usually chose loose terms and hedged them: "It was circa the fourth hour of the night." Their handling of days and weeks was likewise vague: "I met her on the street a week ago last Tuesday, if I remember rightly" or "I got to know him before Lent just past."

Renaissance time also differed in its being not consistent and universal—the same for everyone—but particular to places and persons. Every city and village had its own time of day, linked to the sunrise and sunset right there. The communal bells rang with their particular timing, frequency, and pattern. The peal could mark collective identity; by ringing its own time a town asserted itself. The cultural packaging of time also depended on ways of life. Peasants, merchants, artisans, notaries, and nuns understood time differently. Some groups followed the earth's natural temporal rhythms, while others needed more precise, artificial time-keeping, marked and enforced by human authorities.

Now, beginning with the smallest units and proceeding upward through the scale, let us trace in more detail the many ways that concepts of time shaped Renaissance lives.

MINUTES AND HOURS

The ancient Babylonians devised the minute, but premodern Italians made scant use of that invention. Although Renaissance scientists, in theoretical discussions, wrote of minutes, and even seconds, in daily life these units had no place. Medieval clocks told the hours, but through the fifteenth century we have little evidence that a clock recorded minutes. Though sandglasses could measure time's smaller steps, people rarely felt the need. When referring to brief stretches of time, they spoke of fractions of hours, halves or, less often, quarters. For short intervals, phrasing often drew on religious vocabulary, measuring duration with common prayers: the Paternoster, the Ave Maria, and the Credo. These measures from the sacred realm could describe both natural phenomena and government work. So, in 1456, a Florentine in Naples, gauging an earthquake precisely, wrote home that it "lasted the duration it would take to say a Miserere quite slowly and more specifically one and a half times." No less committed to exactitude, notaries for the criminal courts in Rome also used the Miserere psalm to measure and record a round of torture.

The Renaissance found the hour, unlike the minute, useful; it distinguished the parts of day and night. The term, however, had many senses, dependent on the circumstances of its use. Ancient Rome bequeathed to medieval Europe one system for dividing daylight. Romans numbered twelve hours of notionally equal length, stressing groupings of three. Thus, Prime (first), Terce (third), Sext (sixth), and None (ninth) hours divided up the day. The sun's place in the sky was a key: the First Hour followed sunrise, the Sixth Hour came at midday, and the Twelfth Hour sat at sunset. Monasticism preserved this system, because central to their rule was a daily seven-part cycle of prayers, known as "hours" and named, in part, Prime, Terce, Sext, and None. Yet this monkish "hour" was conceptual, not technical. It denoted neither a measured length of time nor a precise moment in the sun's passage. Rather, it was a step in a round of bells and prayers. Over the centuries, the timing of the monastic day shifted to fit the seasons and institutional convenience. Thus, houses varied in singing Sext; some chanted just before the sun reached its height, others an hour and a half earlier. And the None—the Ninth Hour—drifted from mid-afternoon toward midday and gave us our word *noon*.

Traditional technologies for tracking hours involved observing the movements of celestial bodies, and measuring shadows on a sundial, or they noted the duration of sand falling in a glass. Between the easily fixed points of sunrise and sunset, it was hard to measure consistent hours. First, the day's length shifted with the seasons, so that, as one-twelfth of the day, an hour stretched or shrank. Second, the sun itself was an unreliable gauge. How many degrees of angle actually marked an hour? And what if the sun was out of sight or the horizon was hilly? With practice and the right conditions—in good weather, at sea, or on land with sky-view clear—a fair estimate of the hour should have been easy. But often—at night, or with cloudy sky—time-telling was guesswork. While, properly positioned and read, a sundial could give greater accuracy, such devices mostly belonged to institutions or the elite. Knowing the hour was for specialists. For most, it was neither easy nor needed.

During the Middle Ages, clearer meanings for the "hour" did begin to reach more people. As urban governments adapted the monastic sounded hours to secular uses, church bells came to mark administrative time. To serve new uses, the ringing patterns became more elaborate. Markets opened and closed with bells. For workers, they announced the start and end of work, and even breaks and meals. For civic officials, bells called court sessions and council meetings. In fourteenth-century Venice, the four bells of San Marco rang daily in distinctive combinations at twelve irregular intervals. Six signals involved long tollings lasting a quarter or a half an hour, for a clangor of two to three hours per day. Add to these the calls to Mass, peals for special events and celebrations, and tolling for deaths, plus the bells from all the other city's churches. This proliferation of bongs and clanks threatened cacophony and confusion.

A remedy came in a novel instrument: the public mechanical clock, which from the mid-fourteenth century spread through northern and central Italy. The pendulum, tripping a clock's escapement wheel, brought new precision. With its consistent, countable motions, the machinery could assign the hour a fixed duration and strike the hours clearly and efficiently. As an emblem of civic pride, ambitious communes installed a clock in the tower of the city hall. But the spread of these novelties was slow. Where they were in place, the complicated church bell codes gradually gave way. In Rome in the fifteenth century, a simplified round of two bells at dusk and dawn, both called the *Ave Maria* (or, in English, the Angelus), marked the day's end points. In 1456, Pope Calixtus III mandated a third bell, at midday, to signal a prayer to ward off the Ottomans.

During the Renaissance, especially in cities, clocks fostered the measured hour. But that fit awkwardly into the old day made of two stretchy sets of twelve hours—one for the darkness, the other for the light. Both forms persisted in parallel use. For Italy, the count started with sundown, followed by the first hour of the night, and so on. Clocks were expensive to install and maintain. They needed frequent adjustment to absorb the day's fluctuating duration. Nevertheless, civic authorities and employers installed clocks to tighten discipline. Large workplaces, such as the Venetian Arsenal or palace construction sites, regulated labor with their own clocks. It became normal to expect city dwellers to know the hour and to comply with ordinances that heeded it. Similarly, siege commanders issued ultimatums demanding response by a specific hour. Still, only a few people had means of precise timekeeping at home or in their neighborhood, and for most everyday purposes the looser forms continued to serve.

DAYS, WEEKS, AND MONTHS

The Renaissance day could be long. Although people moved about and worked mostly during the hours of light, they might extend the day at either end. Some, including women, rose before dawn to prepare for work or to attend early Mass. Many stayed up after dark, to socialize, to work, to patrol their fields, or to go raiding. Although loosely divided into roughly equal segments, *mattina* (morning) and *sera* (evening), the day's organization adapted to activities afoot. Meals came at the end of each division, but not at set times. *Pranzo* (dinner) was a serious meal sometime around midday, and *cena* (supper) typically came soon after dark.

The week of seven days went back to ancient times, and the Italian names of the days were mostly from Roman gods: Mars, Mercury, Jove, Venus. Yet in Renaissance the week's rhythms owed much to Christianity. Wednesdays and Fridays, for example, were especially penitential, and the scrupulous might abstain then from meat and sex. Renaissance folk distinguished holy days from ordinary days, but they knew no "weekend." Sunday, *Domenica* or the Lord's Day, was for God, although cities offered many occasions for liturgy on other days as well. Before, after, or instead of church, Sunday was also time for sociability. Moral reformers repeatedly denounced the open taverns and weekly ball games that competed with worship. Even for the pious, Sunday was no day of universal rest. Montaigne noted that many Italians, even officials, worked on Sunday, and court testimony bears him out.

Renaissance Italians continued to use the Roman calendar, part lunar, part solar, that divided the year into twelve months. These bore the ancient names that we still use. Yet the Roman practice of counting days in the month from both the Kalends (first day) and Ides (thirteenth or fifteenth day) was cumbersome, so the Renaissance just numbered them consecutively, as we do. A month-by-month rotation of agricultural activities was a favorite theme in art. In frescos, tapestries, and illuminated prayer books, we see pruning in February, planting in March, harvesting grapes in September, and butchering pigs in November or December.[3] Similarly, cut into the stone floor of Siena's cathedral was another annual cycle of twelve, the signs of the zodiac. For these, learned culture drew on the classical Greek representations of planetary movements against the backdrop of stars. By arcane readings of celestial bodies astrologers sought auspicious days to undertake a war or a wedding, or calendrical explanations for puzzling past and present events. Astral calculus sometimes trickled into sermons and popular texts to foretell earthquakes or other calamities that bespoke God's wrath. Reactions to these prognostications were mixed; they could sow fear or be met with laughter, especially when dire claims failed.

As careful dating of events and their documentary record gained importance, the system based on the solar calendar using day, month, and year served well. It was handier than using saints' days for tracking duration and missed deadlines. Debts came due on specific dates, and interest payments and penalties counted the days past due. Birth dates governed eligibility for government office, and times of death could govern a property's distribution. Governments measured officials' terms, with their swift, precise rotation. Still, vagaries of location vexed dating. In particular, Italian cities started their year on different days. While Rome's New Year's fell on January 1, it came in Venice on March 1 and in Florence on March 25, the Feast of the Annunciation. Consequently, on legal paper, Rome's January 26,1491, was Florence's January 26,1490. Furthermore, after fifteen centuries of too much Leap Year, the real movements of the sun and the nominal solar dates had parted company. By the sixteenth century, the equinox fell around the eleventh of March instead of the twenty-first. To haul things back into line, lest spring begin too soon, Pope Gregory XIII in 1582 decreed calendrical reform and suppressed ten days. His improved "Gregorian" calendar is still in use today.

YEARS

The year measured fundamental cycles in both natural and sacred time that together strongly shaped Renaissance experience. Mediterranean patterns of temperature and rainfall governed the agricultural rhythm and the movement of workers and herds up and down the landscape. The winter, chilly and punctuated by rains, or by snow in the mountains, was a fairly quiet season for people on the land, a time to mend gear and practice home industry, to migrate to the lowlands for work, or just to rest. Then came spring, temperate and well watered. Peasants kept busy, pruning vines and orchards before buds opened, then hoeing, plowing, and planting summer crops. After lambing, shepherds drove their flocks from lowland winter pastures into the hills and began to make cheese. As summer arrived, bringing Mediterranean heat and dryness, farmers reaped last winter's grain and made hay. In fall, as the temperature moderated, came another round of harvesting, as well as processing grapes and olives and gathering chestnuts. Before the heavy rains of late autumn, peasants planted the winter grain crop, and herdsmen brought the flocks back down. The great diversity of Italian landscape and crops could shift the weight and timing of these moments, but some such seasonal pattern set the rhythm for most Renaissance lives.

These rotations of agricultural tasks intertwined with religious holidays. The prehistoric observance of the sun's annual cycle was grafted onto major Christian celebrations, with Christmas marking the winter solstice, Easter tracking the spring equinox, and John the Baptist's day falling at midsummer. Similarly, fertility ceremonies clustered at the Ascension, in late spring; processions went into the fields to bless the crops. At Venice, instead, a bishop blessed the Adriatic while the doge, for the city, ritually married the sea, the source of wealth. Particular saints' days marked out the agricultural regime. For the shepherds and wool merchants in Apulia, the year's two great transitions—when the flocks left the lowlands for summer pastures and when they descended— were linked to Saint Michael feasts (May 8 and September 29). The warrior archangel, believed to have perched on looming Mount Gargano, was a mighty local patron. In early May, devotees made pilgrimages to his seaside mountain shrine, and to a lowland sanctuary harboring the Virgin of the Sacred Wood of the Incoronata. The herds' spring movements and these observances coincided with big wool fairs at Foggia, when merchants bought and sold the year's fleeces and paid the government for winter pasturage.[4]

Yet, because the seasons varied from year to year, nature's timing and religion's did not always align as expected. Furthermore, the church calendar had its own uncertainties, as some feasts fell on dates pinned to the solar schedule and others shifted against them with the movements of the moon. Occasional upsets of what felt normal could breed anxiety. When, in 1383, as rarely happened, the lunar holiday Easter occurred before the fixed solar Feast of the Annunciation (March 25), the Florentine notary Naddo da Monte-catini urged his readers to beware "that great novelties ought to be in the world from which God in his pity guard us."[5]

The Christian year was a crammed roster of holidays. Only monks and nuns observed all the many lesser ones, but major religious holidays punctuated the year for all Renaissance Italians and gave them reference points in time. This cycle reenacted over the year's course the redeeming history of Jesus and, secondarily, the life of the Virgin Mary. The religious year included two major sequences of observances, Christmas and Easter, the first fixed by the solar calendar and second shifting with the moon. Other holidays followed Easter's timing: Ascension Day, commemorating Christ's rising into heaven, came forty days after and Pentecost, fifty days after. Also timed by Easter, since the thirteenth century, a very popular, often elaborate celebration dedicated to the Corpus Christi, the body of Christ made visible as the Eucharistic host, followed in June. Interspersed through the year with these Christ-focused occasions were three important solar holidays honoring the Virgin Mary: February 2 marked her Purification after the birth of Jesus, March 25 recalled the angel's Annunciation of her divine pregnancy, and August 15 celebrated her bodily Assumption into heaven.

Though distinctly lesser than Easter, Christmas, a joyful observance of the birth of Jesus, was a principal religious feast. Its cycle began with four weeks of Advent, a penitential season for the pious to pray, fast, and shun sex. At its end, on December 24, the vigil of the Nativity, people customarily went to church at night. In Rome, where unaccompanied women were not allowed to circulate after dark, zealous police sometimes arrested lone churchgoers. Also, as witnessed by the traveler Montaigne, on Christmas Day, the pope, assisted by several cardinals, celebrated a very solemn Mass at Saint Peter's basilica. Another pageant, attributed first to the medieval Saint Francis of Assisi, was the display of the manger scene with a doll as the holy infant; such a crèche was recorded in a Florentine friars' church in 1498. On Christmas's twelfth and final day, January 6, Epiphany marked the embassy of the biblical three kings. In Florence, again, from the late fourteenth century, the Company of the Magi staged mounted processions and enacted the tale of the royal visitors to Herod. Like other religious festivals, Christmas involved shared offerings of food, but other gift-giving was modest, such as coins dispensed by lords to their dependents.

Easter, a lunar, movable feast in March or April, anchored the year's longest and most important celebratory cycle. The season started with a bang: Carnival, several weeks of license that figured vividly in the popular temporal imagination. Beginning soon after the twelve days of Christmas—in Venice, even overlapping them— Carnival echoed the ancient Roman year-end Saturnalia. It was a time for parties, masquerades, comedies, athletic contests, music, street dances, general high jinx, and bloody mayhem. Social license allowed ranks and genders to mix, leading to deflorations, forbidden sexual encounters, and violence. Cruel spectacles attracted crowds. In Rome, stigmatized Jews and prostitutes raced down the long, straight Corso. In Venice, where Carnival was already famous, people thronged on Fat Thursday to watch a gory ritual where a bull and twelve pigs were formally condemned to death, chased around the piazza at the doge's palace, decapitated, and dismembered. Afterward, presiding dignitaries shared out the meat. Festivities accelerated toward Fat Tuesday (*Martedi Grasso*), and then, on Ash Wednesday, activity veered abruptly to renunciation and penance.

After Carnival came its inversion, Lent, a period of Forty Days (*Quadragesima*) to prepare for the highest holiday, Easter. People were asked to try harder than usual to purify the spirit by denying the flesh: abstaining from eating meat altogether rather than just on weekly fast days; restricting play and sex; hearing sermons and doing penances. While observance no doubt varied, declines in births nine months after Lent and Advent suggest some more sexual continence during these penitential seasons. The run-up to Easter, and especially the Holy Week just before, was the peak of the religious year. Processions, rituals, and passion plays retold the story of Jesus's sacrifice and resurrection. On Holy Thursday, the pope, nobles, and their ladies imitated Christ's charity and humility by washing paupers' feet. Good Friday recalled Jesus's crucifixion and liturgy reenacted his death and burial. On this bitter and sorrowful day, emotions ran high, and even blood flowed. Confraternities of flagellants so harshly beat their bodies that bishops, especially in the South, repeatedly banned their self-mortifications.

Rome's passion play staged in the Colosseum moved its audience to attack the Jews, so in 1539 it was abolished. Churches on Easter Sunday itself celebrated the resurrection, light and joy contrasting with the dark pain of the days just past. During the Renaissance, most Catholics seldom confessed and took communion. As reiterated in the decrees of the Council of Trent, Easter was the moment to perform the minimal duty of an annual communion. By the late sixteenth century, priests had to compile a census of parishioners and then record those who did or did not do their Easter duty.

Besides these elaborate cycles of Christ-focused holidays, the religious calendar recognized a crowded pantheon of saints. Communities of many sorts and sizes—villages, cities, guilds, confraternities, and families—had particular holy patrons who were honored with festivities on their saints' days. These occasions often blended broad Christian and more local meanings. Boons received, threats averted, military victories or miraculous apparitions were often tied to the religious calendar for veneration and thanksgiving. Thus, the feasts of Saint Mark in Venice (April 25), Saint John the Baptist in Florence (June 24), Saint Gennaro in Naples (September 19), and Saint Nicholas in Bari (December 6) were both religious holidays and times for civic identity and pride.

HISTORY AND TIME'S END

Although the cycles of days, months, and years dominated most of their experience of time, Renaissance Italians sometimes also placed themselves in long-term, linear courses of history. The Christian eschatological vision set a principal model. Looking backward, Renaissance culture framed its epoch as beginning with the birth of Jesus, before which Old Testament time counted generations back to Creation. Looking forward, all anticipated history's ending in an apocalypse that would usher in the Second Coming of Christ and the Last Judgment. No one knew when this end would come, but, even with no millennium on the calendar, a few prophets and their followers believed it might be nigh. On a less godly or cosmic plane, writers began to scan an earthly past with largely human import. From the Middle Ages chroniclers recorded notable events, year by year. In the Renaissance, histories acquired a new dimension, as scholars and statesmen began to assign meanings, logical connections, and narrative line to events' sequence, all less tethered to heaven's frame. To insert firm rungs on history's long ladder, lining up and conjoining distant events, some sacred, others secular, took hard intellectual work. For many ordinary folk, however, the past probably seemed less an unbroken line than a clutter of isolated noteworthy moments: hardships, losses, anomalies, occasionally a victory or heroic feat. As reminder or as heirloom, things from the past that cast glory were treasured. Yet, the record of the past was very malleable, readily reshaped to serve present needs. (See Chapter 8.) Major events in living memory could serve as temporal markers. Someone might tie a lesser happening to a greater, as before or after the big flood or fire or when the soldiers marched off to war. Speaking of the more distant past, however, most Italians would re-create stories but seldom evoke periods, let alone precise years or centuries.

NOTES

1. On time-keeping, Gerhard Dohrn-Van Rossum, *History of the Hour: Clocks and Modern Temporal Orders* (Chicago, 1996), and, on calendars and ritual, Muir, *Ritual in Early Modern Europe*, 55–80.

2. ASR, GTC, Processi, 16th c., busta 103, f. 897 and following.

3. For example, the large Trivulzio tapestries in the Castello Sforzesco museum in Milan.

4. John Marino, *Pastoral Economics in the Kingdom of Naples* (Baltimore, 1988), 40–44.

5. Quoted in Richard Trexler, *Public Life in Renaissance Florence* (New York, 1980), 81.

11

LIFE CYCLES: FROM BIRTH THROUGH YOUTH

LIFE STAGES AND LIFE EXPECTANCY

Renaissance Europeans, following ancient and medieval models, imagined human life as a series of stages. The "ages of man," appeared, for example, in illustrations in early printed books that showed the life span divided into three or seven or more phases. Although the number of steps varied, this imagery always represented human life as a neat staircase of waxing and waning capacities. The simplest models distinguished only childhood, maturity, and old age; the longer sequences broke the ascending and descending slopes. Some writers ascribed conventional ages, typically at rough multiples of seven years. The fifteenth-century Florentine Matteo Palmieri, in a treatise on the good conduct of civic life, used a well-known version with six stages. While his age markers did highlight abilities gained or lost, Palmieri hewed only partially to the count by sevens. Following birth, first came infancy, which, etymologically, means "without speech." Of course, babies learned to talk long before the stage's end at seven. Childhood, the second step, lasted until the youngster, supposedly around age fourteen, achieved "discretion," by word-sense, the capacity to "discern" good from bad and make sound decisions. Next, youth extended from the mid-teens to age twenty-eight, two sevens later. Only in the next "age," virility ("man-ly-ness" in Latin), did a man attain full powers, which he would enjoy for a full four sevens, to fifty-six. Thereafter, decline set in, though gradually in first old age until seventy, and then collapse—decrepitude. With this vision of the life cycle, we, like Renaissance writers, mention only men. A women's pattern was occasionally represented; there standard practice, as in thought's other spheres, showed females as mere mirrors of males.[1]

This traditional imagining of a long life cycle glossed over harsh realities. After the Black Death, life expectancy fell sharply and long stayed low. At some points it dipped below twenty years, though after 1450 it crept back to forty. Stillbirths and infant deaths were rife; they brought the statistics down. Even if one survived the early culling, by the age of thirty-five, death already seemed plausible. Consequently, Renaissance Italy had a young population of whom many had lost parents, struck down early. Nevertheless, some people did reach ripe seventy, eighty, or more. A cohort of elders did live long enough to tread the tidily symmetrical stages of the "ages of man" imagery.[2]

Although the intellectuals' neat schemes about life's cycle failed in face of the Grim Reaper's furious haste, Renaissance Italians still expected life to trace a pattern. Several of Christianity's seven sacraments set major rites of passage that marked life stages. Baptism signaled birth, and extreme unction sealed death. Between them, marriage was a turning point most survivors experienced, although the church's direct role there grew central only late. Other less resonant moments, some ritualized and others not, punctuated maturation. Some men passed through entry ceremonies such as the ordaining of priests, the dubbing of knights, or the reception of masters into guilds. But even where ceremonies were absent, the physiological and social lives of men and women had general stages we can trace.

Ideas About Childhood

To discern Renaissance childhood, we peer through a distorting lens. First, we easily project onto the past our modern, charged pre-conceptions concerning children. Second, our historical evidence is uneven: as usual, most comes from elites, from Florence especially. For the bulk of the population in other classes or places, we must build on inference. Also, the sources are often prescriptive rather than descriptive. In treatises and manuals, privileged authorities—moralists and medical practitioners—advised and admonished parents and teachers on how to rear the young. Did their normative words represent accepted wisdom and reflect what many people actually did? Or did these instructions aim to correct faulty care-giving, because common practice did the preachment's opposite? How do we interpret the experts' frequent contradictions? With too few descriptive documents to test the written precepts, we easily misjudge how Renaissance society treated its children.

Wrestling with these conceptual and documentary constraints, historians of childhood have debated whether, due to their society's attitudes and behavior, premodern European youngsters suffered. In the 1970s, the French historian Philippe Ariès reshaped the field by arguing that before the seventeenth century childhood had no distinct identity or place, as children were treated as small adults. Citing this presumed conceptual vacuum, plus fragmentary data, some scholars conjured up widespread neglect and abuse. Studies have highlighted as harmful premodern parental feelings and practices that violated more recent child-centered dogmas. Against this rather bleak picture, other historians softened the assessment, challenging Ariès's hypothesis about miniature adults and mustering evidence of parental concern, love, delight, and grief. On balance, it is best to eschew sweeping judgments and see Renaissance childhood as a mix of difficult and happy experiences. The early modern circumstances that shaped the fates of premodern children and the challenges facing their caretakers were different from today's. The past had both stresses and good efforts, and the results, as now, varied. Here we survey the practices and circumstances that shaped the lives of Renaissance youngsters, in struggle and in contentment.

COMING INTO THE WORLD

Birth

In the Renaissance a new baby's arrival was both welcomed and feared. There was little control over whether, when, or how many babies came. Children were the natural consequence of marriage and the fulfillment of the biblical injunction to multiply. They were also the family's future, often the foundation of its continuing economic and social well-being; to the poor, they were also more mouths to feed. Parents greeted new children with acceptance and often warmth and praise to God. At the same time, birth was a focus of anxiety and stress. The delivery was dangerous for both mother and baby, and death lurked nearby. Unlike modern parents, Renaissance ones could never count on a happy outcome.

While families embraced the arrival of both boys and girls, males were especially welcome. High-ranking couples marked firstborn sons with special parties. A ruling dynasty, when an heir was born, funded rejoicing throughout its domain. The fragile infant embodied an elite family's surviving lineage name and promised its economic and political security. A daughter or two, whose marriages would build alliances, were a boon, but also a worry and a burden. Their precarious chastity risked the family honor, and their dowries depleted its fortune. Surplus daughters seemed expensive. While one Florentine father professed equal pleasure with girls and boys, another, upon the birth of a friend's daughter, sent joking condolences. Responding to the desire for sons, advisers on family life taught how to conceive a boy. Humor theory associated masculinity with warmth. Since the right side of the body was deemed warmer, organizing sex crossways, lodging seed from the right testicle on the womb's right side, helped. So too might warming herbal treatments or the mother's consumption of malmsey wine. One writer recommended intercourse in a virile setting, perfumed with musk and bedecked with paintings of valorous men.

Typically, Italians entered the world in the family home. One or several women attended the delivering mother, including, if possible, an experienced midwife. She knew a repertoire of moves to steer the baby along its course and, in dire necessity, to try to extract it by force; to ease the labor, she might also deploy herbal teas, potions, and salves of her own making. Yet her skills were limited. She offered neither the relative security nor the intrusiveness of modern obstetrical medicine. Healthy newborns underwent the stresses natural to the process but escaped such prophylactic interventions as eye-drops or, for boys, circumcision. Difficult deliveries often endangered mothers and damaged babies, many of whom were disabled or died. Once born, the baby was washed, wrapped tight, and placed in the bed with the mother or in a cradle.[3]

Baptism

Baptism, the ceremonial acknowledgment of the new arrival, gave it a social identity and a Christian soul. Normally the baby was carried by the midwife and accompanied by a few friends and neighbors to the church or baptistery. Baptism was what anthropologists call a rite of passage, in which a person moves from one life stage into another through a sequence of ceremonial steps: first, separation from the past, then an intermediary limbo, and finally incorporation into a new social state. Thus, baptism began in front of the building, where a priest exorcised the child, banishing the evil spirits into whose reach, as a descendant of Adam, it had been born. The party then moved the newcomer, now in limbo, without sin but still without identity, into the sacred space. Immersed or sprinkled at the baptismal font, the baby received a name and acceptance into the Christian community, membership necessary for salvation. Because the child's soul was in peril, baptism had best come within a day or two of birth. If the newborn seemed unlikely to survive so long, the church authorized fathers or, more often, midwives to perform emergency baptism at the bedside. Indeed, they were to christen even a protruding arm or leg when they feared that the baby would not emerge alive.

At baptism, godparents, not parents, were central. Although the father could attend, the mother could not. She was still recovering from childbirth, which, also, rendered her unclean; by custom she was not to enter a sacred precinct until some forty days after, when a churching ceremony purified her. For godparents, each baby had from outside the family at least one man and one woman who undertook to steer their charge into a righteous life. Receiving the child from the hands of the priest, they incorporated it into the community. Godparents might serve their ceremonial offspring as patrons in worldly life as well. Parents chose them with a careful eye to connections useful both to the child and to the whole family. Therefore, ambitious families might give their children several sponsors at the font. Prestigious godparents were expected to bestow honorific gifts. A rich Florentine merchant wrote that two large cakes, boxes of spiced cookies, and handfuls of candles and small torches were customary godparental contributions to the party that followed the rite. Often, however, not only modest folk, but also the affluent, sought godparents among ordinary neighbors or friends. Inviting a social inferior, even a pauper, to serve not only bolstered local alliances but also reenacted the humility and charity that Jesus had modeled.[4]

Naming

Along with a collective identity as a Christian and community member, baptism gave the baby an individual identity marked by a name. Elite fathers wrote of choosing what to call their progeny, but mothers must sometimes have helped pick. Certainly, when, as often, at the time of birth the father was away, the mother or even the midwife or priest might give the name. Most children carried a single tag, but some received two. Some double-barreled pairs, like Giovanni Battista or Pietropaolo, were customary. But ease of use encouraged shorter names. Parents who gave two names at baptism chose one for everyday use. Convenience compacted nicknames too. Giovanni Battista easily shrank to Titta, Tommaso to Maso, and Elisabetta to Betta. To distinguish people, a second playful practice re-lengthened these contractions with evocative endings. Thus, Florentines called two fine painters Masolino—little Tom—and Masaccio—bad Tom, and a Betta might become Bettuccia—cute, little Betty. Baptismal names were just the first step in a naming process that shaped and tracked a child's identity.

The name received at baptism could come from several sources. The repertoire of names was regional. Local saints, heroes, and rulers furnished models, as did family traditions. Infants were named after ancestors and kin, especially those not long dead, including lost siblings; fathers then spoke of "remaking" a lineage member. Unusual names often came from local traditions. Another colorful tag invoked blessings or good fortune: the given name of the goldsmith Cellini, Benvenuto, meant "welcome." Naming practices also followed policy and fashion. By the fifteenth century, the name pool had shrunken. In Tuscany, for example, nearly half the male population bore one of only some fifteen names. Most honored prominent saints, including Antonio, Francesco, Giovanni, and Bartolomeo. Similarly, many women bore female versions of these same names, but the favorite was Caterina, after the Sienese mystic. Birth around the saint's feast day might set the choice, or a parent's special devotion, or even a vow in hope of safe delivery. But other kinds of names circulated. In Florence, despite the new interest in Roman and Greek classics, classical appellations were few. In sixteenth-century Rome, the ancient names flourished: Pompeo, Bruto, Marco Antonio, or Giulio Cesare, and, among women, Lucrezia, Camilla, Portia, or Livia.

Identifying people by a precise birth date and stable formal name only gradually became common practice. By medieval custom that continued into the Renaissance, names were various and fluid, and, in life, a person might be known by several. By the fifteenth century, however, church and government alike sought to stabilize names for recordkeeping and, from the mid-sixteenth, enjoined parish priests to register systematically all the baptisms, marriages, and deaths they oversaw. Yet most men and women had little use for these official records. They knew their names but did not count their years or celebrate their birthdays. If anything, they observed the day of their patron saint. For a long time, the richest personal records were not public, but private, kept by the same literate merchants on whose diaries historians have so depended.

Bringing Children into the World: An Example

In his business ledger, the international merchant Gregorio Dati (Chapter 2) recorded the births and names, and often the deaths of his twenty-six children by four wives and one slave. Bandecca, his first "beloved wife," died of a miscarriage in their second year of marriage. Dati's first child, borne him the next year in Spain by his Tartar slave, was a son, whom he brought to Italy and raised at home. His second wife, Betta, delivered eight children between 1394 and 1402. Their first daughter Dati called Bandecca in memory of his deceased spouse, a naming custom observed by other fathers too. The next born, his first legitimate son, the merchant named Stagio, after his own father. Alas, four years later,

> Our Lord God pleased to take to himself the fruits which He had lent us, and he took . . . our most beloved, Stagio, our darling and blessed first born [son]. He died of the plague on the morning of Friday, 30 July 1400, in Florence without my seeing him for I was in the country. . . . May God bless him and grant that he pray for us.

The next year, God "lent" the couple a seventh child, a son again called Stagio, adding as a hopeful second name Benedetto, meaning "blessed." But shortly "Divine Providence was pleased to take him back and for this too may he be praised and thanked."

Of Betta's last child Dati recorded:

> On 5 July 1402, before the hour of terce, Betta gave birth to our eighth child. We had him baptized straight after terce in the love of God. His godparents were Nardo and blind Margherita, and we called him Piero Antonio because of Betta's special devotion to Sant' Antonio. God bless him and grant that he become a good man.[5]

This son survived to adolescence, but his mother died shortly after his birth.

INFANCY

Renaissance Italian portrayals of infancy reflected the same ambivalence that birth evoked. On the one hand, delighted love for young children shines in so many religious paintings. Increasingly naturalistic portraits of the infant Jesus, tenderly held and gazed on by a Madonna and sometimes handed toys by a boyish playmate, John the Baptist, graced hundreds of churches and private chapels. Artists attuned to the market, reflecting a warm and hopeful appreciation of idealized youngsters, filled acres of painted background with chubby putti and sweet child-angels. On the other hand, as with Dati, there were the unrelenting losses to mishap and disease. A quarter died in life's first year, and another quarter or more before maturity. Modern historians, weighing the impact on parents of such losses, have imputed stolid resignation or callous numbness. The most bearable way to cope, they suggest, would be not to invest until sure an infant would survive a while. Demographers have discovered that censuses undercounted babies; it might fit such an attitude. Dati's rhetoric—"God gives and God takes away"—could testify to indifference, or it might enjoin grief's solace in religious consolation. Certainly, numerous anecdotes show fathers and mothers emotionally engaged with youngsters: tending their needs, worrying over their illnesses, happily watching them play. Taken together, the various sources from Renaissance Italy show us a society that cared about its children and, trying to bring them to adulthood, battled many obstacles.

Infants belonged in the domain of women. Mothering was, however, just one of women's many responsibilities, and seldom the most crucial for the family's well-being. Although tasks varied between city and country, and up and down the social scale, few mothers had the luxury to dedicate much time to childcare. Consequently, infants and children had to share limited attention with siblings and maternal distractions, and also found it with other people. Their care routinely fell into the hands of other women—wet nurses, servants, older sisters, or grandmothers.

The customs and techniques of handling the very young passed by word and example from woman to woman and from one generation to the next. During the Renaissance, however, male experts also began to pronounce on pregnancy, infant care, and raising families. Though sermons might be in Italian, much of this literature remained in Latin. Even when, from the late fifteenth century, printing brought these texts into wider circulation, only educated men—and a very few women—could read them. The one guide in the vernacular, by Michele Savonarola, addressed to the women of Ferrara, remained in manuscript, probably known to a mere handful of its intended audience. These books thus were remote from what women actually did but do hint at what learned contemporaries thought they should be doing.

Mother's Milk

The central and most worrisome part of infant care was feeding.[6] All babies, with a few bereft exceptions, were fed at the breast. While the doctors warned against overfeeding, the commoner problem was lack of breast milk. Because a woman's supply might fail, emergencies cropped up; backup had to be found quickly. If no wet nurse was available, informal sharing by nursing women was the best solution. One offered the breast to another's baby, hoping that another time someone would do the same for her. Analogous to this Christian gesture, the classical allegory of "Roman charity" appeared in paintings as a woman offering her breast to her father, left to starve to death in jail.

When no woman with milk stepped in, infants were no doubt offered risky alternatives. The experts expressed grave distrust of other foods, and with reason. Animal milk, where available, was unsafe; other liquids, such as almond water, or solid foods, such as boiled wheat porridge, did not provide what the baby needed and often troubled its digestion. Such food, people thought, might even addle the child's mind. A mid-fourteenth-century author, Pietro da Certaldo, cautioned against giving "the baby the milk of a goat or sheep or ass or some other animal because the child, boy or girl, nourished on animal milk doesn't have perfect wits like one fed on women's milk, but always looks stupid and vacant and not right in the head."[7] Many of those fed substitutes died, but not all. The biographer Giorgio Vasari wrote of one artist who, as a two-month-old, after the plague killed his mother, was suckled by a goat.

Procuring not only enough milk but also "good" milk posed a challenge. Male authorities urged mothers, for moral as well as medical reasons, to nurse their own children. To the mind of these educated men, milk was a powerful fluid, concocted of the woman's blood that, like it, bore the imprint of her body and soul. Therefore, milk gave the infant not only physical benefits but also psychological ones. A nurse's character and social attributes flowed to the nursling. And what traits better suited babies than the heritage of their parents? Nevertheless, mothers sometimes found breast-feeding hard. Besides weakness after pregnancy and delivery, there were assorted impediments for which physicians' books suggested remedies. For example, one 1577 text showed a woman using a breast pump, a bulb with a long tube, probably glass, to suck out painful excess milk. For others it was hard to produce enough. Some mothers could not nurse; others for social and economic reasons chose not to. Among the well-born, wet nursing, not maternal feeding, was usual practice. The reasons, according to indignant commentators, were inconvenience and selfishness: women's vanity and husbands' chafing at the taboo on sex while nursing. Forgoing lactation's contraceptive effect also fostered pregnancies and the big families that fortified a lineage. But not only the nobility withheld mother's milk from babies. Especially in the city, middling sorts frequently imitated the patricians, as did even some artisans, who held their wives' other work too valuable to sacrifice. Babies whose mothers could or would not feed them came into the arms of paid wet nurses. Would their milk be "good" enough?

Wet Nursing

The difficulties of finding and keeping a suitable wet nurse, or *balia*, preoccupied both parents and medical experts. While women handled most infants' needs, the selection and payment of wet nurses was one responsibility in which fathers took part. Wet nurses were typically lower-status women who needed income. Their socially superior employers harbored chronic doubts about the health and moral character of these women on whose milk their infants would depend for their lives and even their personalities. Parenting guides offered detailed counsel on how to choose. Savonarola recommended a woman in her thirties, sturdy but not fat, with skin unblemished and milk a good white, not pale and watery. If she had last born a boy, her milk would be warmer and purer. She should be good tempered, not melancholic. Unless a widow, she must have a husband willing, for income's sake, to sacrifice his marital rights, for pregnancy spoiled good milk. Evidently, such a paragon was about as likely, Savonarola joked, as a white crow.

Wet nurses' acceptance of paid employment often placed them in uneasy binds. The *balia* had to have milk; that is, she had to have recently given birth or been nursing a child. Furthermore, a commercial wet nurse promised exclusive access to her client. That

meant either that her own baby had just died or been weaned, or
that she had to sacrifice it, abandoning her infant as a foundling or
shunting it to an inferior while she took a paying customer. Paradoxically, foundling hospitals were themselves a major employer
of wet nurses. Hard choices, which seemed necessary to the wet
nurse or her husband, amplified the client's suspicions of her character. With a keen eye to fraud, fathers worried that the nurse they
hired might try secretly to divide the milk between two babies.
Thus, even with a wet nurse, a steady flow of good milk was hard
to ensure.

Although the wet nurse was hired for her milk, she shouldered
the infant's full care. Typically, she became a more or less attentive surrogate mother. Children sometimes developed an enduring affection for their "milk mothers," who might retain for years a
connection with the family. It was more common, perhaps, to experience interrupted relationships. Displaced by nurses' illnesses or
pregnancies, a child often suckled from a series of women. Where
money and space permitted, parents preferred a live-in *balia*. Mothers could then enjoy their children's company and oversee their
care. Meanwhile, employers could monitor the wet nurse's own
regime of nutrition, sleep, and behavior; to prevent expense and
harm to the baby, she was to eat and drink moderately, avoiding
heavy wines and foods too salty or full of garlic and onions. A good
resident wet nurse was neither cheap nor easily found. A domestic slave was one solution, or a lone woman stranded by misfortune. Otherwise one had to negotiate the nurse's absence from her
own family, at further cost. Providing a scarce resource on favored
terms, the live-in *balia* enjoyed a fairly privileged position. Most
often, in large, wealthy households, she worked as a well-paid
servant, but occasionally, especially in smaller ones, she became a
mother's companion. If the *balia* could not dwell in the house, better she live nearby. Florentine wet nurses were known to ship their
own babies to the countryside, to supply their milk to the high-end
urban market at premium prices.

For many parents, to use a wet nurse meant sending the child
away, usually to the country. Thus, only a few hours or days
after birth, a city-born infant left its natal family to spend many
months—even years—in a modest rural household. The distance
caused stress. While some parents perhaps gave little thought to
their absent offspring, others clearly worried, seeking reports on
their health and arranging visits. Concern and forethought might
also appear in rich families' record books, which sometimes

cataloged elaborate layettes sent along for the infants' needs. In one book, the provisions include "a branch of coral with a silver ring," likely intended as both toy and amulet. Many children died in wet nurses' care. Condemned as ignorant, slovenly, and greedy, these surrogates were often blamed; grieving parents charged them with neglect and cutting corners. But infants died everywhere. It is hard to say whether the country, as a nurse's paying guest, was riskier than the more contagious city, in the hands of domestic servants.

Experts recommended that infants feed from the breast, but not indefinitely. In most views, weaning came best for girls at eighteen months and for boys at two years. Actual ages probably varied greatly, dependent on chance events like those that shunted infants from nurse to nurse. At some point it became easier to nourish youngsters entirely with other food. Probably they had already sampled foods deemed suitable for infants. Boiled wheat porridge, fed through a hollowed horn, was a good beginning. Sops of bread dipped in broth, oil, or watered wine also served. Childcare manuals discouraged fruit as hard to digest. Other adult food, pre-chewed by the mother or nurse, could be introduced gradually. Once eating such adapted forms of regular food, infants could come home from the wet nurse, if their families were ready to receive them. For those youngsters, the change in diet spelled a dramatic shift of life. It might be the first time they knew their parents and siblings.

Swaddling

Besides nursing with its many arrangements, a defining feature of earliest life was swaddling. Fresh delivered, the newborn was washed and dressed in loose garments and diapers. Then the baby's limbs were carefully straightened, and strips of fabric were wound around from toe to head, often leaving only the face exposed. Experts claimed that swaddling kept the baby warmly secure from drafts and discouraged dangerous movements. The wrapping was to be careful, to prevent pressure on fragile organs. Savonarola warned against left-handed women, who would swaddle badly. Snugly bound, the infant lay in a cradle that could be moved about, but probably mostly stayed near the mother or nurse. Fittingly, doctors expected infants to sleep a lot.

A good regime of care recommended unbound times, for hygiene, stimulation, and exercise. Diaper cloths were to be changed several times a day, and experts recommended frequent baths. One should wash babies oftener than adults bathed. Besides offering cleanliness and comfort, bathing let the child move and stretch, free of swaddling. Caregivers could seize these moments to cuddle and play. The friar Giovanni Dominici, who austerely advised a widow against petting, embracing, or kissing her son after age three, clearly expected such intimacies with infants. These bouts of interaction probably also helped children learn to speak, although our sources say next to nothing about this essential early skill. Busy, likely harried, and often poor, women surely could not easily fulfill the male pundits' many injunctions, but we should not assume that, by the standards of the time, babies were routinely mistreated or neglected. How long the swaddling stayed on we do not know: a week, a month, several months? Perhaps it ran longer in the winter. Certainly, into their second year, children were expected to be mobile, and playing with other youngsters. Children learned to walk, it seems, amid the characteristic Renaissance mix of parental delight and fear. Protective devices reduced the risks: harnesses, wooden-frame walkers that in the sixteenth century acquired wheels, and, in Rome, light cotton helmets, secured by silk strips crossways atop the head.

Foundlings

Some infants grew up in foundling homes. These charitable institutions multiplied during the Renaissance to care for unwanted and abandoned children. From the mid-fifteenth century in Florence, Bologna, Siena, and other northern cities, specialized hospitals opened to combat a perceived spread of infanticide, especially by neglect. Funded by communes and charitable religious companies, these houses accepted infants whom parents would or could not keep. Many foundlings came from illegal unions, involving slaves or priests, or from pregnant servant girls unable to secure a husband. In times of crisis, the poor also deposited youngsters whom, for the while, they could not support. These parents sometimes left pitiful letters, expressing hopes to reclaim the child in better times. In Florence, the Hospital of the Innocenti kept careful records of admissions, including tokens left to identify the foundlings.[8] More girls than boys ended up there, as if parents more readily sacrificed daughters. Although called hospitals, these asylums offered little medical care. Rather, they kept their charges according to a regimen set by age. Once received, infants stayed only briefly; they soon went to country wet nurses, where mortality was very high.

Renaissance cities often built charitable hospitals to serve those without homes or families, including abandoned children. This detail from a fresco by Domenico de Bartolo (Siena, 1442) represents the reception of swaddled foundlings and their care. (Leemage/UIG via Getty Images)

After weaning at age two or three, survivors returned to the city, where the hospital trained them to take jobs and support themselves as soon as possible.[9]

CHILDHOOD

Children, weaned from the breast and capable of speech and independent movement, entered a new phase of life. Their parents should start to teach them the values, attitudes, and skills that would enable them to function as adults. Some such knowledge, such as religious and lay moralities, was nearly universal. Other lessons fit the niche to which gender and rank destined the child. When, as often happened, given high mortality, father, mother, or both were gone, others might step in, more or less willingly and capably. Older sisters, aunts, grandparents, servants, workers in the family business, tutors, masters, or others replaced or supplemented parental efforts. In farm families, or among Florentine patricians, where widowers remarried swiftly, stepmothers were common. As in infancy, caregivers and adult models might well rotate. Youngsters learned to compete for attention. To rely on multiple caregivers came easier because few social environments segregated age groups. While, by convention, males and females sometimes had separate spaces, the old and the young mixed readily. Renaissance children did not often pass long hours in dedicated rooms or spaces. Again, this mixing did not mean they were seen as "miniature adults." Children had their own capacities and inclinations, but practiced them in companies and spaces that also served adult affairs.[10]

Until age six or seven, children remained largely on women's turf. Fathers sometimes showed great interest in their younger offspring but generally expressed it in visits to domestic spaces. For instance, Alessandro Pallantieri, a Roman lawyer and high bureaucrat, and in many ways a thoroughly wicked man, kept the child of his horribly abused young mistress, the daughter of a lute maker, in the artisan's house across the street. To his own family's distress, in the evenings the lawyer would often slip over, to enjoy the singing and dancing of his four-year-old bastard son.[11] Around age six, as children took first steps toward future adult roles, fathers began to participate more directly. They assumed responsibility for sons' education, overseeing whatever training they did not themselves impart. For girls at six, in Florence, a father started paying into the civic dowry fund, the Monte delle Doti, so that at sixteen the daughter could marry. As these paternal activities suggest, at this stage gender differentiation intensified. Earlier, although parental expectations for girls and boys diverged, their care and experiences had much in common. They wore similar clothes and played similar games.

Before the age of six, children had few obligations. While some began early to acquire mature skills—Pallantieri's four-year-old son's singing and dancing, Giovanni de' Medici's spelling at the same age—in spirit these seem to have been less earnest preparation than easy play. Nevertheless, such things soon led toward more serious learning about religion, work, and, for some, book knowledge.

Religion was fundamental knowledge and practice shared by Renaissance Christians of whatsoever rank. So pervasive was it that youngsters must have begun acquiring Christian culture as soon as they awoke to things outside themselves. To their ears came prayers muttered over them, invocations of the holy in excitement, surprise, or fear, and cautionary and inspirational tales told by mothers or nurses. Their eyes saw printed images tacked to homely walls and street-corner Madonnas honored with votive candles. In wealthy houses, colorful holy paintings featuring youngsters like themselves may have struck a chord. The touch met protective amulets dangling from the wrist, or pinned to bedclothes. For the spiritually precocious, these early encounters resonated. According to their biographies, as children future saints often played house in caves as hermits, acted out holy rituals, or vowed virginity.

For urban children between six and twelve, these impressionistic early lessons set the stage for more formal religious education and observance. In fifteenth-century Florence, confraternities, especially for boys, taught religious rites and duties. Aimed originally at youth between the ages twelve to fifteen, they came to admit boys of eight or even six. Meeting on Sundays, they sought to enhance piety and edify leisure time, leavening the dose of religion with ball games and virtuous play. Catechism classes, multiplying everywhere in the sixteenth century, prepared children ages six to twelve for first communion. Their lessons taught basic beliefs and practices to those of modest means. In Bologna such schools reached more than half the boys. Girls, for whom activities so public were deemed unsuitable, were seldom included. Yet, this same age frame did shape some females' religious life. Daughters of affluent Florentines destined—by family strategy or personal vocation—for the convent typically moved in at six or seven, took the veil as novices sometime between nine and eleven, and swore final vows at twelve or thirteen.

Between ages six and twelve, in city and country, at homes, workshops and farms, youngsters began to learn the elementary practices of adult work. Girls observed housekeeping tasks—for example, preparing foods, fetching water, sweeping, and feeding and minding small animals—and took up the simpler ones. Boys too gradually acquired basic skills, while their orbit of activity expanded beyond the domestic compass to streets and hillsides where they ran errands and watched over grazing animals. For many boys and a few girls, education in reading, writing, and arithmetic also began in these years. While elite boys might have home tutoring, assorted schools trained city children (Chapter 8). Despite the earnest training, children still played, girls at home, and boys, often rough and tumble, roaming the town or village, little supervised. In trials we glimpse them scrapping, gambling, improvising ball games, up to assorted mischief, swiftly learning worldly skills.

Economic stress, illnesses, and demographic accidents often unsettled childhood. It was common for children to lose one parent, or sometimes two. At worst, some youngsters found themselves without sustenance and adult care. Alone or with peers, such children coped on their own: their lot, often, was wandering, begging, and thieving. While forced to prey on others, they were themselves very vulnerable to exploitation. Other children, though not wholly abandoned, lived with too little to go around. In the absence of maternal supervision or to reduce the number of mouths to feed, youngsters were sometimes sent to serve in other people's houses. By general custom, children below the age of eleven were not deemed able to earn their own keep. Younger girls and boys might be fostered in others' houses as an act of charity or on payment of a fee by their guardians. From ages eleven or twelve children's work earned bed and board, and, with luck, the promise of money or goods at the end to help set them up as adults. Thus, Anna da Cattaro, an orphan from the Venetian hospital of Santi Zanipolo, served from age nine through seventeen as a "little housekeeper" to a goldsmith. In like fashion, adoptions or less formal arrangements installed young poor relatives or other children as de facto servants of rich households. But less fragile families could also choose service, even early, for the training and connections. A resident from Egypt who placed his ten-year-old son with a Venetian nobleman may well have intended such benefits. Exceptionally, in a few North Italian towns, thousands of children aged seven to fourteen worked regularly in the semiskilled industry of knitting hats (Chapter 15).

ADOLESCENCE

Somewhere between the ages of twelve and fourteen, childhood merged into what moderns call "adolescence," but what the Renaissance more often called "youth." Becoming adolescent, youngsters gradually acquired new physical, sexual, moral, and intellectual capacities. These in turn brought greater social, economic, and legal responsibilities but seldom full autonomy. Over years, even a decade, bodily growth delivered size, strength, and sexual potential. Mental and moral skills expanded in parallel. According to Renaissance thinking, younger children, while possessed of sufficient reason for primary learning and taking communion, lacked full judgment to discern good from evil. Adolescents, in contrast, were expected to have greater discretion and were held more liable for consequences. As physical and moral maturation often did not align neatly, their disjunction called for adult oversight. With these emergent capacities, the stage of youth, both male and female, typically involved beginning to earn one's own keep and acquiring the necessary training, engaging with a larger social world and sometimes leaving home, and managing maturing sexuality. Most youngsters entered this transition with neither a sharp break nor a major rite of passage. Leaving youth for adulthood often had clearer markers—for example, marriage or reception into a profession—although these rituals did not correspond to a sudden physical or psychological transformation. Though essential for all, these processes took different forms for the elite and lower social ranks, and for young men and women.[12]

Female Youth

Italian and, more broadly, European culture did not often articulate a distinctive life stage of female youth. Girls nonetheless reached adulthood not abruptly from childhood, but rather through a series of personal and social transformations. These changes largely took place in domestic settings, although not always at home. As young women seldom had a documented civic face, scholarship often overlooks them. For example, although many teenaged girls went into domestic service, few had access to apprenticeships in guilded trades. Nor did they participate in groups with other young people as part of local festivities. Nevertheless, for female teenagers, adolescent steps toward social and economic maturity and more individual agency were crucial.

The language used to describe female adolescents pertained less to age than to family relationships and sexuality. Classified in relation to men, a woman was a daughter, a virgin, a wife, or a widow. While moral discourse tended to reduce the female life pattern to a schematic threesome of child/virgin, bride/wife, and old crone, data about ages reveal an unlabeled but experientially important stage of youth. The minimum age for a girl to consent to marriage, set by the ancient Romans and still canon law in the Renaissance, was twelve (Chapter 12). This stipulation presumed the capacity to have sex and bear children, although few medical authors believed that girls so young had passed menarche. A more likely time for achieving that milestone was fourteen or fifteen, and indeed that is the age, with a few exceptions, of younger brides. Nevertheless, especially among the vast majority of non-elite people, women tended to marry later—in their early to mid-twenties, and even noble brides were usually at least in their later teens. Therefore, for most, if not all, young women there was a period of several years, or more, for the transformations of youth.[13]

A girl's sexual maturity and its attractiveness to men was her youth's most fraught dimension. Women, overall, were seen as creatures of desire and deemed poor at self-control. A girl's allure thus threatened not only her own honor, but her family's too. When law courts prosecuted defloration, an adolescent girl, not presumed innocent, had to prove her resistance. To protect her from abusers, seducers, and her own weakness, a teenager's guardians—father, brother, mother, master, or mistress—were to hedge her movements and supervise her contacts with men. In practice, the application of these modesty precepts varied with social status. The elite could afford to chaperone and sometimes seclude its nubile daughters, but working families had no such luxury. Bandello wrote a tragic *novella* of a poor girl, raped when, to support her family, she worked the fields alone; afterward, all she could do to save honor was drown herself in the river. The story's moral, however, emphasized the unusual virtue of even a peasant girl. Such idealization was far from everyday experience. While surveilled, teenagers were not in fact routinely shut away. The dangers and costs of sexual exploitation were real, yet loss of virginity, while it might bring a less good marriage, did not condemn an errant young woman to permanent shame or social perdition.

Male Youth

Adolescent boys' experiences differed markedly from those of their female age-mates. The growing physical strength and sexual appetites of male youth, although potentially disruptive, did not invite so much anxiety and repression. Sometimes, their energy was harnessed to social use in a variety of occasional public roles. Most importantly, for many men youth was the time for the organized training and higher levels of Latinate education that prepared them for careers from which women were largely excluded.

As male adolescents grew stronger, their sexual desires burgeoned. The emergence of a beard crossed a cultural boundary, marking masculinity more clearly. While church law allowed males to marry at fourteen, they very rarely did so until their mid-twenties at least, and usually later. In the meantime, male sexuality posed social risks, as youths might have illicit encounters with women, respectable or mercenary, and with men. Unlike with girls, whose virginity society aimed to wall in, authorities allowed young men some satisfaction but tried to channel them in the less socially harmful directions. Prostitution, said Saint Thomas Aquinas, served the public good as did a sewer; it disposed of noxious wastes, lest they contaminate the virtuous. In this spirit Renaissance city fathers typically tolerated sex workers if suitably labeled and contained in discrete districts. Florence encouraged them as a deflection from offenses to respectable women and from widely practiced homosexuality. For such sexual transgressions the courts might assign some legal responsibility to boys even as young as ten. Not until age fourteen, however, or, in some places, eighteen did the law hold them fully accountable.

Economically and politically, young men remained incompletely adult from their mid-teens to their mid-twenties, or sometimes longer. Though still in many respects dependent, city boys entered the economy through formal apprenticeships or informal training in commerce and crafts. Florence offers the clearest age-linked staircase up this stage of life. There, fourteen was the official age for beginning formal apprenticeships. Adolescents also began to take on civic personality, becoming eligible for the head tax—country boys at fourteen and city dwellers at eighteen. They would not, however, qualify for election to government offices until twenty-five for some posts, thirty for others, and older yet for the highest positions. In some families, however, fathers adopted a strategy of legal emancipation by which they formally relinquished authority over sons, to let them conduct business on their own. Although twenty was the average age of emancipation, in the fifteenth century some merchants took the step at fifteen and sixteen. While the young man acquired ostensible autonomy, this maneuver was usually a ploy to spread and shield the family's debt. Already discouraged in some cities, with time emancipation receded in Florence too. Across the peninsula, young men destined for the church or the professions studied on into university, a few remaining at their books till thirty. Others launched careers by accepting junior posts in the bureaucracies and courts.

In contrast to their domestic sisters, male adolescents played roles in the public sphere. Youth groups, almost exclusively male, sometimes served a city's collective conscience. The notion of youth's innocence had moral force. Processions of children and adolescents invoking God and true religion were a familiar urban sight. Apparently spontaneous congregations might coalesce in times of crisis. In 1483, at Brescia, during a severe drought, and in 1505, at Bologna, after terrible earthquakes, youngsters trooped the streets imploring divine mercy. The spectators hoped fervently that God would heed the youthful cries. Moreover, mendicant preachers drew on the boys' confraternities to organize phalanxes of adolescents, sometimes dressed as angels, to parade the streets promoting virtue. The radical Dominican politician Girolamo Savonarola sent boys prowling Florence to spy out moral lapses and to collect "vanities"—dice, cards, gaming boards, pagan paintings, and licentious books—to burn on the piazza in purifying bonfires. The preacher deployed the spectacle of youthful virtue to shame elders out of worldly behavior.

On the other hand, male youth was often violent. Wielding fists, sticks, stones, knives, and, with time, guns, young men battled for personal honor, and for the standing of their quarter, faction, or city. Grown men observing them could vent, vicariously, strong emotions they also felt but deemed unfitting or risky to express. This youth violence has parallels with gang wars today. Authorities tried to quell mayhem and harness youthful vitality. One strategy was to ritualize violence. A common custom was to hold competitions and mock battles with a ritual order that moderated the damage. In cities across northern and central Italy, from Perugia to Modena to Milan, groups of young men, often representing their sections of town, gathered to brawl for victory and prestige. Combat's protocols varied with place and time. Bridges marking neighborhood boundaries were a characteristic site. Often youths struggled *en masse*; sometimes a single champion fought for each side, reducing the danger. Even when the playfulness was obvious, as when "mounted" warriors rode staffs like hobbyhorses, fighters risked injury and even death. In some cities, regimes tamed these melees into more elegant diversions. Led and subsidized by gilded scions of the elite, the "brigades" of Florence, named "of the Parrot" and "of the Flower," for instance, conducted jousts and feats of arms. In "most serene" Venice, "stocking companies" of young noblemen, garbed in their group's multicolored hose, sponsored festivities, usually comedies and parties devoid of combat's ruckus. Such events echoed tamely the fierce rivalries that rattled Renaissance political life; they also allowed the young to strut before a large audience, displaying virile prowess, with little bloodshed.

In another, more occasional form of violence, crowds of young males embellished the judicial punishment of tyrants or despised criminals. When someone particularly heinous was executed, a mob of adolescents sometimes captured, shamed, and desecrated the corpse. For example, in 1478, after the hanging of Jacopo Pazzi, ringleader of the conspiracy that killed Giuliano de' Medici and nearly killed Lorenzo, a crowd of boys dug up his body, dragged it by the hangman's cord around the city and past his house, and then dumped it disparagingly in the river. Chroniclers told similar stories of dismemberment and even cannibalism. At times older men instigated these shaming ceremonies and accompanied the boys, but the young people's actions had resonance. As incomplete adults, they both embodied vitality and the future, and retained vestiges of irresponsibility and even innocence. The young could thus go overboard, to castigate a culprit on behalf of the whole society. When they did so, they signaled the enormity of the offense. At the same time, extreme or impulsive deeds, upsetting in mature men, were tolerable in boys. Thus, the ambiguous, fluid nature that Renaissance culture ascribed to adolescence, while in some ways troublesome, could still be put to use. The unsettled shifts between virtue and violence helped express and manage, if not resolve, some of society's entrenched tensions.[14]

CONCLUSION

The young of Renaissance Italy who survived the cull of disease and hardship passed through a sequence of life stages. Although the transitions between them often lacked distinct times or ritual markers, the steps and pathways were functional and widely understood. With passing years came more difference between the genders. Where male youth took on some public roles that tapped their scarcely trammeled energy, girls' maturation occurred in domestic spaces where adults restrained them, aiming to shield them from risk.

NOTES

1. On life stages, Bell, *How to Do It*, 177–78.
2. On life expectancies, David Herlihy and Christiane Klapisch-Zuber, *Tuscans and Their Families* (New Haven, CT, 1985), 83–86.
3. On pregnancy and birth, Bell, *How to Do It*, chap. 3.
4. On baptism, Muir, *Ritual in Early Modern Europe*, 20–27.
5. Gregorio Dati, "Diary," in *Readings in Medieval History*, ed. P. Geary (Toronto, 2010), 795–97.
6. On infant feeding and wet nurses, Bell, *How to Do It*, 124–45.

7. Quoted in James Bruce Ross, "The Middle-Class Child in Urban Italy, Fourteenth to Early Sixteenth Century," in *History of Childhood*, ed. L. DeMause (New York, 1974), 187.

8. The renovated museum of the Ospedale degli Innocenti in Florence is an excellent resource.

9. On the care of orphans, Nicholas Terpstra, *Abandoned Children of the Italian Renaissance: Orphan Care in Florence and Bologna* (Baltimore, 2005).

10. On childhood and child rearing, Bell, *How to Do It*, 145–74.

11. Cohen, *Love and Death*, 125–70.

12. On adolescence, Bell, *How to Do It*, chap. 5; Stanley Chojnacki, "Measuring Adulthood: Adolescence and Gender," in *Women and Men in Renaissance Venice*, ed. S. Chojnacki (Baltimore, 2000), 185–205.

13. On female youth, see essays by Megan Moran, Michele Robinson, and Elizabeth Cohen in *The Youth of Early Modern Women*, ed. E. Cohen and M. Reeves (Amsterdam, 2018).

14. On the public roles of male youth, Andrea Zorzi, "Rituals of Youthful Violence in Late Medieval Italian Urban Societies," in *Late Medieval and Early Modern Ritual*, ed. S. Cohn, et al. (Turnhout, 2013), 235–66.

12

LIFE CYCLES: FROM MARRIAGE THROUGH DEATH

Adulthood had many dimensions; one moved into and through it by increments. Maturity demanded respect and conveyed responsibility, but only to a few did it promptly bring social and economic autonomy. Yet, for all its limitations, adulthood was the peak—the goal toward which all earlier stages built. While circumstances and timing varied with social class, for women marriage marked a major change. Although subordinate to the husband, a wife, along with the motherhood that was expected to follow, earned recognition and honor. While elite brides often moved into extended families, a working-class wife usually became the assistant head of a new household and an auxiliary in the family's livelihood. A minority of women never married—for example, nuns and dowryless poor— but they too gradually left childhood behind. For men, marriage, signaling dominance over a household, wife, and children, also marked adulthood. Maturity also brought men new economic roles, but their freedom of action much depended on the family's business and on paternal longevity. Although an adult male had the physical strength and technical skills to earn a living, senior men often exploited or controlled his labor. For social and political autonomy, a grown man had room to maneuver, hedged however by his niche in the hierarchy and his responsibilities to his peers and dependents. Then, at some, unmarked point, for both men and women, maturity gave way to decline and, unpredictably, sooner or later to death.

MARRIAGE

Fundamentally, for women, but also significantly for men, marriage was a banner of adulthood. For many Italians, marriage coincided with passage out from under the power of fathers, who held authority over youths. Although a woman's marriage often just exchanged one obedience for another, it signaled a major break with earlier life. A wedding rearranged one's closest social relationships. Most adult Italians married. Elite families, for honor and thrift, did send some children into celibate careers as priests or nuns; for surplus daughters, a convent dowry was far cheaper than a worldly one. Yet even nuns were sometimes said to marry Christ or the church. Renaissance people had a hard time imagining a mature life without a spouse—divine for a few, human for the rest. It was possible to live singly, and some men and women did so, delaying marriage for economic or other reasons until death caught them. But to most minds never to have married appeared an anomaly, a misfortune.

Renaissance ideas about so important an institution as marriage were not simple; they came from at least two crucial sources. Religion construed marriage as a pillar of the earthly order, that advanced salvation. Social traditions, meanwhile, looked to marriage to secure a family's well-being in this world by cultivating alliances with other families and ensuring a line's survival into future generations. Neither approach to marriage shared the modern stress on romantic love, companionship, and psychological fulfillment.

Religious Concepts

For the Catholic Church of the Renaissance, a wedding was a sacrament, a divine intervention that sanctified its participants. Yet, before the mid-sixteenth century, a man and a woman could—and often did—contract a religiously binding alliance without a priest present. By church law, the core of a marriage was the free consent of the two parties in "words in the present tense." These are reciprocal vows in the form—"I, Caterina, take you, Pietro, to be my husband"—that remain at the crux of the Christian ritual to our day. This exchange of commitments, once sealed by sexual consummation, created an unbreakable bond. Earlier public statements of the intention to marry "in the future tense," witnesses to such vows, and a priestly benediction were all desirable. Still, even without publicity and blessing, a secret marriage was legal and binding. From the medieval church's point of view, the couple and their obligations to one another were the center. The purposes of marriage were to procreate and to aid one another, especially toward salvation. In particular, marriage avoided sin by providing sexual appetite a legitimate outlet. Sex was a marital right; husbands owed it to their wives, not only vice versa. While, in the early Renaissance, many married without the church's sacrament, these religious ideas nevertheless colored everyone's experience of matrimony. With the reform decrees issued by the Council of Trent in 1563, the church's role grew. Thereafter, parish priests had to preside over the exchange of vows, as well as to make public the proposed union, three times, in advance.[1]

Social and Economic Concepts

Regarding matrimony, social traditions had concerns quite different from those of religion. The dominant model, reflecting elite views and practices, saw marriage as linking not merely two persons but two families. Exchanging economic and political resources and cementing social alliances, it benefited not only the bridal pair but also wider networks of kin and associates. Reflecting the concerns of household heads, this way of thinking put group interests ahead of personal comfort. The private inclinations of the couple had little priority. While the bride might have strong preferences and certainly a great stake in the outcome, her role in the matchmaking was largely passive. She was the principal object in a complex exchange, in which responsibility for her body and honor passed from her father and male kin to her new husband.

In the exchanges that were key to marriage, each side gave and received, but the offerings did not balance. On one side, a family gave its daughter, including her sexuality, fertility, skills, and labor power, to the husband and his family, but there was more. Up and down the social scale, where there were means, and even where they were lacking, a girl needed a dowry to marry. The dowry, complemented by a trousseau of linens and household wares, was a sizable chunk of assets that underpinned the new unit economically. Its mix varying with the family's rank and occupation, the dowry's capital included cash, credits, and sometimes real estate, as well as household goods, tools, clothing, and jewelry. Socially, a fat dowry also manifested the honor of the bride and her family. So, to maximize both alliances and honor, where the market for good husbands was competitive, dowries tended to inflate. Consequently, dowries burdened patrimonies; the daughters' portions sometimes even outstripped the sons' inheritance. Lawmakers' efforts failed to curb their rise. Among nobles and patricians, inflation got so steep that families had to limit the number of marrying daughters and to find honorable accommodation for the others—as many as 50 percent of Venice's patrician daughters in the sixteenth century—in nunneries. On the other side of the marriage bargain, having received the fair boons of woman and dowry, the groom then reciprocated with gifts to the bride. In wealthy families, these often included jewelry, clothing, and adornments for the nuptial chamber, whose cost might be worth a third of the dowry. Sometimes the completion of the marriage depended on down payment of enough dowry to afford the groom the funds to buy these presents for his bride. Besides these ceremonial donations, which the husband might later repossess, he also committed himself to support his wife during his lifetime and, at his death, to restore the dowry to support her needs. A widow's claim on her often quite substantial dowry threatened to disrupt her marital family's well-being; it often led to drawn-out, tense negotiations.

These imbalanced exchanges and the anxieties and disappointments they provoked were most dramatic at society's upper ranges, where marriage worked as an alliance of large lineages. Lower down the economic ladder, marriages also involved dowries, but, mainly, the union focused on the couple, not on kin. In those classes, marriage still assumed gender hierarchy and male responsibility for female honor, but, because women's labor supported household income, the pair functioned as a fuller partnership. Across society, marriage brought both husband and wife status, greater responsibility, and somewhat more independence than they had enjoyed in their pre-adult condition.

Age of Marriage

The considerations on when to marry differed for women and for men. For females, the precariousness of honor pushed for early marriage, but the search for dowry argued for delay. By these logics, girls from families rich enough to dower them from wealth on hand wed younger than those from poor ones, who had to earn more money first. Demographic pressures and the heat of the marriage market also affected ages of first marriage. Brides' average age varied: between city and country, class and class, and one epoch and another. Although young brides were desirable, Shakespeare's fourteen-year-old Juliet was unusual. No one was surprised by a married fifteen- or sixteen-year-old, but, even in Florence, where average ages were among the youngest, the usual age fell at seventeen to eighteen. In smaller towns, in the countryside, and toward 1600, brides were older yet, twenty and above. Everywhere, nearly all women became wives (and sometimes even widows) by the age of twenty-five.

Concerning marriage, men had some other things to think about. For them, thanks to the double standard around sex and honor, and the availability of prostitutes and, illicitly, serving girls, the hurry was less. Moreover, the need for means to support a family urged prudent slowness. In the country, the supply of land and local labor practices determined whether an early wife helped or hindered a man's career. In the city, if an artisan was not yet master of a shop, before marrying he needed at least to complete his training and find steady work. Advice manuals discouraged men from marrying before age twenty-five, and, anticipating elite readers, they sometimes recommended thirty-five or forty. But quantitative evidence suggests that most people ignored these pundits. In patterns that invert those for women, country men usually married sooner than city-dwelling Florentines, at twenty-five to twenty-seven on average instead of thirty-one or thirty-two. As a result, the age gap between rural brides and grooms was typically five or more years, not the fifteen years common among urban patricians.

Making a Match

So how did Renaissance Italians find a mate? While they generally did not practice formal endogamy, that is, marry only inside a restricted group, as a rule they chose partners among those who were familiar, with whom they shared social rank, neighborhood, or economic ties. While marrying well was a strategy for rising in the world, most people aimed just to secure their position by marrying someone fairly like themselves, whose economic interests and honor matched their own. Alongside material assets and social connections, appearance and health counted. Elite girls, mostly shut in at home, were looked over when they appeared in church. A desirable spouse also should have at least a compatible temperament. Too quarrelsome a domestic life subverted a marriage. Normally, for cooperation's sake, men sought a docile female. These criteria so narrowed the field of potential mates that finding a suitable choice at the right moment and winning her family's agreement posed a challenge. The bargaining was often a delicate business, and the stakes, in wealth and prestige, were high. To save face in the bargaining, many families resorted to third parties.

In theory, church law firmly demanded the free consent of bride and groom, but in practice often, and among the elite always, the match was negotiated and made by others. Making marriages for their offspring was a parental responsibility; for daughters especially, it was a critical part of launching them into adulthood. So weighty was the dowry that giving or receiving one affected the larger family's well-being. Therefore, heads of households saw marriages as a major concern. Property issues shaped parental decisions: how many matches, who, to whom, when, and at what price? During marriage negotiations, through emissaries and directly, the two families dickered over who would give what when. In a competitive and nosy society, this stage cherished secrecy. Men usually conducted the face-to-face negotiations, but women—the mother, even the bride, or veteran female servants—might have their say. Thus, a Florentine patrician had to haggle for a satin dress requested by his daughter, though he himself thought this bid too lavish and it threatened to stir up jealousy in her unwed cousin.

Where parents were absent or needed help, other family members or even non-kin often stepped in to secure a match. Relatives and friends pointed out possible candidates and served as go-betweens. Masters and mistresses might arrange respectable marriages for their servant girls. Rather than resent such matchmaking as a threat to autonomy and future happiness, many young people likely welcomed their elders' assistance. To assemble a solid partner and a reasonable dowry often took more effort and more resources than two young people possessed.[2]

The dowry, the largest piece of the property exchange, could call on assets from a network of sources, both male and female. While fathers had a duty to dower their daughters as best they could, this was a burden not easily shouldered alone. Contributing to dowries was a favorite good deed. Mothers, masters and mistresses, senior male relatives, friends, and allies would make donations, sometimes as deathbed bequests. Young working women saved their earnings in order to marry. Yet the specter of the dowryless poor girl, teetering on the brink of concubinage or worse, beckoned to the charitable. From the late fifteenth century, special confraternities in many Italian cities devoted themselves to showering hundreds of dowries on vulnerable virgins. For example, an energetic congregation at Santa Maria sopra Minerva in Rome promised a respectable, though not lavish, sum to poor girls over the age of fourteen, of good and "honest" local parentage; later, "foreigners" too could apply. Annually, on the feast of the Annunciation, the candidates, demurely dressed, paraded through the neighborhood, attracting a crowd; watchers seeking wives passed their choices to the administrators and, after proving suitability and good intentions, received their brides, properly endowed.

The couple's own part in making matches ran the gamut, from almost nil to doing it all themselves. For elite families, where the stakes of honor and property were very high, the nuptial pair often had almost no control. A man, if fully mature, especially if his father had died, could make his own choices, but still might leave the initiative in others' experienced hands. Typically, at this elite level, bride and groom first met during the wedding ceremonies. Courtship consisted of negotiations over material matters and ritual gestures, extended through "ambassadors." Among those of lower status, some imitated such arrangements as best they could, others not. In both city and country, they sometimes found their own partners. They met on the job, in the street, or at public festivities. While girls of this class had honor that they and their guardians sought to protect, they did not live under steady supervision. Men could pay court to them with conversations at doors and windows or across the rooftops, and with serenades, gifts, and trysts. Hoping to marry, the couple might then seek parental backing and enlist others to help muster the needed funds. Some young people had disapproving parents or mentors; some had no one.

Thus, many couples were on their own. Putting together a dowry entailed long delays. In the meantime, the couple, having promised each other to marry in the future, might embark on a sexual relationship. Among the plebeian classes, girls who had lost their virginity might not claim as good a dowry, but they were not ostracized. Before the Council of Trent tightened policy, the combination of agreement and sexual companionship was, in many people's minds, binding, like a marriage. Once the pair had "carnal knowledge" of one another, authorities, public and familial, usually wanted to regularize their alliance. If a pregnant girl claimed convincingly to have received marriage promises, both community pressure and church courts would lean hard on a reluctant suitor. This strategy did not serve every seduced woman; some men fled, others were not free to marry. Firmer couples balked by family opposition might exploit the same logic, by having sex to extract grudging consent.

Weddings

The rituals of the wedding itself had three phases. These might bunch together over a few days but could also stretch over weeks or months. The solemnities had no single crowning moment; thus, when trouble intervened before all the steps had been completed, disputes might arise over whether the couple were in fact married. The first formality was the signing of the contract. At this all-male assembly before a notary, supporters from both parties witnessed the groom's and bride's fathers affix their names to a legal document detailing the agreement. Exchanging handshakes or kisses, the men made public their reciprocal commitments. Only at another gathering did the bride herself appear. This second stage of the wedding took place at her house. With a small escort, the groom came and, before a company of her kin and friends and a notary, exchanged consent with the bride, marking the event by giving her a ring. He also bestowed other gifts that made up the "counter-dowry." The bride's family then sponsored a banquet and festivities for the groom's party. The ring ceremony initiated the symbolic transfer of the woman out of her natal family and her incorporation into her marital one. This transition was completed only during the third phase of the nuptial rite of passage, with the physical movement of her person and goods to the home of her new husband. In a highly visible procession, the bride, clothed in her finery and accompanied by her trousseau, went to her new residence. There the man's family offered further celebrations and gifts. As part of the display, wealthy families liked to have chests, and even walls, lavishly painted on nuptial themes. The consummation of the marriage, which definitively displayed the bride's honor and placed it in her husband's hands, traditionally occurred that night; guests might make much ado of bedding the new couple. The wedding night and the morning after often featured playful, noisy, and often bawdy revelry. If, however, families expected delay in this "translation" of the bride, sexual relations might begin after the ring ceremony, at the bride's house.[3]

Living Together, Making a Family

After all the wedding steps, usually the new couple set up on their own. They had to learn to live together and to collaborate in earning a livelihood and running a household. Often the husband and wife had many of the skills already, but had not been in charge before. They could continue to draw on the advice of family and neighbors. Sometimes, however, rural or patrician newlyweds began married life in a larger, existing household. There, as they adapted to one another, they would have both more help and less privacy. (See Chapter 4 on the behavior expected of good husbands and wives.)

Producing and raising children was a principal function of marriage. Advice books directed parents, for the child's sake, to conceive it very soberly. According to Alberti's dialogue on the family,

> Husbands . . . should be careful not to give themselves to their wives while their mental state is troubled by anger, fear, or some other kind of disturbing emotion. The passions that oppress the spirit slow up and weaken our vital strength. Those passions that inflame and excite the mind disturb and provoke to rebellion the masters whose task it is at that moment to form the human image. Hence it may be found that a father who is ardent and strong and wise has begotten a son who is fearful, weak, and foolish. Sometimes from a moderate and reasonable man springs a mad and bestial youth.[4]

Whether or not they monitored their mood in bed, couples could expect a long chain of pregnancies at intervals of about two years. Six or seven deliveries were common; many women had more. Sometimes, especially if several children survived infancy, some couples may have sought to contain their numbers. The available means were not very effective, and the demographic evidence for a concerted practice of family limitation is not strong. Barrenness, meanwhile, was a hardship, even a curse. Sufferers sought remedies through prayer at special shrines dedicated to the Virgin Mary, Saint Margaret, or the archangel Michael at Gargano. If that failed, they might turn to magic.

Women faced childbirth with fear. While we should not exaggerate the numbers who died, we should recognize its costs to women's life, health, and tranquility. Before childbirth, many made a will, with good reason. Anxiety had its antidote in the female solidarity that supported the new mother. Besides the midwife, other matrons gathered around the laboring woman and, after the delivery, female relatives and friends assembled to celebrate with conversation, jokes, and delicacies. Rich Florentines used birth trays, finely painted with classical allusions and lineage emblems, to transport gifts of food for these festivities.

Not all marriages were successful, let alone happy.[5] Husbands sometimes drank and beat their wives, not only temperately for

"just correction," but excessively. Occasionally women fled.
Also, not infrequently, a man abandoned his wife and children—
deliberately, or through inadvertence—and left them without support. Wives, too, fell short; they scolded and hit their spouse, or
even tried to poison him. Now and again, a wife not only ran off
with another man; she also hauled away the linens and furniture.
Some young wives got bored and went looking for fun in adultery. Boccaccio's *Decameron* is full of such tales; not to be taken
literally, these stories entertain by showing what might be imagined. Although honor justified irate husbands in killing their errant
wives, we have little evidence that this happened often. In contrast,
Renaissance rulers and even on occasion popes kept mistresses
who lived under the veiled respectability of complaisant husbands.
Courts, both church and lay, did sometimes take up failed marriages, but punishment for sexual transgression was usually not
their goal. Rather they strove to return the couple to proper cohabi-
tation. That could well prove impossible. Many troubled couples
probably lapsed into cold war or de facto separations.

Alternative Partnerships

Although religion, law, or other social logics constrained Renaissance Italians' opportunities to form and live in comfortable partnerships, there were unsanctioned, but tolerated, practices that
helped some. Following Jesus's teaching that no man should sun-
der a married couple, the church resisted unbinding those who had
been joined by a sacrament. In canon law, marriage was understood
as, especially for the woman, a guarantee and therefore, for her
sake, to be kept sacrosanct and unbreakable for any but the gravest
of causes. Accordingly, annulments, retroactively cancelling a marriage usually on technical grounds, were slow and rare. The only
other official recourse for an unhappy spouse was a trammeled
separation of "bed and board." These decrees, also cumbersome to
secure, left the marriage in place, while suppressing its obligations;
while both lived, the partners could not wed again. Despite the
impediments, however, some women did successfully pursue their
own welfare through the church courts. Under this mostly unre-
sponsive regime, many bad or even just tired marriages instead
succumbed to forms of de facto divorce. Among ordinary people,
many husbands and wives went their own way, leaving the marital household and not infrequently finding another partner with
whom to live. Especially before the mid sixteenth century, when

the Council of Trent undertook to tighten up lay moral behavior, informal concubinage was common in the big cities.[6] Some couples lived undisturbed as if married, even attending church and communion, for months or years. Neighbors might know the history, but they often would not speak out unless some local problem brought the couple into the limelight. An unusual adaption of concubinage occurred in an elite setting in the late sixteenth-century Venice. Sons of the patriciate whom the high cost of dowries, making brides too scarce, excluded from marriage within their class sometimes established long-standing "common law" bonds with highly respectable daughters of the families of ranks below the patriciate. The marriage rules were real, but social practice could soften them for some.

Remarriage

Cruel demography broke up many marriages before old age. Death had no high season. Mortality, not divorce, left partners newly single. Men were much likelier than women to remarry. For men, a new wife and dowry paid well. Because the marriage market favored them, widowers often snatched up scarce young brides. Gregorio Dati, who professed respect and affection for his wives, was nevertheless remarried three times and promptly. Women's chances depended on age and circumstances. If she reclaimed her dowry, a widow could use it to wed again, but to the cost of her children by the first marriage, who often lost both capital and maternal care. More experienced and less dependent than when they first married, widows sometimes had more say about whether, and whom, to remarry. Young widows, however—those most likely to attract a profitable rematch—could again fall subject to their fathers' strategies. Older widows, as fertility ended, would not easily find another partner. Opting for tranquility and their soul's salvation, they often preferred a divine spouse and entered a convent.

OLD AGE

Renaissance understandings of old age were full of contradictions. On the one hand, growing old was a thing to dread. Muscular, mental, and reproductive powers all waned; looks faded. The old, at least in literature, were the object of scorn and obloquy. Old women, when cast as spiteful crones, might suffer persecution and even suspicion of witchcraft. But the old of both sexes could also invite charitable solicitude, condescending, or mingled with respect for years. Meanwhile, the classical notion that age brought wisdom and judgment persisted, and among the powerful one found old men. Thus, for some, age brought poverty and neglect; for others, great wealth, prestige, and power. The fortunate old were numerous and vigorous enough to wield substantial influence.

The borders of old age lacked sharp definition. They were largely subjective. There was nothing like modern retirement, sharply defined and enshrined in laws and rites of passage. Some people did retire from public roles or private business, but as a choice about lifestyle. No set age imposed or prompted the decision. Some wrote that, having reached a peak at thirty-five or forty, they should now prepare for death. Others were going strong at sixty and seventy and beyond. Renaissance bodies suffered such wear and tear that one seldom blamed pain and weakness on years. Rather, old age came with decrepitude, whenever it hit rather than at an expected time. The poor and sickly became "old" early, while the vigorous and successful carried on without much change of life. The condottiere Bartolomeo Colleone led his last battle at age sixty-seven; for five years more he kept receiving—and declining—offers of commissions from the pope and the Duke of Burgundy. Popes were usually old; in the sixteenth century, average age at election was sixty-one years, eight months. The doges of Venice were often no less venerable. The Genoese admiral Andrea Doria beat the warrior's odds and died four days before his ninety-fourth birthday. Artists, too, stayed in harness. Michelangelo, sixty-five when he began his *Last Judgment*, worked on it and other projects for another twenty years. His contemporary, the Venetian artist Titian, was still painting when plague took him at ninety-nine.[7]

Old age was harder on women than on men. In the fifteenth century the long-lived tended to be males, though in the sixteenth century the life expectancies of older women somewhat increased. In either time, women were much less likely to enjoy a comfortable, potent old age. Old women, despite the theoretical claim to support from their dowries, were very often poor. Opportunities to earn a living were few. Some older women returned to domestic service, but, as they aged, their capacities declined. When they could no longer work, some masters sent them away, but some let them stay on as dependents, "for the love of God." Other women were reduced to begging. Past their thirties, women did not readily remarry. Although they sometimes lived with their adult children, they were often forced to live alone or with other poor women. And, more and more, the charitable hospitals gave food and shelter to the aged. Those who could pay their keep sometimes sheltered in nunneries.

Overall old men fared better. They were likelier to hang on to money and to the resources to earn it. They rarely lived as solitaries, but, holding the economic reins, continued to rule a household of their offspring and servants. Or else they remarried and begat more children. Fiction and drama were full of May-December marriages; doddering December could take fresh female May as his prize, but could not keep her faithful and suffered shame as a cuckold. Although the tales may reflect youth's envy more than age's actual woes, they press the claim that the old took for themselves scarce goods. Such feelings made these matches a common target for *mattinatas*, insulting nocturnal serenades. In the political sphere, likewise, the party of youth railed against the elderly, who held an undue share of power.

DEATH

Death never left the minds of people at any stage of the life cycle. While death felt more imminent in life's later phases, it could and did strike at any time. From Christianity came the notion that all of life prepared for death and for passage to a better life. Although the irredeemably wicked faced eternity in hell, Christians aspired to salvation, in the long run, and to heaven. Most, however, expected a stint in purgatory, an intermediate domain in which sinners—more or less everyone except saints—expiated their transgressions before being admitted to paradise. The belief in purgatory sustained links between the living and the dead. As supernatural patrons, saints and even a family's souls in heaven could intercede with God on behalf of mortals, and living human beings with indulgences, prayers, and Masses could boost the souls in purgatory upward. Thus, the quick and the dead, allies still, continued to foster one another. Providing for the future of one's soul in purgatory was one of feature of a "good death."

The "Good Death"

With death unpredictable and all around, Italians had reason to fear being caught unprepared, their souls unshriven and their families and goods in disarray. Preachers and confessors used this threat to pressure their flocks into good behavior so as always to be ready to face God. You should live well, fearing death. You should die well too. There was a clear picture of what to do with the last hours. The scene at the deathbed was a social and a sacred drama, a moment of gathering for family, associates, a notary, and a priest. While some people prepared their wills in advance, many did not. Some used their last breaths to make or remake the arrangements, as the possible beneficiaries hung about grieving and comforting, but also vying to protect their interests. The death of a wealthy paterfamilias with many dependents to provide for was particularly intense. Wills settled worldly matters, parceling out assets among the heirs and showering gifts in cash and kind well spelled out—clothing, jewelry, weapons, art—on kin, friends, and faithful dependents. Testaments also attended to the life beyond. Donations to charity and the church to rectify specific sins such as usury were intended to unburden the soul of part of the transgression. In the later Renaissance, dying penitents made fewer such designated bequests, but left more and more funds to religious institutions to pray and say Masses for their souls and those of deceased family members. On their deathbeds, people strove to make their purgatory short and light. With the future of the testator and the kin as secured as best could be, the dying person then confessed and received the sacrament of extreme unction.

A Hero's Last Moments

In 1584, the Italian baron Marcantonio Colonna, the hero of the great naval defeat of the Turks at Lepanto, died in Spain at the age of forty-five after a brief illness. A member of his household sent home a long, detailed report on his care. Clearly, to the anonymous author's approving eye, the nobleman had died a good death: "He asked for extreme unction, . . . saying it should come quickly, and father Luis gave it to him, and gave him many reminders, asking him questions and to everything he answered literally, and with attention, and after that he spoke no more, but remained with his eyes fixed on the most holy cross, and when the Creed had been sung he expired with no travail or movement of any sort." Because the man had been important, the physicians opened the corpse to find the cause of illness.[8]

Funerals

Death set in motion a further series of customs and rituals. As with other rites of passage, arrangements, from grand to miserable, varied. They depended on the wealth and tastes of the deceased and the mourners and also on the death's circumstances. In plague times, funerals were rudimentary and hurried. We describe here the full panoply of observances with the understanding that for many people these were truncated or plainer.

The first stage was a vigil around the corpse in the family house. Family members and neighbors burned candles and kept watch. Tradition called for women to mourn dramatically, crying out, unbinding their hair, and tearing their skin and clothing. Women also washed the body and dressed it for burial, usually in its best apparel. Sometimes preparing the corpse, as well as transporting it, fell to specialists such as Florence's *beccamorti* (corpse handlers), but usually this task went to ordinary women readily on call. After the domestic vigil came the public stages of the funeral: the procession, requiem, and burial. These usually took place the day after the death, although, in the sixteenth century, for the great the final steps might tarry to await a more splendid crowd. Earlier, even for state obsequies, the period for viewing and paying respect to the dead usually lasted a mere few hours. Techniques for slowing decomposition were ineffective, and only the very holy were allowed to remain more than a day unburied. One mark of sainthood was a supernatural preservation of the body, which gave off not the stench of sin but the sweet "odor of sanctity." Allowing time for this miracle tested or confirmed sainthood and invited veneration.

The public rites focused on honor. They both cared for and celebrated the dead and affirmed the continuity through time of the collectivity, especially the family. Funerals, made for the dead, bolstered the living, who shared in their honor. The procession was often marked by great pomp. Troops of clergy to accompany the body, crowds of mourners, family members in somber but rich garb, caparisoned horses, banners and drapery, many candles and torches all proclaimed the prestige of the deceased, but also that of the family or the corporate bodies to which he or she had belonged. The grandest obsequies glorified rulers and others who had nobly served city or community. In the same spirit, rich families would seize a funeral to celebrate their past or trumpet their even greater present. Thus, while lavish rites as a rule marked the deaths of men, a socially aspiring husband or son might also stage a handsome funeral for his wife or mother, milking pomp to extol the lineage. For ordinary people, death rituals were less grand affairs. Nevertheless, commoners' desires for a decent funeral reflected similar attitudes. Guilds or, especially, confraternities allowed members with fewer assets to enjoy some funeral splendor. These corporations served as burial societies; they provided mourners, regalia, and funds to convey their members to the grave with due honor.[9]

The procession moved from the dead person's house to the church, the usual place of burial. For the important dead, to exalt the occasion the mourners might trace a longer route. Benches set out along the route could seat mourners and gawkers. The typical procession had three sections. First walked the clergy; for a high-status event, since more was better, several religious communities would be invited, at a price, to swell the ranks. In the middle, on a bier, came the body, usually wrapped, but without a coffin. At fancy funerals the corpse might sport expensive scarlet or purple fabric. Some persons of rank, however, preferred to go to their tombs in the guise of Christian humility; these requested for their grave clothes the ostentatious poverty of a plain religious habit. In third position, the mourners followed, with family members and other prestigious associates marching nearest to the body while lesser folk and those with looser ties brought up the rear. In the procession, only men were welcome, for the occasion combined public display and decorum. Women, whose presumed fragile self-control might not avail to stem their grief, should not make a wailing spectacle of themselves in the streets; therefore, they better mourned indoors—at home or in the church at the requiem.

The requiem was a Mass offered on behalf of the dead. A priest officiated before the gathered mourners, male and female. A bid for honor might clothe the chief women in luxurious black fabric, and expensive veils and mantles, some fur-lined. The requiem, in response to the social rupture caused by death, reincorporated the survivors, male and female, into an intact community. The liturgy might end with a sermon eulogy. In Florence, the preacher, nodding to collective continuity, praised the family as much as the deceased.

The burial itself attracted less fuss. Unless a will asked otherwise, people were normally buried in their parish—in the church or churchyard. When room ran out, external cemeteries were used. Collective tombs, for families or corporations such as confraternities, were common. When testators asked for burial outside their parish, it was usually in the church of an admired religious community or with entombed kinfolk. The wealthy buried their dead in a family chapel inside a church they patronized. After observances at church, family and guests might repair to the house for a mourning banquet.

Through this ritual process, the dead and the living, having both acknowledged their connections, were freed to pursue their now-separate paths. The dead, duly helped on their way to their next existence, should not hang around as errant spirits, as some thought they could, to harass those left behind. Their worldly goods passed to their survivors, as did their outstanding debts and credits, thorny matters for a designated "universal heir." Family and friends would pray for their souls in purgatory and perhaps attend commemorative Masses funded by the testament. But, affirming the vitality of the surviving community, the living would also carry on with their earthly tasks.

CONCLUSION

Renaissance Italians understood life as a series of stages, each with its own capacities, concerns, and rituals. For men, full physical and social maturity knew no single moment of arrival, but for most women marriage served as a ritual induction into adulthood. After the prime of life, the later steps, for many, though not all, brought loss. Many women and some men found themselves weak and vulnerable. Despite the damage wreaked on the old by illness, hard work, and misfortune, other men continued to work, deal, command, and govern until very ripe ages. Sooner or later, death came to all. Its customs arranged that what the deceased abandoned be distributed for honor, profit, and economic closure. For most, the soul headed to purgatory with a hope for heaven. Of the worldly remains, the bones rested in fitting sites where mourners could pray for and revere their ancestors. Properties and credits passed to family and church to support the living.

NOTES

1. On canon law of marriage, James Brundage, *Law, Sex and Christian Society in Medieval Europe* (Chicago, 1987), chaps. 9 and 10.

2. On matchmaking and family strategies, Anthony Molho, *Marriage Alliance in Late Medieval Florence* (Cambridge, MA, 1994).

3. On marriage rituals, Muir, *Ritual in Early Modern Europe*, 31–41.

4. Alberti, *The Family*, 120.

5. On marital relationships and troubled marriages, Bell, *How to Do It*, chap. 6; Joanne Ferraro, *Marriage Wars in Late Renaissance Venice* (Oxford, 2001).

6. On concubinage and the church's response, Cecilia Cristellon, *Marriage, the Church and Its Judges in Renaissance Venice, 1420–1545* (New York, 2017).

7. On old age, Georges Minois, *History of Old Age from Antiquity to the Renaissance* (Chicago, 1987), chaps. 8 and 9; Erin Campbell, *Old Women and Art in the Early Modern Italian Domestic Interior* (Farnham, UK, 2015).

8. BAV, Vat. Lat. 7031, 292r–93v.

9. On death rituals, Muir, *Ritual in Early Modern Europe*, 44–51.

13

HOUSES, FOOD, AND CLOTHING

TENDING BODILY NEEDS

Daily life takes its flavor not only from people and their relation-ships but also from the routine activities that sustain the body—eating, sleeping, and hygiene—and the everyday objects that support them—furniture, clothing, storage vessels, wells, hearths, brooms, bedding, cooking pots, and so on. Renaissance Italians had to meet the basic human needs for food, rest, and shelter under much greater constraints than ours. They lacked our technology and energy resources. Their bodies were routinely assaulted by physical dangers and irritations, ranging from plague to lice, from crippling injuries to smoke-red eyes, that most readers of this book encounter rarely. They drew on what resources in time and mate-rial there were. Some burdens weighed alike on rich and poor, but wealth or poverty gave great diversity to material circumstances.

Well-being linked to both physical and social condition. Not just life and livelihood were at stake, for bodies were prime social and cultural markers. Beauty and good carriage, smooth features and straight limbs, nimbleness, and strength all fed honor (Chapter 5). Clothing and cosmetics highlighted a body's assets or covered up its flaws. Norms set expectations keyed to status, age, and gender. Given the physical and social challenges, few could display the peak of health and allure, but daily routines helped keep people as well and healthy-looking as possible.

Renaissance Italians, who found honor in health and good appearance, did not flinch from showing or seeing bodies. Though heirs to Christian traditions that feared flesh as a distraction from spiritual things, they enjoyed the display of physical beauty. Though attentive to reputation and wary of affronts to female sexual propriety, they were not prudish. They were indeed often quite matter-of-fact about bodies, and their fluids and excretions. The abhorrence of nudity and visible sexuality we call "Victorian"—our picture mislabels and exaggerates that prudery—hardly infected premodern behavior. In Renaissance Italy, men sometimes appeared publicly seminude or nude. Book illustrations show bare-legged agricultural workers stomping grapes in vats and working in the fields. Men swam naked in the Tiber in the center of Rome. The English traveler Thomas Coryate commented with northern surprise at scant or absent clothing. In Padua, he reported, a bankrupt would escape his debts if he sat three days at the Palace of Justice with his buttocks exposed, a shameful but thinkable choice.[1] In Piedmont in June the Englishman saw bare-bottomed children scamper near women workers in light smocks, who to him seemed scarcely clad. He credited the warm climate, but local norms about the body were also at work. Overall, gender rules allowed women less bare flesh than men, but another observer told of seeing through open windows city women with little on, as if modesty's demands were lax. Nor was sex easily shrouded. Couples might seek a modicum of privacy, but between crowded domestic quarters and outside spaces where others might stumble by, it was hard to be alone. Shame attached to public and improper sexuality, but one encountered or discussed it without squeamishness.

Evidence of exposed bodies also comes from preachers and moralists. Sermons targeted the vanity of women and especially—they said—lewd décolletage and even uncovered breasts. These jeremiads were conventional, but pictures of women's dress lend them plausibility. Other moralists of a humanist bent advocated female modesty and general civility by veiling the body and its functions. Giovanni Della Casa's mid-sixteenth-century handbook on genteel manners was keen to ban bodily displays in public, such as yawning, scratching, cleaning teeth, or even being seen washing hands after excretion, lest one remind others of what one had just done. "And when you have blown your nose," hectored Della Casa, "you should not open your handkerchief to look inside, as if pearls or rubies might have descended from your brain."[2] Reading this ban on the nigh-unthinkable, we now blush or giggle. But in the

Renaissance the novel rules seemed useful, if one aspired to fit in among the best. For most people, the body with its shameful parts and its nail parings, phlegm, urine, blood, and milk were familiar and routine. Conventions shaped their handling but did not banish them from sight, touch, or talk.

Most Renaissance Italians ate, slept, washed, and dressed at home, but not in our familiar private, isolated settings. Renaissance bedrooms often had semipublic functions, and a bathroom like ours did not exist. Domestic space was porous. Rooms served multiple purposes; people came and went—core family, servants, workers, and guests. In the countryside and even in cities, animals too might live close by. Many Italians also routinely tended their bodily needs in other settings. Monasteries and hospitals housed substantial numbers. Others ate and slept in taverns and boarding houses. Wanderers—migrant workers, shepherds, soldiers, bandits—camped out for months.

Although the wealthy enjoyed greater comfort than the poor, by modern standards all Renaissance houses were quite primitive. Without electricity, artificial illumination required controlled burning, always dim, dangerous, and costly. With few exceptions, there was no private running water and no piped sewage. Poor heating and ventilation left winter rooms drafty, smoky, and smelly. Against summer's heat, the sole remedy was to preserve the cool of night or winter as long as possible inside dark, thick-walled dwellings; ice was a rare luxury. To succor the body amid these stresses, household goods and possessions were relatively few. Those few were solid, treasured, cared for, and much reused. Much furniture, equipment, and clothing did daily service for years, even for a lifetime, and then passed to the next generation. Many items showed signs of repeated repair; others remained in use though worn or tattered. Some belongings were inventively adapted to new purposes. People knew their few things intimately and could describe them in great detail; they distinguished carefully between old and new.

As the Renaissance went on, Italians acquired more goods for their bodies and homes, and the wealthy, especially, consumed many more, richer and finer. Fifteenth-century Italians produced astonishing art in many media, some of which embellished private palaces as, to mark rank, elites increasingly invested in handsome surroundings. The notion of high fashion, not new to Italians in the Renaissance, commandeered much attention and material investment. Italian taste set the style for all of Europe. By the sixteenth century, appetites for domestic elegance supported abundant fine wall painting, hangings, ceramics, metalwork, and ornamented furniture. Meanwhile, even high-placed Italians lacked basic physical comforts we now take for granted.

Acquiring domestic goods took various forms, but buyers did not go to a store, pick out a mass-produced item, and pay a ticketed sum. For furniture and clothing, shoppers often commissioned what they wanted from the maker, specifying materials, approximate size, and ornaments desired and discussing a price. For food ordinary city dwellers visited markets, where the merchandise was seasonal, or shops that offered a limited mix of items—a butcher, a baker, a greengrocer, or dry goods merchant. For bulky purchases, a porter could be engaged to deliver them. Under the direction of a purser (*spenditore*), large households ordered food from wholesale brokers and sometimes direct from producers, even paying a premium in order to ensure supply. Small items of value like drugs, cosmetics, accessories, and books came from specialist traders, some of whom, like apothecaries, kept shops, but many also attended at the houses of the patrician elites. Women were certainly among those listed in merchant's or craftsmen's account books as owing monies, although it is not clear whether they had visited the shop itself.[3]

DOMESTIC SETTINGS

Walls, Ceilings, and Floors

Domestic spaces could be large or small (Chapter 9). Most people lived in only one or a few rooms, but the rich occupied long chains of chambers, built tall and broad. Walls, especially in cities, were of brick or stone, often faced with plaster. Such construction discouraged fire. Maintenance was haphazard; weather's wear and tear, and man-made damage, raddled surfaces. Life's escapades might well turn on information overheard through a wall's chinks or a surreptitious letter slipped through. Walls, sometimes several feet thick, could be cut for window seats, niches, and shelves. The affluent embellished their internal walls in colorful ways, with paint on plaster (fresco), canvas, or leather. More routine treatments featured geometric designs or stripes shaded to evoke draped hangings; more ambitious were mythological paintings or images that evoked the family—its achievements, legends, and heraldry. Walls could also be hung with tapestries, gold-framed mirrors, or pictures tiered to the high ceiling. Sculptured moldings or stucco work sometimes divided and accented rooms. Fancy ceilings often

showed off their beams, embellished with bright designs and carv-
ings. Rich Italians beautified their homes for their pleasure and to
awe their guests. In an ironic Bandello *novella*, a visitor to a courtesan's lavish home spits in his servant's face, explaining that he has
chosen the only ugly thing in sight.[4] In more modest houses, however, rafters were rough-hewn, and only a cheap religious print
might relieve the bareness of walls. Humble packed dirt or wide
boards made many more floors than the wealthy man's herring-
bone brick, ceramic tiles, or marble.

Openings, Light, and Heat

The openings in the walls of Italian homes—doors and windows—
demanded deft management by the occupants. The social and
physical environment both penetrated. Goods, people, creatures,
sounds, air, dust, heat, and light came and went. Some arrivals
were welcome, others not. Security of both honor and property,
and comfort, urged control of human and environmental traffic.
Warmth was to treasure in winter and shun in summer. Light was
often scarce, but sometimes too bright and hot. The design and use
of doors and windows thus balanced contradictory claims. Doors
came large and small. Palace portals ten and twelve feet high
admitted light as well as goods and persons, even some on horseback or in coaches. Inside, people traversed grand public rooms
through big doors elegantly framed with classical moldings. Doors
into more private or modest quarters could be small and narrow—
sometimes little more than five feet high and two feet wide. These
let scant light in, only if left open. Italians, living close together and
worried about their property and reputations, preferred to keep
street doors closed and, at night, latched and locked. By modern
standards, door keys were often big and cumbersome. As police
records show, these precautions discouraged but did not always
bar insistent intruders. And they sometimes inconvenienced both
residents and visitors. Romans, who typically dwelled in upper
stories above workshops, could unlatch the door below by pulling
an upstairs string.

While medieval windows were often few, small, and haphazardly
placed, during the Renaissance they grew larger and more regular. They faced onto both interior courtyards and streets. Flower
pots might grace their sills. For protection and privacy, indoor or
outdoor wooden shutters with assorted panels adjusted the flow
of light and air. Watching from windows, residents—especially

women—tracked local goings-on. Instead of glass, translucent blinds made of oiled cloth on frames of wood and wire provided some slight illumination while checking drafts. Many windows remained unfilled. From the fifteenth century, the rich began to install window glass. Cloudy and cluttered with much leading, the small panes were hard to see through. When natural light fell short, the fireplace, candles, oil lamps, lanterns, and torches made good the lack, at some cost and risk. Brackets and hooks high on walls supported burning lights, out of harm's way. But only the wealthy could afford the brilliance of chandeliers. Overall, despite more windows and supplemental light from controlled fire, indoor life was often rather dim.

In cold seasons, domestic life lacked not only light but heat. Although Italy's Mediterranean climate was temperate, in winter many regions, especially the North and mountain districts, were cold and damp. The illuminated manuscript calendars classically illustrate January by depicting huddled folk by an indoor fire. Such comfort was precious, for heating was poor. A simple household had a single fire for warmth and cooking. In primitive houses, it burned at the center of the main room, set on the floor or in a mud hearth or metal brazier. Smoke found its own way out eventually, through a hole in the ceiling, but wandered the room en route. Better houses had fireplaces and chimneys. A hood might speed cooking by catching the heat. Concentrating the warmth, however, deprived far corners of the poorly insulated space. People hung cloth over openings and along walls to cut drafts. So, besides all-too-common accidental burns and scaldings, such heating taxed health as bad ventilation irritated eyes, windpipes, and lungs. Among the wealthy, fireplaces, built against the wall and served by a chimney that carried smoke outside, multiplied rapidly in the fifteenth century. But even among the rich many rooms remained unheated. In chiller quarters, metal pans filled with heated stones or coals and ceramic containers of hot water to warm beds and hands gave slight comfort.

Such pesky environmental aggravations made Renaissance housekeeping a chore. There was plenty of work keeping a family or household running and caring for its goods. Nevertheless, our image of the cloistered housewife keeping a "home" chock full of stuff in sparkling order does not fit the Renaissance. Ordinary women, including servants, spoke of making beds and sweeping; the always-handy broomstick was a common weapon in female street fights. Yet cleaning and embellishing a domestic space claimed little attention.

Water and the Lack of Plumbing

A major challenge for Renaissance housekeeping was water. It was sometimes neither clean nor safe, and was often inconveniently located. Some houses had private wells, and by the late fifteenth century a very few well-appointed, innovative palaces, as at Urbino, deployed pipes and drains that brought more and less clean water for different uses to parts of the building. But most people relied on the river or on public wells and fountains. From the late Middle Ages, many cities invested in civic works to bring water to their neighborhoods. For example, Perugia's great thirteenth-century fountain is the proud symbol of the city. In sixteenth-century Rome, popes restored aqueducts feeding fountains that proclaimed their largess. Women fetched water at the public source, stopping briefly to chat, negotiate, and argue, before carrying it home on their heads in jugs. Because it was heavy, for some tasks it was easier to bring materials to water than vice versa. Thus, washing—clothes, but also dishes—often took place in public, not at home. Laundry was spread to dry on grassy banks or, in cities, hung on lines strung in loggias or between houses. Tempers sometimes flared around the stresses of doing laundry and getting it home clean. Women squabbled over good hanging space and "accidentally" splattered dirt on their rivals' clean linens.

People also used water to wash themselves. How and how often is hard to say. In towns there were commercial bathhouses, where men and women—preferably at separate times or locations—went not only to get clean but also to socialize, as in *hammams* of the Islamic world. By the sixteenth century, condemned for presumed links with prostitution and venereal disease, many such premises had closed. We have a few references to bathing in tubs at home and more to washing hair. Scholars have suggested that by 1600 the motives that shuttered bathhouses discouraged bathing itself.[5] Washing face and hands remained routine, but a full-body ablution became an uncommon rite, often to mark a major life passage. Personal hygiene for the elite moved to applying powders and perfumes rather than washing off sweat and dirt. Increasingly, smell became a marker of social status. Without deodorants, however, it was hard to fulfill Giovanni Della Casa's injunction that a gentleman should smell neither foul like a beggar nor sweet like a harlot. Nor did teeth cleaning rely on water. Della Casa implies that people customarily did this at meals, rinsing their mouths with wine and then using napkins, fingers, or toothpicks hung on strings around their necks to dislodge anything left behind.[6]

With scant piped water and, hence, no flush toilets, Renaissance arrangements for excretion were primitive. People did not agree on what was proper behavior. In Rome, for example, on the one hand, a man caught urinating in the street might invite residents' sharp rebukes; on the other, a respectable notary could joke about hearing men pissing in the courtyard of his office. So the management of human waste posed architects and housekeepers an eternal problem. Ordinary householders used latrines outside, but during the night or for those who could not move, there were chamber pots that had to be emptied. In dense communities, latrines were hard to place, for heaped excrement bred stink and illness. Where possible, they could jut from the backs of buildings, venting directly onto unused terrain. Or they could occupy a courtyard nook far from public activities. In cities servants and lower-status folk sometimes enjoyed the scant privacy at many-holed banks of seats suspended over a pit or void, a convivial arrangement with antecedents in the ancient world. Elites, however, wished not to trudge to inconvenient, smelly corners. The better-off used individual close-stools—chairs with chamber pots inside—typically lodged in bedrooms, from which, in a well-run house, the servants would carry away the refuse. Even better were tiny, separate rooms, close at hand, sometimes nestled in the outer walls, and just large enough for a one-seat privy.

Furniture and Household Goods

To a modern eye, even in a wealthy Renaissance house the furniture would have looked sparse, and bulky. Built solidly and simply, the basic types and designs of furniture were few: beds, seats, tables, and chests. A mix of heavy pieces, often only a few per chamber, lined walls throughout the house, but moved as occasion required. During the fifteenth and especially the sixteenth centuries, the rich eagerly purchased fancy, decorated pieces—embellished in Renaissance styles evoking ancient architecture, with carving and inlay and upholstered with tassels, scallops, and fringes.[7]

The bed was, both symbolically and functionally, a house's center. When a newly married couple set up home, the bed was their principal acquisition. Lucky ones might receive an heirloom. Its bedding and sometimes its frame were usual parts of the trousseau. In this bed the next generation would be conceived; there women would later gather to congratulate the new mother and greet her child. Suitably, the bedroom was often better furnished, decorated, and warmed than other rooms. Located as far as possible from the outside world, it was also the strong room; Italian men and women hid not only jewelry, papers, and money in, under, or near the bed, but also their grain, arms, and armor. Paradoxically, beds and bedrooms were also sites for sociability. Not only women after childbirth, but also men, even officials, sometimes entertained guests and petitioners from their beds. Beds were also shared for sleeping. Assorted family members commonly slept in the same bed, as, sometimes, did mistresses and their servants, or friends, or even strangers thrown together in an inn. No one equated shared beds with sex.

Beds varied greatly in size and comfort. Those of sixteenth-century saints Filippo Neri and Giuseppe Calansanzio, preserved at Roman shrines, are fittingly narrow and, in Neri's case, very short. These holy activists put comfort last. Many other beds were wide, ample for several sleepers. The simplest bed frames consisted of planks or rough boxes set on low trestles. The best beds were substantial wooden structures built tall and flanked by low, flat-topped chests, where guests might sit or servants sleep. In fifteenth-century Florence, where luxury furniture-making flourished, a buyer might pay a skilled worker's annual wage for a highly decorated bed or chest. From the 1490s, good beds boasted columns at the corners to support hangings. Even before four-poster beds came in, curtains suspended from walls and ceilings facilitated sleep. Draperies in winter held warmth in and in summer kept bugs out. As elsewhere, rich fabrics heralded affluence and glamour. As in Giulio Romano's painting of "Two Lovers," courtesans liked to sport a "pavilion"— a crown of drapery spread to the sides of the bed. In daytime, bed curtains were looped into knots to raise them out of the way.

Bedding, with other linens such as tablecloths, napkins, and towels, made up much of the value of many people's household goods. Mattresses, pillows, and sheets made beds comfortable—the more the better, if one could afford them. In cities poor or transient people could rent mattresses and sheets separately from a space to sleep. Bedding might be the currency of survival, all the poor could pawn.

Though less central than beds, tables and seating were common furniture. Like beds, tables ran a gamut from simple, easily dismantled rigs of boards and trestles to solid pieces of fine carpentry now seen in museums and historic castles. An ordinary household might well have only one table used for meals, and also for work, recreation, and sleep, as needs arose. When people sat—at the table, by the fire, or elsewhere—what few seats there were may have been uncomfortable. Sometimes they sat directly on ground or floor or cross-legged on platforms, like tailors sewing; even patrician women might be painted sitting with only a cushion for support. But there were seats. Pictures of peasant houses feature wooden stools and benches. These are depicted in urban and wealthier settings too, but chairs of several sorts also appear. Some were barely more than narrow-backed stools; some had seats of woven fiber; others folded for easy portability. For the grand, who bought more ease and prestige, there were armchairs, sometimes upholstered in leather or gold-embroidered velvet.

Chests were the other staple home furnishing. Storage—of food, dishes, clothing, linens, tools, work supplies, weapons, jewelry, money, books, papers, playthings, and so on—was a crucial function. Accessibility and security both mattered. For clothes in frequent use, wall pegs were handy. Foodstuffs could hang above vermin, suspended from ceiling hooks. Barrels stored bulky goods compactly. A household stowed much of its worth, however, in chests of many sizes. Some small ones enclosed valuables, while others, for clothing, were large enough to hide a lover, as in several of Boccaccio's salty stories. To secure them, chests were frequently fitted with locks and sometimes strapped with stout metal bands. Into the sixteenth century, most chests stuck to a basic rectangular shape. Elegant inlay or narrative painting from a premier workshop could make even a straight-sided wooden box a luxury item. Fancy chests bore high honor; when transporting the trousseau at a patrician wedding, or bestowed on a foreign potentate, they flaunted status. In the later Renaissance, the chest elaborated took new forms; some, acquiring legs, doors, and drawers, became more like cupboards and wardrobes. The credenza, a sideboard-chest supporting shelves for showing off dishes and silverware, was one popular variant. Even ordinary homes or inns might sport a credenza. Personal desks, which multiplied in the Renaissance alongside literacy, evolved into storage chests for small books and papers. Beautiful examples of artful Italian chests grace museum collections, but we should remember that most people stored their belongings in rather plain and functional pieces.

Besides these larger pieces of furniture, a Renaissance home also contained a motley of other useful equipment and goods. Notarized postmortem inventories help show who had what. Besides serviceable belongings heirs might desire, these lists catalog countless worn or broken items, kept perhaps with an eye to repair or recycling. Houses often stored tools and materials, including horse gear and weapons. Women kept spindles, embroidery frames, and sewing supplies. For recreation there might be musical instruments and games; some householders kept birds in cages. The literate acquired books, and rich connoisseurs bought art and antiquities. Many homes had holy icons, plain or splendid, most often featuring the Madonna.

FOOD

Eating and Serving

Among the household goods were also the equipment and dishes for preparing and consuming food. For everyday fare, Renaissance Italians used plates, bowls, trays, and pitchers made of dull metal or simple terracotta. For banquets and display, the rich favored silver, or fancy majolica, a new Italian specialty, admired across Europe. These tin-glazed ceramics featured colorful pictures, often outlined in blue against a light background. Although only the wealthy could afford large pieces, smaller, simpler ones bearing a name or simple picture were in reach of artisans or monks and nuns. Apothecary shops also stored ingredients in glazed ceramic vessels, some of fine majolica. Tableware consisted of usually rather large spoons and knives; forks for individual use, a Renaissance novelty, spread from Italy to other parts of Europe, usually moving from the top of society downward.

Sometimes larger groups of people ate together. Local communities sometimes gathered in solidarity at a feast to celebrate a wedding or patron saint's day. A more individual yen to show off one's taste and largesse led among the wealthy to ever more elaborate banquets with bevies of guests. To make a stunning impression, hosts ordered up many courses of fancy food and laid on stylish entertainment.[8] The décor of the room and the presentation of the dishes became themselves a spectacle. Since few aspiring families owned enough silver serving dishes and utensils or wall hangings to make a fulsome display, it was customary to borrow for the occasion from the well-stocked storerooms (*guardaroba*) of one or more neighbors or patrons. On banquet day, sometimes underlings were allowed to glimpse and marvel as their betters gorged themselves, and afterward leftovers might be distributed to the poor.[9]

Eating, although often shared with friends as well as family, was commonly a domestic activity. While eating together was enjoyed, there is little protocol around ordinary mealtimes; those on hand when food was ready ate, and those missing ate when they could. In large palaces, servants and other menials dined in a separate refectory (*tinello*). Ever more courtly manners for eating came to distinguish high table etiquette. In cities, inns, wine shops, and street vendors fed many people. At the *ostaria* (tavern) guests bought beverages and meals of meat, fish for fast days, and even artichokes. Even at a simpler wine shop, customers might bring in clams and sardines to wash down with drink. Take-out, although not pizza as we know it, was familiar to many who ate at home or on their own. Besides purchasing the staples bread and wine, people ordered cooked meat and other dishes from the inns, sometimes for delivery by servants. Peddlers sold fruit, chestnuts, and baked treats.

Not all homes had kitchens, but better houses had a dedicated room for cooking, with the necessary fireplaces, andirons, hooks, spits, and cauldrons, and occasionally even running water. Because cooking produced heat, smoke, smells, noise, and some danger, the well-to-do preferred to locate the kitchen away from living spaces, at the back or in a garret. Some apartments had a separate kitchen elsewhere in the building. Simpler dwellings used the fire in the main room or had no facilities at all. Especially in modest accommodations but even in well-equipped ones, cooking was physically demanding. It involved much squatting and kneeling on the floor, bending to lift hot and heavy containers, and care to avoid burns and fires. Wood and water had to be fetched. In a large household with many mouths, the cook, often male, usually had helpers. In an ordinary family, cooking was one of many jobs the housekeeper juggled—be she mother or servant.

Diet

The Renaissance diet lacked many foods central to Italian eating today: tomatoes, corn, potatoes, chili pepper, chocolate, and coffee. Gelato had yet to be invented, though, late in the period, drinks chilled by stored snow delighted a few rich men. Pizza was a simple, flat bread, not ubiquitous and never red. Pasta was no staple, but an occasional treat, often eaten sweet. Mostly, these missing ingredients would come from the New World, whose culinary gifts first infiltrated Europe only in the mid-sixteenth century. At first they were for occasional or special uses. Tomatoes, for example, served first as medicine and aphrodisiac, then enlivened salads, but sauced spaghetti only in the 1800s. Similarly, maize was cultivated in Veneto from the 1540s, but corn-based polenta fed few North Italian peasants until the eighteenth century. Potatoes' victory came no earlier. The Americas also provided new meats; at Renaissance banquets turkey sometimes stood in for local fowl, while Newfoundland codfish, dried and salted as *baccalà*, caught on as cheap fare for fasts. Some new foods came from the East. Coffee, for instance, wandered from Arabia via Egypt, arrived at Venice late in the sixteenth century and diffused rapidly from there. Italians probably also owed the Arabs for pasta, made from special hard-grained wheat. The Middle Ages knew pasta, but during the Renaissance it still cost three times more than bread. It served special events only. Not until the seventeenth century, in Naples, and later elsewhere, was pasta daily fare.

As a rule, Renaissance Italians enjoyed an ample, varied, balanced diet. Famine was a risk, but, between 1400 and 1580, grave shortages were local, and rare. When supplies ran short, town governments stepped in quickly to ensure that food, especially bread, was available at a reasonable price. Epidemics' death toll kept population from pressing hard on land's capacity, and helped keep survivors well nourished. Indeed, early modern Italians were on average bigger and more robust than they would be in the poorer centuries to follow; even 1900 was less healthy than 1500. In structure, their diet, however, differed from ours. While many Renaissance Italians ate a fair bit of meat and other animal protein, they depended on carbohydrates, including those in alcohol, for most calories. Fats, rather than a health hazard, were desirable, for overall intake was low, much of it coming from healthful olive oil and fish.

Carbohydrates were central to Renaissance nutrition, ever more so as the population rose. Because land yielded five times as many calories per acre from grain as from meat, bread was the staple that fed more people. Baking bread was heavy work. It took energetic kneading in a wooden trough, often on the ground. In cities and villages, specialized artisans made most bread. Typically, it was dense, perhaps lumpy, with thick crust. Such loaves kept well but required serious chewing, even when fresh. Rather than making sandwiches, ordinary Italians often ate their bread plain, in hunks, perhaps seasoned in peasant fashion with a bite of raw garlic or onion or perhaps olives preserved in brine. As a moister alternative, bread might serve as a plate under a helping of meat or cooked vegetable or as a sop dipped in an individual bowl or in a common pot. For folk with missing or damaged teeth, such a meal was easier than plain bread. Most ordinary bread was brown. Wheat was the

preferred grain, and the more refined white bread, while providing less nutrition, commanded more prestige and a higher price.
In southern Italy and in northern cities, everybody, even the poor,
ate wheat bread. Elsewhere, peasants often had to eat loaves made
at least partly with lesser grains, cheaper and easier to grow but
harder to digest. Regional diets included millet, oats, rye, barley,
and spelt. In the high country, chestnut flour, a major starch, supported villages in the colder months. In addition to bread, Italians
consumed much carbohydrate in the form of boiled grain, as mush
(thick), porridge (thinner), or *minestra* (thinnest).

At the top of the scale, grain foods included rice and pasta. In the
fifteenth-century Po valley, rice cultivation spread, a luxury crop for
soups and medicines. Pasta, made from special hard wheat flour, was
rolled, cut, and dried on frames. It already came in different shapes
with regional names—macaroni, ravioli, tortelli, papardelli, lasagne—
and local recipes. It served for special events, or a Sunday treat for
monks, not with our savory tomato sauces, but either plain with meat
or fish, or dressed with cheese and "sweet" spices like cinnamon.

Eating Well

This description of preparing pasta is one of many recipes
offered by Platina in his late fifteenth-century guide to health
and good eating.[10]

Sicilian Macaroni

Beat well-sifted white flour with egg white and rose water and
plain water. When it is mixed, draw out into thin strips of dough
in the manner of straw half a foot long. Hollow them out with a
very thin iron rod. When you draw out the iron, you will leave
them hollow. When it is dried in the sun, the pasta of this sort
will last two or three years, especially if it was under the waning moon of August. If it is cooked in rich broth and poured into
serving dishes, it should be sprinkled with fresh, new butter
and sweet spices. The dish requires two hours' cooking.

Renaissance people consumed many carbohydrates, but far less
sugar than they do now. The sugar in wine, however, was a big
source of calories. Almost everyone drank it, straight or watered, as

the principal beverage (upward of two-thirds of a liter per person per day). Most people drank cheaper local wines, but the affluent prized fine vintages such as Chianti whites or the sweeter wines of Naples, which traveled well. Besides wine, Italians consumed sugars in sauces for meats, in fruit preserves and syrups, and a few pastries such as marzipan and *mostacciolo*, a dense fruit cake. Italians certainly liked sweet tastes, but the ingredients inflated a food budget. Sweet therefore was long associated with the elite palate, while salt—a preservative—was dominant for ordinary folk. In most Renaissance recipes, cane sugar, grown in Cyprus under Venetian monopoly in the fifteenth century, and later raised in New World plantations, replaced honey. Medical texts recommended sugar to aid digestion and, for health, prescribed sweet alcoholic cordials.

While carbohydrates supplied the bulk of Renaissance calories, meat and other animal proteins were reasonably plentiful. The fifteenth century marked consumption's high point. Thereafter a rising population needed grain that competed for productive acreage; higher prices reduced meat eating. Around 1600, in Rome, children at an orphanage enjoyed about one-third of a pound of meat per day, while the Jesuits' adolescent male students ate twice that. The poor who received no charity would likely see meat rarely. In general, however, more people ate more flesh than in succeeding centuries. Cooks prepared meat by boiling and roasting, sometimes in combination. Long cooking, which helped kill microbes, left meat soft, bland, and ready for a sweet or tangy sauce. Nuts, fruits, and "sweet" spices such as cinnamon, cloves, nutmeg, and ginger were welcome components, yielding a flavor akin to our mincemeat, derived from medieval cookery, which originally had meat in it. Saffron, another favorite seasoning, besides adding taste, gave the dish a golden hue that suggested well-being.

The meat consumed varied with the season and the eater's wealth. Except for Lent and fast days, when they ate fish, Italians, especially the well-to-do, ate beef, available all year-round. But many people looked to cheaper animals, whose availability shifted with the season. Pork, killed in early winter and preserved as ham and sausages, was eaten until Lent; lamb, born in spring and symbolically tied to Easter, went into early summer. For variety there were chicken and rabbit, and wild game. Aristocratic banquets featured a stunning display of exotic meats, prepared to delight both eye and taste buds: boar, venison, peacock, swan, crane, and cormorant. Renaissance elites increasingly chose the lighter flesh of fowl and fish over the meaty tang of big game. Though linked with fasting, fish was much enjoyed, especially freshwater sorts, including migratory eel and lamprey, transported alive in barrels or baskets. Not only the patricians relished such delicacies. One police chief in Rome raged jealously at his concubine because of an eel that, he believed, a rival lover had given her.[11]

Though seldom abundant in Renaissance diets, fats were very important for a balanced nutrition and for cooking, as well as for lighting and making soap. Besides fats were tasty. Their costs limited consumption, as did the religious calendar of fasts, which restricted meat, lard, and butter. The rich treats of "Fat Tuesday," the day before the "forty-day" Lenten abstinence, reminded celebrants of lean weeks to come. For cooking, much of Italy—the alpine lake district and the regions south from Tuscany—relied on olive oil. Good oil was prized; in the fifteenth century, the best was said to come from Apulia. At that time, Lombardy, in the upper Po valley, was adopting the butter that reigned across the Alps, while some of Tuscany used lard and liquefied pork fat. Where olive oil was not standard, Jews met their dietary rules with goose fat. Eggs and dairy products, specifically cheese, were another fat source. Fresh milk was generally unsafe to drink and did not keep. As cheese, however, it could be processed during the summer, in the mountains, and then, especially in its hard and dry forms, saved for eating year long. Cheese was popular; the richer in fat, the pricier, it appeared in many dishes, including pasta. As today, there were countless kinds; a treatise by a fifteenth-century physician from Turin cataloged a host of varieties.

Europeans from the North remarked on the Italian diet's copious vegetables and fruits. The Mediterranean climate permitted their consumption fresh, as well as preserved in brines and syrups. Renaissance Italians made good use of protein-rich pulses such as beans and chickpeas. They ate cabbage, squashes, artichokes, spinach, and other greens as well as garlic, onions, and leeks. Selection varied with the season. Vegetables were served both stewed and raw; salads—dressed with ample oil, moderate salt, and a dash of vinegar—were widely popular. Although not costly and eaten by modest folk, such dishes appealed also to the elite. Thus, recipes for condiments redolent of the garlic and onions associated with peasants appeared regularly in cookbooks for the upper-class table. Fresh fruits, including apples, grapes, peaches, pears, and oranges, were more of a treat. Still, market demand supported, for example, the orange vendors in Rome's streets. People gave prized fruits, like melons or pomegranates, as gifts. Fruit preserves also featured as delicacies at banquets.

CLOTHING

To Renaissance Italians, clothing was immensely important. As in many cultures, clothes not only protected the body from the elements but also marked people's social identities and thus shaped their daily transactions. Frequent civic regulations specified what types and styles of apparel should be worn by different social ranks. While these sumptuary laws sought to ensure modesty and social propriety, they also aimed to cut costs. As clothes and body ornaments were often pricey, city authorities aimed to curb splurging. Cloth itself, which came in many qualities, weights, fibers, and colors, was often quite valuable. Unworked bolts of fabric figure in wills as significant bequests. Good cloth was substantial and tough, meant to last; like many other goods, it was used and reused. Nonetheless, aside from shirts and collars, many garments got washed seldom, if ever. Most people, owning few items, wore the same clothes all the time. When witnesses in criminal investigations described culprits by their clothing, they could reasonably expect that the identification would hold because most had few other garments. The rich had much larger wardrobes, but even for them, a new cloak or dress was a serious investment.[12] The clothing a patrician groom bought for his bride might cost a third of the dowry he received from her father.

Because cloth and clothing were so valuable, their manufacture loomed large in the Renaissance economy. Many people made part of or all their living in the range of crafts that moved material from fiber to yarn to cloth to garments or to draperies, bedding, and table linens. Specialized artisans produced the lace, gold thread, embroidery, and buttons that ornamented fancy dress. In the Middle Ages, clothing was made largely of linen and wool; under wool, a linen undergarment was recommended, to prevent chafing. During the Renaissance, silk, which earlier had been manufactured in the East, began to compete with the other fibers. Its softness and sheen were prized; dyed in brilliant colors—red, purple, saffron, indigo— it could be woven into thick velvets and multicolored damasks. By the later fifteenth century Italy itself was producing much silk cloth, though mostly of lighter and less expensive grades than the medieval imports. The fashion for silk thus spread and moved into the wardrobes of women of middling means.

While most clothing was custom-made and intended for a particular wearer, use and reuse meant that fit was often approximate. For something quick and ready-made, people looked for

an old-clothes seller, a trade commonly plied by Jews, and made
do with what they found. Buyers wanting something new and to
a particular design needed more time. They might purchase the
fabric and decorations themselves and find a tailor to make it up;
or they might ask the tailor's advice in choosing and buying the
materials. A tailor was a cutter as the English-French word suggests. He knew the shapes and sizes of pieces for a gown, doublet,
or cloak and, if skillful, how to lay them out, with little fabric
wasted, to maximize comfort and sturdiness. Then he stitched,
finished, and fitted the garment in consultation with the customer. A tailor also happily altered old clothing as it passed to
a new use or wearer. Even so, although some Renaissance styles
fitted more closely than their medieval predecessors, the sizes
of garments remained irregular. The cut and design of clothing,
both male and female, left room for adjustment without resort to
the needle. Laces at crucial junctions, instead of seams, made fitting easier.

Among the forms of social place that clothing announced, gender stood out. Regulations forbade either sex the apparel of the
other. Cross-dressing did occur, for both practical and transgressive reasons. While men sometimes donned female garb as a carnival masquerade, women more often got caught cross-dressing.
Some dressed as males to travel more safely and freely, incog-
nito. Most notorious, however, were courtesans, who played
their trade's moral ambiguities to titillate customers. These rare
exceptions only stressed the general commitment to different
male and female appearance. Hair styles, headgear, necklines,
and the coverage of the lower body were among the sharpest
markers.

Basic male attire was a shirt and tunic with hose. The shirt, a
loosely fitted linen shift worn against the skin, was the garment most
often changed and washed. Over it, men usually wore some form of
tunic or jacket that extended partway down the legs and cinched at
the waist or hips. With the belt, length could be adjusted to accommodate one's work. Lacking zippers or elastic and using few buttons, Renaissance men kept their close-fitting hose up by tying laces
through holes in the upper and lower garments. Early on, hose had
two separate legs not seamed together. This drafty arrangement,
while convenient for excretion, depended on the overhanging tunic
for modesty. As the Renaissance progressed, the two columns

of fabric came to be joined at least partway around. Short breeches also covered the gap; in the sixteenth century, for fashion-conscious men, these became quite puffy and might sport a fat codpiece. Hose tended to wear through at the knees. So, for warmth and protection, working men sometimes wore extra leggings bound around the lower leg and over the knee. A cloth cape—sometimes trimmed or lined with fur for the wealthy— usually completed the ensemble. Such were the usual elements of the male "short" costume. For reasons of age, civic office, or professional or clerical station other men wore "long" garb,

Both men and women wore long shirts as basic, readily washable undergarments. Because they were heavily used, these garments rarely survived, but the intricate embroidery on this sixteenth-century example likely led to its preservation. (The Metropolitan Museum of Art)

which replaced or covered the thigh-length tunic with a straight or flowing robe down to near the ankles. Caps and hats came in a variety of colors and silhouettes: some, of cloth, fitting snugly to the head or rising to high, even bulbous crowns and others of felt or straw with broad, flat brims. Toward the end of the sixteenth century, a fashion for large ruffs struck for men of varied rank. These linen collars, known sometimes as "lettuce," required much starch and attention from laundresses. In Rome, if a gentleman wanted to justify a visit to a lower-status woman, he would say he went to get his collars tended.[13] Perched yet higher on the head, a prime site of bodily honor, hats served tastes from the soberly functional to the fashionably flamboyant. Footwear ranged from wooden clogs to thin-soled leather shoes.

Although women's clothing distinguished them from men, breeches aside, it shared many elements with male garb. Under it all went the shirt, for women sometimes cut wider at the neck. Over it went a one-piece dress, with fitted waist, from which fell a long, fairly full skirt. Its folds fell close enough to the body, especially when layered over the tails of a long shirt, to provide warmth and modesty. Italian women wore stockings but only rarely leggings rising to the waist. Nor were they needed before the arrival of the Spanish fashion for bell-shaped hoop skirts that stood out from the body, exposing it to drafts. For much of the Renaissance, the often square-cut neckline was quite open, showing the shirt beneath. Sleeves often came separately and attached to the armholes of the dress with laces; one relatively cheap way to refresh a wardrobe was to get a new pair. When needing another layer of clothing or for sheer display, women wore a flowing overgown that sometimes trailed on the ground. Urban women wore slippers made of colored fabrics. The soles, often wooden, sometimes served as weapons. To rise above mud and water in the streets, in Venice especially, there were platform shoes of wood and cork that lifted the wearer even a foot above the ground; these caused women to hobble precariously, and some critics claimed they led to miscarriages. On their heads, atop often elaborate hairstyles, women generally wore veils.[14] Although those in mourning and nuns shrouded the body and sometimes the face with long and somber folds of fabric, Italian ladies are often depicted with light, sheer, backspread veils that more enhanced than hid their looks.

During the Renaissance, fashion came into its own. For the wealthy, clothing became more elaborately shaped and decorated. Courtiers and their rich imitators began to distinguish cuts and ornaments and to define themselves by wearing what was novel and prestigious. Competitors for status sought not only lavishness but also style. They eyed the cut of sleeves, which, for both men and women, grew wide and layered; arms sometimes emerged through upper slits while the voluminous sleeve drooped almost to the ground. Other sleeves puffed the shoulder but snuggled the forearm. Eye-catching sleeves, like other items of apparel, might be trimmed in gold thread, embroidered with flowers and leaves, or strewn with pearls. Another decorative fad was slashing: cutting holes in the fabric to allow a contrasting underlayer to show through. This fashion discouraged reuse and drew criticism as wasteful. Indeed, the pursuit of fashion in general was frequently condemned as expensive, inconvenient, vain, and immoral. Sermons and sumptuary laws, however, never quenched the appetite to spend and flaunt. While many reproaches targeted women, portraits show that men too invested heavily in an impressive, modish look. In these and other fashions, during much of the Renaissance, Italy was Europe's trendsetter. Francois I, king of France, asked Isabella d'Este, Countess of Mantua, to send a doll in courtly dress as a model for his ladies in Paris. Costume books, after the middle sixteenth century, show the growing awareness of fashion. With pictures and text, Cesare Vecellio, for example, highlighted variations in dress both over time and across Italy. By his time, however, clothing was shifting to a soberer tone. With the emerging "Spanish" mode, paralleling Spain's sway in the peninsula, black replaced the old vibrant colors and décolletage yielded to high collars and ruffs.

Examples of Men's and Women's Dress

In his compendium of Renaissance world clothing, Cesare Vecellio described the layered outdoor attire of married noblewomen of Milan (1590):

> These noblewomen wear a cloth of light silk on their heads, colored or black according to their preference, which leaves visible only small curls framing their foreheads and ruffles at their necks; this cloth . . . is so large that it covers their shoulders entirely. They wear a three-quarter-length *Romana* [overgown] of patterned damask or velvet, fastened with gold buttons down to the waist. The overgowns are worn open from the waist down to the feet, revealing the floor-length *sottana* [undergown] of silk with bands of patterned velvet or gold brocade. Their *zimarra* [another overgown], on top, has open, short sleeves and the wearer's arms emerge from them, showing the sleeves of the sottana. They wear wood-soled slippers, but not too high, and this is how they walk about.[15]

A Spanish pickpocket, on trial in Rome in 1557, described the dress of a soldier, probably a countryman, he had known in Naples:

> He is a man of some thirty years, tall, a little plump, a round face more brown than not, and rather good looking than not. His beard

is brown and long and round, his hair black. He usually wears a red mantle [*tabarro*]in the German fashion, a velvet collar with four long slashes, with five or six gold buttons at the throat and on his chest. And sometimes he wears black hose with cut velvet uppers, and sometimes they are gray, also velvet, and sometimes he wears a red pair, also velvet, and on his head, when he is wearing his red mantle, he wears an embroidered red hat, and when he does not wear his red mantle, he wears a black cape with velvet finishings and a velvet cap.[16]

HAIR AND COSMETICS

A *bella figura* required attention not only to clothing but also to hair and face. Coiffure and cosmetics pertained to women, but men too took pains with their appearance. Males frequently cut their hair at chin or shoulder length. Many are depicted as clean-shaven in the fifteenth century, but a fashion for beards appeared in the sixteenth.[17] Paintings show both head and facial hair as often curly. For some, curls no doubt came naturally, but Della Casa reproved as effeminate those men who crimped their locks with warm irons. Printed recipes for potions "to blacken the hair and beard" suggest men also used dye. Women's hair grew long and was generally worn piled on the head in simple chignons or intricate confections of rolls and braids. At court and for special events, gold chains, gem-studded nets, and other jewelry ornamented these elaborate coiffures. Women took much trouble to keep their hair fashionably beautiful. They plucked their hairlines well back to achieve the admired smooth, high-domed forehead. Because blond was much prized, women devoted long hours to bleaching. According to Coryate, the English visitor, Venetian ladies spent every Saturday afternoon treating their hair with oil and other "drugs." They then spread it over special straw hats with a hole in the center and very broad brims, and sat in the sun to let it dry. Later, they curled the "whitish" locks and wound them into a distinctive two-horned coiffure.

The culture of Italian beauty included cosmetics for the skin. While Della Casa's chastisement implied that some men used makeup, perfecting the skin's appearance was women's business. The Venetian hat that used sun to bleach the hair also kept the face from darkening. Tanned skin signaled not beauty but outdoor toil and low rank. White was the desirable color for a woman's face, hands, and breast. Where nature and precaution did not suffice, women resorted to cosmetics. Preparations drawn from a tradition of herbal wisdom and applied chemistry promised to soften the skin and remove or cover spots and blemishes. Powders or heavy pastes laid a white shell over the face. Other concoctions sought to make the cheeks pink and the eyebrows dark. As with other female vanities, moralists condemned these cosmetics as injurious to soul and body. Associating them with prostitutes, these commentators saw face painting as tempting the flesh and harming the skin. Other men objected because a rigid mask did not in fact entice. This gale of reproach itself suggests that not just prostitutes but also respectable wives used cosmetics. Knowledge of how to make and use them circulated among women, and some made money by making and selling these wares. In the vogue for empirical alchemy among the literate, in 1561 Isabella Cortese published her book of *Secrets*, that went through seven editions before 1599. She offered a host of recipes that people could prepare themselves; mixed among dyestuffs for leather, polishes for metal and semiprecious stones, and cures for impotence and for worms in horses were many varieties of cosmetics, soaps, perfumes, and treatments for the skin and hair.

Cosmetic Recipes

Face-Water from White Beans

Take peeled white beans and put them in white wine to soften for nine days; then pound them and return them to the wine; and take goat's milk and whole barley and boil it with the milk, until the barley grains are broken; then mix together all those things, and add six fresh egg-whites and mix everything well; and set it to distill. Make the water two weeks before you use it; then it can be used, and washing the face with it, it will do very good job.

To Keep Hair Black

Take four or five spoons of quicklime in powder, two pennyworth of lead oxide with gold and two with silver, and put everything in a mortar and grind it with ordinary water; set it to boil as long you would cook a pennyworth of cabbage; remove it from the fire and let it cool until tepid, and then wash your hair with it. After an hour, wash your hair with clean, warm water and no soap, and then wash yourself with ordinary cleaning agent and soap your hair as usual; and do this every week.[18]

CONCLUSION

Renaissance arrangements for homemaking, eating, and clothing met bodily needs and served social and psychological appetites. Both for their own delight and to win the esteem of others, people of high status and wealth invested money and taste in embellishing their households, possessions, and selves. The privileged few, clothed in colorful and ornamented silks, lived in handsome palaces bedecked with beautiful paintings, and banqueted on peacock and eel. But the vast majority of folk, while they might see gorgeous art in churches or ogle nobles in the street, lived with few and modest belongings. They ate their bread with an onion or a hunk of ham. These goods, however, sustained them, shaped their lives, and commanded close attention. The poor kept a sharp eye to what they and their neighbors owned and used. They struggled to acquire and hang onto what they needed and made patient and inventive use of recycling. While the rich certainly enjoyed greater physical security and comfort than their less fortunate compatriots, even they faced the inconveniences of domestic life without good heating and ventilation, reliable lighting, or, of course, refrigeration and air-conditioning. The material culture of Renaissance Italy was a dazzling mosaic of contradictions.

NOTES

1. Coryate, *Coryat's Crudities*, 280; Fynes Moryson, *Shakespeare's Europe* (New York, 1903), 165.

2. Della Casa, *Galateo*, 7.

3. See Evelyn Welch, *Shopping in the Renaissance: Consumer Cultures in Italy, 1400–1600* (New Haven, CT, 2005).

4. Matteo Bandello, *Novelle* (Milan, 1978), Day III, story 42.

5. On hygiene and its challenges, Douglas Biow, *The Culture of Cleanliness in Renaissance Italy* (Ithaca, NY, 2006).

6. Della Casa, *Galateo*, 54, 57.

7. On furnishings, Peter Thornton, *The Italian Renaissance Interior, 1400–1600* (New York, 1991).

8. By the banquet chef to two popes, Bartolomeo Scappi, *Opera of Bartolomeo Scappi (1570)* (Toronto, 2008).

9. On food for lords and for commoners, Katherine A. McIver, *Cooking and Eating in Renaissance Italy: From Kitchen to Table* (New York, 2015).

10. Platina, *On Right Pleasure and Good Health*, ed. M. Milham (Tempe, 1998), 333.

11. ASR, GTC, Processi, 1600–1619, busta 23, f. 110 v.

12. On patricians' clothing and the people who made it, Carole Collier Frick, *Dressing Renaissance Florence: Families, Fortunes, and Fine Clothing* (Baltimore, 2002).

13. ASR, GTC, Costituti, busta 506 ff. 62v–65v.

14. On veils, shoes, gloves, and handkerchiefs, see essays by Paulicelli, Laughran and Vianello, Welch, and Mirabella in *Ornamentalism: The Art of Renaissance Accessories*, ed. B. Mirabella (Ann Arbor, 2011).

15. Quoted, with simplification, from Margaret Rosenthal and Ann Rosalind Jones, *Cesare Vecellio's Habiti antichi e moderni: The Clothing of the Renaissance World* (London, 2008), 237–38. This book is a rich resource on the clothing of men and women of many classes across Italy, Venice's *stato da mar*, and beyond.

16. ASR, GTC, Processi, 16th c., busta 31, case 7, f. 417v.

17. On facial hair, Douglas Biow, *On the Importance of Being an Individual in Renaissance Italy: Men, Their Professions, and Their Beards* (Philadelphia, 2015).

18. Isabella Cortese, *I Secreti della Signora Isabella Cortese* (reprint Milan, 1995), 80, 140 (our translation). See Meredith K. Ray, *Daughters of Alchemy: Women and Scientific Culture in Early Modern Italy* (Cambridge, MA, 2015), 46–72.

14

DISEASE AND HEALTH

Disease is a facet of the natural world that we still face and fight, but it threatened the people of the Renaissance infinitely more than us. The difference between then and now was stark. In the eyes of modern epidemiology, disease is a curious part of nature, for most disease organisms live, as parasites, in intimate contact with their human hosts. They are therefore a part of nature that is more inside us than out in the wild. We are our microbes' ecological niche, to which they have adapted by sly Darwinian tricks. The same is true of that other, altogether inner foe, the successful cancer cell. Our modern picture of disease has several elements: contagion, personal and social susceptibility, and efficient medicine.

The Renaissance perception of disease had some elements in common with ours and others that were radically different. It is worth pausing to reflect on the raw experience of disease. Although our medicine is far from omnipotent, we trust its powers to shield us from many dangers and, above all, to dull or even banish pain. A fundamental fact: the Renaissance had no aspirin, or other pills, for pain. Headaches and toothaches—and they were common—had merely to be borne. Fever victims burned or shivered, and sweated, and waited for relief. And childbirth hurt a great deal more than it does today. Furthermore, without reliable antiseptics or anesthesia, internal surgery was extremely perilous. A condition like hernia, now cured by a simple operation, had no safe fix; its victims might go years or decades with their intestines, painfully bloated, sheathed in trusses outside their bellies. Italians, like other Europeans, learned to live with pain. They also lacked cures for infection. Thus, they feared untimely death. They had their remedies, and their hopes in them, but lacked our luxury (now imperiled by bacterial evolution) of trusting one antibiotic or another to do its job and save us. Hope therefore was shot through with an anxiety that we, despite Ebola, Zika, and other new diseases, can scarcely comprehend.

MEDICAL THEORIES

The Renaissance conception of patterns of infection was unlike ours. Like us, Italians were aware of isolated illnesses and of epidemics, waves of sickness that swept through houses, towns, and districts. To them, as to us, these were manifestations of the natural world. However, for Christian reasons, they were also part of a larger divine plan—God's providence. Thus, one response to infection was prayer and ceremonies. There were other differences in response as well. Only in the mid-nineteenth century did medicine discover germs and work out a clear theory of contagion. Renaissance learned medicine, though aware of contagion, still hewed to ancient Greek theories that held that sickness commonly came from imbalances in the body. The four humors (body fluids: blood, phlegm, black and yellow bile) were out of healthy equilibrium. Each humor combined two factors: hot or cold, wet or dry. Thus, if sickness struck, the goal was to restore deficiencies and to remove excess: to warm the cold-wet sufferer and bleed the hot-wet one and so on. To sustain health, one should aim, physicians said, for a temperate life, regulating food, drink, sleep, exercise, and sex, cultivating peace of mind and a quiet soul. Proper diet, everyone agreed, was crucial. Humor theory taught Renaissance Italians to keep the body balanced. For example, when cold and damp, drink warm dry wines. When heated, eat cooling foods![1] Diseases, then, came from God, from the natural world, from the *distemper* of human souls and bodies. But they also proceeded by infection, and the vectors were not organisms but miasmas. Vapors. Smells. Malaria, for instance, means just "bad air."

The bad air theory galvanized authorities. Ignorant of germs, they went after smells, and in doing so probably improved the general health. In the sixteenth century, the Grand Duchy of Tuscany had a vigorous body of health inspectors, who collected reports on the air of towns and villages. Their reports of manure piles, garbage-strewn streets, open sewers, and casual latrines remind us that the Renaissance had its stenches. Where successful, the officials' efforts at hygiene probably curtailed water-borne diseases. They were, however, irrelevant to respiratory ailments and to the grave or deadly sicknesses borne, as we now know, by insects: malaria, typhus, and bubonic plague.

The whole complex of Renaissance theories of infection thus called forth an elaborate program to defend public health. Authorities, with an eye to general welfare, developed a series of measures—some in fact appropriate, and others either irrelevant or even harmful—to hedge the spread of epidemics. Infected travelers could carry serious illnesses from one city to another. Thus, early on, cities learned that they could sometimes ward off an epidemic by barring suspect travelers. The English word *quarantine*, of Italian origin, traces to the practice of making incoming ships from plague-ridden ports anchor in isolation for forty (*quaranta*) days. It often worked; the wait was long enough to kill off the crew or prove a vessel clean. It was much harder to prevent contagion's spread overland; terrestrial human traffic was both heavier and more diffuse. As, for grave epizootics like rinderpest, was the drift of migrant livestock. Nevertheless, since cities were walled, they could close their gates to travelers from infected zones. During epidemics, travelers had to show a certificate to prove they came from uninfested places. Although open to corruption and cheating, these measures afforded some protection.

By the same logic, when highly infectious diseases did strike, one response was to isolate the victims. The authorities often sequestered the poorer patients in a hospital. The measure, though it might help the populace as a whole, was often deadly to the sick. Renaissance hospitals, for all their good intentions, lacked efficacious medicines. Crowding and the plethora of diseases in cramped spaces made them fairly deadly. A second recourse, often tried against bubonic plague, was to seal up a house if one resident fell sick, and not unseal it until the dying stopped. Due to the complex epidemiology of plague, this measure did little good and much harm, for the rats could leave and flea-filled houses were actually more contagious than their denizens. Unable to flee, imprisoned households were thus at far greater risk. The experience of plague had taught Italians that flight was the most prudent remedy. For example, in 1462, Pope Pius II and his court were in Viterbo, celebrating the feast of

Corpus Christi with sumptuous processions. Pestilence cut short
the festivities. He records in his autobiography:

> But what joys of mortals are lasting? All that pleases is too brief. Grief
> succeeds happiness. Lamentation follows hard on laughter. While the
> Curia was exulting over such a state of affairs [a festival] and the
> city was elated with excessive joy, they were stricken with a sudden
> plague. A wasting poison and fatal pestilence carried off many, both
> citizens and curials [members of the papal court], so that the terrified
> cardinals asked that the Curia be moved. The Pope kept a few with
> him and allowed the rest to go where they pleased to escape the fatal
> sickness.[2]

The papal court's reaction here was normal. The rich, with their
villas, were better placed to flee the city; though they too at times
succumbed, plague increasingly smote mainly the lower classes.

INFECTIOUS DISEASES

Patterns of Morbidity

Among infections, plague, a spectacular killer, was not alone.
Historians find it hard to lay out a statistical balance of its morbid
rivals. For one thing, medical terminology was vague; for another,
the actual symptoms of some diseases have changed as both the
microorganisms, and their victims' responses, have evolved.
Despite DNA analysis of old bones, medical historians still have
much detective work to do. Nevertheless, they can point to some
general patterns. As with us, but worse, the winters, when families huddled in damp, close quarters, were the season for respiratory infections, including bronchitis and influenza, at times deadly,
and pneumonia, yet more perilous. These diseases most afflicted
the very young and the old. Unlike us now, with our refrigeration
and clean water, Italy had sickly summers. Minor stomachaches
and serious dysentery were rampant. In infants, easily dehydrated,
severe diarrhea could kill swiftly. The hot season therefore took a
heavy toll of babies once they consumed any foods besides breast
milk. Poor, malnourished infants were particularly susceptible. As
we shall see shortly, some other diseases also had their seasonal
patterns.

Of all causes of death, bubonic plague far outweighed the others.
Fifteenth-century Florentine records dating from six quiet years
bracketed by bigger outbreaks still blamed perhaps two-thirds of

all the city's mortality on the illness. Plague fell most heavily on children and adolescents. Older Florentines, who had survived earlier epidemics, less often succumbed. Given the records' imprecision, these statistics are uncertain. Nevertheless, they give some sense of the extraordinary power of that pestilence and the reasons for its grip on the collective imagination.

Three Insect-Borne Infections: Malaria, Typhus, and Plague

Some of the gravest illnesses had insect vectors. These diseases had geographic and seasonal patterns linked to the life cycle of their carriers. Malaria was very common. The disease's name came from the dank "bad air" (*mal aria*) that was thought to spread fever. Although they had no notion of mosquitoes' role in propagation, Italians knew well that the illness somehow came from swamps. Although summer was the infection's season, sufferers could carry the microbe for years and unexpectedly relapse at any time. The great campaigns to drain swamps had the express goal not only to reclaim land for the plow but also to drive off fever. Commonly, malarial fevers are cyclical, in synchrony with the life cycle of the parasite that infests the blood. In the Renaissance, therefore, countless Italians complained of falling sick with *febbre terziana* or *quartana*, an acute fever that hits every three or every four days, when the parasites break out of cells. Despite the vagueness both of fever and of these common terms, most often, malaria must have been the cause. Sometimes fatal, malaria was and is debilitating.

A second insect-borne infestation was typhus: fever, exhaustion, delirium, and little spots all over. Transmitted by lice, it came in epidemics, newly in Italy, from the 1490s. Although almost everyone had body lice, the poor were more often stricken, for they had fewer changes of clothing, less money to spend on bathhouses or washerwomen, more reasons for sharing beds and for living at close quarters. Winter weather, when one huddled under infested wraps, fostered epidemics.

The third and by far the deadliest insect-borne pestilence was the bubonic plague. This utterly terrifying disease seems (the bacillus for sure says DNA analysis, but the bubo lumps less certain) to have first returned to Europe in 1347 after six centuries of reprieve; it afflicted Italy and the rest of Western Europe for more than three hundred years and then, for reasons still hotly debated by historians of medicine, retreated eastward. Wherever it went, plague spread appalling devastation. Generally, it was an urban disease, sometimes endemic, but often appearing in massive epidemics. Through much of the Renaissance and down to the 1650s, these would hit a city perhaps once a generation. The epidemiology of bubonic plague is fascinatingly complex, for it involves four organisms: bacilli, fleas, rats, and humans. The course and rhythms of the disease, and the efficacy of remedies, depended on the biology of all four organisms and the material culture of the human hosts. Occasionally plague took a pneumonic form, spreading from human to human. Generally, however, humans caught it from the bite of a rat flea. Although plague bacilli do not make fleas ill, they clog their digestive tracks. Unfortunately for humans, when rat fleas bite, they also regurgitate, spitting up bacteria. What complicates the picture is that, for a rat flea, a human, as a meal, is no treat. So it was only when there was an epizootic—a great dying off of infected rats—that their hungry fleas would leap, reluctantly, onto unpalatable human prey. Meanwhile, humans had their own fleas in itchy plenty, but our insect species—because they do not regurgitate—are inefficient vectors. The lessons of all these facts are several. For one, humans were not themselves a major source of contagion. Rather, it was usually sick rats on the move that brought the disease to an uninfected, vulnerable rat population, from which it spread to humans only when most of the local rats took sick and died. That is why ships, often rat infested, were so dangerous and quarantine so useful. This pattern also shows why locking stricken families in houses was a mistake, for it was the house, with its dying rats and ravenous rat fleas, that was dangerous, not the inhabitants, even if already infected.[3] Those who fled town, like Pope Pius and his court, thus took the prudent course. At the same time, some of the other plague remedies, such as burning the clothing of the dead or sitting near hot fires, killed or repelled fleas and probably did some good.

The medical effects of the plague were dramatic. The characteristic mark of the disease was the appearance of buboes, great swellings of the lymph nodes of the armpits and groin. Mortality usually exceeded 60 percent, and death came within days. The social effects of a serious epidemic were almost as dramatic. Boccaccio's famous description in his *Decameron* of the 1347 plague depicts the dissolution of human ties. When the disease appeared, he writes, as people fled in terror, many of the bonds that held society together collapsed. Even family, the primary social institution, dissolved, leaving the sick in the hands of mercenary caretakers, men and women of low station who for pay risked all. The obsequies for the dead suffered the same fate. In normal times, a proper funeral and a requiem were moments of solidarity that served both the grieving survivors and the soul of the deceased. In a raging epidemic, there were corpses everywhere, and almost no one left to bury them. Carts, driven by brave, desperate men, might gather the dead from streets and houses and haul them unceremoniously to a mass grave. In a world where the solidarity of the living and the dead was precious, this disruption of good funerary order appalled everyone.

Syphilis: A New Disease

Another disease that especially frightened Renaissance Italians was syphilis. The novelty of the ailment baffled physicians; there was nothing like it in the ancient Greek and Roman doctrines of their textbooks. Some medical commentators looked to the stars; baleful Saturn had been in the house of genital Scorpio. Most, however, soon agreed that sexual contact was a likely cause. Its particularly disgusting symptoms struck terror. The great Veronese physician Fracastoro, whose long poem on the subject gave this ailment its modern name, described it as follows:

> In the majority of cases, small ulcers began to appear on the sexual organs [and they were] intractable and did not depart. . . . Next the skin broke out with encrusted pustules . . . and they soon grew little by little till they were the size of the cup of an acorn, which they in fact resembled. . . . Next these ulcerated pustules ate away the skin . . . and they sometimes infected not only the fleshy parts but even the very bones as well. In cases where the malady was firmly established in the upper parts of the body, the patients suffered from pernicious catarrh [respiratory infection] which eroded the palate or the uvula or the pharynx or tonsils. In some cases the lips or eyes were eaten away, or in others the whole of the sexual organs. Moreover, many patients suffered from the great deformity of *gummata* [rubbery lumps] which developed on the members; these were often as large as an egg or a roll of bread. . . . Besides all the above symptoms, as if they were not bad enough, violent pains attacked the muscles. . . . [T]hese pains were persistent, tormented the sufferer chiefly at night, and were the most cruel of all the symptoms.[4]

In Fracastoro's day, almost no one in Italy called this terrifying, shameful ailment "syphilis." Rather, they called it "the French disease." Much of Europe followed suit; Shakespeare's England called it "the French pox." The French, who abhorred this credit, rather called it "the Neapolitan disease." Both appellations made good sense, for the malady seems first to have appeared, dramatically, as if from nowhere, when a French army in 1495 laid siege to Naples. The French in 1496 retreated up the peninsula, frequenting prostitutes in the usual military way and leaving behind them a trail of pustules, racking pains, and slow death. One proposed remedy was to test the prostitutes and lock the sick ones up. But, since a lively sexual commerce was tolerated and legal, no such thing happened, and with astonishing speed the illness spread through all social classes, infecting commoners, princes, and cardinals. As with many new diseases, syphilis was very contagious and virulent. With time, microbes evolved into milder forms.

Although Renaissance medicine could not overcome the scourge, it proposed some treatments. One was to roast the disease out; poor sufferers would be shut in barrels for several hours, with hot stones piled around them to make them sweat. A common remedy was the application of mercury to the sores, a risky measure giving some relief. Physicians already knew that mercury was severely poisonous, and many urged a light dose. This therapy continued into the twentieth century, when effective antibiotics at last appeared. Another cure was "holy wood" (*lignum vitae*), a resin derived from the guaiacum tree, native to the Caribbean. Powdered and quaffed as an infusion, this gum did in fact ease the pain of the awful pustules; a great transatlantic trade grew up to feed the appetite for relief. The big Roman hospital of San Giacomo of the Incurables in a year could consume almost four tons to treat some 2,000 patients. San Giacomo, a working hospital until 2008, was refounded in 1515, with ample papal blessings, for the poor sufferers of "incurable diseases," mainly cancer and syphilis. One goal was the relief of suffering, another the clearing of the city streets of putrid, pustular beggars. Similar foundations sprang up in many Italian cities. Administered by energetic religious orders, they served at once two contrary urges of the elite: compassion and stern social discipline.

Treating the Pox

Here are the recommendations of the papal physician Gaspar Torella for a psychological and physical regime to ward off or cure the French disease:

As for prevention, the person should avoid anger or melancholy. Who was likely to contract the pox? Those who "make use of salt or sharp or bitter foods or drink . . . who do not take baths as they used to do, who do not change their clothes; who do not take any exercise or massage; who take meals or medicine that brings matter to the skin; who drink sharp and old wines or those sweet and heated too long."

As for treatment, optimistic confidence on the patient's part would help a cure. To remove the "morbific" matter or "peccant" humors (bad fluids), according to standard medical doctrines, he recommended evacuation (bleeding), resolution and desiccation (the sweat box, to drive the humors to the surface), and consumption (removing the lesions where the humors had gathered from the skin).

For this last step, to remove the lesions, Torella recommended ointments, liniments, and lotions. From the surgeons, he took recipes for corrosive and abrasive mineral substances designed to clear the skin: mercury, yellow litharge (lead monoxide), sulfur, ceruse (white lead), watered and live calx (residue of various burned minerals), ammonia and verdigris (copper acetate), alum (potassium aluminum sulfate), rock salt, tartar emetic (a poisonous salt of potassium), ink, vitriol (metallic sulfate or sulfuric acid), and aqua fortis (nitric acid). To these minerals and acids, he recommended adding substances of vegetable origin: turpentine, incense, and three gums—mastic (aromatic, from a Mediterranean shrub), myrrh (sweet-smelling, from East Africa and Arabia), and galbanum (stinking, from West Asia).

These recipes, typical of early modern medicine, show several things. For one, such treatments were only for the rich, for the many ingredients were exotic and expensive. For another, the minerals, especially the mercury, but the copper and lead as well, were toxic and the acids painful. As with many other diseases, with syphilis, professional physicians probably did more harm than good.[5]

POSSESSION: BETWEEN THE DEVIL AND DISEASE

Lacking a theory of microbial infection, Renaissance Italians were usually less likely to see sickness as an invasion of the body from without than as a disorder (distemper) of its internal components.

There was one great exception to this diagnostic habit, on the boundaries of what we today would call mental health. Like other early modern Europeans, Italians took demonic possession seriously. In their eyes, real demons—sometimes one, sometimes a whole rowdy pack—could enter a victim, commandeering thought, speech, and actions. *Spiritati* (spirit-possessed) and *indiavolati* (devil-possessed) were not rare. Some of these were persons we might diagnose as suffering a serious mental illness. Others almost surely were sane but believed themselves haunted. In either case, the possessed often followed a well-known traditional script. They gnashed their teeth, rolled and thrashed, spoke in altered voices, and lashed out at bystanders and at things held sacred. Sometimes the possessed blamed others for their condition; an ill-wisher, using magic powders or other diabolical devices, had infected them. This grave accusation could instigate prosecution for witchcraft. Thus, the possessed sometimes had sly agency; even unwittingly, a sufferer might fall into an altered state to take revenge. In other cases, when an intractable physical illness baffled diagnosis and cure, experts could inject into a patient the notion of diabolical possession.

To cure possession often required the aid of an official exorcist, whose job it was, with the aid of prayers, holy water, and astute arguments or stubborn exhortations, to refute, vanquish, and banish the devils, thereby restoring health. Exorcism, a venerable practice dating from the first years of the Christian faith, remained for the Renaissance church a lively activity. There were other remedies as well; friends and family could take the patient to a miracle-working image, usually a Madonna, to pray for succor. On the flanks of orthodoxy were lay exorcists and sorcerers, willing to try their hands at an unlicensed cure.

A Young Bride Possessed

Here is a case of bewitchment and exorcism that shows many of the elements of such tangled stories. It takes place in Naples, in 1573–74, and 1580:

> Laura, the beautiful daughter of a tax collector, lives in a fishermen's quarter. Liso, a ship captain, with her father's approval seeks her hand in marriage. But, defying her parents, she instead espouses Giovanni Battista Marsicano. It is a love match. But shortly after the wedding, Laura begins to act possessed, to hate

her new husband, calling him a devil, and to yearn instead for Liso. A few days later, her husband also starts to act as though he has the devil in him. Suspicion falls at once on Dianora, Liso's mother. The district midwife, she is feared as a magic worker and witch; people say she murders newborn babes. Speaking through the newlyweds' mouths, the resident devils accuse the midwife, her son, Liso, and a teacher, himself a reputed sorcerer. The neighbors believe the devils' charges. Furthermore, they have heard Liso and his mother say that they want revenge for the failed courtship. One day a stranger, also crazy, comes to Laura, claiming to be possessed by the souls of two murdered men, and blaming Liso's mother.

It is a hard case: multiple possession. A physician gives up the cure. Clerical exorcists fail. A pilgrimage to a famous healing church does no good. The only thing that quiets Laura's soul is hearing that the distant sails she sees from her window belong to the ship of her now-beloved Liso.

More possessions follow; Laura's sister falls into possession, as do two cousins, daughters of the groom's brother, and the daughter of a local fisherman. All these, through their devils, accuse Liso, his mother, and the teacher. At this point, the archbishop's court is called in to take depositions.

The bishop hears testimony about Dianora's past career of magic, her using powders, nail parings, hair, and blood to patch up a marriage. Laura's physician reports she has wanted to jump out the window and asked the devil to take her soul. When the exorcist came in, says the doctor, Laura swore and writhed and asked to be taken to Dianora's house, saying that the tools of magic would be there. The court, skeptical, asks the doctor if Laura might not instead have melancholy, but he is sure that this is different. Still, the court does not yet press the case.

Note several lessons. First, the first two victims of possession, the young married couple, could be using their affliction as a weapon against their supposed bewitcher. Second, the accused is often very vulnerable, especially if, like Dianora and many other women, she practices magical remedies. Strangers flock to give evidence of her guilt. Third, possession itself is contagious, by suggestion, within a family and among neighbors. So, clearly, it is not always the expression of neurosis. Rather, possession can offer an avenue for saying things one otherwise dares not say.[6]

VARIETIES OF HEALERS

A varied hierarchy of practitioners addressed the diseases of the body. At top were the university-trained physicians, long-robed, bookish dignitaries who did not deign to touch their patients. They peered intently, however, at glass vials of urine, for its color was a key diagnostic tool. The rich consulted these learned doctors, as did the big charitable hospitals, which employed them to tend their inmates.[7] Most Italians had little traffic with physicians, but generally turned for cures to other professionals, semiprofessionals, and amateurs. In cities, wounds, broken bones, and skin problems were in the purview of the surgeons and barbers. Thus, the usual aftermath of a bloody fight was an urgent message to the surgeon to come clean up the havoc. Apothecaries prepared medicines from a smorgasbord of flowers, roots, gums, minerals, and other exotic materials, stored in handsome labeled jars on their shelves; a guild usually regulated their work, as it did that of the "empirics," narrow specialists low on the ladder of prestige. Skilled spectacle-makers, first Florentines, then Venetians with their better lenses, exported eyeglasses throughout Italy and abroad.[8]

There was also a busy lower echelon

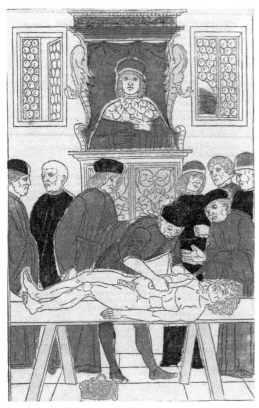

In an illustration of an anatomy lesson, a surgeon, less prestigious and more practical, wields the knife while robed physicians confirm book knowledge by observation. This image appeared in an Italian translation, published in Venice (1494), of a German medical compendium. (The Metropolitan Museum of Art)

of healers. Other remedies, often with secret ingredients, came from itinerant medicine sellers. In many places, these men too fell under the supervision of the medical inspector's office. Some of these patent remedy merchants were skilled hucksters, akin to the snake oil salesmen of North American legend. Indeed, not rarely, snakes and venom were part of the pitch and stock in trade. The showmen were called *ciarlatani*, a word derived from a verb meaning "to chatter." Our modern *charlatan* evokes the old suspicion that greeted their patter. Also called *montebanchi*, these hucksters mounted a *banco*, a low stage, to pitch their wares. All these curers and sales folk belonged to the world of medical practice, as supervised by the public health authorities.

Mountebanks

The English traveler Thomas Coryate has left a fine picture of a late sixteenth-century Venetian mountebank at work (we modernize his spelling, but not his vocabulary and grammar):

> While the music plays, the principal Mountebank which is the captain and ring-leader of all the rest, opens his trunk, and sets abroach his wares; after the music hath ceased, he maketh an oration to the audience of half an hour long, or almost an hour. . . . [He] maketh an extemporal speech, which he doth eftsoons intermingle with such savory jests (but spiced now and then with singular scurrility) that they minister passing mirth and laughter to the whole company, which may perhaps consist of a thousand people that flock together about one of their stages. . . . I have observed marvelous strange matters done by some of these Mountebanks. For I saw one of them hold a viper in his hand, and play with his sting a quarter of an hour together, and yet receive no hurt; though another man should have been presently [right away] stung to death with it. . . . Also I have seen a Mountebank hackle [slash] and gash his naked arm with a knife most pitifully to behold, so that the blood hath streamed out in great abundance, and by and by after hath applied a certain oil unto it, wherewith he hath incontinent [right away] both stanched the blood, and so thoroughly healed the wounds and gashes, that when he hath afterward showed us his arm again, we could not possibly perceive the least token of a gash.[9]

Folk Healers and Magicians

Still another sort of lay medical practitioners were men and very often women who prepared folk remedies. These were mostly people of modest means and scant literacy. Their concoctions typically combined herbs and other natural substances, gathered in the fields and woods or cultivated in gardens, and then processed according to recipes passed through oral tradition. A body of venerable but uninstitutionalized knowledge guided these preparations, but their makers—often called *magare*, magic makers—could also improvise, following their own intuitions and experiments. These lay healers were specialists within a larger domain of informal, do-it-yourself health care that occupied much of the female population. One consulted the wise woman when the usual home remedies did not avail. As an alternative, sixteenth-century printers began to offer literate women published compendia with specialized household recipes for treating many ills. By the later Renaissance, the wisewomen faced pressures from several directions. Not only had they to compete with these books and with other more prestigious medical practitioners, but, also, increasingly meddlesome courts more and more suspected them as purveyors of not cures but harmful spells.

The difficulties of the wisewomen and men arose from the close ties between their preparations of herbal remedies and the practices of magic. Ointments to cool fever and salves to induce or banish love looked quite alike, and the underlying principles understood to do the job were often the same. Though medical in intent, cures might well call on supernatural as well as natural powers. Even the devil might be invoked, as when, for example, the healer deemed the illness to be brought on by a curse that could be countered only by a like force. Thus, sufferers might seek out magic itself to ease their pain or weakness.

Magic, as a shield against illness, was, unlike medicine and religion, an ethically ambiguous force, sometimes benign but often malevolent (or both at once). That which helped one person often hurt another. For example, many believed that love magic could bring on love-sickness, sometimes called "the hammer" (*martello*), a yearning that nailed down and enthralled the victim's emotions and weakened his or her body; this served the pining lover but harmed the reluctant beloved. Such charms could also rattle proper gender hierarchy by taming a man, subjecting him to a woman's will. In the hands of a jealous woman, magic could cause impotence in a straying man. Similarly, a resentful competitor or a vengeful neighbor might buy from a sorcerer or witch a spell to cause bodily illness, diabolical possession, or death. Not all magic intended harm, nor was human health its only domain. People also sought out magic workers to divine outcomes, locate water, find treasure or lost objects, or cure livestock.

Magical beliefs belonged not just to commoners. Some humanists cultivated a speculative magic, arcane and philosophical, and some well-born Italians dabbled in magical practices. Among men accused of sorcery there were priests. Learned churchmen and magistrates took applied magic seriously, because, to their eyes, it was not mere silliness but perhaps the devil's work. The sixteenth-century religious reforms mounted an ever sharper campaign against magical practices and witchcraft. Nonetheless, to curb Satan and his disciples, the Italian authorities often adopted relatively mild tactics. While the Inquisitions prosecuted hundreds of women and men for illicit magic and witchcraft, unlike in some parts of Europe, courts executed few.

CONCLUSION

Against the fearsome powers of disease, Italians of the Renaissance resorted to three kinds of helpers: first, churchmen, second, medical people (physicians, surgeons, barbers, apothecaries, and, at or below the boundary, empirics and charlatans), and, third, workers of traditional remedies and of magic. A comparison shows their complex borrowings and ties. The first two groups had access to prestige and to elite, Latinate education. As professionals, they were allies who respected one another's spheres of competence. The third group, non-elite and largely severed from Latin high culture, was scorned and sometimes persecuted by the other two. In the eyes of the elite curers, this third zone shared some of their professional traits, but lack of schooling perverted and debased them. Like physicians and apothecaries, the practitioners of folk medicine and magic used ointments, powders, plasters, and other materials that worked in opaque ways, but they often resorted to the supernatural to make them work. These therapies might have their inherent powers, but, often, to make them work, special prayers and spells were helpful or necessary. Thus, folk healers also trespassed on the clergy's zone of competence, the manipulation of the providential power of God and the saints. Some healers also trafficked with the devil. Because the boundary between high and popular culture was porous, magic workers appropriated and modified materials and formulas from their social superiors.

The great variety of helps against disease, secular and sacred, shows how preoccupied Italians were by the risks of illness. Although this rich multiplicity of curers was in some ways reassuring, it could also be confusing. Moreover, no helpers, from whatever zone, inspired great confidence.

NOTES

1. On cultivating health, Sandra Cavallo and Tessa Storey, *Healthy Living in Late Renaissance Italy* (Oxford, 2013).

2. Pius II, *Memoirs of a Renaissance Pope: The Commentaries of Pius II: An Abridgment*, trans. F. A. Gragg (New York, 1962), 269.

3. On Florence's plague history, Ann G. Carmichael, *Plague and the Poor in Renaissance Florence* (Cambridge, 1986).

4. Quoted in Jon Arrizabalaga, John Henderson, and Roger French, *The Great Pox: The French Disease in Renaissance Europe* (New Haven, CT, 1997), 205–6.

5. Ibid., 134–44.

6. Giovanni Romeo, *Inquisitori, esorcisti e streghe nell'Italia della Controriforma* (Florence, 1990), 109–11, 127.

7. On hospitals, John Henderson, *The Renaissance Hospital: Healing the Body and Healing the Soul* (New Haven, CT, 2006).

8. On eyeglasses, Vincent Ilardi, *Renaissance Vision from Spectacles to Telescopes* (Philadelphia, 2007).

9. Coryate, *Coryat's Crudities*, 410–12.

15

WORK

To comprehend work as the foundation of Renaissance life, we have to put aside some modern assumptions. We usually think of work as labor exchanged for income, normally done outside the home. Although our model imagines a public market, with its jobs, pay scales, and contracts, not all our work follows this notion. Yet, because unpaid, housework, schoolwork, volunteering, and much care of dependents are seldom counted by economists or included when studying work. Now, for the Renaissance, we must conceive of work in the largest sense as many kinds of purposeful effort, whether for money or not, that often traversed our conceptual boundaries. Note four chief differences. First, in modern thinking, we distinguish work and public identities from our private lives and domesticity. But, for the Renaissance economy, no pervasive private–public distinction made sense at all. Second, and related, in thought, if not in practice, we cast work and social life, including play, as ideally separate realms. Our work should be sober, purposive, and evaluated on impersonal grounds. In the Renaissance, work, economic success, and social entanglements could never be sundered. Third, we moderns distinguish paid from unpaid work. While money is our prevalent and concrete marker of value, the Renaissance economy, cash-poor, had many other, looser forms of earnings and of payment schedules. Money sums blended with gifts and services that blurred the line between economy and society. Fourth, many services—education, health care, public ceremonies, and recreation—that we now purchase or pay for with taxes were available to most people only in their own homes or from church-supported charitable institutions. The clergy and other professionals often led these efforts, but much ritual work and many activities that sustained the common good relied heavily on do-it-yourself and volunteer labor.

WORKING TO LIVE: STRUCTURES

In this broad sense, the vast majority of Renaissance Italians worked. They worked in many settings and at a great variety of tasks organized in different ways. Work took place outdoors in fields and woods, in farmyards, on boats at sea, and inside in palaces, shops, and homes. Country work was the lot of most people, but urban work—in government, commerce, luxury production, and culture—drove the distinctively Renaissance economy. Much of this effort contributed to sustaining life, although often its yield did not translate directly into money. In non-elite households everyone who was able was expected to contribute to the collective livelihood. In some of the more highly capitalized or highly skilled and specialized kinds of work, persons would spend much of their time in a particular enterprise or craft. Many workers, however, in both country and city, rotated their activities with the seasons, the materials on hand, and the demand for labor. In theory, division of labor looked to age, gender, physical capacities, and levels of skills and education; in practice, it also much depended on who was available.

At one extreme, work was sometimes solitary; at the other, it might involve large groups. On occasion, as at the Arsenal in Venice that built, equipped, and repaired galleys, a big labor force gathered in collective workplaces, not unlike our later factories. A major building project—a church or fortification, for instance—assembled gangs of workers, as did a military campaign. In a very different setting, in asylums for girls at risk such as the Casa della Pietà in Florence, dozens of wards worked together at textile production as well as routine food preparation and laundry.

Household

In most locales, however, people typically worked in small groups on the model of the household. In this frame, which embraced farms in the countryside and crafts, businesses, and even some offices in the city, the places of work and domesticity largely overlapped. Although there were differences by gender, age, and skills in what coworkers—family members, servants, apprentices, and assistants—did, no sharp boundary distinguished the "public" domain of work from "private" domesticity. Not only women but also many men, not only adults but also often the young worked "at home," and paid laborers often lived where they worked. Classically, a household was shaped around a family, with husband, wife, children, sometimes other relatives, and often servants and subordinate laborers. In practice, however, households, like people, passed through life stage cycles, and too often death and disability truncated the labor force and contorted the usual divisions of labor. Large, more complete households had more economic resilience, while the poor often dwelled in fragmentary clusters sustained by improvised livelihoods. In principle, the head of the household, normally a senior male, though not always, was responsible for the basic sustenance of all. He directed and allocated activities, exercised discipline, paid taxes and represented the group to outside bodies, collected income, and distributed resources as appropriate. The support of his wife as auxiliary manager of not only the family but also the economic enterprise could be a key to prosperity. Training workers through formal or informal apprenticeship was a regular part of the household model of economy. Younger or less able members of the household shouldered more routine domestic tasks like drawing water or minding children and animals.

Some household members were too young, too old, or too weak to work. Youngsters gradually did take on tasks as their strength and dexterity grew. Children placed in service at the age of ten or eleven barely merited their own keep. From the age of twelve or so, their efforts began to earn some additional rewards. Yet, in some circumstances, small young fingers even with relatively limited skills could be a useful fount of cheap labor. Mantua in 1494 or Verona in the late sixteenth century employed thousands of children, including wards of the orphanage, knitting wool hats. As for retirement, the Renaissance had neither the concept nor the legal framework. High mortality swallowed many before senescence sapped their powers. Those who lasted to the age of decline often just tapered off productive work. On the other hand, some truly old or disabled folk, too weak to support themselves, along with young children, were called *bocche inutili*—"useless mouths." The lucky few had families to tend them. Many, often women, were poor and alone. One gave them alms, or took them in as lodgers "for the love of God"—for charity. Some unfortunates took rough shelter in hospitals.

Discipline and Compensation

The fragmentation of production often freed Italians from the systematic scrutiny that characterizes much of twenty-first-century employment. Since the Renaissance economy reflected the constraints of solidarity and hierarchy, workers had to answer to others and to the law (Chapters 4 and 5). For example, according to a lease's stipulations, peasant tenants had to grow specified crops and conserve the farm—pruning vines, repairing buildings, ditching fields, and maintaining watercourses. But they set their own daily pace. On the other hand, teams, be they harvesters, construction workers, or policemen, had to reckon with their foremen. And servants fell under the watchful eye of masters and mistresses. The large staffs of palaces had a complex internal hierarchy; a groom or chambermaid obeyed high-ranking servitors, who in turn took orders from the house's head. Many master artisans, despite their independence, had also to reckon with the collective, fitful scrutiny of the guilds they must join. A guild could inspect the worksite to assess the materials and the product. It set limits to prices and wages, and regulated the hiring and treatment of apprentices and the placement of shops; there were fines for breach of rules. Mostly, though, masters followed their own inclinations. Renaissance work, although often flexible, was seldom at total liberty.

The demand for labor shifted with seasons and localities. Especially where workers were mobile, labor was fairly abundant and so relatively cheap. Even for luxury goods where materials could be expensive, highly skilled labor could count for only a modest part of the cost. The most common kinds of work—field labor, watching animals, moving materials for construction, spinning, knitting—required some strength or dexterity and basic familiarity with the tasks. Yet such skills, widely available in the general population, were easy to find. The specialized knowledge of master craftsmen or professionals was rarer and more valuable. Obligatory membership in guilds or colleges often protected these special skills and raised their profit. Many of these men of middling prosperity were known by their crafts and businesses. But, like the rest of life, occupations and successes were often volatile, and not everyone could count on an orderly "career."

Although Renaissance work was not defined by or limited to effort expended for pay, much labor did ensure a livelihood. It expected compensation. Under the household model, payment for goods and services usually went to the master who supported his family or other employees. Workers often received part or all of their reward in kind, as food, shelter, or clothing. Work for pay was often measured by the piece—be it a pound of spun flax, a tailored doublet, a painting, or a legal writ. Other work, including a wide variety of services—from domestic drudgery and farm labor to soldiering—earned at least nominally a wage by day or month or year. Workers did not, however, collect their pay regularly. With cash in chronic short supply, workers frequently got paid only in lump sums, as at the end of a stint of employment—if then. Army stipends were notoriously in arrears, and unpaid troops sometimes ran amuck, as during the Sack of Rome in 1527. Nor, if the workers were dependents, was the money paid to them directly. Overall, most work was not bounded by precise job descriptions, nor did people identify themselves by how much they earned. As payments were so unpredictable, computing one's income was hard.

Gender

With a sharp dichotomy between public and private spheres projected backward, it is still common to imagine that women of the past were confined at home and did not work. Even for noblewomen such a dismissive image is misleading; for non-elite women it is certainly wrong. In keeping with the Renaissance understandings that we present here, most Italian women regularly worked, and their families depended on it. This labor did not make women "equal" to men, but it did shape their lives and their relations with the people around them. Most women, like many men, worked within household settings, but we should not discount their efforts as merely "domestic." Our sense of "housekeeping" risks trivializing the welter of substantial tasks, falling largely to women, that sustained the workforce (called "reproduction" in some political sociology). Also, in some stages of their lives, many women produced babies. Nevertheless, pregnancy and childbirth, while dangerous, did not bar or excuse women from work. Women, both rural and urban, regularly took part in production or marketing as well. The mistress of a prosperous worker's household oversaw the domestic realm that sustained family, children, and other workers. But much of the hands-on labor and child care fell to servants,

older women, or youngsters whose time and skills were less valuable to the family enterprise than hers. Even more than men's work,
women's time was divided among many kinds of tasks. Although
women sometimes acquired a few specialized skills such as lace-
making and embroidery, the full roster of abilities required for
most crafts, especially those learned through apprenticeship and
certified by guilds, were inaccessible. On the other hand, where,
as often, it served the family, a mistress of the household might
become proficient enough to manage dependent workers, to help
run the shop or a market stall, and to perform some processes of
manufacture. In other cases, women carried on a separate trade
that brought in income. Indeed, many urban women, lacking male
partners due to death, abandonment, or other causes, were on their
own and had to improvise their livelihoods.[1] Non-elite women's
work varied by age, familial circumstances, skills, and capacities.
They were rarely in charge like the rich male peasant or master
craftsman, but many male workers spent their lives in subordinate
roles as well.

WORKING TO LIVE: ACROSS THE ECONOMY

Rural Work

While work in Renaissance Italy took many forms, the production of goods, from the routine necessities of life to the refined luxuries that embellished the era, was a major sector. By weight and by
its value for basic sustenance, the bulk of production took place in
the countryside. Agricultural work produced food: plants including grain and vegetables; grapes for wine; and tree crops like olives,
nuts, and fruit; as well as animals for meat, cheese, and eggs. Farms
also yielded materials for producing other goods, such as fibers for
textiles and rope, and animal skins for leather. Hunting and gathering also supplemented rural production. The tasks were many and
varied with the seasons and climate, so that demand for quantities and kinds of labor fluctuated. Peasants sometimes worked in
part on their own lands, but more commonly by arrangements with
landlords such as sharecropping. Others worked by the day or the
task.[2] Migration from place to place and into other kinds of work
was common, especially in more marginal regions or in bad years.
Besides agricultural work, in the hinterlands of those cities with
lively textile industries, country women and men also labored for
income on materials provided by urban entrepreneurs under the

"putting-out" system. Over them all, a small cohort of the lord's stewards and the clergy mediated between those who owned the land and those who made it bear fruit. Notaries and officials from the cities also appeared from time to time to conduct business.

Production and Commerce

As sites of government and culture as well as production, cities were more complicated places than villages, and urban work was more diverse and more specialized.[3] In some crafts, such as baking, shoemaking, and cooperage, the classic artisan workshop carried through an entire process from raw materials to finished product that was sold to customers. High-end craftsmen such as goldsmiths, armorers, and printers used this organization as well. But other economic enterprises involved a carefully orchestrated chain of activities by different kinds of workers. Probably

As rendered beautifully by artist Francesco Bassano around 1580, country work involved a panoply of tasks; many of them are seasonal like shearing sheep or cutting and bundling grain. At intense moments such as the harvest, everyone turned out. (Fine Art Images/Heritage Images/Getty Images)

the most differentiated industry in medieval and Renaissance Italy was the production of high-end cloth, first wool and later silk. The many patient steps varied with the cloth: cleaning and preparing the fiber, spinning, dying, weaving, fulling, stretching, cutting, and trimming. In Florence, for instance, where textiles and banking made the city's fortune, wealthy merchants supplied capital and oversaw a complex industry, as the materials moved from shop to busy shop and hand to well-trained hand. Textile manufacture claimed much labor, including that of many women, combing and spinning, for instance, but their work was typically less structured and worse paid. Even nuns often supported themselves with weaving, sewing, and embroidery. Yet as fashion and demand evolved, the kinds of fabric changed and the gendered mix of labor along with it. Turning cloth to clothing, especially for fine garments with costly fabrics, fell to professionals, generally men. But many seamstresses earned a livelihood from mending and alterations, and also fashioned lighter items like shirts, headcloths, and towels. Other women made lace or embroidery for the market.

Differently organized, major construction projects, especially ones that had to accommodate particularities of landscape, took years of work and the coordinated efforts and skills of many men. Such was the renewal of an aqueduct to bring more good water into Rome. So, too, in Venice did building a palace (called a "house") or a public institution on the soft lagoon bed. Acting somewhat like general contractors, master builders oversaw the work of many trades including stonemasons and carpenters. These projects began with designs and required approvals from government agencies, moved on to amassing materials and sinking hundreds of timber pilings to support the heavy structures, and concluded much later with the decoration of the walls and ceilings.

The business of buying, selling, and distributing goods occupied another group of workers who ranged from the very modest to the fabulously wealthy. Although artisans and food purveyors often sold directly to consumers, lesser retailers, both men and women, shopkeepers, secondhand dealers, and peddlers, spread commerce more widely. The *pizzicarolo*, for example, retailed salami, cheese, and dry goods. At the glittering top of commerce were the famous merchants and bankers who dealt internationally. In a still quite opaque economy where information of many sorts was scarce, brokers and appraisers facilitated Renaissance transactions. As middlemen, they took fees for providing specialized knowledge to solve problems of pricing and deal-making. How good is this piece of cloth? What is the value of a painting? Where can we find a buyer? How reliable is this customer? Brokers, often self-appointed, were everywhere. Even a Roman beggar woman on Saint Peter's steps sought tips for helping servants find a willing master.

Services

Besides producing and circulating goods, many workers delivered a panoply of services. Most common were the many forms of domestic service that employed both females and males at a welter of routine but necessary tasks. Women both young and adult served even in very modest households. Their tasks included not only housekeeping and food preparation but also running errands and accompanying their mistresses in the street. Many women did laundry, a heavy job, and others hired out occasionally for special needs such as wet nursing, hair arranging, or practical care for the sick. The great *famiglie* of nobles, patricians, and prelates employed many tiers of servants, including men from the major-domo atop it all down to footmen, stable hands, and even soldiers. The hospitality business—inns, taverns, wine shops, and boarding houses—employed men but also women, either as spouses or alone. In cities prostitution, too, belonged to the terrain of domestic service, as women peddled not only sex but also companionship, and even storage of goods to men with no local household. Mostly self-employed and sometimes supporting dependents, prostitutes ranged from affluent courtesans to bedraggled streetwalkers.[4] The costs of the profession's stigma varied with women's means, but many took part in their neighborhoods. In a fractious, risky trade, facing social or legal problems, lucky ones might seek help from clients. Male services also included transportation of persons, possessions, and produce—the work of coachmen, carters, porters, and boatmen. Footmen bore torches in dark streets or scattered the crowd from around a master's steed.

Other urban workers engaged in various professional services. At the top these practitioners wielded high literacy, but their domains of activity drew also on the hands-on support and oral knowledge of others. In an economy where information was scarce and often private, communication was a swelling sector, crucial to the economy and to states and churches (Chapter 8). Although many of those who dealt in goods needed, sought out, and shared news, for other workers communication was the central task. Preachers, secretaries, notaries, teachers, publishers, and proto-journalists dealt in little else. The same is true, in the oral zone, of storytellers, mountebanks, prophets, and freelance spies, who might easily mix truth and fantasies. Governing and keeping order was another major zone of literate labor, supported by rough enforcers (Chapter 7). Although bureaucracies and disciplinary institutions were growing, by modern standards government employment was small. Nevertheless, for states and cities down through guilds and corporate bodies, officials on many levels worked: keeping records, writing and interpreting rules, buying supplies, judging offenders, and running jails. What we would call health care likewise gave work to a roster of practitioners, some trained by books, many others by more or less formal apprenticeship—physicians, barber-surgeons, apothecaries, midwives, tooth-pullers, and peddlers of remedies (Chapter 14).

Ritual and Charitable Work

On the margins of the economy, much energy went into what anthropologists call "ritual work." These efforts ranged from public ceremonies and festivities to quiet charitable help for one's fellows. While Christian values justified these activities and the clergy led the sacred formalities, the volunteer participation of lay men and women through confraternities and as individuals contributed to the well-being of the collectivity. Rites and processions upheld state and church, cemented social relations, and petitioned God's grace and the saints' benevolence. They also consoled the faithful and lifted their spirits. A civic observance of a patron's holy day, a pilgrimage, a family funeral, or a wedding banquet absorbed much labor—physical, organizational, spiritual, and emotional. In this zone where work and play readily blended, ritual often bled into festivity. Lay energy and materials also went into the staging of a feast or picnic, of a ball game or joust, that enlivened many a holiday. People, too, benefited privately from informal work undertaken in a spirit of charity. For example, below the literate elites, instruction in prayers and bible stories, and even in how to read, could be a work of piety and altruism. In a world where illnesses were frequent and deaths all too common, much nursing and consoling fell to family and friends. Confraternity brothers comforted condemned criminals all the way to the gallows.

WORK'S VALUE

Work or labor as a category did not figure in Renaissance ideology as it does for us moderns. Italians then did not share our belief that work validates our lives and gives us a potent social identity. They lacked our "work ethic," our compulsion to be productive and our prejudice against idleness. They also had none of our political rhetoric that bestows dignity on idealized toil. Renaissance Italians did, however, have ideas about work that bespoke social and economic hierarchy. Work looked both good and bad, depending on who was looking. Some middling sorts boasted of their craft or profession and propped their self-esteem on the work they did. Lower down, productive labor raised the working commoners above the lazy and the indigent. Those who lacked special skills talked of their effort, and those who could not support themselves invoked Christian pity for their poverty. For those at society's summit, however, work undercut elite status. Nobles vaunted their superiority over any work at all.

Work as Effort and Craft

The laboring classes, when they talked of work, had a rich vocabulary for effort. Since bodily labor brought sweat, hunger, thirst, and aching muscles, men and women might render the verb "to work" as *fatigare* (to get fatigued) or *stentare* (to make an effort). Peasants groaned and complained: "We, by the strength of our arms, pulled all the wood into the castle. It was a great effort and fatigue," or "The garden and the hunting park were made with the sweat of everybody in the village."[5] Immigrants to the city used similar language: a man reported "I came [to Rome] to labor and to make an effort with my hoe," and a woman said she intended to make an effort as a servant.[6] Women supporting themselves, including a widow, formerly a slave, frequently used the phrase "I live from my fatigues."[7]

At the same time, working men could stress their occupation's dignity. In this less plaintive mode, they often called their work an *arte*. This term had a double meaning. Indicating a "craft," it connoted skill and respectability. In this sense, "arte" applied not only to the work of urban artisans and merchants of many levels of skill and prestige but also to the toil of peasants. As one casual laborer testified with modest pride, "I enjoy laboring in the vineyards, and leading horses, and other activities [*arti*] of the outdoors."[8]

Meanwhile, "arte" also named an institution, the "guild," that also gave work weight and luster. In that second sense, it glowed with traditions of solidarity and sometimes of political participation. Even women, although they rarely claimed an *arte*, were guild members in some cities and manufactures, especially where the work's precious materials, like silk or gold, gave it high value. Men below—unskilled laborers, beggars, and thieves—however busy or adroit at shady practices, never dared boast an "art." Having an *arte* distinguished a man from the shiftless, the helpless, and the dispossessed who thronged the cities; it was a badge of worthiness.

Work and Noble Status

For the nobility, the idea of work subverted status. So when lords sold the products of their estates or oversaw commercial investments, to them it was not work. Happy to strain and sweat at fencing or the pursuit of deer and boar, nobles sneered at underlings' more fruitful exertions. The proper activities of a man of noble rank were to fight and to govern or to attend at court, but also to manage lands, urban properties, and investments on which his income depended. Noble widows or wives with absent husbands sometimes took a hand in this critical family business. Often the regular supervision of estates fell in fact to paid agents, but attentive lords kept a sharp eye on the overseers and on major sales or construction projects. Unlike the country-based lords of much of Europe, in North Italian cities, patricians did engage in commerce and in the liberal professions, at least until the sixteenth century. Then, however, these families increasingly deserted trade for landed income.

As elsewhere in Europe's old regime, newcomers below noble rank struggled for social elevation. However rich a family grew, the snobbery of the idle held new money down. Fathers therefore strategized to purge their children from the reek of productive work. Merchants and officials who waxed rich, honestly or crookedly, married their accomplished daughters with fat dowries into the idle elite. They also cleansed male progeny by buying them sinecures, real offices, knighthoods, military commands, and sufficient lands to support a life of prestigious leisure. In the later sixteenth century, the papal Curia was another ladder of ascent so useful that elite families sometimes destined their first-born for the church, hoping to reap a cardinalate with all its patronage. Prelates, running the church and the Papal State, did indeed work hard, but governance—deemed clean, prestigious employment—still sat well with elite status.

ENVIRONMENTS OF WORK

Renaissance working conditions were very different from ours. The difficulty of transmitting or concentrating energy helped keep most workplaces small. Employment therefore had a sparse geography that encouraged the movement of workers from place to place and task to task. The lower ranks of the labor force were especially mobile. Because production was fragmented and legislation spasmodic, work's schedules—in the day, the year, and the lifetime—were also supple.

Energy

For the past 200 years, our economy has relied on abundant energy easily stored, and readily sped by wire across distance. Motors transport us; machinery supplants muscle. Carbon-based fuels and, more recently, split atoms largely sustain us. The Renaissance world had little of the pervasive power, movement, and illumination that we take for granted. Lacking these potent and accessible resources, premodern economies fell back on something far more diffuse: current sunlight. The sun, through evaporation, raised water that fell on hills as rain and then powered river mills. Yet, mills only worked where water flow allowed. The sun's heat, lifting warm air, caused wind that propelled ships and windmill sails. Sunlight caught by the leaves of trees became wood that, burning, warmed the house or cooked food, melted glass and metal, baked bricks, and heated water for washing, dyeing, and other uses. Other plants made oils and, with insect help, beeswax for illumination. Muscle power, animal and human, also traced back down the food chain to green plants. Since other energy did not transport readily, muscle was crucial for moving things. The only conversion of heat to motion came from gunpowder, superb for hoisting fireworks, bullets, cannon balls, or an enemy bastion into the air, but so brief and violent as to be useless for anything but pyrotechnics or destruction.

Even by premodern standards, Italy was energy poor. Scantily endowed with rivers and forests, it harvested little power from falling water and burning wood. Short of summer grass for grazing beasts of burden, it lacked abundant hoofed muscle to pull and carry. It did use intensively what resources it had, enhancing them with ingenuity. Mills cropped up in unlikely places by damming minor streams or tethering floating machinery off urban riverbanks. Italian craftsmen and engineers devised clever windlasses and rigs of block and tackle, screws, shafts, gears, bearings, and levers that captured and transmitted water power and muscle energy, both animal and human. Such engines could transform and carry energy and force, though only so far as their cables, wheels, and beams could reach. Construction yards and cannon foundries were full of such devices. Leonardo da Vinci's ingenious machines thus grew out of a long tradition of making the most of a scarce resource.[9] Yet much work was powered simply, by unmediated human and animal force.

Time

In both country and city, work fit into the Renaissance's purposeful but flexible senses of time (Chapter 10). Sometimes work made heavy demands, and other times it allowed considerable leisure. Overall, for a mix of social and technological reasons, few Renaissance people labored with the intensity that modern work regimes expect. Seasonality counted. In summer and especially for harvests, countryfolk worked long days in the fields. In winter and other slack times, they turned their hands to other tasks—repairing equipment, hunting, put-out piecework, or migrant labor. In the city, although more work was indoors, the annual and especially the diurnal cycles still made their mark. Fluctuations in demand and supplies of materials gave some urban crafts their own rhythms around the year. In dim, short winter days work contracted, although, lit by candles or firelight, people often labored after dark. In some towns church bells tolled the start and end of the day on some work sites. The official six-hour December schedule of the Venetian Arsenal stretched in summer to eleven. Sacred time also impinged. For example, between Sundays and holidays, the Arsenal closed 100 days a year. In the many small shops that made up most of the urban economy, however, individual masters often chose just when to work and how long. Schedules lacked synchrony. No rush hour! Yet where much work was paid by the piece, less work time meant less income. Subordinate employees had little control over their hours.

Space

Renaissance work had complex spatial arrangements. Many men and women, from peasants and artisans through merchants and officials, up even to the rulers, worked where they ate and slept. If they could, peasant families settled, like barnacles, in a single location.

Others had to commute. In towns, distances were fairly short, but country workers often trekked far between village and fields.

While in the countryside almost everybody did the same tasks, the geography of urban work was much more varied. In towns, financial means governed what premises a household could own or rent. Some better streets offered more elegant housing, but more modest quarters in lesser alleys were seldom far away. Thus, a city neighborhood usually housed people of varied status and diverse occupations. While some crafts clustered, like with like, many others scattered. Bakers, tailors, notaries settled everywhere, not just on a single street. Masons, straw braiders, apothecaries, tavern keepers, landlords, and laundresses could live and labor side by side. There were exceptions to this promiscuity, set by law, custom, or practical considerations. Facilities like a port, a market, or running water might concentrate some trades. Moreover, at times, legislation pushed dirty activities like glass-making, dyeing, tanning, and butchery into a remote corner. And some forms of commerce, banking especially, worked better when practitioners settled side by side.

While the elites of the workforce enjoyed greater occupational stability, the less fortunate were forever shifting, not only job but also place. For some Renaissance workers, their livelihood required mobility. This applied to some of prominent rank. International merchants, early in their careers especially, often traveled far and long. Some judges and officials had itinerant posts; to keep them honest and detached from local networks, they could not preside too long in one place. For some of lesser status—sailors, soldiers, mule drivers, coachmen, carters, and herdsmen—crossing country was part of the job. For still others, especially the less fortunate, itinerancy or migration was the only way to find a job and survive. Those many with little capital—in learning, cash, land, tools, a shop, skills, or contacts—scrambled. In villages, while those with enough acreage sat tight, neighbors with skimpy holdings came and went. Men ducked in and out of tending stables, watching flocks, guarding fields, driving livestock, and harvesting. When local work ran short, the poor ventured further in anxious search of income. Some shifted a few miles at most, while other wanderers trekked long. Both city and countryside were full of workers from far parts of Italy, some stable immigrants, but many others transients. Some returned to work their lands part time; others drifted off for good. In cities, too, those with routine skills and few assets that they could not carry bounced from post to post. If jobs grew scarce, they tried another town or went home to their village.

DOING BUSINESS: MONEY AND CREDIT

The same improvisation that marked labor also infected commercial exchange. Despite medieval Italy's invention of banking and bookkeeping, by our standards its monetary system was ramshackle. It had problems with what economists call liquidity—easy payment and the rapid circulation of money in all its forms. Making change, collecting a payment or wages owed, converting currencies, raising cash for a purchase or capital for an investment—all these things go better when liquidity is high and money moves fast. In this department, Renaissance Italians faced shortages and frictions. With various devices they adapted flexibly to the quirks and drawbacks of their premodern economy.

One great obstacle to liquidity was the hideous complexity of the currency. There was no paper money, only coins minted from gold, silver, and copper. Coins took their value from their bullion's mass and purity. Buyers and sellers had to be alert, for their money's weight and worth kept shifting. The three metals fluctuated in their relative values. And governments, to cover debt, sometimes debased their coinage. Counterfeiting made matters worse. Furthermore, many currencies circulated side by side. Each Italian state minted its own. The major cities—Venice, with its ducats, Florence with its florins, Rome with its scudi—set a measure for the others. Foreign coins also moved, especially in the commercial centers. In Venice, the Englishman Coryate encountered not only local money but French crowns, German ducats, Spanish pistolets, and Hungarian coins.[10] Trading across these shifting currencies was always intricate.

To the vagaries of exchange, one antidote for business and government was money of account. This bookkeeping convenience, a form of virtual money, was never a tangible piece of metal. Moneys of account were flexible, stable, widely recognized, and largely free from governmental tampering. Best of all, there was no need to scrounge them up among the bankers. Therefore, they were much used in accounting, administration, and contracts. The usual currency of account was the lira, meaning a pound (*libbra*) of silver. But the lira's value varied from city to city. Thus it took arithmetic skill to figure out the equivalents between assorted lire and the varieties of coin. Thus, money of account, while it helped liquidity, did not solve all problems.

Another major barrier to economic liquidity was a general shortage of ready cash. This caused almost all Italians to turn to credit.

Big transactions—a dowry, the purchase of lands and houses, of a public office or a ship's cargo—and even modest sales routinely deferred payment. Borrowing and debt were everywhere. While many debts remained informal oral agreements, borrowers also issued promissory notes and letters of credit. These became a form of currency, for one could pass them to third parties as payment. Some credits drew on bankers, but many more stemmed from private persons. Rather than put money in the bank, wealthy families often bought private bonds. A borrower put up as collateral his houses and estates and issued the bond, promising steady interest and eventual redemption. If he defaulted, unforgiving creditors could swallow the ancestral lands. Big transactions often had rickety scaffolding, rigged out of interlocking private loans. Mortgaging and pawning ran the social scale. Peasants, often drastically indebted to their landlords, hocked their vineyards to pay rents and fines; soldiers pawned their swords and armor to pay for food, wine, and lodgings at the inn. It was a common but risky gambit. Since debtors could be jailed and held hostage until they paid, some grabbed their remaining lighter valuables and fled town. For rich and poor alike, bad luck could bring ruin; bankruptcy was a painful escape from debts. At the same time, to a degree, Italians used their webs of debt and credit as a device for social solidarity and control (Chapter 7). Yet wide-flung borrowing also served economic necessity; quick cash was hard to raise, so one played one's network to muster coin and promises.

In the face of these monetary difficulties, entrepreneurial Italians had since the Middle Ages turned to the *compagnia*, an association that joined investors with active partners. Merchants, artisans, mercenary captains, or rural enterprisers pooled resources to raise capital, aid operations, and spread risk. Often some partners put up funds, while others saw to the work. Companies—big and small, enduring and brief, sealed by charter and by handshake—were everywhere, in production, in commerce, and in venal government "offices" that did no work. Also in the countryside, many noble landlords barely cultivated their estates, but instead rented out the rights to cut timber or graze animals to a *compagnia*. In such contracts, two or three sheep capitalists pooled resources to buy their beasts and secure the rights to set loose vast woolly flocks.

For both private enterprise and institutions, another way to raise cash efficiently and fast was the practice of "farming out." This was a disguised form of borrowing. As those sheep contracts also show, landlords settled for less money, sooner, without effort. Those with resources—forests, grazing lands, mines, or commercial monopolies, for example—leased the running of an enterprise to a stand-in who reaped the eventual profits. Public services that earned money were also an asset to rent out. Cash-hungry states often farmed out their revenue-bearing operations—courts, jails, customs, taxes, and levies on Jews or transhumant sheep—to private operators who paid promptly. Feudal lords auctioned off the running of their mills and taverns.

Another response to low liquidity and short cash was barter and payment in kind. This strategy survived in myriad forms, especially for retail exchanges among ordinary people. Masters and mistresses paid their servants in shelter, food, and clothing. Towns and states rounded out the stipends of functionaries with hams, melons, barrels of flour, and casks of wine. Cultivators often paid their sharecrop or feudal rents and court fines with the products of their fields. And shepherds signed on to run a mixed flock for several years, replete with rented guard dogs rigged with wolf-proof spiked collars and great cheese molds, in exchange for annual lambs and kids, and half the cheeses. Landlords also rented out dairy cattle and beehives, to be paid in calves and honey. With officials, payments in kind easily blurred with gifts and bribes. The same economic mélange of fees and gifts surfaced in the sex trade, where men plied their hired consorts with meat pies, fish, wine, slippers, cloth, and even domestic furnishings. One grateful, if shady, customer even dropped off a heavy bed, nimbly stolen from a cardinal's house.[11] These modes of payment exemplify how versatile were Renaissance financial arrangements.

TWO EXAMPLES

To round out our picture of Renaissance work, let us follow some workers through a day. As usual, trial records supply telling vignettes.

In the Country

In the hill town of Fara, north of Rome, Agostino, a serving man recently immigrated from eastern Italy, is murdered in October 1555, well after midnight, as he drives a gray, droop-eared donkey, laden with newly ground flour, homeward from the mill. When last seen, as he drives the beast, he is singing to himself. Shortly after, some villagers hear a shot, and a few even see the flash of powder. Early next morning, several women, having risen early and descended, jug on head, to fetch water at the spring, discover Agostino's corpse, shot and beaten, by the Hawk Fountain. Both donkey and cargo have vanished.

Suspicion falls on two boys, the brothers Lorenzo and Giacobo. Since, on the morning of the crime, they were seen carrying a long gun, the local court arrests them and makes them account for their movements. The lads, it eventually turns out, were innocent. The bloody hands belonged to a notoriously thuggish thief, exiled from a nearby village. But their testimony illustrates the rhythms of rural labor.

The night Agostino dies, around two in the morning, the boys rise from the bed they share with their mother and their brother, and head off to patrol their fields. Normally, for safety on such outings, Lorenzo carries a sword and Giacobo a battle-axe, but, having left these arms in another house, they have borrowed the friar's loaded gun, a powder flask, and one extra bullet. The pair goes first to a grove of oaks at Little Fountain Hill to be sure no thieves are in their acorns. All is well. They then go to a vineyard of theirs, at Mangle-Wolves Hill, and find that some of the threshers who roam the district, renting out horses for trampling loose the grain, have broken in to loose their beasts to feed. The gun persuades the intruders to surrender a knife; this the boys will deposit at the village court as surety that the threshers will show up to be fined for damages inflicted. Fines for trespass and abuse to crops, fences, walls, and other outworks are the daily meat of rural justice. Having shooed the men and their horses from the vineyard, Lorenzo and Giacobo check their oak grove again, find it secure, and then go over to a house, where they eat a light meal. They then cross to a nearby meadow, where they join two herdsmen, acquaintances down from Ornaro, a village some miles to the east. The herdsmen have lit a predawn fire to warm themselves as they watch their oxen. In the gray early light of a foggy morning, the boys leave the fire and their companions' conversation to make one more tour of inspection, first to their vineyard and then to their oaks, and then head back toward Fara, high on its hilltop. First, however, in an outbuilding of theirs they stow the gun under a pile of hemp. As the youngsters start up the slope, they hear the Ave Maria bell, calling the village to morning prayer. One hour after a foggy sunrise, Giacobo joins his mother, harvesting olives in a family plot. Lorenzo goes not to the fields but to the village school, to recite his lessons, and then, when school is over, joins the others picking olives.[12]

Country work adapted to the patterns of time and interdependency that we have described. It had no clocks or tyranny of time, no immediate boss, no cleavage of labor from the rest of life. The boys' work was loosely scheduled and open at the edges. The two young guardians slipped easily, or groggily, from bed to armed patrol, and from there to snacks and fireside talk. On the other hand, as often in the Renaissance, their labor was long, hard, and dangerous. Giacobo and Lorenzo risked injury to guard their lands. They spent a cold October night prowling fields and then, at the break of day, instead of crawling into bed, went to school or set off to pick olives.

The boys' household of interdependent workers juggled a shifting kaleidoscope of tasks. One man alone could hardly cultivate his lands and guard them from nocturnal intruders. Although a farm required multiple hands with diverse skills, the Renaissance family was notoriously fragile. Since demography never stood still, the workforce waxed and waned. Hired men—like the murder victim, Agostino—helped keep the balance. Lorenzo and Giacobo belonged to a family team that practiced a mixed agriculture, typical of small holdings in hill country. The lads, their brother, and their mother must do many things. To know their crops, we can follow the walk that night. The family had acorns to gather, for sale or for feeding their own pigs. They grew olives they had to prune, graft, harvest, and transport to a press for crushing and boiling. For the grapes, before picking, hauling, pressing, and fermenting them, there were vines to trim, stake, ditch, weed, and guard from livestock, birds, and thieves. And, finally, the brothers stored hemp; they would probably extract the fiber, which their mother might comb and spin for making rope and burlap. And, probably, like other villagers, the family grew grain for which they plowed, once or several times. Then they must sow, cut, gather, and haul it to the threshing floor so horses could trample it free of the stalks. Like most peasants, this family were not specialists. Yet each crop exacted knowledge, effort, and time.

In Town

In the city also, work and sociability intermingled, and time and place were flexible. Artisanal conditions, however, were less often heavy. An episode from Rome shows how, on a Sunday, a purported day of worship and repose, work still interlocked with the rest of life.

Late on a Sunday afternoon in February 1572, a gang of thirty nobles and their servants marshals in Piazza Altieri, in central Rome, spoiling for a fight. Though nothing bad ever happens, the next day, an anxious criminal court calls in thirteen of the piazza's artisans: five shoemakers, three tailors, two saddlers, a carpenter, a box maker, and a fruit seller's helper. With his usual guile, the judge says only, "Tell us what you did yesterday," and then lets the witnesses reveal the rhythms of their lives.

Andrea the saddler, for instance, rises late, about an hour and a half after winter sunrise. His first errand takes him to the nearby Caetani palaces to discuss a velvet saddle with the master of the accounts. Andrea then goes to his guild's church, San Salvatore della Pietra, where he lights a candle to honor Sunday and stays for Mass. He returns home, fetches his mallet and balls, and heads to the Colosseum—fifteen minutes away—for a bout of *palla maglia*, robust croquet. He returns home for the midday meal and finds his workmate, Giulio, back from church, attaching fringes to horse gear. Giulio informs him that two gentlemen from the Conti palace have stopped by to demand a saddle of theirs. Right away! So Andrea, though hungry, loads the saddle on a horse. The two partners and Niccolo, their agent, go to the Conti, back by the Colosseum. After delivering horse and saddle, the three saddlers eat their midday meal at a nearby inn. Then Andrea and Niccolo take the *palla maglia* gear to the church of San Vitale—another fifteen-minute walk away—to spend the afternoon at play. Giulio, the partner, returns to the shop, hangs around with the local artisans, and then strolls sociably along the Corso, Rome's main street. Home before the others, he arrives in time to see the menacing crowd, to pick up gossip about the wounding that provoked it, and to warn Francesco, a tailor, to stay home lest trouble brew. When Andrea returns, all is calm; he finds Giulio reading and takes him to supper at an inn.[13]

The Sundays of the other men have these same elements: work, play, sociability, and repose, plus worship. Sunday, not a normal workday, mixes their labor with leisure and church. Of the eleven artisans who tell full stories, seven spend part of the day at their trades, and an eighth devotes all of Sunday to errands for his kinfolk. But only one, an underling, works all day. One man plays all day long, one visits and worships, and one spends his Sunday—at play or worship, we know not which—at the far basilica, Saint Paul Outside the Walls. Of the men who work, five stay in their shop, four call on wealthy houses to deliver or fashion goods, and one, a fruit seller's shop boy, peddles wares around town. As in the country, work is mobile. As for church, most go, some once, others twice, both before and after the midday meal; one goes twice in an afternoon. These working men have no local church of choice; while several hear sermons in the nearby Franciscan church, the Aracoeli, others go all over the city. Their recreations also vary; the men play, gossip, stroll, visit their friends. One dines with his mother. Unlike the saddlers, most take meals at home. Are there cooks in the house, or, more likely, do they bring in bought food? The narratives are strikingly male; all customers, messengers, friends, gossipers, and partners in work and play are men. The tailor's mother dining with her son is the only woman to appear. Nevertheless, urban women were surely all around—on doorsteps, in courtyards, and in the streets.

CONCLUSION

Renaissance work was larger than the economy, as many aspects of daily life required effort, planning, and a sense of purpose. For men and women alike, work varied hugely; it pervaded daily life but did not take it over. In the absence of a modern work ethic, Italians were less likely to define themselves or shape their lives by work alone. Productive labor mingled with many things: governance, celebration, worship, leisure, and companionship. The unclarity of work's edges was typical of most Renaissance activities, as was work's flexibility in place and time. Short resources imposed adaptiveness. The boundary between work and sociability blurred. Italians also invested in leisure and active forms of play (Chapter 16). Thus the Renaissance, though hierarchic, rule-conscious, and sometimes harsh, never pinned working people in a single posture or penned them in a narrow band of labors. Rather, it let them adapt and improvise, for rigidity in some places demanded give in others.

NOTES

1. On Venice, Monica Chojnacka, *Working Women of Early Modern Venice* (Baltimore, 2001).

2. On peasants' work life, Gregory Hanlon, *Human Nature in Rural Tuscany: An Early Modern History* (New York, 2007); Duccio Balestracci, *The Renaissance in the Fields: Family Memoirs of a Fifteenth-Century Tuscan Peasant* (University Park, PA, 1999).

3. On the urban economy, Richard A. Goldthwaite, *The Economy of Renaissance Florence* (Baltimore, 2009).

4. Joanne M. Ferraro, "Making a Living: The Sex Trade in Early Modern Venice," *American Historical Review* 123:1 (2018), 30–59.

5. ASR, GTC, Processi, 16th c., busta 25, ff. 111r, 126r, 190v.

6. ASR, GTC, Costituti, busta 169, f. 90r; Processi, 1600–1619, busta 6, f. 218v.

7. ASR, GTC, Costituti, busta 599, f. 88.

8. ASR, GTC, Costituti, busta 170, f. 88v.

9. For Leonardo's machines and their links with earlier devices, Martin Kemp and Jane Roberts, *Leonardo da Vinci* (New Haven, CT, 1989), 218–32, 236–41.

10. Coryate, *Coryat's Crudities*, 422.

11. ASR, GTC, Investigazioni, busta 80, f. 86r.

12. ASR, GTC, Processi, 16th c., busta 26, case 2, ff. 634r–58v.

13. ASR, GTC, Processi, 16th c., busta 177, case 2.

16

PLAY

Renaissance Italians had a strong sense of play that ran through life's many times and places and took many forms and tones. Often, playfulness was joyful or raucous. Other times, it had deliberate design and serious, even bloody consequences. Play could be scripted, hewing to custom and the holiday calendar, or it could improvise. It embraced large and populous events from sports, contests, and ritual battles, to festive ceremonies and banquets with music and dancing. On a smaller scale, there were parties, excursions, practical jokes, and the rites of courtship. In the street, on the doorstep, or before the fire, family, friends, and coworkers enjoyed games, gossip, song, and plain idling to watch the passing scene. A small but growing cohort savored solitary private reading.

Despite these myriad forms, Renaissance play had characteristic traits. First, it sought bodily well-being and sensory or mental stimulation. Second, play belonged to leisure: action freely done for pleasure or release—from labor, discomfort, and constraint, or from abstinence and self-control. Renaissance play, though sometimes separate, often permeated more purposeful activities like livelihood, politics, and even religion. As activities, play and work could have much in common, but their experiences differed in pace, tone, and style. Third, low-stress activities that allowed good company—like women embroidering or men fishing—engaged

A young man and young woman play chess, watched by their peers, suggesting the romantic stratagems of courtship. Liberale da Verona painted this wooden panel around 1475 in Siena to decorate a cassone, a large chest used often for wedding goods. (The Metropolitan Museum of Art)

sociability. Shared enjoyment in groups, large or small, lightened the heart. Gatherings, harmonious or competitive, refreshed their participants, eased tensions, and fortified solidarities.

Italians took their leisure, and often lived their lives, as on a stage, where playfulness and zest for performance converged before an audience. If, in any culture, people shuffle familiar social scripts to shape their words and actions, Renaissance Italians did this with gusto, flair, and theatricality that caught the traveler's eye. They stepped into roles built from a great repertoire of stories, proverbs, stunts, and stock characters. From a heritage of wisecracks, taunts, excuses, and consolations, they invented new versions. Italians shifted easily from performer to spectator and back. In formal ceremonies and in everyday exchanges, they both dramatized themselves and relished others' shows, praising, counseling, or heckling the actors. From princely court to urban street, practical jokes played well, often at the expense of social underlings in ways that offend modern egalitarian ideals. In a section of the *Courtier* little read today, Castiglione praised such antics for the court at Urbino. But nothing better distills Renaissance everyday sensibility than Manetti's Florentine story of Filippo Brunelleschi's elaborate practical joke. Because his Fat Woodcarver had declined to dine with his fellows, the famous artist-architect organized a large cast to mortify their friend by convincing him that he was not himself.

Like Renaissance people everywhere, most ordinary Italians lived deeply in their bodies, and everyday repose or recreation involved meeting those needs, often best done in friendly company. Rest soothed drained limbs and tired brains. Food filled the belly and restored energy. Drink warmed the blood and left a pleasing buzz. At home, on shop-front benches, at taverns, people ate and drank with companions and family. These comforting shared activities firmed up old ties or forged new ones. *Commensality*, from Latin, meant "sharing a table"; it suggested friendship and alliance. The table-mates were *compagni*, literally "sharers of bread." Magistrates probing crimes often asked, "Do they eat together? Do they drink together?" One witness, shocked by knifing in a sudden quarrel over a woman, remarked, "The two of them were *compagni*, and that very day they had drunk together."[1] Judges even asked if suspects "had slept together"—a marker not of sex, but of friendly corporeal trust.

Stimulating the senses also gave pleasure. Much leisure went into taking in attractive things, both natural and artful. A fertile landscape or urban prospect, a handsome man, woman, or animal, a bright costume, virtuoso painting, well-laid feast, harmonious facade, or clever machine all pleased the playful eye. People also marveled, puzzled, and scowled at accidents, prodigies, and the unfolding social scene. Ears relished birdsong, the splash of fountains, as well as the human creations of song, storytelling, and wit. Smell savored flowers, perfumes, and incense as an antidote to carrion and sewers. Taste lapped the sweetness of fruit, the tang of garlic, and the zest of pepper, cinnamon, and ginger. Touch skimmed the smooth nap of velvet, the slickness of worn leather, and the softness of human skin.

TIMES AND PLACES

Play could happen anytime, but some parts of day and seasons of the year gave particular opportunity. Everyday recreations favored the hours after work, in the late afternoon or evening or, despite the church, on Sundays and religious holidays. Occasionally, an exceptional event—a peace, coronation, royal entry, or princely birth—invited workers to down tools and celebrate. Some seasons were unusually given to play. In Venice, the months between mid-August and Christmas saw interparish rivalry tested in games and fights.[2] In much of Italy, the spring, after Easter, was for courtship, amid jousts, parades, and dances. The season par excellence for fun and wildness was Carnival (Chapter 10). Fat, bibulous, and ribald, Carnival gave a hierarchic society badly needed time out to let loose. Besides organized spectacles performed by amateurs and professionals, informal theater surfaced in masquerade. Masks, obscuring the honor-bearing face, unleashed impudence. Protected by disguise, people broke rules, refusing deference, flirting outrageously, and courting violence. A gentle form was throwing eggs; from carriages and balconies, from horseback and the street, Italians pelted one another. Some eggs were benign—gilded, perfumed, and others putrid. Other revelers resorted to snowballs, sloppy mud, hard turnips, rotten apples, and assorted garbage. Another medium of violence was satire and mime. Crueler mockery figured in races such as Rome's infamous four where first "naked" Jews (clad in turbans, shoes, and drawers), then old men, donkeys, and lastly placid mozzarella-buffaloes were forced to run the length of town past jeering, jostling, filth-throwing spectators. In many cities, wider violence traditionally broke out in massive inter-district fights. This customary mayhem covered the not-so-playful, bloody settlement of many private accounts.

Green Spaces

Similarly, play happened everywhere, but Italians found some settings especially suited and agreeable. Urban Italians loved leisure amid space, light, good air, and greenery. They often fled their houses and workplaces in search of natural settings to soothe and stimulate town-worn senses. Although the countryside had its dangers, too, nearby sites attracted visitors. Riverbanks invited strolling and fishing. Some rivers and lakes attracted swimmers and boaters, and the rare times when they froze solid, supported games, races, and impromptu markets. The sea, however, was not to toy with; beaches served working fishermen, not the idle. Natural hot springs, scattered across volcanic western Italy, lured people seeking cures and, like a modern spa, pleasant, healthful leisure. Pursuing treatment for his kidney stones at several Italian baths,

Montaigne soaked long in hot and tepid pools, drank prodigious quantities of smelly water, and chronicled his belly's every stirring. Between aquatic forays, he attended dances, exchanged gifts, and conversed with other well-born guests.

For their pleasures, Renaissance elites built new kinds of artful gardens. Lacking our cult of untamed wilderness, they preferred a safely ordered, if sometimes fantastical, domain stocked with pleasing flora and fauna. This appetite and its architecture took its pedigree from the ancient Romans. Later, the European Middle Ages reformulated Near Eastern images of paradise (an old Persian word meaning "garden") as monastic cloisters and walled gardens. In turn, Renaissance landscape architects and their patrons, steeped in humanistic admiration of classical ways, transformed the simple medieval close, with its modest geometric plots of herbs and flowers, into elegant spaces, traversed by tunneled arbors and broad, straight lanes and ornamented by patterned beds, fountains, cascades, artificial grottoes, and ancient and modern statuary. Peacocks might peck and strut under orange, lemon, pear, and well-tailored live oak trees. Gardens served some as places of private solace and others as venues for hospitality. The grander ones had ample lanes for jousting and racing horses, and paths for bowling and mallet ball. Elite gardens also hosted intellectual and cultural life, both sober and playful. Circles of learned men, sometimes constituting themselves as academies, gathered to discuss politics and literature, recite poems and orations, put on plays, or hear music. These gatherings also punned and joked; participants might take mock-serious classical names and celebrate a literary hero or debate a daring proposition. Many gardens opened to the public. Some posted Latin inscriptions that cited the ancient Roman custom of inviting strollers to enter. Montaigne, in Rome, reports such casual visits, remarking that he enjoyed the birds, fish, and art, and also a nap.

Some elegant Renaissance gardens lay inside or near the city walls, while others attached to rural mansions called villas. These were a Renaissance development, as the unruly medieval countryside had discouraged pleasure buildings. Many villas began as farms or forts, but added elegant, classicizing pavilions and spacious grounds. Cicero had praised such retreats for fostering a civil life of leisured reflection. Like the ancient Romans they admired, urban elites retreated to a villa to relax with rural pastimes—and to delight and awe their guests. While owners sometimes oversaw leisured agriculture, many villas put beauty and entertainment well ahead of function. For example, fanciful waterworks that wed art to engineering were a favorite showpiece. The famous sixteenth-century fountains of the Cardinal d'Este at Tivoli still spout and spray. In their heyday, they featured a water-driven musical organ and bronze birds that sang till hushed by the approach of a statue owl. There were also practical jokes, hidden nozzles, triggered by trick paving stones, to douse the unsuspecting guest, and oozing benches to soak unwary bottoms.

Around Rome, a different, favored space for play was the suburban *vigna*, conveniently set apart from the intrusive surveillance of city life. Although the term means "vineyard," a typical *vigna*, worked by a sharecropper, was a terrain for raising not just grapes, but also vegetables, fruit trees, and sometimes even rabbits, chickens, or pigeons. The owners used them for summer outings and picnics. Roman court records swarm with *vigna* matters—squabbles over boundary ditches, thefts of fruit and water, but also troubles arising from play gone awry: raucous parties, seductions, and brawls. A trial of 1563 shows how varied a crowd—clergy, laity, men, women, Christians, Jews, parents and offspring, masters and servants—could enjoy these suburban retreats. A police official, Captain Ottavio, rode back at dusk one July Sunday from a vineyard dinner. With him were friends, kinsmen, and retainers—two clergymen, a prosecutor with his wife, a butcher, the captain's son and daughter, servants of both sexes, and five Jews wearing yellow hats imposed by law. Abraham, Jewish lutenist, paunchy, bearded, and bent, strummed as he ambled while a woman sang. Eschewing non-kosher meat, the Jews had dined, at their small table, off cucumbers, bread, and mozzarella. In the evening gloom, at a tight spot, a pack train, outward bound, forced the women against a looming wall. "The street is plenty large! No need to crowd the ladies," the captain said. Harsh words ricocheted, and soon the servants hurled stones atop their insults at the drivers' backs. Had his party but known that one horseman was the pope's own groom escorting a fragile gift of papal wine to a great lord, they would have been beyond polite, the flustered captain later told the judge.[3]

Urban Settings

Dwellings—from modest apartment to cavernous palace—were a prime site for play. The basic pleasures of eating, drinking, sleeping, and keeping company typically took place at home. More occasionally, parties did as well. For the wealthy, another domestic pleasure was to relish the sun or breeze while admiring the panorama. Renaissance palace builders favored a high, open porch or gallery high called a *belvedere* (meaning "beautiful view"). The most famous one, a long, open passage atop the Vatican, still bears the name and murals by Raphael's workshop. On the ground, recreation also enlivened the boundaries of the house, especially for women. They idled at their windows or on their doorsteps, watching the scene, minding children, and calling to passers-by. This surveillance and the gossip that accompanied it was fun, but it also helped regulate local behavior. For processions and spectacles, even noblewomen, dressed up to join the show, appeared at balconies or windows.

City streets too were playgrounds. Working men readily took their ease not only at home, but also in one another's shops or in the streets, walking *a spasso* (for pleasure), joining a card game, flirting with prostitutes, picking fights. Peddlers sold hot chestnuts in season and *ciambelle*, circular cakes, fast food for strollers. From the mid-sixteenth century, women and mixed company took to coaches to take in the urban scene. Non-elite women also moved routinely about town, on foot. Although they usually described their purposes as work or church, they went for recreation, too. Likewise, women's gatherings at fountains and washing places or in the market served sociability as well as practical needs.

Taverns and inns likewise combined utility and recreation. Simple wine shops and slightly grander inns with beds and stables were everywhere, in towns and villages and along the road. Some taverns hosted strangers, while others served a local clientele. Most users were men, but not all. In a "home away from home," guests drank, ate, warmed themselves by the fire, exchanged news, played cards and dice, told stories, made friends, and sometimes brawled. They also, as trials show, arranged deals and plotted crimes. (To find a good hit-man, scout a tavern.) Preachers, of course, eternally flayed inns as dens of vice that distracted the faithful. An early sixteenth-century Florentine devotional painting with nine framed scenes—the pious tale of a man who drank, gambled, lost, cursed, stomped off to stone a painted holy Virgin, hanged for sacrilege, and died repentant—begins with a clear, if homely, picture of the tavern where the trouble started. The Inn of the Fig, as painted, was a simple affair, a courtyard paved in rough flagstones, with one big table lined with benches. One wall sports a mural of a woman and a big fig tree. Three fateful dice lie on the table; while one player dozes off, the winner raises exultant hands as the loser, a devil at his ear, stalks off raging. To one side stands a crude bench with a simple tablecloth, a jug, and two ceramic mugs. To the other is an indoor kitchen open to the courtyard, where a servant ladles food from two wide bowls resting on a cloth-covered table. Devil aside, we see tavern life at its most normal: food, drink, sleep, play, and dudgeon.[4]

Cities often had a red-light district, typically well furnished with taverns. In these hot zones, the authorities' major concerns were not sexual misconduct and debauched women, but rather the raucous brawling and too-frequent bloodshed that attended drink, sexual jealousy, and proneness to insult among armed young men. Although both honor and religion condemned the prostitute, commerce with her had little stigma. This paradox had complex roots. Medieval theology acknowledged prostitution as a necessary evil that, like a sewer, served public hygiene. The trade protected the established sexual order, as it deflected men from either seducing chaste women, or, as Florentine authorities much feared, pursuing young men instead. For much of the Renaissance, therefore, city fathers allowed districts of toleration. Clients were supposed to be unattached men. Husbands and even clerics, however, though officially banned, sometimes joined in the sociability. In sixteenth-century Rome prostitutes, though clustered in certain streets, did not work in licensed houses. They typically operated independently and entertained in their own rooms (Chapter 15). Those more affluent and more cultured women called "courtesans" offered plusher accommodations, more courtly manners and conversation, and a higher class of entertainment. At whatever social level, however, friends and colleagues often gathered at the lodgings of someone's current hired lover. For sex, a man usually withdrew behind a bedroom door, or at least into a separate bed.

An Evening Chez Alessandra

In 1557, to supply an alibi for Francesco, a Roman tailor, a prostitute called Alessandra described a normal evening in her quarters.

It was Thursday evening, around the second hour of the night. [8 p.m.] Francesco came to my house with three companions; one of them was Geronimo, and Paganino the book-seller, and another one I do not know. And they brought supper [from an inn], though they hadn't said that they intended to have supper with me. . . .

> I don't know who paid. They brought bread, wine, and roast and stewed meat. At my house, there was my mother, and her husband, Antonio, and me. At that time, my sister, Caterina, was in jail. We were seven in all. . . . after we ate, we kidded around until the fourth hour of the night, and then two of them left, and two, that is Geronimo and Francesco, stayed to sleep in my house. . . . And both of them slept in my sister's bed in the bedroom. I slept on a mattress in the same room, near their bed.[5]

> Alessandra claimed that she had sex with Francesco, while Geronimo just spent the night.

ACTIVITIES

Music and Dance

Renaissance people produced and consumed music prodigiously. Without electricity, all music was made and heard on the spot. Streets, houses, even shops could be full of pleasant sound. Much music was do-it-yourself: singing, and playing lutes, pipes, drums, and keyboards. To amuse themselves and friends, some Italians studied with music teachers to master instruments and sophisticated vocal harmonies. Artisans, to believe *novelle*, might sing Dante's poetry while working. In Chapter 15, the peasant Antonio, singing as he drove his mule, ambled to his sudden death. In the city, Gypsies (Roma), among others, played in search of coin. Evening idlers sat on steps, plucking a *chitarra*, and would-be lovers serenaded girls, to the consternation of nuns in earshot. Revelers bent on shaming their victims strummed and caterwauled insults below the windows. Occupations had their street music: soldiers marched to drums and trumpets; clergy and devout flock processed to psalms and *laudes*, songs of praise to God. Secular liturgy—pageants, jousts, parades, and banquets—also came with songs.

Professional musicians also attracted eager patronage. Musical performance embellished elite ceremonies and festivities, particularly at court. Combining multiple voices and instruments in motets and madrigals, musicians devised new polyphonic woven harmonies. The papal chapel also employed and imported the best singers and composers. Professional women singers were a novelty; in the 1580s the Duke of Ferrara formed the soon-famous *Concert of Women*. Toward 1600, more complex forms attracted admiration: song, dance, and storytelling were yoked to create the first ballets and operas, and music, sacred narrative, and prayer merged to produce the splendid oratorio.

Music animated dancing, a festive pastime fun for both participants and spectators, at court and in ordinary homes, in cities and villages. Elite dance both fed off and nourished a vital, now less visible, popular tradition. Dance marked special occasions: weddings, May Day, and Carnival especially. Jews danced for Purim, their brief spring carnival, full of wine, masks, and mischief. Choreography was richly varied. Group dances, often accompanied by bagpipes, shared traits with modern country dancing, which indeed descends from Renaissance court dance. Couples held one another by the hand, waist, or shoulder. In facing rows or circles, dancers "reverenced" or honored one another and moved through symmetrical patterns. Many dances enacted stylized courtship. Others were games, and some for men mimed combat. Dancing masters recorded, invented, and published steps, carrying court forms far and wide. Teachers readily found work, as dance flourished at schools for gentlemen, for agile footwork was a social grace. Even in villages, masters sometimes gave lessons. Commoners, schooled or self-taught, danced for pleasure, but also entertained the public. One Roman Carnival company, led by a stocking maker and including a weaver, a slipper maker, a saddler, and a shoemaker, practiced their *moresca* in a cardinal's garden before performing in the city.[6]

Formal courtly dance we know well, from paintings, instruction manuals, and celebration accounts. The elite danced to small bands of a drum, pipes, and several shawms (old-style oboes). Tempos varied from the slow *bassa dansa* to the quick *saltarello* and *piva*. In rhythm and movement, Renaissance dance was unlike much modern choreography. On the beat, dancers rose, not fell. They held the upper body gracefully upright, with hands mostly low. The most lively movement was in the legs, where intricate steps, kicks, hops, and stamps showed style and virtuosity. Improvisation was prized. Men, in hose and short tunics, had more room—and encouragement—to show off. Images of dancing show them kicking merrily, while their female partners, demure in long gowns, lift a hem to reveal not feet, but a fancy undergown. Though encumbered by skirts and proprieties, women dancers were admired for skill and elegance. A girl might solo with her teacher to entertain the court. Images also often feature women dancing in circles, holding hands. Other court performances featured couples who flaunted steps in turn. At its most flamboyant, court dance produced great pageants, splendid allegories, or mythic dramas with costumes and stage machinery, where the prince inevitably danced Hercules or Jupiter, while the squires and maids-in-waiting played mere centaurs, nymphs, and shepherdesses.

How to Bow

In this lesson, laid out in dialogue by dancing teacher Fabritio Caroso (1600), a master (M) instructs a hopelessly dull disciple (D) on how to bow:

D.   Please tell me whence comes this term, "Reverence"?

M.   This term derives from "to revere," since by humbling your body a bit, drawing back your left foot [and] bending your knees a little, you revere that person toward whom you make a *Reverence*.

D.   With which foot should it be done—with your right foot, or with your left?

M.   Let me say that it should always be done with your left foot.

D.   Why with your left, and not with your right? For you have just told me, Sir, that in doffing your bonnet, you must use your right hand, since it is nobler than your left. Please clarify this point for me.

M.   You should make a *Reverence* with your left foot for the following reasons. First, your right foot provides strength and stability for your body, and since it is its fortress, you should do this movement with your left foot, because it is weaker than your right; now this is the first reason. The second is that you honor that individual who is close to your heart and toward whom you wish to make a *Reverence*, and since your left foot is the limb corresponding to the side wherein your heart lies, you should always make it with your left foot.[7]

Spectacles

The Renaissance, in its architecture and arts, was keen to put on shows and spectators loved to watch them. Music and dancing lent themselves to spectacle, as did many other arts. Churches and lay regimes, corporate bodies, schools, youth groups, and private persons performed themselves with energy. Alongside solemnity and ceremonious aplomb, there was play in performance, both professional and amateur. Play also suffused watching, as audiences, in a world before electronic screens or hushed theaters, were seldom passive. They responded with voice and body, so that, at many a spectacle, the crowd, flocking to learn, gawk, marvel, and cheer, took their own lively part. Spectacles brought time out, a change of pace, sociability, and the thrill of shared experience.

The church had long used spectacle to inspire, comfort, and persuade. Its ceremonies fed all the senses, even more so as the Catholic Reformation took hold, using every art to glorify the faith and keep the faithful fervent and loyal. The campaign succeeded. In a middle zone, where sober duty mingled with sociability and recreation, Italians attended liturgy, watched processions, and went on pilgrimage. Religion also offered more intimate dramas. One might visit special churches, like Santa Maria del Popolo in Rome, to watch a riveting exorcism, a priest's harrowing struggle to drive tenacious demons from a writhing sufferer. And, in the shadowy zone between religion and magic, one might huddle in a downstairs room, hoping that, by the guttering light of a holy candle, the magical prayers of a priest, a female adept, and very virginal girl would coax a prophetic spirit from the White Angel, a magic mirror, to signal a woman's future.[8] Like religion, magic was a zone where work and play intertwined.

Like the church, the state too performed itself in spectacles, and, salvation aside, the experience was little different from what one had from holy ceremonies. A grand occasion set in motion solemnity's machinery (Chapter 7). Bells, cannons, bonfires, triumphal arches, fireworks, torches, bright finery and glittering metal on men and beasts, the blare of trumpets, the thump of drums and marching feet, the clatter of massed hooves all put on a show to shiver the spine and stir the soul. Italians participated by looking, shouting, or calling out their feelings.

Lavish spectacles also took place in private palaces, and sometimes ordinary folk caught glimpses. Grand banquets, for example, caught public notice. The proto-journalist *avvisi* authors published breathless accounts of heaped-up magnificence. The silent precision of the liveried servants, the dexterity of the head carver, the dazzling dishes of gold and silver, the lights, music, costumed dances, and display of the food itself all feasted the eye and ear. There were food tricks: live rabbits, birds, or piglets baked into a pie, while guests feasted on their late brethren. Fish swimming in aspic. Roast birds refeathered. And edible statues, antique gods of sugar, and course on course, in dazzling variety, for hours and hours.

Competition and Combat

Like their medieval forebears, Renaissance Italians, as participants or watchers, relished violent play. Their real warfare sometimes had its playful side, and much of their play was warlike. Many Italian towns enjoyed ritualized street battles. Sportive brawling throve in Carnival and burst readily forth whenever neighborhoods or parishes skirmished for place, as when marshaling a procession. Teams of young men, summoned by their captains, would march on the chosen day to the appointed field, square, or bridge. Their adversaries were denizens of another part of town, ancestral foe against whom they sang insulting songs and shouted slogans. There might first come a provocatory sally, when a reckless few dashed madly into hostile turf to taunt or cow with a show of force, and scooted back home before defenders rallied. On the big day, fighters came armed with swords and clubs of hardened wood, and wicker shields and helmets. A clash, with its single combats and grand melee, could last for hours. Almost always, there were wounded and, not rarely, several corpses.

This fighting, however playful, threatened civic order and religious peace. The usual preachers preached the usual indignant sermons, and town councils passed countless futile ordinances. Only very gradually did this mayhem lose its cutting edge. Swords and clubs yielded to stones and fists, but those remained in plenty. In Venice, the elite backed champion pugilists and flocked to see the bridge-top fist wars from their gondolas, keeping just a little back to avoid the knots of brawling men who tumbled still grappling into the canal. Against the general trend, fist-fighting throve well into the eighteenth century. Ludic violence was tamed, but more slowly than in some other parts of Europe.

In parallel, sons of the elite, while still given to rough sports, deserted some of this street fighting for safer, more elegant combat. Patricians turned more to expensive formal competitions, pantomiming old rites of chivalry. Drawing on the myths of medieval romances, they played at knights in shining armor who entered military contests to win honor and the hand of a lady love. Wellborn sponsors of ritual fighting wrapped the whole occasion in fancy rhetoric, writing pompous challenges and evoking allegories of love, youth, fidelity, and other overblown virtues. These elaborate ceremonies and play combats partook more of nostalgic fantasy than of the robust crudity of real medieval warfare. A tourney was a set-piece mock battle, with field combat and perhaps a siege or naval fight. A joust pitched riders, lance in arm, one on one, or ran them at a target, perhaps a dummy or a hanging ring. Lance splitting set riders noisily ramming weapons against a barrier. All three sports featured gorgeous costumes and fancy horseman-ship. Helmet plumes stood six feet tall. Riders wore costly armor, exquisitely wrought and flashing with gems, and rode fine horses with brocaded coats, jingling bells, and sparkling trim. Alongside walked retainers, adorned in chivalric devices. The spectacle played at courtship. Ladies praised riders and accepted dedicated prizes. A tourney was costly. Besides the fighting gear, it required jousting barriers, seats, and judges' booths. Sponsors funded floats, decorations, a banquet, and perhaps a firework finale. Extravagance and feudal trappings distinguished these combats from neighborhood street battles. Their chivalric nostalgia flattered elite families and prettified autocratic regimes just when, ironically, real warfare's improved gunnery undid the mounted knight.

From the end of the fifteenth century, dueling sometimes deflected elite men from less formal brawls with enemies. The duel was a hybrid thing, at once a masculine fashion show, a rule-bound game akin to jousting, and combat where the loser could finish dead. In theory, as trial by combat, it was a judicial process to settle the charge, "thou liest!" The practice came wrapped in legalistic moves and doctrines about procedure and judgment. Into the six-teenth century, big duels were great spectacles, chaired by princes who provided the grounds, saw to their good order, and declared the winner. Crowds flocked to the "free field," and chroniclers lovingly detailed the mounts, the tack, the gorgeous fabrics, and fine armor, before cataloguing the blows, gore, and agony that settled the question of who indeed spoke truth. After Trent's prohibition, dueling crept underground and lost its ludic streak. Yet the cere-mony and punctilio, and endless wrangling over rules and actions, often by pen and printed broadside, lived on for centuries.

Animals: From Blood Sport to Pets

The hunting and fishing that supplemented commoners' diet, though akin to work, also had their pleasures. A judge asked, "Are you and the suspect friends?" The witness replied, "At times we fished together, and he told me one thing and another."[9] Thus, like commensality, a shared river bank, net or rod in hand, signaled alliance. Bird catching too was companionable; it was a theme of sixteenth-century art, a cloying image of rustic sociability. Italians, who ate birds of every size and shape, had ingenious devices for catching them: gooey limed twigs, hidden nets, caged songbirds to call the wild ones down, dummy birds of prey, and insidious baited traps.

In the later Middle Ages, lords commandeered much hunting for themselves, shouldering ordinary folk off the good grounds and into poaching. *Signori* laid claim to river rights and sold fishing privileges. They closed communal woodlands and grabbed the meatier, more prestigious big game: boar and deer. Princes built great hunting lodges, with stables and kennels, to support lavish forays, with participants in the dozens, or even hundreds. Nonetheless, by the Renaissance, rising population and shrinking habitat had cramped the nobles' hunt as well. A fancy picnic crossed with butchery, it survived in pockets of the Po valley and in the empty landscape near Rome. Popes, cardinals, and princes did not chase their prey but camped at a suitable spot while a horde of dogs, mounted huntsmen, and beaters traversed the woodland, barking, shouting, thrashing underbrush, and spreading smoke to drive the wild animals toward nets and traps, where the patrons could slaughter them at leisure. Women might join this stationary hunt and share its risks: "Lady Alda has been badly wounded in the leg by a boar, because our Lord insisted on all the women taking spears and staying at their posts."[10]

Our notion that animals may have rights or feelings worth respecting never crossed the Renaissance mind. Alongside the hunt were other cruelties. An animal's death struggle was a common entertainment, not only during Carnival but also at other times. There were still bears enough to furnish the odd baiting. Some cities staged bullfights; Naples had a *corrida*, with cape and sword on the classic Spanish model, but elsewhere the fight was more a crazy melee, but bloodier, as men with swords and spears dodged and thrust among the animals. In 1584, a Roman duke, to show his wealth, staged a three-way fight, pitting a lion against a bull and dogs. To spectators' chagrin, the lion, terrified of the bull, wasted his ferocity on the dogs. Why this sadistic sport? Italians saw death, animal and human, all the time. What drew them to such slaughters was not agony but the unpredictable fight, the confrontation with fear, and the ticklish confusion of the boundary between beasts and men locked in struggle.

Cruelty to some animals did not bar treasuring others. Renaissance Italians, both nobles and commoners, kept pets. Some people had favorite horses such as those lovingly portrayed on the walls of Mantua's Palazzo del Te for Federico II Gonzaga. For others it was dogs. An earlier duke of Mantua, Ludovico III, had painted into the famous family portrait in the Camera degli Sposi a woolly-coated *spinone* and a huge red-brown beast snuggled under the ducal throne. In the city, many a quarrel flared over a dog stolen, borrowed overlong, or hurt. Women on occasion fondly nursed puppies at the breast. Cats were another matter, good for catching mice but usually beneath respect or love. Still, since courtesy books warned against letting them onto the table at meals, they must have been indulged. Although medieval falconry was fading by 1600, caged songbirds gladdened many houses and talking parrots were a colorful novelty.

A Pet Bird at the Scene of the Crime

The following vignette of almost cinematic irony is in the words of a young man in the bird-cage trade. Captain Giacomo, the victim of imminent murder, had brought in his cage for repair.

And Captain Giacomo stayed there in the shop. He was standing, leaning on the counter, and dragging back and forth some little bags, and a green bird was pulling its food and drink from him, for it was inside those little bags. And while the bird was pulling the bags with his beak—they were tied by a string—Captain Giacomo was pulling them away, and the bird kept coming back to pull them up. And while Captain Giacomo was standing like that with his back to the street, I saw a man come in through the door of the shop, and without a word, with a broad dagger, he struck Captain Giacomo on the head with the cutting edge.[11]

Games

Many games appealed to children and adults alike, but gender shaped the repertoire. Men and boys competed in stick-throwing and jumping matches and in ball games with assorted balls and rules. There was a form of indoor tennis, with down-filled leather balls, and a raucous kind of wall-ball, where one vied to catch the rebound. *Bocce*, where you try to knock your rival's well-placed ball away from scoring, was already popular. A related pastime was *palla maglia* (mallet ball), a robust ancestor of croquet. While visual imagery shows us few girls playing outdoor games, some elite women did ride horses. Males and females both played cards, and dice, often for stakes, and board games. Women, like men, might learn chess, as we see in Sofonisba Anguissola's painting of two sisters at the board under a tree.

Also widely enjoyed was a ball game, generically called *pallone*, a rough-and-tumble version of rugby or soccer (in the United Kingdom, football). The rules could vary. In Florence, the Medici regime sponsored matches, and elite youth played in public, for an eager crowd, on the great square by the church of Santa Croce. They played rough, on a field of sand. As *calcio fiorentino*, the rambunctious game survives today, The English traveler Thomas Coryate visited a *pallone* match in Venice, with different rules and gear. He described both the play and mixed audience:

> Every Sunday and holy day in the evening the young men of the city do exercise themselves at a certain play that they call Balloon, which is thus: six or seven young men or thereabout wear certain round things upon their arms made of timber, which are full of sharp pointed knobs cut out of the same matter. In these exercizes they put off their doublets, and having put this round instrument upon one of their arms, they toss up and down a great ball. . . ; sometimes they will toss the ball with this instrument, as high as a common church, and about one hundred paces at least from them. About them sit the Clarissimos [gentlemen] of Venice, with many strangers that repair thither to see their game. I have seen at least a thousand or fifteen hundred people there. If you will have a stool, it will cost you a gazette, which is almost a penny.[12]

Dice and cards were among the commonest sedentary games. Already on the scene from the 1370s, playing cards caught on fast and attracted mixed reactions from the church. In Bologna, in 1423, severe Bernardino of Siena staged a cards bonfire. But a fifteenth-century bishop of Pavia commissioned elegant painted packs, just like his own, for his sisters in their nunnery. But only in the sixteenth century did print let cheap decks spread. By the seventeenth, they were ubiquitous; ragged card players, perched on wagons, walls, or handy lumps of ruin, became a painter's emblem of the daily life of commoners. As for the dice games, there were several variants. In one, a player called out the total of three dice before the throw. In another, called *zara*, contestants moved colored pieces—squares, circles, stars—on a checkered board, taking turns. If one threw a seven or less, or a fourteen or more, one lost one's turn. Players, when blocked, shouted *Zara!* A good moment for an oath! Another favorite indoor game, *morra*, required no equipment. Much like our "rock, paper, and scissors," it had players guess how many fingers would be extended. At the inn, a bout of *morra* might decide who bought the next round.

The popularity of cards and dice linked closely to betting. Players wagered at dice and cards, at *morra*, and also on future events: who would be elected pope or what sex a child would have. Some operators made a living off this appetite, making book, renting out dice and tables, or, like the Florentine diplomat Buonaccorso Pitti, playing the palace for high stakes. This love of gambling horrified moralists, both clerical and lay. To them, betting—the ruin of fortunes, the calamity of heirs—provoked blasphemy and fights. Yet gambling appealed to the taste for risk and love of strategy and calculation so central to Italian culture. Furthermore, although it made for quarreling, it also bolstered alliances. There can be solidarity in sustained rivalry; in many societies, internal foes often lock ranks against outside enemies. Gambling also spun webs of debt that, though fractious, also sustained solidarities (Chapter 7).

As with prostitution, rather than strive in vain to banish a vice, regimes often sought to curtail and channel gambling. Campaigns to abolish betting met dogged popular resistance. According to the memoirs of the Spanish buccaneer Contreras, for example, the captain of a Maltese privateer, to avoid the usual ructions, tossed overboard all dice and cards. Undaunted, the crew of many nations carved concentric circles on the deck; then each man rummaged in hair and clothes, caught his racing louse, at the signal placed it in the center, and cheered its progress to the finish line. Winner took all. The captain just gave up.[13] Unlike the thwarted captain, many governments tried compromise. Some authorities, preferring to keep things in the open, permitted certain days or places. Others, to profit from what they could not quench, auctioned off the rights to run a game or house.

A Crooked Gambler

Ascanio Giustini, the son of a prominent Roman lawyer, disgraced his family as a notorious cheat. (We met Ascanio in Chapter 6, in a slanging match and sword fight with his brothers). Below, from a trial of 1555, is testimony against him by a noble partner at *primiera*, a cousin of poker where one bets from a four-card hand. He was asked if he had ever seen Ascanio cheat:

> Your Lordship, yes, I have seen him cheat. For once he was playing with me, and I had a 49. Ascanio showed me a 51. He had a card, slipped under another, so you could not see it. But [a friend] made me a sign that he [Ascanio] had another card hidden underneath, so I pulled out the cards that he had in his hand and discovered the other card, and found that there were five of them. I got furious, and he returned my money. . . . He also brought loaded dice, and he settled down to play with me, with [assorted friends] . . . and others. And when I and the other men saw that he always made things go his way with these dice, we sent out to purchase other dice. And when he played, he would always let the dice fall onto the floor, and when he went to look for them, he would fetch his own [instead], in such a way that nobody noticed. And we kept playing with those dice of his, and we thought we were playing with our own, the ones we had sent out for. And at the end of the game, Giulio Girone wanted to keep the dice, and Ascanio replied that they were his. When Giulio said that they were his, Ascanio left and took his dice. And that time he won a lot of *scudi*.[14]

CONCLUSION

To leisure and sociability, we can add theatricality that pervaded almost all the activities we have seen. These several pleasures ran through Carnival and other spectacles, through fighting, hunting, and gambling. They also shaped gardens, villas, palaces, and churches—spaces crafted as backdrops to human events. Theatricality touched ordinary conversations, learned and rough, and even reading. The quiet, solitary novel reader had not yet been invented, nor had the companionable novel. In the Renaissance, very often one read aloud, often to others. The learned did sometimes retreat to the privacy of the *studio*, there to ponder, alone—as did Machiavelli, fallen from his job, in his tedious rural exile from Florence and politics. Nevertheless, even in his solitude, Machiavelli did not shrug drama off. At the climax of what surely is the Renaissance's most famous private letter, he describes to his friend Francesco Vettori how, after a day of country trivia, he returns to his true friends, his books:

> When evening comes, I return home and go into my study. On the threshold I strip off the muddy, sweaty clothes of everyday, and put

on the robes of court and palace, and in this graver dress I enter the antique courts of the ancients where, being welcomed by them, I taste the food that alone is mine, for which I was born. And there I make bold to speak to them and ask the motives of their actions. And they, in their humanity, reply to me.[15]

Machiavelli's robes of court and palace may perhaps have been ironic metaphors, not real clothing, but his idea illustrates a feature of his culture. Even reading, that most reclusive entertainment, as he pictured it to self and friend, was a form of play, a conversation, a social moment for the spirit. One had to dress the part, as always.

NOTES

1. ASR, GTC, Atti 22, f. 484v.

2. Robert Davis, "The Trouble with Bulls," *Histoire Sociale/Social History* 29:58 (1996), 288.

3. ASR, GTC, Processi, 16th c., busta 85, case 9.

4. William J. Connell and Giles Constable, *Sacrilege and Redemption in Renaissance Florence: The Case of Antonio Rinaldeschi*, 2nd edition (Toronto, 2008); for the picture, 73.

5. ASR, GTC, Atti 22, ff. 51r–v.

6. ASR, GTC, Costituti, busta 526, ff. 167v–71r.

7. Fabritio Caroso, *Courtly Dance of the Renaissance: A New Translation and Edition of the Nobiltà di Dame* (1600), ed. J. Sutton (New York, 1995), 97.

8. ASR, GTC, Processi, 16th c., busta 115, case 29.

9. ASR, GTC, Costituti, busta 52, f. 34r.

10. Letter of Lorenzo Strozzi to Federico Gonzaga, 1512, quoted from Victoria and Albert Museum website, http://www.vam.ac.uk/content/articles/r/renaissance-women-at-leisure/.

11. ASR, GTC, Processi, 16th c., busta 85, case 14, f. 492.

12. Coryate, *Coryat's Crudities*, 385.

13. Alonso de Contreras, *The Adventures of Captain Alonso de Contreras* (New York, 1989), 23–24.

14. ASR, GTC, Processi, 16th c., busta 20, case 4, ff. 376v–79v.

15. J. R. Hale, *Machiavelli and Renaissance Italy* (Harmondsworth, 1961), 112.

17

COMING AND GOING: ITALY AND THE WORLD

To round out our picture of daily life, we adjust our focal length to look at Renaissance Italy in broader European and global contexts. Sited in the midst of the Mediterranean Sea, Italy had for centuries been at the center of busy circulations of goods, of ideas, and of people. Much of the celebrated culture that Renaissance Italy branded and exported had roots in other lands and in earlier times, not only the ancient world but also the medieval Middle East. Italy, especially though not only its cities, was a place where many foreigners came and went. At the same time, for commerce, war, religion, art, and curiosity, Italians often carried their ambitions and their skills abroad. This chapter highlights the wider, churning connectivity of Renaissance Italian life through two directions of experiences: non-Italians and non-Christians inside Italy, and Italians who went to live and work elsewhere. For both these sorts of travelers, notional boundaries linked to geographies of origin, religion, and familial and occupational ties set them apart from most local folk. On the other hand, many people came to speak more than one language. More than others in this book, this chapter portrays people who were distinct in their talents or experiences. Even if not typical, these men and women show us the complex textures that everyday life could assume.

Geohistorical Background

Renaissance Italy's many links to the larger world had roots deep in the Middle Ages. From culturally sophisticated shores of the eastern Mediterranean and the pilgrimage hubs of the Holy Land to the busy fairs of France and the Low Countries, Italians had for centuries figured prominently in Europe's long-distance commerce. Using both overland routes and convoys of seaborne galleys, Italian merchants and bankers facilitated the economies of northern Europe, bringing luxuries from the East, and returning to the peninsula with wool for manufacture, and other commodities. The maritime powers of Genoa and Venice, located on the western and eastern cuffs of the Italian boot, had long vied for dominance in the Mediterranean. By the mid-fifteenth century, Venice had laid its hand on most of the eastern trade and established a commercial empire of a network of small colonies strung along the Balkan coasts and perched on islands in the Ionian and Aegean Seas. In the west, on the other hand, the Genoese sustained lively ties with Iberia, including the surviving remnants of the Islamic al-Andalus. Hostilities between European powers, and especially war with the swelling Ottoman Empire and the corsairing it spawned meant that maritime success required military as well as commercial prowess.

As historical categories, neither "Europe" nor the "clash of civilizations" works in making sense of Renaissance self-understanding. Before the emergence of new "global" approaches in the 1990s, much European history-writing reflected, often unconsciously, a self-centered and triumphalist narrative shaped in the nineteenth century. In this version of the story, modern Europe had come through its special prowess to dominate the world, technologically, economically, and, as imperialism, politically and culturally. The "Renaissance" in Italy figured as a highly polished cornerstone of this ascent. Another strut in this edifice of European greatness was the maritime enterprise, launched in the fifteenth century, through which Europeans explored and colonized, over time, much of the rest of the world. Nevertheless, although we now speak readily of "European" culture, during the Renaissance even elites had no clear notion of "Europe" as a geographic, political, economic, and cultural unity. Nor did those elites see themselves as dominating the globe.

On the contrary, politically and religiously, Europe's fifteenth and sixteenth centuries were marked by stress, internal conflict, and fragmentation. There was scant energy for jointly defending even

Christendom. Let us take the example of Italy. Population rose, and there was considerable, if fluctuating and often ill-distributed, prosperity. Some Italian states grew by suppressing the autonomy of their neighbors, and another large chunk of the peninsula lived under Spanish rule. Nevertheless, there was little will or resources to take on external enemies, even in the name of religion. Popes, notably the humanist Pius II in the mid-fifteenth century, preached crusade, but no rescue of the Holy Land materialized. Instead, the surging Ottomans captured Constantinople in 1453, gobbled up the Balkans and then much of Hungary, threatening the Hapsburgs' very seat at Vienna. Among Italian states, only the Venetians, themselves pressed, sustained a chain of colonies in the eastern Mediterranean.[1] They did so less by challenging the Ottoman foe than by negotiating with it. Indeed, rather than making a common Christian front against the Turkish infidels, in first half of the sixteenth century European rulers repeatedly put their own needs first and failed to mobilize forces to meet the threat. Not until 1571 did a combined force of Spanish, Venetian, Genoese, Tuscan, and Maltese ships stem the advance with a victory at Lepanto clinched by the Roman captain general Marcantonio Colonna. Yet the Mediterranean remained a contested sea.[2]

Sixteenth-century Italian readers were fascinated by powerful leaders, near and far. This image of the Persian king, Shah Abbas, comes from an album depicting contemporary rulers, *Effigie naturali dei maggior prencipii*, published by Giacomo Franco in Venice (1596). (The Metropolitan Museum of Art)

In these circumstances European cultures did not always feel the brash confidence that we may project back onto them. A substrate of uncertainty helped shape responses to the new lands and societies that maritime expansion brought into Europe's ken. The established customs and categories for recognizing and engaging with foreigners—such as the known peoples of Egypt and Ethiopia, or of distant Central Asia—now met major new challenges. As boats bore explorers, soldiers, businessmen, and missionaries to the Americas and to and around Africa to South and East Asia, the appetite for knowledge of far and unfamiliar worlds swelled. Imbued with excitement and puzzlement, intellectuals' texts and artists' images circulated both questions and answers. Besides morality-infused, often idiosyncratic firsthand reports from travelers, this literature drew on familiar authorities—the Bible, ancient classics, and medieval fables. The newfound worlds were enormous, places full of wonder, but also of strangeness and threat. The elites who promoted, programed, and funded European outreach knew that the world was neither flat nor populated with monsters. But it took many decades to begin to fill out the cognitive and visual maps that differentiated the Americas from India and all Asia. As can be tracked in the rapidly developing art and science of cartography, in, for example, the world maps of the Piedmontese Giacomo Gastaldi, it was only *after* the Renaissance that Europeans consolidated our empirical images of global geography and its peoples.

IMPORT AND EXPORT

Food and Fiber

Peninsular Italy's imports ranged from the prosaic but fundamental foodstuffs to art's most refined products. With their many cities and limited arable land, Italians had since the ancient Roman Empire often been dependent on imported grain from Sicily and North Africa. As the population recovered from the Black Death, this demand resurged. Meat, too, once more came from afar with cattle driven from the Hungarian plain across the Alps. Other eatables brought from the eastern Mediterranean were luxuries like sugar, grown in Cyprus and Crete, dried fruits, and spices, especially pepper. Italy's major textile industries, producing not only personal clothing and bedding but also commercial equipment like sails and awnings, had during the Middle Ages relied on imported fibers and dyestuffs. Between 1400 and 1600, the quality and sources of fibers shifted, but Italian production of lighter weight fabrics did well. The woolen industry that sold to the Levant, declining but slowly, then used Spanish and local materials instead of the high-end English and Flemish ones. Silk yarn, formerly bought in the Middle East, was largely replaced by locally grown and wound thread. Cotton fibers, least expensive and often overlooked, arrived in rising quantities, the best from Turkey and those of lesser quality from Sicily.

Arts

In another dimension, the renowned artistic production of Renaissance Italy had deep international roots. Medieval commerce had brought many decorative arts to Italy from far away: from distant Central Asia and even China; from Syria and the Middle East via Byzantium; and from Andalusia in the western Mediterranean. Among these goods were exquisite works in textiles, ceramics, glass, metal, gemstones, and marquetry. These arts, though less valued by European posterity than painting and sculpture, attracted the admiration and investment of wealthy patrons. By the fifteenth century Italians had acquired many of the technologies and styles and had adapted and elaborated them for their own markets and profit. Richly patterned damasks and velvets and glazed ceramics were prized examples.

Exchanges between Italians and other Europeans contributed also to the Renaissance painting and the other visual arts that claim so much of our admiration. Elite Italians, both clerical and secular, supported not only local artists but also many from elsewhere. Thus, Italians abroad bought and carried home influential paintings, notably from Flanders, as, for example, the famous altarpiece commissioned by the Florentine banker Tommaso Portinari who had lived long in Bruges. In turn, foreigners resident in Italy, including cardinals, patronized the arts including early work by Michelangelo. With travel a common part of a successful artistic career, foreign artists flourished in Italy. Bringing with them elements of their local practices, painters and engravers from the Low Countries, Germany, France, and other parts of Europe came to Florence, Venice, and Rome to study the classical monuments, to learn from other art makers gathered there, and to find work or, with luck or talent, fame and prosperity. Some foreign artists died in Italy, but others went home bearing with them skills and tastes. For example, two trips to Venice in 1494–95 and 1505–1507 shaped the work of the German painter and printmaker Albrecht Dürer.

In the performing arts, Italy was likewise an importer as well as exporter of talent. In music, it was northerners who led innovation in sacred polyphony. Yet Italian patrons were keen for the new sounds and invited leading Flemish performer/composers to their courts. Josquin des Prez worked in Italy for much of twenty years after the mid-1480s, including an influential stint in the papal choir, and Orlando Lassus spent a formative early decade there in the 1550s. Both musicians took Italian experiences with them when they returned across the Alps. During these years the printing of music books, a speciality in Venice, contributed to the diffusion of musical styles to wider audiences. On the stage the *commedia dell'arte* matured, and Italian players—male and female—performed in Paris and London in the 1570s.

FOREIGNERS IN ITALY

Although some presume that "traditional" societies were static, Renaissance Italy teemed with people on the move and readily crossing local and more distant boundaries. Within the peninsula and the islands, people migrated from hills and mountains to plain and coast, from country to city, from region to region, from city to city, and back again. Across Europe, all cities depended on country migrants to sustain and swell their populations, and for an unusually urban society like Renaissance Italy, that mobility was great indeed. The reasons to move were many: looking for work, fleeing creditors, exiled by politics, banished for crime, begging a handout, pursuing a lawsuit, avoiding an epidemic, praying for a miracle, fulfilling a vow, or just plain restless. Amid all this coming and going, a prominent marker of personal identity was *patria* or *paese*, a locale that someone or his or her ancestors came from, and the language and traditions associated with it. A label based on home place gave names to many Italians, from the famous like Leonardo da Vinci to the ordinary witnesses in criminal court records—"Giovanni fiorentino" or "Caterina da Macerata." Notably, such terms had meaning only if someone was away from home. The upshot was that many urban Italians who had not traveled abroad were nonetheless accustomed to adapting to new settings and new associates.

From outside Italy, many and diverse foreigners came in turn to Italy to work, to make deals, to pray and reap indulgences, to litigate, to study, to marry, and to party. These visitors faced further hurdles, both formal and functional. Legal restrictions coupled with lack of cultural familiarity reduced outsiders' access to power and to material and social resources. Yet representing foreigners' historical situations only in reductionist binary terms—"us" versus "the other"—seriously misleads. First, in the Renaissance's hierarchical world with its sharply distinguished privileges and obligations, being an "insider" did not carry any systematic benefit. At the same time, arriving outsiders brought highly varied assets, statuses, and connections. Some carried stigma and faced heavy disabilities, but others brought prestige and valued skills.

"Nations" of Europe

"National" or "ethnic" identity did not have our modern meanings, but some sense of belonging, linked to shared place, language, and customs, did matter. The term *natio* or homeland applied to groups of "foreigners" in various contexts. A "national" community of compatriots could provide support and a safe haven, even across religious lines. In Rome, the Florentines with their church of San Giovanni and Confraternity of the Gonfalone were a nation. So also were the "German" merchants with their *fondaco* (trading place and lodgings) in Venice. Universities also attracted foreign students who were organized by "nation." At the University of Bologna a corporation of "ultramontane" (beyond the Alps) students hailed from more than a dozen nations, including the French, Spanish, English, German, Hungarian, and Polish. In the sixteenth century, these students included Protestants as did some businessmen and tourists. Although regulations required inn-keepers and others to report Protestants, economic interests and a hope that Italian religiosity would lead them to convert left most quiet dissenters in peace. There was always a risk of denunciation, if you rubbed someone the wrong way. In Rome Protestant foreigners who stayed for long often found it more convenient to join the Catholics. In another setting, after the Council of Trent, popes and religious orders sometimes reached out to foreign, that is eastern, Christians to bring them into the Roman Catholic orbit. Colleges were founded in Rome to shelter, for example, Maronite and Ethiopian scholars and clerics who were willing to recognize papal authority. To serve this campaign, the Typografia Medicea began to print religious texts in Arabic and other scripts. Some foreigners sojourned in Italy only a year or so, and others remained long or died there. Some assimilated readily, while others sustained close ties with compatriots, in Italy and at home.

Spaniards, from the top of society and the bottom, were many, brought by the designs of their monarchy to expand. With its viceroy ruling over southern Italy and Sicily, and its governor controlling Milan, Spain sponsored military campaigns that intermittently marched across northern and central Italy, between the 1490s and the 1550s. In the South, noble Spanish men and women presided over large estates and populated the court at Naples. Spanish cardinals had a potent presence in Roman curia, and the aristocratic bride, Eleonora of Toledo became Duchess of Tuscany. Spaniards of lesser rank followed in goodly numbers to serve their masters and to seek their fortunes. The Hapsburgs wars needed many soldiers, among whom were Spanish *tercios* and the German *Landesknechts*, who got blamed for much damage, notably the imperial army's Sack of Rome in 1527. Soldiers of any nationality, especially when, as often, not paid, earned popular notoriety for brutish behavior, and foreign soldiers seemed worse. There were also Spanish prostitutes and thieves. Furthermore, Spanish royal policies toward Jews and Muslims contributed to Italian experiences of these non-Christians.

Profile: Juan Gomez, Soldier and Thief

Juan Gomez (active 1550s), a veteran Spanish soldier, found his way to North Italy and in 1551 enlisted to fight for his king against the French. Condemned for thefts and brawling in camp, he rowed as galley slave until, in 1555, two Spanish friends bailed him out and brought him penniless to Rome. The three companions took lodgings and, one Saturday, picked pockets. The next afternoon, Juan stood guard while his companions snatched from a house fine silver trays and bowls. At dusk, the trio buried their loot in ruins in the ancient Forum. On Monday, they unloaded half their treasure to a fence, but, returning to their stash, found the rest was gone. Suspecting one another, the thieves quarreled and sulked. On Tuesday, the police collared two of them, betrayed by the third or by the fence. The court, keen to trace the still missing silver, tortured Juan with fire to his feet. We last see him in the documents, in agony, protesting his innocence.[3]

Vying with Spain for influence in Rome and for territorial purchase in Italy, the French monarchy named its cardinals and repeatedly sent its soldiers. King Charles VIII's troops of 1494 sparked a Renaissance health crisis by rapidly spreading the new pathogen of syphilis. Ultimately, the Valois lost the Italian wars in the mid sixteenth century and withdrew from the peninsula for some sixty years. But French men and women continued to flock over the Alps. They often practiced more pacific trades such as pastry-making, engraving, and painting.

Religious and Cultural "Others"

These "nations" were, with a few exceptions, Christian and European. On the other end of the spectrum of acceptance were the Roma, then known with routine disparagement as "Gypsies" (*zingari*), who lived apart from the larger society. Their itinerant bands, who first appeared in Italy in the later fifteenth century, were never many, but they quickly attracted city regulations to send them packing. Nevertheless, *zingari* continued to pop up here and there in local records, earning a tenuous livelihood at the margins of the economy: men traded in horses, picked up odd jobs, played music, and sometimes stole or fenced goods, while women told fortunes and begged.

Venice and its *stato da mar* (maritime state) was a terrain for rich and complex national mixing. In the colonies, not only Venetians but also a polyglot and religiously diverse population, including Dalmatian Slavs, Greeks, and others, served as merchants, administrators, mariners, and soldiers and occasionally as spies. Albanian light cavalrymen often served in Italian armies. Intermarriage took place even across religious lines—not uncommonly between Eastern and Roman Christians and once in a while between Christians and Muslims. A few fascinating tales have emerged of women and men who played these semi-porous religious boundaries to protect themselves or advance their families.[4] In parallel, as the Ottomans engrossed more and more territory, some Greeks took refuge on the Italian peninsula. Venice itself had a growing community of Greeks that acquired first its own confraternity (*scuola*) and then a church. Other Greeks migrated to the rural South. Albanians, though in fewer numbers, likewise were busy agents in the Venetian colonies. In the 1450s and 1460s, some fled the Balkans to settle in Calabria. Immigrant villages, both Greek and Albanian, retained distinctive languages and identities into the twentieth century.

Jews

Jews were outsiders because they did not share the faith that underpinned the culture of Christian Italy and Europe. At the same time, Jews had lived in parts of Italy since the ancient Roman Republic and the early years of Christianity. Over the centuries religious difference sometimes sparked violence, in which the Jews, outnumbered and disenfranchised, came out the worse. Nevertheless, though few and often persecuted, with restrictions on how they made a living, they served usefully in several economic niches. A few wealthy ones acted as creditors to princes, but most were far from rich and worked as traders, pawnbrokers, and small-scale moneylenders. Italy's Jews also sustained cultural traditions both high and popular. Hebrew learning attracted the interest of Renaissance humanists, and vernacular texts of Jewish customs and stories circulated in manuscript and print.

In response to developments in Iberia and Europe more broadly, the Jewish worlds of Renaissance Italy became more complicated from the end of the fifteenth century. Before then, Italian Jews lived scattered across small towns and cities—a few families here and there—with about half of their population concentrated in Sicily. After the 1490s Jews in Spain and Portugal, and in Spanish-ruled Sicily and southern Italy, were forced either to convert to Christianity or to leave. The Iberian expulsions echoed across Europe, triggering much mobility, new settlement patterns, and layered identities. Although Jews from different places recognized each other as co-religionists, groups often had their own leaders, traditions, and cultural practices, and founded new synagogues. Many Sephardic Jews migrated to and through Italy in their search for a new home. These migrants also included *conversos*, former Jews converted under pressure, who posed special problems for Catholic society. Though Jews were allowed to live and work in the Papal States and northern Italy, during the sixteenth century they faced mounting harshness propelled by Christian movements for religious reform. Jews increasingly assembled in a few larger urban communities, where they could better muster leadership and provide religious services to their community. Shaping these was the imposition of the first formally instituted ghettos—Venice was the prototype in 1516—where at curfew residents were locked inside. Counter-Reformation legislation excluded Jews from many economic and social activities that they had once shared with the Christian majority. At times, they suffered persecution: book burnings, trials for alleged abuse of Christian sacraments, and persistent Inquisitorial pressures, especially against apostasy when converts relapsed from Christianity. Yet prosperous Jews with their networks of connections across Europe and into the Ottoman Empire continued to attract princely support. In the later sixteenth century Duke Cosimo I de' Medici promoted his new free-port at Livorno with legislation that protected Jews and other foreigners.[5]

Elite Muslims

Besides the Jews who were both insiders and outsiders, small numbers of other non-Christians, mostly Muslims, found themselves in Italy by varied routes from the late fifteenth century. Among these were a few men of high status whose stays were fairly comfortable but not necessarily free. When Cem Sultan failed to pre-empt the succession of his older half-brother to the Ottoman sultanate in 1481, he fled first to Egypt, then to the island of Rhodes, next to France, and finally to Italy. Along this path Cem became effectively a cosseted prisoner, because the Sultan paid the Europeans well for keeping him out of Turkish circulation, until his death in Naples in 1495. A little later, a Moroccan diplomat and author, Al-Wazzan al Fasi, was captured and enslaved by Christian corsairs in 1518. Because of his unusual intellectual talents, he was sent as a gift to the pope in Rome. Soon freed and converted to Christianity, taking the name of his papal sponsor, as Leo Africanus al-Wazzan spent several years in Rome and other parts of Italy in conversation with Italian intellectuals. He completed his most famous Latin treatise, the *Description of Africa* in 1526, but soon after returned to Tunis and the Muslim faith.[6] A later exotic visitor was the prince Fakhr al-Din of the dissident Druze sect of Islam, who fled Lebanon with his family and entourage during political troubles with the Ottomans. After a harrowing voyage, the party was given refuge in 1613 in Livorno by the Grand Duke of Tuscany and later in Sicily. Fakhr al-Din failed to enlist Italian military support against the Ottomans, but returned to the Levant several years later with a printing press and several clerics engaged to improve education. Much more common were the experiences of ordinary Muslims enslaved at sea.

Slaves

The most disadvantaged foreigners who came to Renaissance Italy were slaves. Most felt alien to Italian locals, for both their distant origins and religion. Among them were some black Africans, but most came from other places. Some slaves worked growing sugar for Italians in Cyprus. Yet, slaves in the Italian peninsula had different fates from those who worked the American plantations. Christians and Muslims both took part in the Mediterranean slave trade. Neither was supposed to enslave co-religionists, but practice sometimes did not honor this principle. Thus, in the Middle Ages eastern Christians were sometimes among those captured by western Catholic slavers, who then sold them on to Muslims. Furthermore, the Roman Church allowed masters to retain as slaves those who converted to Christianity.

Between the fourteenth and seventeenth centuries, the activities and geographic origins of enslaved foreigners in Italy shifted. Early on, most slaves were women, who served in prosperous urban households. Owners also rented out their slaves' services, such as wet nursing. Masters expected sexual access; other men who tried to take advantage could unsettle household relationships. Relatively expensive and declining in numbers, many of these slaves came from the Balkans, the Crimea, and the Caucasus. In general, a paler skin claimed a greater price.[7] In the later Middle Ages, men who rowed the galleys were not slaves but convicts or poor men pressed into service. In the sixteenth century slaving changed. As antagonisms waxed in the Mediterranean between the Muslim Ottomans and the Christian Europeans, prisoners of war multiplied and corsairs on both sides preyed on shipping and raided enemy coasts. At sea and on shore, many Italians played roles in these dramas. The pirates' captives, now mostly, though not only men, were enslaved. Muslims took their human booty to markets in North Africa and Constantinople.[8] Christians took their slaves to Malta, and in Italy to Naples and Genoa.[9] Since Muslim rulers were not quick to ransom their religious brothers, thousands were put to hard labor— rowing galleys, mining, or building fortifications; many died.

Black Africans

Categories of "race" began to take on new meanings in the later Middle Ages and Renaissance. Although much of the momentum between 1400 and 1600 came from Iberia, Italy participated in these broader European developments. In the mid-fifteenth century, voyages sponsored by the king of Portugal along the coast of Africa brought that continent and its peoples to renewed European attention. Although we know of only a few Italians among the early adventurers, interest in Africa did feature in sixteenth-century Italian literary texts. As elsewhere, *black* and *moor* were ambiguous terms, and distinctions between North African societies and sub-Saharan ones were often unclear. Nevertheless, stereotypes were emerging. For example, Giovanni Battista Giraldi, nicknamed Cinzio, published in 1560 a short story about a Moorish sea captain who married a Venetian noblewoman with tragic results. This frequently reprinted version of the tale gave its plot to Shakespeare's *Othello*. More historically, Filippo Pigafetta published in 1591 a secondhand account of the kingdom of Congo, where a century earlier the king had led many of his subjects to adopt Christianity. Some Italians were involved in the western Mediterranean slave trade that from the fifteenth century brought more blacks, largely enslaved, to Europe. In much of Italy, compared to other foreigners, black Africans were few, but their numbers increased, especially in the South. In the arts, black faces and bodies attracted attention. As exotic figures, they appeared in devotional paintings as one of the three magi and as servants in portraits. The art patron Isabella d'Este had a special interest in pictures of black women and children. And, based partly on the evidence of paintings, the mother of Alessandro de' Medici, Duke of Florence, is believed to have been a peasant woman of black or Moorish heritage. In Italian sculpture, too, especially after the European victory at Lepanto, blacks appeared many times as figures of bondage.[10]

ITALIANS ABROAD

The border crossings that we show here went both ways. Not only did diverse foreigners come to Italy, but also many Italians of different ranks and skills carried their works and their ambitions abroad. Men went to trade and to make war, and some were enslaved. Others went to serve local rulers who patronized the new Renaissance culture in its many forms. Similarly, some high-born women traveled to marry and carried Italian manners and tastes with them.

Italians bearing their Renaissance cultural and intellectual achievements were welcome abroad. Princely patrons in foreign lands invited scholars, artists, and artisans to bring their prestigious Italian ideas and styles. In the mid-fifteenth century King Mattias Corvinus of Hungary was one of the earliest rulers to welcome Italian humanists to an east European court. Also, according to Antonio Manetti's story, fifteenth-century Hungary was where the "Fat Woodcarver," the butt of Brunelleschi's famous practical joke, went to redeem his reputation with highly prized skills. In Poland, too, Italians had an influential presence. Around 1470, the humanist Filippo Buonaccorsi, fleeing trouble in Italy, took refuge at the court of Poland, where he became a royal tutor, administrator, and diplomat. After, in 1518, Bona Sforza of Milan married the Polish king, she introduced further Italian manners, art, music, and, to the diet, she added vegetables. Italian architects and engineers were also active, introducing new construction techniques and decorative styles. In a peripatetic career, Ridolfo "Aristotele" Fioravanti, after designing palaces in Florence, Milan, and Bologna, went to Budapest in 1467, and then to Moscow in 1475, where he built the Kremlin's cathedral of the Dormition. Later, after being waylaid by the Tatar Khan to design a palace in Crimea, Aloisio "the New" finally arrived in Russia to construct the Church of the Archangel and ten other churches for Tsar Ivan III.

During the later Renaissance also, European rulers sought out Italians to help build and ornament stylish new palaces and gardens. In France after 1528 the architect Serlio and the painter Rosso Fiorentino, and later other Italians, designed and decorated the great gallery of King François I at Fontainebleau. His son, Henri II, married the Tuscan princess, Catherine de' Medici, who carried on the work at the palace and also presided over a general Italianizing of manners. Similarly, across Europe, a succession of Hapsburg emperors from Ferdinand I to Rudolph II imported many Italians, among other artists, to expand and beautify the royal castle and gardens at Prague. For example, the inventive Giuseppe Arcimboldo served all three emperors as court portraitist.

Italians with different talents left the peninsula to serve in maritime adventure or war. When in the later fifteenth century Europeans began to set their sights on transoceanic adventure, small Italian states chose not to speculate with their own resources. Yet several of the Atlantic mariners famous—or infamous—for their discoveries in the "New World" were Italians commissioned by rulers of other countries to find a route to China or the Indies. The Genoese Christopher Columbus worked for the Spanish crowns of Ferdinand and Isabella on four voyages to the Caribbean between 1492 and 1504. Just after 1500, the Florentine Amerigo Vespucci, who gave his name to "America," took part in Iberian explorations further south. Around the same time, John Cabot, a citizen of Venice, landed in Newfoundland for the king of England, and in the 1520s, the Tuscan Giovanni da Verrazzano scoped out the shores of New York for the French.

War, a major Renaissance enterprise, was often fought by mercenaries. Many Italians served as foot soldiers in foreign armies.

Some elite men rose to prominence as *condottieri,* hired by states abroad to raise troops and turn their force wherever the paymaster pointed. In this tradition the Spanish Hapsburgs were keen employers of Italian military talent. Italian engineering of geometric fortifications to resist gun warfare was in demand by many powers. Bautista Antonelli, of a prestigious family of military engineers, served the Hapsburg monarchs in Spain, North Africa, and the Americas. In the later sixteenth century, commanders such as Alessandro Farnese, Duke of Parma and great-grandson of Pope Paul III, and the Genoese Ambrogio Spinola successfully led armies for the Spanish against the Dutch.[11]

A special cluster of expatriate Italians ran Venice's commercial empire and represented its interests inside the Ottoman Empire, sometimes even as renegades. When the Ottomans took control of most of the eastern Mediterranean, exchanges with Italy and especially Venice continued. The entangled interests of the Venetians and Ottomans, despite their being nominal enemies, produced on occasion a slippery fluidity of identities that challenged the ideologies on both sides. In Constantinople, a distinct community of Europeans occupied the district of Galata, where Venetian leadership under an officer called the *bailio* was key. This mission was served by an agile cohort of dragomans, linguistic and cultural interpreters. The Ottoman regime itself also habitually made good use of talented foreigners. Some were temporary imports. Mehmed II, for example, made repeated diplomatic requests that Venice supply him with skilled artisans including metal founders. In a cryptic incident, the city in 1479 did send the sultan one of its leading painters, Gentile Bellini, who produced, among the very few surviving images, an unusual, rather European portrait of Mehmed. As the sultan's more conservative successor later insisted, Islam forbade such depictions. It seems likely, indeed, that Mehmed desired the portrait not for Ottoman consumption but perhaps to present himself to Europeans. More typical and influential was the Ottoman practice, analogous to the story of Leo Africanus in Rome, of selecting talented enslaved Europeans, inviting them to convert, and promoting them to high positions in the imperial administration. Scipione Cicala, captured with his father, a Genoese patrician, after the Battle of Djerba, ended up as a janissary in palace service in Constantinople; having "turned Turk," he rose, as Sinan Pasha, to become grand admiral of the Ottoman fleet and, briefly, grand vizier. Power was precarious, and not all such stories ended well. Much more common were the slaves who did hard labor and died in miserable captivity. But some, having escaped or been ransomed, returned to Europe. From the 1580s the Inquisition at Malta was busy overseeing the reentry to Christianity of Italian and other European renegades.

As elsewhere in Europe, some Italians favored aspects of religious reform, but as the Protestant challenge clarified and the Catholic Church mobilized against it in the mid-sixteenth century, it became riskier for dissenters to stay home. Intellectuals, both clerical and lay, with Protestant sympathies or suspect philosophies chose prudently to slip past the Inquisition and depart. Among the early self-exiles was an obscure but highly skilled female Latinist, Olympia Morata, the daughter of a prominent humanist and teacher at Ferrara's court, where Calvinist ideas briefly flourished. Morata herself embraced reformed religion; as it fell out of favor, she married, for love, a German physician and left Italy in 1550.[12] Much more famous was Giordano Bruno, a Dominican friar with inventive mathematical and scientific interests, including the art of memory and controversial cosmologies. In 1579 Bruno left Italy and spent the next twelve years as an itinerant intellectual, crisscrossing the continent and England to teach, share his ideas, and publish. In 1592, he risked a return to Venice, but the Inquisition soon grabbed him and, after seven years of trials for heresy, burned him at the stake in Rome in 1600.

Other stories illustrate not only religious displacement but also the value of Italian language and manners that exiles brought, notably to later sixteenth-century England. Michelangelo Florio, a Franciscan friar, adopted Protestantism. When his preaching in Venice and Naples attracted the baleful eye of the Inquisition, he fled to London where, in 1550, he served as pastor to the Italian Protestant community and taught his language to courtiers of King Edward VI. His son, John Florio, was born in London but educated by Protestants in Germany. Under Queen Elizabeth, John, a friend of Giordano Bruno, tutored in foreign languages at Oxford and published innovative manuals to cultivate European linguistic finesse among the English elite. The first edition of his still-useful Italian/English dictionary, *A World of Words*, was published in 1598. In parallel, Giacomo Castelvetro at the age of seventeen left his home in Modena to join his heterodox humanist uncle in Geneva. He, too, knocked around Protestant-friendly European towns for years, seeking patronage and teaching Italian. He returned to Italy twice, but, fearing the Inquisition, did not stay. Among his expatriate contributions, toward the end of his life, he wrote for the

English Countess of Bedford a promotion of Italian vegetables by season—for spring, delicacies included artichokes and "good, thick asparagus."[13]

CONCLUSION

Italy was a very lively place during the Renaissance, enriched by many cultures and languages. To describe the intricate tangle of differences, the word we have used in this chapter—*foreign*—is handy, but on inspection any clear boundaries it implies tend to dissolve. The peninsula itself was such a mosaic of regions and dialects that Italians from one end of it to the other often appeared quite "foreign" to one another. But people from farther afield were more different yet. Italy imported goods, styles, and ideas, especially from other parts of the Mediterranean where the ancient cultures of the Greeks had encountered the traditions of Asia and the arts and sciences of Islam. Renaissance Italians in turn took pieces from this amalgam and created novelties that made their culture stand out in its time. In this process Italy imported a mix of foreigners—some talented, enterprising, or strong, others poor, fugitive, or enslaved. These travelers brought things with them to Italy and took others away. As it had done for centuries, Italy also sent its sons and daughters out into the larger world where they served or married foreign rulers, did business, introduced refined manners and arts, or slipped out from under the heavy hand of the church. Both Italy and the larger world benefitted from the busy churn across frontiers of people, goods, and ideas.

NOTES

1. For historical background, Monique O'Connell and Eric Dursteler, *The Mediterranean World from the Fall of Rome to the Rise of Napoleon* (Baltimore, 2016), chaps. 8, 9, 10.

2. A good yarn on military themes, Roger Crowley, *Empires of the Sea: The Siege of Malta, the Battle of Lepanto, and the Contest for the Center of the World* (New York, 2009).

3. Thomas V. Cohen, "Three Forms of Jeopardy: Honor, Pain, and Truth-Telling in a Sixteenth-Century Italian Courtroom," *Sixteenth Century Journal* 29:4 (1998), 975–98.

4. Several case studies in Eric Dursteler, *Renegade Women: Gender, Identity and Boundaries in the Early Modern Mediterranean* (Baltimore, 2011).

5. Elliott Horowitz, "Families and Their Fortunes: The Jews of Early Modern Italy," in *Cultures of the Jews*. Vol. 2, *Diversities of Diaspora*, ed.

D. Biale (New York, 2002), 271–334. See also the exhibition catalog, *Venice and the Jews of Europe, 1516–2016,* ed. D. Calabi (Venice, 2016).

6. Natalie Zemon Davis, *Trickster Travels: A Sixteenth Century Muslim Between Worlds* (New York, 2006).

7. Sally McKee, "Domestic Slavery in Renaissance Italy," *Slavery and Abolition* 29 (2008), 305–26.

8. Robert C. Davis, *Christian Slaves, Muslim Masters: White Slavery in the Mediterranean, the Barbary Coast and Italy, 1500–1800* (New York, 2003).

9. Robert C. Davis, "The Geography of Slaving in the Early Modern Mediterranean, 1500–1800," *Journal of Medieval and Early Modern Studies* 37 (2007), 57–74.

10. See essays by K.J.P. Lowe, Paul Kaplan, Lorenz Seelig, Sergio Tognetti, and John Brackett in *Black Africans in Renaissance Europe,* ed. T. F. Earle and K.J.P. Lowe (New York, 2005).

11. Gregory Hanlon, *The Twilight of a Military Tradition: Italian Aristocrats and European Conflicts, 1560–1800* (New York, 1998), chaps. 1 and 2.

12. Olympia Morata, *The Complete Writings of an Italian Heretic* (Chicago, 2003).

13. Giacomo Castelvetro, *The Fruit, Herbs, and Vegetables of Italy (1614)* (Totnes, UK, 2012).

18

LAST WORDS

Renaissance Italy was a complicated place. Its internal variety—ecological, economic, political, linguistic—was great. Furthermore, a land of long coasts and many islands athwart the Mediterranean, the peninsula continued through the sixteenth century, as it had in the Middle Ages, to experience a rich ebb and flow of people, goods, and ideas. Italy was thoroughly enmeshed in a wider world. Its Renaissance, which is now often portrayed as a cultural export, owed colors and styles in good part to imports from far away and long ago.

Renaissance Italy differed from our twenty-first-century world in its natural and physical environment and in institutional and cultural responses to it. Those Italians had their own sense both of time and space and of the human order they could build in these dimensions. True, they shared with us all a basic humanity and held religious beliefs akin to those some of us hold today. Nevertheless, Renaissance Italians experienced themselves and lived their daily lives inside a web of circumstances and understandings that together made them very distinct. To know them well, we must recognize and respect both their closeness to us and their real remoteness. To do so takes a leap of historical imagination, a rich adventure of the mind.

Daily life is an all but endless topic. Yet, for past times, the everyday, that most common of experiences, is often the hardest to reconstruct well. We always know better how princes mustered armies than how people cleaned their teeth. In the broadest sense, daily life was the experience of culture. It embraced many things: material goods, activities, social exchanges, beliefs, values, all of consciousness, plus swift instinctive reflex. It involved tastes, habits of vision and understanding, rhythms of sensation and emotion, channels and habits of communication. It was a zone of agency. That is, people, even if poor and disadvantaged, made choices, the better to survive and to make the best of things. At the same time, for no one—high or low alike—was choice ever free. Some of the will's impediments were material, others far less tangible. Any fully rounded history of daily life keeps at center stage both tangible things and mental culture, tracing myriad connections.

Though distant in time, Renaissance Italy has left many traces of its everyday ways. Its material legacy—prolific writing, naturalistic arts, religious and secular buildings with their assorted furnishings—and its much loving, expert preservation has bequeathed historians wonderful matter for research and imagination. Yet, it takes detective work and inference to sketch an image of the everyday past. Our picture is still half smudge and shadow. For one thing, some of Italy's regions and people have, far more than others, claimed the historian's eye. Vibrant Florence, Venice, and Rome, with their arts and intellectual culture, bedazzle those looking backward. It is less easy to see other lively urban centers and hard indeed the countryside, where most people lived and worked. Similarly, the wealthy and educated strata loom larger than their numbers warrant. Their opportunities and ambitions, though colorful and engaging, scarcely typify the experience of the vast majority: peasants, carters, soldiers, weavers, bakers, boatmen, washerwomen, beggars, and prostitutes.

Yet there were some things that all Renaissance lives shared. One theme, obstacle, and stimulus was danger. The prosperity and safety of persons, families, and larger communities was always precarious. Scarcity, disease, violence, and loss to natural catastrophe, theft, or war lurked and haunted. By historical measures, Renaissance Italy was only middling rich, wealthier in general than in the Middle Ages or the three centuries after 1600, though far poorer than today. Goods were very precious, not only as social markers but also as sources of modest security and as potential tokens of exchange. Insecurity at once repelled and fascinated Renaissance people. It awakened fear and anxious prayer and supplication. But, at the same time, it also appealed to a widespread yen for taking chances. Commerce, politics, social life, and play itself all awakened a gambler's taste for calculated wagering in hopes of profit in the face of uncertainty.

Renaissance life offered at least two broad antidotes to danger. The first, looking to the divine, was worship. God could be angry and punish his errant flocks, but much Renaissance religion took its energy from its links to safety, of soul and body, of self and of community. Religion had its rules and ritual disciplines, but for ordinary Italians the church and its priests, friars, and nuns did not routinely appear as God's strident henchmen. Persons, singly or in family, guild and confraternity, or as whole villages and towns, paid respects to divinity in hopes of shelter from all possible ills. Spilling across much of daily life, religion intermingled with magic and medicine. It also marked time and shaped the life cycle.

Danger's second, this-worldly, remedy was human solidarity. In the face of pervasive threat and uncertainty, social ties with one's fellows, as with God and other supernatural partisans, were at once precious and costly. One invested in alliances, formal and informal, and made sacrifices to keep them strong. Yet many risks were themselves of human origin. As a consequence, all sorts of dealings, at work and play, were shot through with urgency, as Italians strove to tighten bonds and stave off betrayal. Thus, shared pleasure, though a good in itself, was not only end but also means. Play, feasting, carousing, singing, dancing, and sharing the kaleidoscopic spectacle of life shored up friendships and coalitions. Not that Italians were cynics, endlessly conniving. Their calculations were often subtle and instinctive, even barely self-aware. Nonetheless, the urge to ally was alert and active.

Inside solidarities and indeed across Renaissance life, another distinctive theme was the anxious calibration of social place. The ideal order was hierarchical, and status and precedence mattered hugely. Yet, there were multiple standards: relative place varied with context, and encounters led to tacit or sometimes noisy negotiation. Social rank trumped many other status claims but was never the whole story. Contests for prestige or honor, Italy's long yardstick of worth and worthiness, could rearrange the field of play. Those who worked with their hands, women, the poor, the young tended to defer. But the female condition, for all its drawbacks, still left goodly room for agency and serious work. For standing, money also counted, especially for those who lacked it. For the rich, wealth and goods served, more than for their own sake, as a main means to acquire and enact honor. The Renaissance itself was, among other things, an exercise in cultivating status through refined taste and uncommon knowledge; it stimulated connoisseurship. The production, consumption, and display of material goods thus served a double purpose: satisfying bodily needs and marking worldly position. In this pattern, for us today, there is nothing new, but what distinguished Italy from now was how formalized was the hierarchy of worth and how sharply agonistic were the contests. Food, dress, architecture, furnishings, speech, body language, ceremonies, dueling rites, and even games all accoutered rituals of status rivalry and social definition.

Let us end by highlighting the drama that shot through Renaissance Italian daily life. Acting and spectating gave pleasure and served useful ends. Italians forever improvised on well-known roles. By choice and reflex, they played themselves on great and little stages, before audiences as big as a piazza crowd or packed cathedral or as small as a solitary enemy, friend, or lover. In these theatrics, convention and invention mingled. As often in art, the tension between the expected and the unexpected gave piquancy, and drew and held a crowd of watchers. The humdrum was there, but well punctuated with lively moments. Daily life, then, was full of dramas on every scale.

RESOURCES AND BIBLIOGRAPHY

FURTHER READING

See also bibliographical suggestions on specific topics in chapter notes.

Sarah Bradford, *Lucrezia Borgia: Life, Love and Death in Renaissance Italy*. New York, 2004.

Patricia Fortini Brown, *Private Lives in Renaissance Venice: Art, Architecture and the Family*. New Haven, CT, 2004.

Gene Brucker, *Giovanni and Lusanna: Love and Marriage in Renaissance Florence*. Berkeley, 1986.

William Connell and Giles Constable, *Sacrilege and Redemption in Renaissance Florence: The Case of Antonio Rinaldeschi*. Second edition. Toronto, 2008.

Roger Crowley, *City of Fortune: How Venice Ruled the Seas*. New York, 2011.

Robert Davis and Beth Lindsmith, *Renaissance People: Lives That Shaped the Modern Age*. Los Angeles, 2011.

Valeria Finucci, *The Prince's Body: Vincenzo Gonzaga and Renaissance Medicine*. Cambridge, MA, 2015.

Catherine Fletcher, *The Black Prince of Florence: The Spectacular and Treacherous World of Alessandro de' Medici*. London, 2016.

Carlo Ginzburg, *The Cheese and the Worms: The Cosmos of the Sixteenth-Century Miller*. Baltimore, 1980.

Richard Goy, *Building Renaissance Venice: Patrons, Architects, and Builders, c. 1430–1500*. New Haven, CT, 2006.

Mary Hollingsworth, *The Cardinal's Hat: Money, Ambition, and Everyday Life in a Renaissance Court*. London, 2004.

Claire Judde de la Rivière, *The Revolt of Snowballs: Murano Confronts Venice, 1511*. London, 2018.

Ross King, *Brunelleschi's Dome: How a Renaissance Genius Reinvented Architecture*. New York, 2001.

Ross King, *Michelangelo and the Pope's Ceiling*. New York, 2003.

Christiane Klapisch-Zuber, *Women, Family, and Ritual in Renaissance Italy*. Chicago, 1985.

Mary Laven, *Virgins of Venice: Enclosed Lives and Broken Vows in the Renaissance Convent*. London, 2002.

Elizabeth Lev, *The Tigress of Forli: Renaissance Italy's Most Courageous and Notorious Countess, Caterina Riario Sforza de' Medici*. Boston, 2011.

Pamela Long, *Engineering the Eternal City: Infrastructure, Topography, and the Culture of Knowledge in Late Sixteenth-Century Rome*. Chicago, 2018.

Rosamund Mack, *Bazaar to Piazza: Islamic Trade and Italian Art, 1300–1600*. Berkeley, 2002.

Lauro Martines, *Fire in the City: Savonarola and the Struggle for the Soul of Renaissance Florence*. Oxford, 2006.

Sara Matthews-Grieco, ed., *Erotic Cultures of Renaissance Italy*. Farnham, UK, 2010.

Caroline Murphy, *The Pope's Daughter: The Extraordinary Life of Felice della Rovere*. New York, 2005.

Jacqueline Murray and Nicholas Terpstra, eds., *Sex, Gender, and Sexuality in Renaissance Italy*. London, 2019.

Jacqueline Musacchio, *Art, Marriage, and Family in the Florentine Renaissance*. New Haven, CT, 2008.

Michelle O'Malley and Evelyn Welch, eds., *The Material Renaissance*. Manchester, 2007.

Richard Peterson, *Looking at Florentine Painting, 13th to 16th Centuries*. Florence, 2014.

Ingrid Rowland and Noah Charney, *The Collector of Lives: Giorgio Vasari and the Invention of Art*. New York, 2017.

Guido Ruggiero, *Machiavelli in Love: Sex, Self and Society in Renaissance Florence*. Baltimore, 2007.

Raffaella Sarti, *Europe at Home: Family and Material Culture, 1500–1800*. New Haven, CT, 2002.

Nicholas Terpstra, *Lost Girls: Sex and Death in Renaissance Florence*. Baltimore, 2010.

Merry Wiesner-Hanks, *Women and Gender in Early Modern Europe*. Fourth edition. Cambridge, 2019.

SELECT RENAISSANCE TEXTS IN ENGLISH TRANSLATION

Pietro Aretino, *Cortigiana* (a play), Ottawa, 2003; and *Dialogues*, Toronto, 2005.

Francesco Barbaro, *Wealth of Wives: A Fifteenth-Century Marriage Manual*. Tempe, 2015.

Michelangelo Buonarroti, *Poems and Letters*. New York, 2017.
Baldassare Castiglione, *The Book of the Courtier*. New York, 2002.
Benvenuto Cellini, *Autobiography*. New York, 2010.
Tullia d'Aragona, *Dialogue on the Infinity of Love*. Chicago, 1997. By a courtesan author.
Isabella d'Este, *Selected Letters*. Tempe, 2017.
Annibal Guasco, *Discourse to Lady Lavinia, His Daughter*. Chicago, 2013.
Niccolò Machiavelli, *Mandragola* (a play), and his letters in various editions.
Lauro Martines, *A Italian Sextet: Six Tales in Renaissance Context*. Toronto, 2004. Includes "The Fat Woodcarver" by Antonio Manetti.
Michel de Montaigne, "Travel Journal" in *The Complete Works: Essays, Travel Journal, Letters*, trans. D. Frame, 1112–1266. New York, 2003.
Alessandra Macinghi Strozzi, *Letters to Her Sons, 1447–1470*. Toronto, 2016.
Giorgio Vasari, *The Lives of the Artists*. Oxford, 1998.

MUSEUMS AND EXHIBITIONS

Museums in North America and Europe have excellent Renaissance collections.

Painting and Sculpture

In Italy: Milan, Pinacoteca di Brera; Venice, Galleria dell'Accademia; Florence, Galleria degli Uffizi; Rome, Musei Vaticani.
In the United States: Washington, DC, National Gallery of Art; New York, Metropolitan Museum of Art; Boston, Isabella Stewart Gardner Museum; Los Angeles, J. Paul Getty Museum.

Collections of Furnishings and Objects

In Italy: Florence, Palazzo Davanzati (a furnished Renaissance house); Milan, municipal museums at the Castello Sforzesco; Naples: Galleria Nazionale di Capodimonte.
In the United Kingdom: London, Victoria and Albert (V&A) Museum. The V&A does good web materials such as Renaissance Women at Leisure, http://www.vam.ac.uk/content/articles/r/renaissance-women-at-leisure/.
In the United States: Chicago, Art Institute; New York, Metropolitan Museum of Art. The Met's fine collection includes a *studiolo* (wood inlayed study) from the Ducal Palace in Gubbio (circa 1480). https://www.metmuseum.org/art/collection/search/198556.

Special Exhibitions and Their Catalogues

Italian Women Artists from Renaissance to Baroque. National Museum of Women in the Arts, Washington, D.C., 2007.

Marta Ajmer-Wollheim and Flora Dennis, ed., *At Home in Renaissance Italy*. Victoria and Albert Museum, London, 2006

Andrea Bayer, ed., *Art and Love in Renaissance Italy*. Metropolitan Museum, New York, 2008.

Julian Brooks, *Taddeo and Federico Zuccaro: Artist-Brothers in Renaissance Rome*. John Paul Getty Museum, Los Angeles, 2007.

Carolyn Campbell and Alan Chong, *Bellini and the East*. National Gallery, London and Isabella Stewart Gardner Museum, Boston, 2006.

Keith Christianson and Stefan Weppelmann, eds., *The Renaissance Portrait: From Donatello to Bellini*. Metropolitan Museum of Art, New York, 2011.

Ludovica Sebregondi and Tim Parks, *Money and Beauty: Bankers, Botticelli, and the Bonfire of the Vanities*. Fondazione Palazzo Strozzi, Florence, 2011.

Elizabeth Semmelhack, *On a Pedestal: From Renaissance Chopines to Baroque Heels*. Bata Shoe Museum, Toronto, 2009.

DIGITAL RESOURCES

The Italian Renaissance on the web.

Wikipedia is mostly solid at providing basic data about notable Renaissance people and their activities. YouTube and other websites offer an array of mini-movies about famous figures, events, or works of art. The broader social, economic, environmental, and technological dimensions of the era that this book aims to sketch are less well represented.

Websites appear, evolve, and sometimes disappear. Any published selection is a snapshot of its moment. The best way to engage is to explore, to follow links, and sometimes to start new searches with keywords.

Sites are not all alike. They vary in their intended audiences and in the goals, topical knowledge, and web savvy of their curators. It is always up to viewers to assess what best serves their purposes. Of the ones identified here, some are aimed at a general audience, and others, though aimed mostly at scholars, include accessible information through short texts, images, maps, and videos.

Television series and novels set in Renaissance Italy are many. Designed to please modern audiences, they vary greatly in their historicity.

Similarly, websites related to Renaissance "fairs," enactment and dressing-up, games and swordplay can be fun. Note, however, that they are often more about modern fantasies and modern marketing—"creative anachronism"—than real history.

An example of a useful site inspired by the *Borgias* TV series concerns clothing. Using Renaissance portraits, it offers a well-organized

array of elite dress from different regions of Italy (http://thebor
gias.wikifoundry-mobile.com/m/page/Italian+Renaissance+
CLOTHING+%26+FASHION).

Walking Tours

Florence

Hidden Florence. Stories linked to walking the city. https://hidden
florence.org. A new, expanded version comes online in summer
2019.
Museums of Florence, Palazzo Davanzati, or the Ancient Florentine home.
http://www.museumsinflorence.com/musei/palazzo_davanzati.
html.

Rome

Roma segreta. Website in Italian with images and itineraries on lost buildings, streets, and so on. https://www.romasegreta.it/.

Venice

Jewish Ghetto. Self-guided walking tours. For example, from GPSMyCity
https://www.gpsmycity.com/tours/ghetto-tour-1956.html.

Renaissance Music

Most easily sampled through YouTube and Spotify.

Some Categories to Explore

Sacred polyphony: Josquin des Prez, Pierluigi da Palestrina
Motets and madrigals
Lute, pipes, and harpsichord
Dance music

Some performing/recording groups: Cappella Artemisia, Cut Circle,
London Early Music Group, Musica secreta, Syntagma Musicum,
Toronto Consort.

Research Sites

DECIMA Project (Digitally Encoded Census Information & Mapping
Archive) (University of Toronto), https://decima-map.net/. Florentine history on an interactive map.

Isabella d'Este Archive (IDEA) (University of California, Santa Cruz), http://isabelladeste.web.unc.edu/. Highlights include videos recreating a "Virtual Studiolo" and "Songs for Isabella d'Este."

Digital Roman Heritage, https://digitalromanheritage.com. A portal for accessing many databases bearing on the history of Rome, many concerning the ancient city, but also including the Renaissance.

For example, Aquae Urbis Romae, LUPA (printed images of the city and its buildings), Rome Reborn (digital modeling of ancient city), Vatican exhibit (virtual museum visit), Views of Rome (interactive 1561 map of the ancient city).

Historic Cities Map Project (Hebrew University of Jerusalem). City maps from the fifteenth to eighteenth centuries. For a variety of Italian cities, see historic-cities.huji.ac.il/italy/italy.html.

INDEX

Note: Page numbers in *italics* indicate illustrations.

About the Authors

ELIZABETH S. COHEN is professor of history at York University, Toronto, Canada. Besides the first edition of *Daily Life in Renaissance Italy*, she is coauthor of *Words and Deeds in Renaissance Rome* and coeditor of *The Youth of Early Modern Women*. She has published many articles on the history of non-elite women in early modern Italy.

THOMAS V. COHEN is professor of history at York University, Toronto, Canada. Besides the first edition of *Daily Life in Renaissance Italy*, he is coauthor of *Words and Deeds in Renaissance Rome*. He is author of *Love and Death in Renaissance Italy* and *Roman Tales: A Reader's Guide to the Art of Microhistory*. He has coedited *Cultural History of Early Modern European Streets* and *Spoken Word and Social Practice: Orality in Europe (1400–1700)*.